LINDLEY J. STILES
Professor of Education for Interdisciplinary Studies
Northwestern University
ADVISORY EDITOR TO DODD, MEAD & COMPANY

The Elementary School
Principalship

The Elementary School Principalship

STEPHEN P. HENCLEY
University of Utah

LLOYD E. McCLEARY
University of Utah

J H McGRATH
Illinois State University

DODD, MEAD & COMPANY

New York   1970

EDITOR'S INTRODUCTION

The Elementary School Principalship brings refined and tested theory, research results, and practical ideas about leadership and management to school administrators who need help the most and have been neglected the longest. The elementary school principal has been treated as a stepchild in the educational hierarchy, a bifurcated teacher by the profession, and almost completely ignored in the literature of educational administration. His professional practice was expected to be modeled after that of the secondary school principal or superintendent of schools with little attention being given by scholars to the unique roles and functions of those who provide leadership for the most vital and comprehensive segment of education—the elementary school.

Only recently has the importance of the function of the elementary school principal come to be recognized. As this position is seen in terms of its unique responsibilities and relationships, professionals and laymen alike are becoming aware that a principal of an elementary school stands at the apex of all educational progress—from kindergarten through college. How he or she manages the job may determine not only how well students learn and continue to develop educationally, but it also has a heavy bearing on the total relationship between citizens and their system of education. For these reasons, the principal of an elementary school stands in the front lines of conflict and controversy about education. He or she has the chance to shape the democratic processes by which people of all cultures can be involved in policy decisions about their schools. The elementary school principal, almost alone at times, has the opportunity to initiate and carry out dialogues between the school system and its various publics. And the principal, along with the school faculty, lives with learning in the raw, before it has been distorted or thwarted by myriads of pressures, procedures, and resulting responses of students, parents, and communities. To help principals of elementary schools to meet the challenges they face, to assist them to elevate their service to professional levels, and to help them to maintain a balance of personal adjustment and development are the purposes of this book.

The sparse literature about the elementary school principalship deals largely with "how-to-do-it" advice. Cookbook-type formulas are presented, apparently on the assumption that people in such positions are incapable of thinking deeply and reflectively about their work. This book pays the elementary school principal the supreme compliment by treating him or her as a professional who is capable of making astute analyses about educational leadership. Its approach is to present a conceptual framework for professional practice of administration in elementary schools. The underlying assumption is that without refined theory and documented knowledge, the principal must confront each situation with little more than his or her instincts and the traditions of practice that have been inherited. With the rationale presented, the principal is offered a guide to decisions and behavior that promises most effective long-range results as well as help in solving day-to-day operational problems. Such conceptualization is rooted in the totality of knowledge about education and its processes as well as in what is known about educational leadership and the unique mission of the elementary school.

Despite the attention given to the theory and characteristics of the elementary school principalship, authors Hencley, McCleary, and McGrath —all experienced administrators—provide useful guidelines for the translation of concepts into professional practice. Also, the book brings the principal into touch with new ideas, new resources, and new relationships that promote growth. Contemporary problems and those anticipated in the future are used to test the validity of administrative strategies. Responsibilities and relationships that result from the elementary school principal's newly recognized leadership role on the system's administrative team are analyzed. The result of these and other emphases is a book that offers a definitive treatment of the unique characteristics of the work and leadership of the elementary school principal. It will help any principal or prospective principal who reads it, and it will contribute to establishing the elementary school principalship as a professional career position of unsurpassed importance in the educational field.

LINDLEY J. STILES

PREFACE

THIS BOOK on the administration of elementary schools is intended as a companion volume to *Secondary School Administration,* which appeared in 1965. In its preparation, the authors have consciously attempted to maintain the same general theoretical perspectives characterizing the earlier work. Thus, theoretical perspectives and constructs were utilized not only to illuminate problems and practices in elementary school administration but also to indicate directions of future development in this field.

In many ways, this book represents a major departure from the typical format of existing works dealing with administration in elementary schools. It is neither a compendium of current information nor a normative treatment consisting of descriptions and principles nor a catalog of "how to do it" recipes for administering elementary schools. Rather, the authors have assumed that potential and practicing school administrators require a solid theoretical perspective and grounding if they are to function effectively in the milieu of forces, functions, and responsibilities that are molding leadership activity in elementary schools.

The authors are indebted to a number of individuals who assisted materially in the preparation of this volume. Lindley J. Stiles provided helpful criticism and advice and gave his full support to the perspectives indicated in this volume. Mr. Claude Cawley and Mr. Mel Sillito, doctoral students in educational administration at the University of Utah, provided outstanding aid as research assistants. Miss Marlene Buchanan, secretary to the Dean, Graduate School of Education, University of Utah, assisted in many ways in the preparation of the manuscript.

STEPHEN P. HENCLEY
LLOYD E. MCCLEARY
J H MCGRATH

CONTENTS

TABLES

FIGURES

Part I

Elementary Education and Administration

Chapter 1

ADMINISTRATION IN
ELEMENTARY SCHOOLS

ADMINISTRATION, as a distinct feature of organized activity, is universally recognized. This is as true in the field of education—from the elementary school through the university—as it is in government, business, industry, military, and other complex and relatively permanent operations. Regardless of the clarity of understanding of administrative problems and processes or the degree of agreement among pupils, parents, teachers, and administrators concerning specific practices, administration is seen as an important element in providing satisfactory programs of education.

Educational administration can be further attested as a distinct and specialized function by the positions created in the schools for the exclusive purpose of administering them. At the elementary school level the position of principal is universal in the United States and many foreign countries. In small building units the position of head teacher is employed while, in large elementary schools, positions such as assistant principal, administrative assistant, coordinator, and director are provided in addition to that of the principal. Descriptions of prescribed duties and responsibilities and job descriptions by incumbents as means of understanding the administration of elementary schools are treated later in this chapter.

Acceptance of the fact that the administrative function is an identifiable element of organized education and acknowledgment of its importance do not mean that sufficient knowledge about it has been attained or that complete agreement exists about its application at various levels of the educational structure. Means are available, however, to characterize and describe administrative practice, and useful

3

approaches have been made to provide understanding of administrative problems and processes.

Two movements, sharply accelerated during the past decade, serve to focus attention upon the administration of elementary schools. First, rapid changes in elementary education—curriculum, instructional practices, and organizational structures and arrangements—call for more perceptive and effective administration. Second, new insights into the administrative function require that a broader meaning and purpose be applied to the administration of elementary schools. Past conceptions of administrative practice are no longer adequate and are becoming increasingly outmoded. In this chapter, the authors attempt an examination of formulations of the administrative function and propose one for use by the reader as a means of giving perspective to his study of administration as it applies to elementary education.

CONTEXT OF ELEMENTARY SCHOOL ADMINISTRATION

Elementary school administration—as does all public administration —derives its character from the context in which it is practiced. It is performed within a matrix of ideals, values, and purposes that are more or less agreed upon and accepted as "right" by those involved. It functions through a system of laws and rules which prescribe and limit actions that can be taken. It is conditioned by the practices of teaching, organization, and management of education itself and by the constraints of the local situation represented by the resources, facilities, quality of staff, and numbers of pupils and the variety of their learning abilities and handicaps, among other factors. The elements noted above, taken together, create the context for administrative activity.

Although adequate information about each aspect of the context of elementary school administration is lacking, data are available that permit certain generalizations to be made about the environments within which administrators must perform. These can be enumerated here.

Local Orientation of Education

In the 1969–70 school year approximately 22,240 local public school districts operated elementary schools in the United States. Of this number, well over 2,500 were separate elementary school districts employing a superintendent and other central office personnel and operating two or more elementary schools. From census data and the biennial reports of the U.S. Office of Education, the authors estimate that slightly more than 1,000,000 teachers and more than 85,000 administrators are currently employed in the elementary schools.

As the reader is likely to be well aware, the determination of policies and practices for a given school and school district are, within broad limits, left to local determination. Without arguing the pros or cons of this condition, the local school and the local community provide a social setting within which the administrator must operate. It is in the local setting that the administrator is confronted with the ideals, values, and expectations that largely determine educational potential. Administration is deeply affected by its setting. This point cannot be left, however, without the observation that administration is also intended to *change* the setting in which it operates.

Broadened Concern for Education

Many forces are now at work to alter the conditions under which education is carried forward at the local level. Most dramatic, of course, has been the impact of federal interest and activity. The Elementary and Secondary Education Act of 1965, the Economic Opportunity Act of 1964, and subsequent federal legislation have introduced a significant new concept of federal activity in the domain of public education. It is the concept that local schools must provide an acceptable proposal for the use of funds and that evidence must be submitted by which an evaluation can be made of the effect of the expenditure. This alters for the first time the principle that federal monies are to be allocated upon an objective formula alone, and it places the federal level of government in a powerful position to effect change in specific directions.

An additional point relating to the federal interest in education is the amount of participation. The first-year allocation of funds under the Elementary and Secondary Education Act was 1.3 billion dollars. Reliable estimates indicate that the federal participation in the support of public education will reach 30 billion dollars within a five-year period. If these estimates are accurate, by 1975 the federal government will double the total amount now spent for all forms of public education.

State governments have been active during the past ten years in strengthening the leadership role of state departments of education. In such areas as the education of the gifted and the handicapped, vocational training, and pupil services, many states have established state-wide programs or have made specific requirements of local districts.

Likewise, the private foundations and the universities have, during the past ten years, greatly increased their influence over public education. Through research, provision of services, demonstration projects, and training programs, the foundations and the universities have considerably broadened their activity not only in the study of public education but in prescribing its direction of development.

Professional Environment

The profession itself presents a changing set of conditions for administration. In 1925, few teachers possessed bachelor's degrees. More than 200,000 elementary teachers had one year or less of college training, about half of the total at that time. By 1970, almost 95 percent held bachelor's degrees, and more than 28 percent held master's degrees; some states reported more than half of their elementary teachers as holding master's degrees.

The dramatic reduction of the number of one-room elementary schools—from more than 200,000 in 1925 to fewer than 18,000 in 1969—is paralleled by the consolidation of school districts—approximately 100,000 in 1925 to about 23,000 in 1970. The effect of this development, along with the increasing school population and the concentration of the general population, is to increase sharply the enrollments of individual elementary schools. The principal is now responsible for more pupils and more teachers than ever before.

Not only are teachers better prepared, the school units larger and more complex, the program broader, and the range of pupil abilities increased, but these conditions have produced the need for new forms and arrangements for the provision of instruction. The introduction of technology—television, teaching machines, laboratories, media centers, and the like—has added a new dimension to the administrative role. New and varied materials, special groupings of pupils, specialized staff and services, and changed deployment of teaching staff have all entered the picture on a wide scale within the past ten years.

Relationship Between School and Community

A social institution, particularly one that is as locally oriented as the elementary school, does not change in isolation from the community. Most would agree that the elementary school typically lags behind the community it serves. This is a most unfortunate condition when the local community itself is likely to be in need of leadership in the processes of social change. The dilemma occurs when the school's leadership looks only to the local community for direction. Too often in such cases the program of the elementary school must be characterized as provincial education.

The advent of a mass society with its centralized and specialized technology, mass communications, and rapid large-scale transportation creates demands upon education far beyond the confines of the local community. The elementary school, if it is to fulfill its function, must become society-centered rather than community-centered. Under these conditions the administrator must mediate between the school and the community where goals and practices necessary to sound education seem incompatible with local values and interests.

The change in role of the elementary school administrator from community servant to community leader is a relatively new and demanding dimension of his task. In textbooks dealing with school administration prior to the 1930's practically no mention was made of the school-community relationship, and none seemed necessary. By the mid-1930's, books frequently dealt with the topic of "public relations," largely with the idea that communities needed to be informed about practices in the schools. In the present decade administrators require a sophisticated knowledge of cultural patterns and values, the relationship of educational goals to societal needs, the means of studying community structures and processes, a knowledge of communication processes and of the means by which controls over schools are established and how they function.

New Expectations for Education

Public education in the United States seems always to have been highly valued. Regardless of whether or not it has received adequate support, influential men in every period have paid tribute to the system of public education. The comments of Jefferson, Adams, de Tocqueville, Eliot, Dewey, Whitehead, Conant, and Johnson span the history of the nation. By and large the expectations held for education and upon which it has been judged center upon three main themes: civic responsibility and patriotism, a command of useful knowledge and information, and vocational preparation for economic self-sufficiency.

The schools have had their critics as well as their advocates, but public faith has never waned. The most recent period of sharp, at times acrimonious, criticism followed the launching of the first Soviet spacecraft in 1957. Even in this period, enrollments in the public schools, per pupil expenditures, and other indices of public support continued largely unaffected.

However, a new and challenging set of expectations is being rapidly formulated. Although its political expression is not yet clarified, simply stated, it is that solutions to the persistent social and economic problems of the nation are, at their roots, educational in nature—that permanent solutions lie not in simply ministering to the symptoms of these problems but in educating the affected segment of society out of its problem. The immediate application of this concept to the culturally disadvantaged, the technologically unemployed, the unemployable, and the impoverished has already been implemented. A second feature is that the schools as social institutions are proper arenas of social conflict and should be used in the resolution of such conflict. The outstanding example, of course, is the assault on the problem of racial discrimination. A third, and perhaps most important, feature is the belief that education can power a scientific and technological revolution whose aim is practically unlimited production of essential economic goods with a minimum of physical labor.

None of the three features listed above are "pie in the sky" dreams of visionaries, nor are they the notions of attraction-seeking politicians. They are based upon substantial evidence—much of which will be examined in later chapters of this book. The important point to be made here is that, if education becomes a central feature of public policy—as it has to a large extent already—then responsibility is placed upon those who seek to exercise educational leadership far beyond that ever demanded of educational leaders in the past.

DIMENSIONS OF ADMINISTRATIVE PRACTICE

Educational administration is an applied field. The nature of its contribution—and certainly the measure of it—must be found in practice. The description in the previous section should be revealing in terms of the possible impact the educational administrator can have, but it also contains the criteria upon which his performance will be judged in the future. Will the elementary school administrator possess adequate knowledge of the variety of processes, operations, and skills needed to meet the challenges of the new conditions? Will he have the insight, the perspective, and the judgment to use them? The authors believe he will, but only if a new conception of the role of the administrator can be fashioned —a formulation of the administrative function suitable to guide both the study of administration and its practice.

Administration in the Local Elementary School

The emergence of the position of elementary school principal—the first reasonably well-identified position in elementary administration—is very recent by any historical standard. The Department of Elementary School Principals of the National Education Association was not organized until 1921; by 1930 fewer than half of the states had organized state associations. In 1920 there were no qualifications for the elementary principalship other than teaching experience, and it is reliably estimated that more than two-thirds of the elementary principals held no academic degree. The few descriptions available indicate that the principal was, as the title implies, the principal teacher and not an administrator at all. Clerical duties, discipline of students, and schedule-making along with teaching comprised almost the total job description.

Responsibilities were added rapidly as school sizes increased and as the trends alluded to in the previous section set in to alter the social environment in which schools existed.[1] By 1956 the Department of Elementary School Principals could identify administrative tasks and responsibilities in such areas as instructional supervision, curriculum development, instructional methods and materials, budget, plant, pupil and staff personnel, district-wide educational policy development, and planning of educational change.[2] The position of principal had emerged as a definite administrative position with significant professional status.

The Principalship:
Focus of Study of Elementary School Administration

Categories of tasks, as noted above, do not define the totality of elementary administration just as they would not provide an adequate

1. The reader might wish to consult: Paul R. Pierce, *The Origin and Development of the Public School Principalship* (Chicago: University of Chicago Press, 1935); Bess Goodykoontz and J. A. Love, *The Elementary School Principal*, Bulletin No. 8 (Washington, D.C.: U.S. Office of Education, 1938); and yearbooks of the Department of Elementary School Principals of the National Education Association, especially 1928 (*Seventh Yearbook*) and 1948 (*Twenty-seventh Yearbook*).

2. Department of Elementary School Principals, *Thirty-seventh Yearbook* (Washington, D.C.: National Education Association, 1958).

description of what the elementary school principal does or how he goes about his work. Such categories do identify the substantive *content* of what the administrator does and the *range* of tasks which he must perform, and, therefore, they do provide one means of describing the job of the principal. The position of principal is the chief administrative position in each school. It becomes defined first, in terms of generally accepted practice; second, according to the specific needs of a particular school; and, finally, by the personal qualities and abilities of the individual occupying the position.

Descriptions of the work of the principal in any given school over a period of time will vary from that of descriptions of the work of principals in other schools whether the task categories or some other classification scheme is used. In some schools certain categories of tasks may be delegated; some categories may not require attention; some may be slighted or dealt with only in a perfunctory way. The point, however, is that an inclusive and generalized conception of administration appropriate to the elementary school principalship is needed which defines the administrative function regardless of the unique characteristics of a given school.

The position of principal is the position of responsibility for the administrative function and is the key position within the principalship whether or not the principal performs all of the administrative tasks himself. Other positions—assistant principal, coordinator, team leader, chairman—may be assigned administrative duties, but they do so as part of the principalship. Even at the district level, positions of superintendent, assistant superintendent, director, or coordinator for elementary education may be provided. The focus of concern, however, is the point at which program plans and professional staff are brought together operationally at the building level. Thus the study of elementary school administration focuses upon the principalship and the position of the principal—the key position of the principalship.

Descriptions of Practice and Job Specifications
Inadequate Basis of Definition

Historically, two approaches have been utilized in the attempt to define the administrative function: (1) descriptions of practice, and (2) job descriptions. Many studies are available in which the investigator observes what principals do on the job, or, more frequently, the principal is asked to describe his job by questionnaire or other device.

A second approach, that of analyzing job specifications, entails the examination of official statements of the duties and directions given to principals. These seemingly straightforward and logical approaches have proven to be of little value in constructing an adequate conception of the principalship.

Descriptions of practice represent the perceptions of principals about what they are doing. At the outset the accuracy and dependability of such statements are questionable; what a respondent thinks is important is often exaggerated and what he feels to be less important—even though it might consume more of his time and energy—he often omits or under-plays. Over a large sample of principals, even though it might be a representative sample, personal characteristics and qualifications influence responses unduly. Some respondents would be experienced, some inexperienced; some would have degrees, some not; some would represent large schools, some small. These and many other conditions influence the kind of data obtained; this procedure can provide a generalized picture but not the basis of a definition. Finally, even if accurate, the descriptions would supposedly be of what principals were doing—not necessarily what they *ought* to be doing.

Job specifications present somewhat the same problem. They are either a listing of duties to be performed or a statement of ideal behaviors and goals the principal is expected to adopt as his own. Even in a single school district where elementary school principals operate under the same set of specifications, considerable variation often occurs. The best that these kinds of statements provide are sets of expectations of the principal. As with descriptions of practice, job specifications are more or less useful for a specific purpose, but they are not very helpful in constructing a generalized conception of the principalship—one that would be useful to guide study and practice.

Need for General Formulation to Guide Study and Practice

The elementary school, partly because of increased size and partly because of the increased competence of the professional staff, has become quite self-directing. Elementary principals—whether in the large city, suburbs, or smaller towns—report considerable independence of action from central office direction, in some instances to a surprising extent. Even though the principal works under a complex assortment of policies, requests, expectations, and requirements, he is usually not given direct or detailed orders regarding the major segments of his activity. Rather, he exercises judgment within a framework of principles and rules. This framework, the authors contend, should be developed as a result of serious professional study and guided experience.

What, then, should be the dimensions of the principalship that give adequate perspective to the administration and leadership required in the elementary school? Can a theoretical formulation of elementary school administration be constructed and employed to identify the essential meaning and purpose of administration and serve as a guide both to its study and its practice? The authors believe that affirmative answers can be given to these questions. The remainder of this chapter is devoted to an examination of formulations already in use and to the proposal of one which serves as the basis of the remainder of this work.

GENERAL FORMULATIONS OF EDUCATIONAL ADMINISTRATION

If the reader is willing to accept the brief statements concerning the development of elementary school administration presented earlier in this chapter, it should be clear that the field of educational administration has developed out of a strongly "practice-oriented" context. The reader will recall that, into the 1920's, the only qualification for the elementary principalship was teaching experience. Knowledge of administration was, and still is, restricted largely to descriptions of normative practice. Knowledge came to be equated with technology—an understanding of how to run a school. Although this is a kind of knowledge, it is not the only kind and, by itself, may not be the most serviceable in the long run.

The methods of study for the "scholar" who creates this kind of knowledge are of two kinds. The first method comprises investigation and data gathering followed by deductions or inferences. The second method is to observe practice, hypothesize about what might produce better results, and test the hypothesis. Both approaches yield findings that become subject matter for study. However, in the main, this kind of subject matter is to be learned and learned primarily for its direct application.

The authors do not disparage this kind of study. It ties the field of practice directly to its study. Practitioners can participate in investigation, and it has produced better practice. It has not, however, produced a disciplined study of administration. Rather it has "manufactured" knowledge out of practice, and it has done so in refined "bits and pieces."

Administration is left without tested concepts that can be brought together into unifying theories.

A recognized field of study, a discipline, possesses a more or less clearly defined territory and clearly defined methods of attack. It is characterized by persistent attention to theory construction which serves to organize what is known and project the investigator into inquiry. One "studies" a discipline; he does not "learn" it. This is not the whole story, of course; but a discipline of administration cannot develop until large numbers of students—neophytes, established administrators, and professors—realize that educational administration cannot be studied as a discipline in "off hours" or "on-the-job." Further, the judgment of whether or not a particular investigation receives cooperation by a school should not depend primarily upon its promise to provide immediate solutions to problems of that school.

There is considerable optimism that the field of educational administration is developing toward "disciplined" as well as "applied" study. The purpose of this section is to outline several general formulations as a means of arriving at a definition of administration and identifying established concepts that might serve to produce a general theoretical formulation.

Investigation and study tend to validate the usefulness of describing educational administration under the headings of (1) administrative tasks, (2) administrative processes, (3) situational factors, and (4) administrative behavior.

Administrative Tasks

The study of the Department of Elementary School Principals, referred to earlier in this chapter, represents an investigation into the discrete tasks being performed by elementary principals. In this study 16 categories were presented, and principals were asked to indicate the duties and responsibilities they performed under each category. Since the number of discrete tasks reported numbered in the hundreds and certain categories seem to overlap, the authors here report only a listing of task areas. These include:

1. Instructional supervision
2. Curriculum development
3. Instructional methods and materials
4. Budget preparation

5. Plant management
6. Pupil and staff personnel
7. District-wide policy making
8. Planning and directing educational change [3]

Another study, perhaps most frequently cited as the source of identification of task areas, is that carried out in the Southern States Cooperative Program (SSCP) in Educational Administration. More than 280 distinct tasks were uncovered, and these were grouped into eight task areas:

1. Instruction and curriculum development
2. Pupil personnel
3. Staff personnel
4. Community-school leadership
5. School plant
6. Organization and structure
7. School finance and business management
8. School transportation and management [4]

Task formulations are the result of *ex post facto* investigations into what school administrators are doing or say they are doing. As pointed out in the introduction to this section, this approach to a definition of the field of educational administration leads to the conception of administration as technology. Most, if not all, of the eight task areas listed above correspond quite closely to individual courses offered as the professional preparation of school administrators. By themselves they provide neither an adequate conception nor a sufficient entrée into an understanding of the important problems and issues of the field.

Administrative Process

The relationship of educational administration to the general field of administration seems to have arisen from attempts to understand administration as consisting of processes. Fayol, a Frenchman, first presented this view of administration in 1916. His major interest was the study of industrial management. He saw the need to incorporate the idea of leadership into administration through the exercise of foresight and the use of judgment on the part of administrators in gearing their organizations to meet anticipated future conditions and problems.

3. Department of Elementary School Principals, *op. cit.,* entire.
4. Southern States Cooperative Program in Educational Administration, *Better Teaching in School Administration* (Nashville, Tenn.: George Peabody College for Teachers, 1955).

Adapted to public administration by Gulick, the processes identified became well known as: planning, organizing, staffing, directing, coordinating, reporting, and budgeting (POSDCORB).[5] (See Part II and Part IV.) The process approach is defined by the Commission on Staff Relations in School Administration: "Administration, then, may be defined as the total of the processes through which appropriate human and material resources are made available and made effective for accomplishing the purposes of an enterprise." [6]

The processes as listed and defined by the Commission are:

1. *Planning,* or the attempt to control the future in the direction of the desired goals through decisions made on the basis of careful estimates of the probable consequences of possible courses of action
2. *Allocation,* or the procurement and allotment of human and material resources in accordance with the operating plan
3. *Stimulation,* or motivation of behavior in terms of the desired outcome
4. *Coordination,* or the process of fitting together the various groups and operations into an integrated pattern of purpose-achieving works
5. *Evaluation,* or the continuous examination of the effects produced by the ways in which the other functions listed are performed [7]

Various other listings of the administrative processes exist. All are quite similar. For example, Gregg, in an excellent treatment of process formulations as they relate to educational administration, favored the following list: decision making, planning, organizing, communicating, influencing, coordinating, and evaluating.[8] Campbell, Corbally, and Ramseyer used: decision making, programing, stimulating, coordinating, and appraising.[9]

Those who use process formulations to describe administration do not deny the existence of tasks, but they see administration as consisting of complex and extended processes which need to be studied as processes. Further, the focus of attention in this approach is upon administrative

5. Luther Gulick, "Notes on the Theory of Organization," in Luther Gulick and L. Urwick (eds.), *Papers on the Science of Administration* (New York: Institute of Public Administration, Columbia University, 1937), p. 13.

6. American Association of School Administrators, *Staff Relations in School Administration, Thirty-third Yearbook* (Washington, D.C.: the Association, 1955), p. 17.

7. *Ibid.*

8. Russell Gregg, "The Administrative Process," in Roald Campbell and Russell Gregg (eds.), *Administrative Behavior in Education* (New York: Harper & Bros., 1957), Chapter VIII, pp. 269–317.

9. Roald Campbell, John Corbally, and John Ramseyer, *Introduction to Educational Administration* (Boston: Allyn and Bacon, 1958), p. 179.

behavior rather than upon the technical aspects of discrete tasks—upon the choices an administrator has and how he proceeds rather than on what information and skill he possesses to do a specific job. It is worth noting that the process approach results from a conceptualization of the administrative act, not from descriptions or reports of practice. In this sense it represents a theoretical definition which can be applied to administration of any type in any setting.

Situational Factors and Administrative Behavior

The most serious shortcoming of both the process and the task approach to administration is their inability to account for situational factors and administrative behavior. These latter considerations provide the only means of taking into account the unique features known to exist from one school to another. In short, process and task definitions yield categories into which data can be sorted and general descriptions obtained; they do not account for the dynamic relationship present in each situation. Moore indicates the need to account for these factors: ". . . . investigators became convinced that the only way to arrive at a definition of educational administration, or, for that matter, to analyze clearly the functions performed by school administrators, was to do so by observing them in actual situations, and to describe them in situational terms. . . ." [10]

A study conducted by The Ohio State University School-Community Development project identified situational and behavioral factors which seemed to affect the solution of problems in the schools studied. They report the following factors as significant:

1. The administrator himself
2. Persons with whom the administrator works
3. Relationships between the administrator and the groups and individuals with whom he works
4. Instructional organization or pattern in which administrative behavior takes place
5. Mores already established in the school community
6. Physical characteristics and legal provisions of the community

They were able to identify problems arising in the following areas: making policy, setting goals, determining roles, coordinating administrative functions and structure, working with community leadership to promote improvements in education, using educational resources of the commu-

10. Hollis A. Moore, *Studies in School Administration* (Washington, D.C.: American Association of School Administrators, 1957), p. 28.

nity, involving people, communicating, and appraising effectiveness.[11]

Schematic Formulations: Because each of the formulations presented seems to be useful in accounting for a significant dimension of administration but not its totality, it is not surprising that attempts have been made to combine them. Lawrence Downey provides such a schematic representation of what he terms the "reality of all administration" with specific emphasis upon what he argues should be the domain of the principalship. With slight adaptation, his schema is given in Table 1–1.

Table 1-1. Totality of Educational Administration–Areas of Commonality, Emphases, and Specialization of the Principalship

The Processes of Administration	Forces in the Administrative Setting	The Tasks of Administration
Commonality { Decision making Communicating Influencing Coordinating Evaluating	Emphasis { External: Political Economic Cultural Internal: Institutional Individual Group	Finance, management Physical facilities Community relations Specialty { Organization Staff personnel Student personnel Instructional leadership

SOURCE: Adapted from Lawrence Downey, "The Secondary School Principal," in Donald J. Leu and Herbert C. Rudman (eds.) Preparation Programs for School Administration (East Lansing, Mich.: College of Education, Michigan State University, 1963), p. 136.

He develops his reasoning in the following way:

1. Process, task, setting, and man approaches, in combination, constitute a useful and comprehensive perspective of the field of educational administration.
2. Each approach has general applicability to any administrative position in the educational system.
3. Processes appear to be generalizable to all administrative positions.
4. Certain differences between the social setting of superintendent and principal require some differentiation in consideration depending upon the position.
5. Tasks performed by the principal are substantially different from the superintendent's and are specialized in the areas of instructional leadership and student personnel.

11. John Ramseyer, *et al., Factors Affecting Educational Administration, School Community Development Monograph*, No. 2 (Columbus, Ohio: Ohio State University Press, 1955).

Downey's formulation was developed for the purpose of identifying areas of training for administrators. He was not concerned with developing a hypothesis-generating model for research or even a device for orienting students to the study of the field of administration. His line of reasoning is an interesting one, however, both in terms of the content he identifies as appropriate for study and for his concern that training within educational administration be differentiated according to position.[12]

Theoretical Formulations: There is not a comprehensive theory of educational administration or of administration in general. Theories of limited application are available and, where appropriate, they are examined in this volume. The body of theory, however, is not substantial, and it is largely unrelated. Efforts are growing to construct rigorous, hypothetical-deductive formulations for the guidance of research, and these efforts are producing systematic, scientific inquiry into the nature of administration.

A growing number of authorities in the field are focusing upon administrative behavior as the strategic element in the construction of theory. The work of Griffiths has been particularly helpful in orienting the field to the need for the development of sound theory to add to, and lead in, the strategies of knowledge production for administration.[13] Before turning to a statement of Griffiths' theory, note should be made that those who pursue the theory approach see their work as appropriate to the study of administration as administration—as applicable to administration in any setting, not just that of the school. There is strong identification with the social and behavioral sciences. This offers the possibility of making fuller use of more basic disciplines and also of making a contribution to these disciplines through research in the educational setting.

Griffiths' theory is here used as illustrative of the theory approach. He views administration as a thoroughgoing problem-solving activity—

12. Lawrence Downey, "The Secondary School Principal," in Donald J. Leu and Herbert C. Rudman (eds.), *Preparation Programs for School Administrators* (East Lansing, Mich.: College of Education, Michigan State University, 1963), pp. 122–136.

13. The reader is encouraged to study the writings of Daniel Griffiths in: *Administrative Theory* (New York: Appleton-Century-Crofts, 1959), and "The Nature of and Meaning of Theory" in Daniel E. Griffiths (ed.), *Behavioral Sciences and Educational Administration, Sixty-third Yearbook of the National Society for the Study of Education* (Chicago: University of Chicago Press, 1964) and *Developing Taxonomies of Organizational Behavior in Education Administration* (Chicago: Rand McNally & Company, 1969).

administrative behavior is seen only in terms of problem-solving acts. He seeks propositions which shed light upon both the *description* and *explanation* of administrative behavior and organizational responses to decision making. He defines the steps in decision making as:

1. Recognize, define, and limit the problem.
2. Analyze and evaluate the problem.
3. Establish criteria or standards by which solutions will be evaluated or judged as acceptable and adequate to the need.
4. Collect data.
5. Formulate and select the preferred solution or solutions.
6. Put into effect the preferred solution.
   a. Program the solution.
   b. Control the activities in the program.
   c. Evaluate the results and the process.[14]

Griffiths argues that decision making is central to all administrative functions because all functions can be interpreted in terms of the decision-making process. Because the decision-making process controls the allocation of resources, communications, groupings in the organization, achievement of goals, and power and authority, all are ordered in relation to that process. Therefore, an understanding of the decision-making process is the key to understanding the essential nature, personnel relationships, and modes of operation of any organization. These statements represent the assumptions upon which Griffiths identifies and defines the concepts he employs in casting a set of testable propositions.

The departure points of a given theory are determined by the assumptions made and observations of practice upon which assumptions are accepted, modified, or rejected. Categories of theory which center upon administrative behavior are: (1) decision-making theories, (2) conflict and accommodation theories centering upon role definition, role and personality incongruences, and the like, (3) motivational theories based upon consideration of individual motives and needs in relation to organizational goals, (4) systems theories—organizations as miniature societies or social systems.[15]

14. Griffiths, *Administrative Theory, op. cit.,* p. 241.
15. The list of readings at the end of this chapter includes a reference to statements of theories illustrative of each category.

FORMULATION OF ADMINISTRATION FOR
ELEMENTARY SCHOOL ADMINISTRATION

Any formulation of elementary school administration must define the substance of administration as it applies to the elementary school and indicate its relationship to factors in the setting in which it functions. As a means of placing in perspective the formulations of administration given in the previous section, the authors offer their own formulation below. The reader is encouraged to analyze critically the following and other formulations, not as an intellectual exercise but as a means of gaining a perspective of the field of educational administration and as a means of constructing a frame of reference for his own use. The formulation presented here may be considered as the basic rationale for the remainder of this volume.

Elementary school administration is a field of specialized professional service. Its practice is performed within three interrelated areas of human concern. These three areas might be isolated and characterized by the following statements.

The first area has already been identified as the setting—social, economic, political, educational—represented by forces upon the school and its program. The immediate environment through which these forces bear upon the school is the local community. The ultimate purpose of the school is to bring the child into ever-broadening contact with the culture in an enlightened, systematic fashion. Whether or not education will be carried forward in a society-oriented climate or whether education will be restricted to the views and values of segments of the local community will rest largely upon the manner in which the administrator approaches program development and implementation.

The second area is elementary education itself. Purposes, methodologies, content, and organization are all profoundly shaped by the profession. The administrator along with the professional staff of the school will, through their knowledge and competencies, give expression to their understanding of the best education possible with the resources available. Possibilities for changing through innovation and growth of knowledge offer exciting challenges and opportunities in this area.

The third area is that of the processes, techniques, operating principles, and ethical values of educational administration. Many of the established tenets of administration are being critically examined and reformulated. How they will be applied to the improvement of elemen-

tary education remains largely in the hands of those who are now enter-
ing this rapidly changing field.

Phases of Administrative Activity

In his work the elementary school administrator is involved in three
fundamentally different, though related, phases of activity. These are
identified as: (1) technical management, (2) organizational leadership,
and (3) broad policy making. The authors' version of a formulation of
administration appropriate to elementary schools is shown in Figure 1–1.
Three levels of administrative activity are shown encompassing the pro-

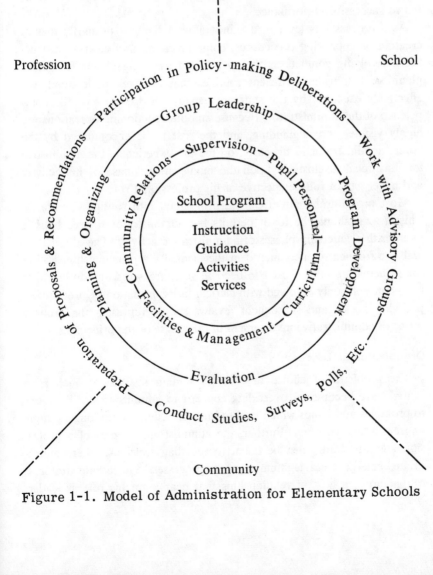

Figure 1-1. Model of Administration for Elementary Schools

gram of the school and subject to conditions and forces arising from the society-community, profession, and the school itself.

Technical Management

The most immediate activity of the administrator—often allowed to become the most demanding—can be characterized as technical management. It involves administrative decisions and actions which ensure successful conduct of instruction, guidance, student activities, and services. Scheduling, assigning, directing, supervising, expediting, inspecting, and correcting are representative activities at the technical management level. Specialized skills and intimate knowledge of school operation are essential to successful performance.

As a process this level of administrative activity is primarily that of creating or approving procedures, communicating and clearing instructions, resolving conflicts as they arise, and assessing results for future planning. Established, efficient routines that are well understood and effectively executed by the staff are usually the first test of the competence of the administrator. Because smooth-functioning operations are highly visible, and demanding, and the first to be encountered by the young administrator in his early, on-the-job experience, the administrator may focus exclusively upon the management phase of his activity and never gain a full perspective of his professional role.

Most procedural matters can be programed into routine operations. This is as it should be for it permits the administrator to free himself to enter the leadership phases of administrative activity. The alternative, and one frequently encountered in the elementary principalship, is that the principal permits himself to become so engrossed with routines that he becomes heavily involved with clerical tasks. Initiation of procedures, periodic checks, and subsequent reviews should represent the primary forms of administrative involvement in this phase of the principal's work.

Organizational Leadership

The problems of choice in complex human institutions such as a school have become an overriding concern to administration. Solutions to problems and issues which lead to lines of action are no longer simple and easily agreed upon. Further, the administrator is part of a professional group. Care must be taken to see that decisions, where appropriate, emerge from legitimate group processes. The administrator is caught up in a host of relationships that bear upon his role as leader.

He receives communications of the judgments and decisions of others, and he uses them as a basis for his own actions.

Planning and organizing form the major tasks of the organizational leader. Whenever certain outcomes are sought, planning takes place. Planning implies an attempt to make decisions based upon a consideration of consequences. For the educational administrator, adequate planning requires concern for educational goals and the design of the program to accomplish them.

Planning leads to organizational decisions and to organizing for goal accomplishment. The administrator exercises organizational power and influence to rearrange the working relationships of individuals and the distribution of resources. In fact, the administration decides the distribution of power and influence, of responsibility and task assignment, insofar as it is possible to do so, within the school organization and in its external relationships. Whenever an administrator makes a decision, he organizes and accepts responsibility for school leadership.

The facet of decision making, often overlooked, is the role of evaluation. Individuals are conditioned to expect decisions to bring a matter to a final conclusion. Actually, most decisions—whether part of planning, organizing, leading, or program formulating—should be accepted as tests of new ideas and of current practice. That is, rather than settling an issue once and for all, specific decisions can be looked upon as proposals or hypotheses to be fully confirmed or revised as their consequences become known. Decision making, then, is an extended process with evaluation as an important element of that process.

The elements, outlined above, make up the leadership role within the school organization. The role is a delicate one for it must accommodate itself to district-wide policies and patterns of operation. In this sense the principal has a mediating role—that of developing an aggressive, active school organization without subverting or circumventing school district policy. At the same time organizational leadership functions to guide and give direction to the management activities. Each phase of administrative activity must be integrated with the others and supportive of them. Yet, the authors would argue that the organizational leadership phase is central to the role of the principal; it should be the focus of the elementary school principal's attention.

Participation in Broad Policy Making

The model, Figure 1–1, reveals only representative kinds of administrative activity that pertain to broad policy development. This is so because the administrative role in this area is as yet not well defined. The administrator clearly has a moral obligation to participate in public policy making; yet many ethical questions continue to arise in a changing political and social climate.

Education is a public concern, and all basic policy matters come within the purview of political bodies—school boards, courts, legislatures, and, at times, the total citizenry. If decisions made within the public domain are to be sound decisions, it is hoped that professional knowledge and opinion will be made available at the proper times and in the proper manner. Here the administrator enters the arena of politics. Questions relating to the goals of education, services to be provided, amounts of expenditures, and a host of like questions require decisions based not merely upon factual data but also upon representative value choices based upon beliefs, preferences, and commitment. Expertise is no claim to authority in such matters. Democratic institutions are the only just means of creating public policy.

In theory, public bodies make policy; administrators execute it. Often, however, legislatures and school boards go well beyond the bounds of policy making, and school administrators enforce decisions untested by public judgment. The problem is to find procedures which enable administrators to participate in sound policy development for education and which permit public review of administrative decisions.

The administrator needs to make proposals to appropriate policy-making agencies. Whenever possible he should give service by participating in deliberations of lay councils and formally constituted bodies. At this level, the administrative role is not to seek control of decision-making processes; his role is to know what processes are to be used in a given situation and how he can ethically contribute to policy development.

Considering the model as a whole, Figure 1–1, the authors conceptualize the principalship as encompassing the three related phases of technical management, organizational leadership, and participation in broad policy making. The total framework perhaps can best be interpreted as focusing upon the administrator as a decision maker, for even at the technical management level it is proposed that the school administrator decide upon appropriate procedures and that administration largely ceases as procedures become routine. Further, the administrator must be seen as a communicator. Unless he can establish and maintain communications with a variety of individuals and groups, he cannot function in any of the three phases of administrative activity. To this extent decision making and communicating permeate and tie the three phases of activity together. In Chapter 4, a systems analysis approach is employed to provide a view of the total administrative structure as a functioning performance system. When this is done, administrative processes are conceptualized independently as a fourth dimension.

REFERENCES

Brameld, Theodore, *Education as Power* (New York: Holt, Rinehart and Winston, 1965).

Becker, Howard S., "The Nature of a Profession," in Nelson B. Henry (ed.), *Education for the Professions, The Sixty-first Yearbook of the National Society for the Study of Education,* Part II (Chicago: the Association, 1962), pp. 27–46.

Department of Elementary School Principals, *Better Principals for Our Schools* (Washington, D.C.: National Education Association, 1961).

————, *The Elementary School Principalship in 1968* (Washington, D.C.: National Education Association, 1968).

————, "The Principalship" (theme of entire issue), *The National Elementary Principal,* Vol. XLIV, No. 5, April, 1965.

Griffiths, Daniel E. (ed.), *Behavioral Science and Educational Administration, The Sixty-third Yearbook of the National Society for the Study of Education* (Chicago: the Association, 1964).

————, *Administrative Theory* (New York: Appleton-Century-Crofts, 1959).

Gross, Neal, and Robert E. Herriott, *Staff Leadership in Public Schools* (New York: John Wiley & Sons, 1965).

Leu, Donald J., and Herbert Rudman (eds.), *Preparation Programs for School Administrators: Common and Specialized Learnings* (East Lansing, Mich.: College of Education, Michigan State University, 1963).

National Education Association, *The Changing World of the Elementary School Principal,* Parts I and II (Washington, D.C.: the Association, 1968).

Presthus, Robert, *The Organizational Society* (New York: Alfred A. Knopf, 1962).

Tilles, Seymour, "The Manager's Job—A Systems Approach," *Harvard Business Review,* Vol. XLV, January-February, 1963, pp. 73–81.

Tope, Donald E., *et al., The Social Sciences View School Administration* (Englewood Cliffs, N.J.: Prentice-Hall, 1964).

Wengert, E. S., *et al., The Study of Administration* (Eugene, Ore.: School of Business Administration, University of Oregon, 1961).

Chapter 2

ELEMENTARY SCHOOLS
AS SOCIAL INSTITUTIONS

E LEMENTARY schools represent the first, and perhaps most important, organized attempt to educate the child. At this level the major function of the school is to bring the child into possession of his culture. Although not the only function, it is central; and, in this sense, elementary education might be defined as that education which provides the child (1) knowledge about the group life into which he has been born, and (2) skills to acquire, extend, and make use of that knowledge to become a purposeful member of society.

Lack of achievement of an elementary education, if not accomplished during the period of elementary schooling, is an almost certain indication of future trouble for the individual. Studies of the achievement levels of children in reading and mathematics indicate this to be so—recovery from deficiencies and handicaps, when left uncorrected beyond grades six or seven, is disappointing; and evidence exists that the dropout and and the delinquent can be identified by grade five with reasonable precision. The period from four to ten years of age is perhaps the "make or break" period in terms of becoming an educated person.

Elementary school education is not only crucial to the individual but to society as well. Increasing responsibility has been placed upon the elementary school in the downward extension of responsibility for the child and also in the broadening of instructional programs, school related activities, and service functions. This condition has come about in such a natural way that it is rarely examined in a serious fashion. Society has had to turn more and more to the elementary school to transmit to the child an enormously complex culture that includes not only sophisticated skills and accumulated knowledge but also diffuse—often conflicting—

sets of values, standards, and norms that make up the ideological basis of the cultural heritage. The survival and advance of modern society depend not only upon learning through formal pedagogical procedures, but also upon the preparation of the child to behave in a rational manner as a member of society.

This latter task involves the elementary school in concerns about creating a social as well as an intellectual environment. The child needs to widen his circle of "significant others," have the opportunity to iron out conflicts in values and patterns of behavior he learns from others, develop the capacity to assume a variety of roles, learn to control emotions, to accept responsibility for his own acts, and to experience a host of other important socialization processes.

The elementary school must establish strong institutionalized practices with which the developing child can identify and in which he can participate. The procedures and practices, the groupings and sets of relationships, the sets of expectations and demands, the opportunities for choice, and the exercise of controls—all create an environment, an institutional press, upon the learner. The development of this environment—whether it stimulates or confines, whether it emphasizes one aspect of learning over another—is the responsibility of the administrator. His views of the culture, of societal needs and trends, of learning and the learner will largely determine how he will work with the staff and teachers and the resources at his disposal to create an environment for learning.

Within broad limits the functions to be served by elementary schooling are socially determined. They are influenced in many ways from the highest levels of policy formulation, from the actions of federal and state legislatures or the courts, to the immediate locale through actions of boards of education. The functions are influenced in informal ways as well as the formal ones noted above, for example, as the mass media introduce children to various adult roles and behavior patterns or as the parents of one neighborhood might expect nothing more of the school than to serve as baby-sitter while in another neighborhood parents expect a rigorously organized academic program to be the dominant influence of the elementary school. To gain any appreciation of the administrative role, the elementary school needs to be viewed as an institutionalized unit operating within a larger social system.

The elementary school administrator will give attention to the school-society relationship if he is to mediate between the expectations held for the school and the goals it attempts to realize; if he wishes to create understanding for what the school is doing and improve its impact upon the community; and if he wishes to develop climates for the acceptance of changes that are needed. To do this the administrator needs to understand cultural values and patterns. He needs to know the means by which controls are established and influence is brought to bear upon the school. He needs to gain a perspective of elementary school education—its present status, its function in American society, and the possibilities for its development.

ELEMENTARY EDUCATION: CURRENT GUIDELINES

Leaders of elementary schools are concerned with two major questions as they attempt to move elementary school education into a new phase of development. The first deals with the functions and purposes of elementary education and how they are to be translated into instructional objectives at the operational level in the ongoing school program. The second deals with the nature of the institution required to achieve the objectives. Obviously the two questions are interrelated, but they are also questions that cannot be settled within the confines of professional decision making alone. These are largely matters of public policy.

Fortunately these two questions relative to elementary education have not become matters of intense public conflict as was the case in secondary schools during the past decade. With the exception of the concept of the neighborhood school—which has come under sharp attack in most communities with racial divisions—work has proceeded in more or less orderly fashion with communities willing to support exploratory and experimental projects. This condition will permit the elementary school administrator a sounder base from which to work providing he moves ahead with reasonable plans. An examination of purposes and institutional arrangements may serve to reveal current issues and problems facing the leadership of elementary schools.

STATEMENTS OF EDUCATIONAL PURPOSES: SOCIAL POLICY FOR ELEMENTARY EDUCATION

One means by which the functions of the school can be clarified is through a statement of purposes. Both national and local groups have been formed from time to time and have issued statements that have received wide attention. Two of these statements are the *Seven Cardinal*

Principles of Education (1918) and *The Purposes of Education in American Democracy* (1938). In their time both were able to consolidate opinion, lay as well as professional, concerning the emphasis to be given the development of educational programs. Each of these statements served to support a broader role for the school and to specify pointedly that programs be concerned with social, emotional, and physical development as well as the intellectual.

Of current interest to the reader are the statements of purposes contained in:

> Reports of the White House Conferences on Education, 1956, 1960, 1965.
> *The Pursuit of Excellence* (The Rockefeller Report), 1958.
> *The Contemporary Challenge to American Education* (Educational Policies Commission), 1958.
> *Deciding What to Teach* (National Education Association, Project on Instruction), 1963.
> *The Changing American School* (National Society for the Study of Education), 1966.
> *Imperatives in Education* (American Association of School Administrators), 1966.

These statements represent thoughtful expressions of the expectations of society at large for the education of children and youth. They are formulated as an expression of social policy for schools as a means of consolidating public opinion, providing criteria for assessing the adequacy of educational programs and a framework within which specific instructional goals can be defined.

All of the statements noted above provide a list of purposes that includes the following points:

1. Fundamental skills—reading, writing, spelling, oral and written expression, mathematical skills
2. Effective habits of work, self-discipline, independent study, intellectual curiosity
3. Knowledge and appreciation for the democratic heritage
4. Respect for human values, beliefs of others, ability to work cooperatively
5. Knowledge of civic rights and responsibilities and of American institutions
6. Awareness of relationships with the world community: geographic, political, economic, cultural
7. Understanding of the physical world and man's relation to it in terms of knowledge of the basic sciences

8. Aesthetic experiences and self-expression in the arts
9. Physical and mental health

Many problems exist between the establishment of general statements of purposes and the day-by-day objectives that guide instruction at the classroom level. Considerable freedom is expected to be exercised at the local level in matters of curriculum, activities, and services; yet, such statements have important uses in establishing the scope of the local program, priorities, and directions of program development.

PRIORITIES AMONG GENERAL PURPOSES

Although general statements of purposes represent idealized goals for schools, strong pressures have developed to require schools to devote more attention to them. Most of the statements noted in the previous section assume or specify some level of priority for the elements given. Two examples of the specification of priorities are given here.

The National Education Association statement, *Deciding What to Teach,* carries a pointed statement:

Priorities for the school are the teaching of skills in reading, composition, listening, speaking (both native and foreign languages), and computation ... ways of creative and disciplined thinking, including methods of inquiry and application of knowledge ... competence in self-instruction and independent learning ... fundamental understanding of the humanities and arts, the social sciences and natural sciences, and mathematics ... appreciation of and discriminating taste in literature, music, and the visual arts ... instruction in health education and physical education.

Responsibilities best met by joint efforts of the school and other social agencies include development of values and ideals ... social and civic competence ... vocational preparation.[1]

This statement is clear in its emphasis on organized subject content as the central concern of the school and that social, emotional, and physical development are supplementary concerns. In its full context it does expect the school to take the lead in assessing student needs and in arranging for coordination of activities of existing agencies in the community. In this sense it argues for a set of priorities and for a particular point of view relative to the function of the school.

1. National Education Association, Project on Instruction, *Deciding What to Teach* (Washington, D.C.: the Association, 1963), p. 102.

Another attempt to specify general purposes and assign priorities deserving attention was carried out by Downey and others. He reviewed classical statements from antiquity to the present concerning purposes to be accomplished through formal education and arrived at 16 statements that could be classified into four areas: intellectual, social, personal, and productive. The list is given in Table 2–1. These statements became items of an instrument which was administered to samples of educators and noneducators in various types of communities in five regions of the United States and in Canada. As an indication of a further application of this approach the State of Hawaii, beginning in 1970, conducted a massive study using the Downey instrument and model.

Table 2-1. Purposes for the Public Elementary School

Intellectual
1. A fund of information about many things
2. The basic tools for acquiring and communicating knowledge – the 3 R's
3. The habit of figuring things out for one's self
4. A desire to learn more – the inquiring mind

Social
5. The ability to live and work with others
6. Understanding rights and duties of citizenship and acceptance of reasonable regulations
7. Loyalty to America and the American way of life
8. Knowledge of and appreciation for the peoples of other lands

Personal
9. A well-cared-for, well-developed body
10. An emotionally stable person, able to cope with new situations
11. A sense of right and wrong – a moral standard of behavior
12. Enjoyment of cultural activities – the finer things of life

Productive
13. General awareness of occupational opportunities and how people prepare for them
14. Classification and training for a specific kind of high school program – academic, technical, and the like
15. Understanding the role of various family members
16. An introduction to budgeting and effective use of money and property

Among other things, Downey based his approach upon the notion that the full list represents the total educative task and that a clear distinction should be made between the total educative task and the task of the school. Further, the definition of the school's task is a matter of public decision, but with the participation of the professional. He found close agreement between noneducators and educators (see Table 2–2) relative to the ranking of priorities by the composite samples. He did, however, find differences within subgroupings of his total sample, particularly when divided geographically.

Table 2-2. Ranks of Elementary School Purposes by Composite Educator and Noneducator Samples

Purpose (abbreviated)	Educator Rank	Noneducator Rank
1. Knowledge	11	13
2. Intellectual skills	1	1
3. Creativity	4	4
4. Desire for knowledge	2	2
5. Man-to-man relationships	3	3
6. Citizenship	6	6
7. Patriotism	8	7
8. World citizenship	10	11
9. Physical	9	10
10. Emotional	7	8
11. Ethical	5	5
12. Aesthetic	12	14
13. Vocational-selective	15	12
14. Vocational-preparatory	14	9
15. Home and family	13	15
16. Consumer	16	16

SOURCE: Taken from "Some Suggestions for the Use of the T.P.E. Questionnaire" (Chicago: Midwest Administration Center, 1959), mimeographed, p. 5.

Findings relative to the priorities Downey and his associates attempted to construct are given in Table 2–3. Based upon the sampling of opinion, both lay and professional, Downey proposed a delineation between the school and other child-serving institutions. This approach is a unique attempt to obtain empirical data concerning overall educational purposes, to order the priorities on the basis of responses, and to delineate the purposes of the school from other social institutions.

TRANSLATING PURPOSES INTO OBJECTIVES FOR THE INDIVIDUAL SCHOOL

Latitude is left to local determination in matters of program specification. Diversity of abilities and interests of children, resources and

Table 2-3. The Total Educative Task

Home and Educative Community	The Public School
Primary Tasks 1. Physical health 2. Emotional stability 3. Moral integrity 4. Aesthetic appreciation 5. Social skills 6. Civic competence 7. Consumer skill 8. Patriotism 9. Home and family 10. Occupational preparation	**Primary Tasks** 1. Intellectual skills 2. Creativity and discrimination – habit of applying facts and imagination 3. Desire for knowledge 4. Fund of information about – man – his physical world – his cultural heritage – his ancestors and neighbors – his work – his civic responsibilities
Secondary Task To supplement and reinforce the school in its primary tasks	**Secondary Tasks** To supplement home and community by: 1. Fostering social competence in – man-to-man relationships – civic responsibilities – patriotism 2. Providing an environment for personal well-being in – physical health – emotional stability – moral integrity – aesthetic appreciation

SOURCE: Lawrence W. Downey, The Task of Public Education (Chicago: Midwest Administration Center, 1958), p. 22.

arrangements within schools, values attendant to teachers' exercise of choice in modes of instruction and materials, among other conditions, argue for each school's shaping a unique program in terms of guidelines previously agreed upon. It is in this realm—the translation of purposes into program objectives—that the principal finds one of his greatest opportunities for the exercise of leadership. At the same time, this opportunity is perhaps the most neglected and most inadequately handled aspect of educational administration. In this section two frameworks for the programing of objectives are considered. The dynamics of the principal's tasks are examined in Chapters 4 and 5, and the specific activities relating to curriculum construction and instruction are considered in Chapters 7 and 8.

GRID STRUCTURE FOR OBJECTIVES

One means proposed for the identification of specific objectives and the planning of instructional and other activities to meet them is that of an objectives' grid. The grid, Figure 2–1, provides a schema for the planning of objectives and activities within the context of a set of general purposes. The result, in this illustration, is a 45-cell matrix of which each cell can be examined and discussed by teams of teachers and supervisory personnel in the planning of a unified program.

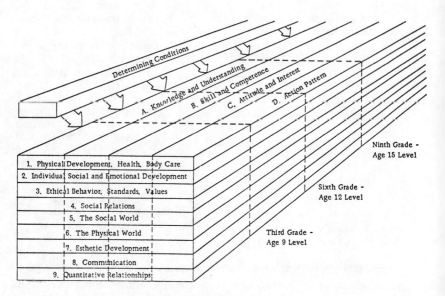

SOURCE: Nolan C. Kearney, Elementary School Objectives (New York: Russell Sage Foundation, 1953) p. 38.

Figure 2-1. Grid of Curriculum Areas with Interesting Behavioral Categories

The general purposes shown in the grid were agreed upon by a select group of educators and evaluated by a panel of critics. However, the grid device is the point of attention here, for it can provide a useful means of identifying specific objectives.[2] Further, it is possible to employ the grid to specify learner behaviors as a framework for evaluation by grade levels or at the completion of planned learning sequences.

Taxonomic Structure of Objectives. Another useful tool for the identification of educational objectives is a taxonomic structure being developed by a group of experts in evaluation. The product is a classification system that has many uses both in the specification of objectives for instruction and the assessment of learning outcomes. All educational objectives are first classified under three categories: cognitive, affective, and psychomotor.[3]

The structure of the taxonomy of the cognitive domain of objectives is given in Table 2–4 as an illustration. Care was taken to ensure that this taxonomy reflects distinctions teachers make among student behaviors as found in curricular plans, instructional materials, and teaching methods. The taxonomy was logically developed and tested for consistency, and an attempt was made to make the classification a purely descriptive scheme so that every educational objective can be represented in a relatively neutral fashion.

In the taxonomy each element is defined and explained; illustrations of objectives are given; and items for testing the objective behaviorally are suggested. Although the cognitive domain is most likely to represent objectives derived from subject matter, the affective and psychomotor domains provide the complete range of possibilities. Therefore, a school might begin with general purposes and spell out instructional objectives that are then tested through the classification represented by this taxonomy, or a school might identify the objectives it is attempting to achieve in its ongoing program and classify them according to the taxonomy to test their adequacy, consistency, and comprehensiveness in terms of overall purposes.

Both the grid and the taxonomy represent rational ways of identifying and evaluating objectives in terms of general purposes. It is important that general purposes are specified and that specific objectives be geared to them through a meaningful plan. This is the challenge of school leadership if time and effort are not to be wasted on less impor-

2. The reader is encouraged to consult the source for the detailed treatment of the development of the grid if purposes are a matter of interest.
3. Benjamin S. Bloom (ed.), *Taxonomy of Educational Objectives; Handbook I: Cognitive Domain* (New York: Longmans, Green and Co., 1956); and Robert Krathwohl (ed.), *Taxonomy of Educational Objectives; Handbook II: Affective Domain* (New York: David McKay, 1964).

Table 2-4. Taxonomy of Educational Objectives:
Categories of the Cognitive Domain

KNOWLEDGE

Knowledge
  Knowledge of specifics
  Knowledge of terminology
  Knowledge of specific facts

Knowledge of ways and means of dealing with specifics
  Knowledge of conventions
  Knowledge of trends and sequences
  Knowledge of classifications and categories
  Knowledge of criteria
  Knowledge of methodology

Knowledge of universals and abstractions in a field
  Knowledge of principles and generalizations
  Knowledge of theories and structures

INTELLECTUAL ABILITIES AND SKILLS

Comprehension
  Translation
  Interpretation
  Extrapolation

Application

Analysis
  Analysis of elements
  Analysis of relationships
  Analysis of organizational principles

Synthesis
  Production of a unique communication
  Production of a plan or proposed set of operations
  Derivation of a set of abstract relations

Evaluation
  Judgments in terms of internal evidence
  Judgments in terms of external criteria

SOURCE: See footnote 3.

tant things and if the school is to have a defensible means of demonstrating its performance.

INSTITUTIONAL MODEL FOR ELEMENTARY EDUCATION:
AN EVOLVING SCHOOL

Educational purposes represent social policy for education, and the
manner in which purposes are being implemented is transforming the

institutional forms and arrangements through which elementary education is being implemented. The idealized model of the elementary school can no longer be described as a neighborhood institution, relatively isolated from community and national affairs, devoted primarily to the activities of childhood as defined by middle-class patterns, and organized as a set of self-contained classes by grades. The picture of a teacher of music, art, or physical education, drawing upon experiences and knowledge cast in locally determined value patterns is now passé.

Pressing social, political, and economic realities have undermined preconceived notions about what the elementary school should be. These realities have brought societal pressures upon the school and change is being powered by influences outside of the formal processes of education itself. The professional leaders from the individual school to the national level are under intense pressure to respond with realistic programs. The transformation of the elementary school from a traditional model of stability and modest, evolutionary improvement is occurring rapidly. A single, clearly defined model is not yet in sight, if indeed a single institutional model will evolve, or is even desirable. The present conditions offer unique opportunities for educational leadership because they open up a range of choice not possible before.

Changing Commitments. Expressions of societal commitments and concerns are having profound effects upon the elementary schools. Precise descriptions of the dynamics of the effects upon the schools are not known. Some can be seen immediately as in the changes in the public perception of teaching and teachers following the pronouncements of President Johnson, particularly when these pronouncements were immediately supported by federal legislation. Others are very subtle, as the change in the view that education ends at some fixed point to the sudden rush into adult education, job training, and the like. Despite this lack of clarity over dynamics, several marked changes have occurred that have already created a response in the institutional arrangements of the elementary school.

1. *Orientation to National Needs.* The basic commitment of the school is shifting in terms of meeting national policies. The school is responding to the call to develop citizens who are knowledgeable about pressing social and political realities that face the nation. It is no longer sufficient to be concerned about development of a literate person but one who is literate about his society and its problems.

2. *Cultivation of Rationality.* The climate of concern about the ele-

mentary school program is that it have substance. Schools are focusing more upon subject matter with the need to staff the elementary schools with subject specialists, to group pupils by academic ability, and to gear instruction to intellectual outcomes.

3. *Acceptance of Uncertainty—Expectations for Change.* Parents, who a decade ago would have protested abandoning the self-contained classroom, now accept the fact that their child will not have a single teacher. The value of flexibility and change over stability is readily accepted in most communities.

These shifts in attitudes have not merely permitted, but required, that many schools change their programs and their institutional arrangements accordingly.

Institutional Responses. Elementary schools have exhibited several kinds of responses to societal needs and changing perspectives about elementary education. Some programs have been dramatic as the break-down of the neighborhood school concept in racially segregated communities and the initiation of busing pupils; another illustration is the extension of programs due to federal initiation as in the Head Start Program. Some changes have been less dramatic but just as pervading, as the shift in school architecture to create flexible spaces, beautify the school environment, and break out of the "series of boxes" approach to educational facilities. The changes felt by the authors to be most pervasive are the following:

1. *Downward and Outward Extension of the Elementary Program.* The almost universal acceptance of kindergarten has led to prekinder-garten and nursery school programs that are true educational and not baby-sitting responses. Head Start is an extension of the school year but also a further extension of the school program into the community. It exemplifies the opening of the school program in a planned way to fuller use of community resources.

2. *Broadening Programs.* Compensatory education,[4] guidance serv-ices, and extensions of standard instructional arrangements have all been added rapidly at the elementary school level. In the latter category are learning laboratories, material resource centers, language and science laboratories, independent study and project facilities, all representative of efforts to create broadening choices and opportunities.

3. *Specialization of Programs and Staff.* The addition of specialists

4. See Benjamin Bloom, *et al., Compensatory Education for Cultural Depriva-tion* (New York: Holt, Rinehart and Winston, 1965).

in large numbers has already been noted—more than 100,000 special teachers are now employed in elementary schools out of a total of slightly more than 1,000,000 teachers. With specialization also comes diversity as well as depth of program. Where specialization of programs and staff is carefully planned into a continuous program, student talents and interests can be more fully developed.

4. *Organizational Patterns.* The elementary schools have been much more flexible and creative than any other unit of the educational ladder in developing new, workable organizational plans. In the present decade the elementary school has successfully demonstrated programs that include nongraded, dual progress, team teaching, continuous progress, and several adaptations of the self-contained classroom. Each of these plans is discussed in Chapters 6 and 15.

The model of the elementary school is an evolving one. Although several dimensions of its evolution are clear, it is unlikely that a single model will prevail as has been true in the past. Fortunately, creative responses to educational needs and societal demands are becoming more possible. Perhaps in another decade the educational park, being advocated in Chicago and tried out experimentally in Pittsburgh, will become the model for the large city, while a highly flexible, multimedia learning center will become the model for some communities, and a modified neighborhood school will prevail elsewhere.

CURRENT STATUS OF ELEMENTARY EDUCATION

Despite the contention that the model of the modern elementary school is an evolving concept, there is little reason to believe that public policy is clear about directions and extent of development, that the structures and controls are being created to support educational change, or that adequate resources are being made available to move ahead with dispatch. Too frequently a few dramatic demonstrations of new approaches to educational problems and challenges lead to the false notion that a new norm has been established and that schools will be able to move ahead unhampered and be given the means to do so.

Most of the new educational features mentioned in this chapter and those discussed in Chapter 3 are reasonably well established in that they have been successfully demonstrated and, to some extent, adopted by a small percentage of schools. They cannot be offered as typical of elementary schools everywhere. In the important areas of direction,

control, and support—areas that depend upon public policy decisions—
elementary schools appear to be seriously hampered.

Lack of Direction. When serious social crises occur that involve important cultural values, society does not quickly consolidate opinion
and turn to a resolution of the crisis. Rather, groups tend to divide into
camps and attempt to hold more closely to their own beliefs and practices. The Cold War is one crisis that, highlighted by the Russian Sputnik,
has created serious differences over education in the United States. Another international crisis of the Cold War, Viet Nam, has caused some
split in educational leadership and some public division because of decisions over resources to be allocated to education. Without doubt, most
important to elementary education over the long term is the lack of
direction and clear commitment relative to problems of poverty and
minority cultures.

Though not the only institution involved, education—primarily elementary education—is undoubtedly the key to the war on poverty and
to the integration of minority cultures. Schools must help children and
youth understand minority cultures; otherwise minority groups and the
poverty stricken will be treated, as now, as though their lot is their own
making and that they must deal individually with problems which are
beyond them. Head Start and Compensatory Education are programs of
promise, but the schools have yet to be permitted to respond adequately
to the problems. This is not to say that educational personnel are geared
and ready to go and are being restrained, but that educational systems
have not been given a mandate and the resources to coordinate educational potential to attack these configurations of problems and solve
them.

Poverty, minority groups, crime, delinquency, and related ills serve
to emphasize the significant social role of the school and the fact that
the school's role has many dimensions. The importance of the school
as a social institution can be seen from the illustration. The war on
poverty must be won, or one of the basic tenets of our culture will be
destroyed; and we shall be less a people than we were—not to realize
the dream of universal education, of freedom, equality, and dignity for
all would be shattering to our cultural and moral life. Our nation must
solve these problems if we are to become a truly educated, intelligent,
and moral society—a truly united society. Education is one of the keys.

Differences over the directions elementary education is to take remain a serious handicap to sound program development. Three rather

distinct views of what the elementary school should be persist today. One position is that the elementary school should be limited to the skills and the intellectual training of children and that the curriculum should be confined almost exclusively to academic subjects. A second view emphasizes the pupil's intellectual development as primary but recognizes the emotional, social, physical, and vocational aspects of the child's growth. This view places the school accountable for the child's total development by making it the coordinating agency in calling upon other social institutions and agencies to share with the school in fulfilling a total educational plan. A third view is that the school must take full responsibility for the range of the child's needs and provide or directly control the programs and services to meet this task. Whenever issues of public policy occur, these three positions are almost sure to appear.[5]

Structures, Controls, and Support. Perhaps most critical of the structures and controls of public education is James B. Conant. In attempting to analyze the structure within which educational policies are developed, Dr. Conant writes, "I defy anyone to describe in a few pages the organization of education in the United States." [6] He further writes, "In urging each state to organize itself so that it can bring about a cooperative enterprise in policy formation, I admit I am indulging in optimistic hopes." [7] Two of the authors of this volume, after study of factors causing diversity in provision for education, concluded:

Critical examination of the factors producing diversity, as they relate to the total context of school administration, reveals a system enormous in size and extent, operated through unrelated and inconsistent organizational patterns, directed through fragmentary and poorly coordinated systems of controls, inadequately and unequally financed, and tampered with in various ways by numerous agencies of at least three levels of government.[8]

There seems little need to document for the reader or to pursue in detail a description of the inequalities of support for schools, of the lack of coordination of programs between districts—to say nothing of coordi-

5. The National Education Association Project on the Instructional Program of the Public Schools identifies these three positions as a result of their investigations. Dorothy M. Frasor (ed.), *Deciding What To Teach* (Washington: National Education Association, 1963), p. 87.

6. James B. Conant, *Shaping Educational Policy* (New York: McGraw-Hill, 1964), p. 18.

7. *Ibid.,* p. 32.

8. Lloyd E. McCleary and Stephen P. Hencley, *Secondary School Administration* (New York: Dodd, Mead & Co., 1965), p. 7.

nation between states, or of the absence of machinery to aid rapid adoption of new materials or instructional innovations. The present structures and patterns of support were designed to maintain a system, not to develop it. The present arrangements assume a slowly developing, static concept of education more concerned with minimum standards than with maximizing potentials.

The elementary administrator needs to study the structures for education which form the context for the functioning of the school in which he works; he needs to concern himself with broad policy formulation— as represented in the model in Chapter 1; he needs to involve himself in the forces and influences that will ultimately shape the institution that elementary schools must become.

ORGANIZATIONAL CONFLICT AND THE PRINCIPAL'S ROLE

Social forces both within the establishment of education—teacher groups, professional associations, school boards, administrators—and forces outside of education are using the educational scene as an arena for conflict. Three kinds of conflicts tend to occur: (1) *individual conflict* occurs when a member of the organization sees (a) alternatives to conditions to be unacceptable to him, (b) uncertainty that the alternatives proposed will resolve a given condition, or (c) the belief that the alternatives being proposed are incompatible; (2) *intergroup conflict* tends to occur when (a) groups believe they do not have sufficient influence in decisions, (b) they perceive their goals to be different from those being pursued, or (c) both of these conditions occur simultaneously; and (3) *interorganizational conflict* usually encompasses some of the same elements as intergroup conflict with the exception that conditions often include very clear power struggles, or when the appeal to power is too uncertain or undesirable to the parties involved, some definite bargaining procedure is agreed upon.[9] A detailed examination of conflict situations is not possible in this volume, but an examination of the position of the principal relative to organizational conflict is in order.

9. The reader wishing to investigate organizational conflict might begin with the study of *Conflict Management in Organizations,* Foundation for Research on Human Behavior (Ann Arbor, Michigan: Center for Research on Conflict Resolution, University of Michigan, 1965); James G. March and Herbert Simon, *Organizations* (New York: John Wiley & Sons, 1958), pp. 113–135, containing models for conflict analysis: and Amitai Etzioni, *Complex Organizations* (New York: The Free Press, 1961).

Donald Erickson has attempted to assess the perceptions principals have of their role. He describes six images principals hold of themselves:

housekeeper—keeps the school in "running" order by arranging schedules, setting up conferences, socializing, and the like. He is much disturbed by the presence of conflict, but he does not see himself as involved and is not apprehensive about conflict.

daddy—stands as the protector of the teachers and identifies strongly with them. In conflict situations he is bypassed or ignored by both teacher groups and administration.

superteacher—sees his role as passing on his expertise to less capable people. He is caught in the middle of any conflict and becomes a target in intergroup struggle; he is incapable of coping with militancy on the part of teachers.

foreman—administers the rules and sees himself as a supervisor of teachers. Since he seldom participates in making the rules, he is often rejected by teacher groups and seen as a bureaucrat by outside groups. In intergroup or interorganizational conflicts he must rely upon the authority of his office rather than upon personal or professional resources—he finds it difficult to maintain his authority since it is usually negotiated away in situations in which he has no voice.

change agent—has carefully thought out leadership strategies and sees his role as staying abreast of current developments, attempting to implement them in the school's program. He sees conflict as one natural condition of change, and he treats it as one variable in his leadership strategies. [See Chapters 5 and 6.]

systems analyst—specializes in defining educational goals in relation to overall purposes and has the technical skills to measure performance levels of his staff and replan the instructional elements of his school accordingly. He makes his voice heard in terms of solid evidence and his knowledge of education, and he is able to provide the feedback and monitoring devices necessary to influence performance. [See Chapters 4–7.] [10]

These six views, to the extent that they represent principal self-images, give an interesting beginning point to an understanding of the stance a given principal might take in a conflict situation and the effectiveness with which he might deal with conflict. Of the three kinds of conflict identified, that of intergroup conflict (that is, conflict between clearly identifiable groups within an organization) contains most of the characteristics of the other two types as far as the principal's role is concerned. This type of conflict is used in the analysis that follows.

10. Donald Erickson, *The Principal as Administrator* (Chicago: Midwest Administration Center, mimeographed, n.d.).

Organizational Response to Conflict

Conflict occurs through the medium of confrontation in each of the three types of organizational conflicts conceptualized at the opening of this section. The administrator usually leads in establishing an organizational response to confrontation, and this response takes one of five forms and often proceeds in stages through two or more of them. These forms of response are: persuasion, accommodation, problem solving, politics, and negotiation. When the arena of conflict is kept confined to the school unit the principal usually has been able to manage the conflict and bring it to resolution in terms of his perceptions of the dissident individual or group purposes and the choice of the form of response that is acceptable and within the alternatives available to the school. The ability to influence both the form of resolution and the arena of conflict are crucial factors to conflict management.

Of the five forms of response, the first three (persuasion, accommodation, and problem solving) represent analytical approaches. That is, the administrator initiates an analysis of organizational and member goals, alternatives, relationships involved, and the like, and he assumes that a resolution is possible without basic organizational realignments, challenge to the authority structure, or intervention from external authority. The latter two forms of response (politics and negotiation) are manipulative and represent patterns in which the only outcome can be bargaining for "who gets what." In the manipulative forms of response the area of conflict is enlarged beyond the school unit and the usual challenges, appeals to the public, falsification of demands, and the like are present.

Teacher Militancy and Conflict Resolution Through Professional Negotiation

The form of conflict that is currently most threatening to the principalship, is most widespread, and will have the most pervasive effect upon educational administration in the future, is that of professional negotiations resulting from teacher militancy in regard to educational decision making. This is not because professional negotiations are undesirable or necessarily destructive to educational excellence. The dangers result from (1) existing cultural conditions that encourage conflict and conflict resolution through the use of power, (2) the patterns being established for professional negotiations, (3) the nature of the bargaining process and the conditions being made subject to the bargaining process, and (4) the effects negotiations are having upon the authority structures of the school.

The school, as viewed throughout this chapter, is an institution that cannot exist without being affected by the dominant values of the culture and by the other institutions that express these values. There seems to be little question that this society is in the process of institutionalizing conflict models as the legitimate means of resolving differences. Impasse procedures and confrontation—boycotts, demonstrations, strikes—on the part of teachers, students, and outside groups are employed without restraint as a means of instituting conflict that can only be resolved by bargaining.

The nature of professional negotiations (bargaining) depends upon the establishment of intergroup power in confrontation with organizational authority. Teachers have now attained sufficient intergroup power to force bargaining procedures concerning many critical factors in the educational process. These include: work loads, nonteaching duties, class size, schedule preferences, professional meeting requirements, the right to exclude children from the classroom (New York City agreement of 1965), and others. The bargaining power of any intergroup seems to depend upon four factors. These are:

1. The intergroup (teachers) perceives itself as critical of organizational operation.
2. The intergroup perceives itself as having the prestige and power to require the board of education to bargain (cost of disagreement to the employer exceeds the cost of agreement).
3. The intergroup accepts the tenet that teachers must be accepted as irreplaceable.
4. The intergroup has the militancy to strike and the cohesiveness to carry it out.[11]

Whenever these conditions are met, teacher groups have attained the power to enforce a bargaining arrangement to resolve conflict. Teacher groups today are fully aware of their strengths concerning each of the four factors and view themselves as having grievances that must be brought to the conflict state and carried to the bargaining stage for resolution.

11. Educational Research and Development Council of the Twin Cities Metropolitan Area, *Teacher, Administrator, School Board Relationships* (Minneapolis, Minn.: the Council, 1967).

The Principal's Role in Professional Conflict

The most serious dilemma confronting the principal is that he is faced with teacher confrontations at the building level and forced to carry out provisions of negotiated contracts with little or no participation in their development. Interviews of principals in a three-state area of the Midwest in which negotiations had just been completed indicated that no principals in any of the districts involved were included in the negotiation process.[12] Results of these negotiations produced changes in the authority structures of the schools and always by limiting the discretionary power of the principal. Apparently, principals need to become aware that they must act for the protection of their own interests in salary, tenure, and other material and welfare issues; and they must also be actively interested in their ability to function as principals. This latter condition points directly at the principal's authority in school organization.

The authors argue in Chapter 1 that, to a substantial degree, the school is a self-contained organizational unit and must function as such. Schools need to be relatively autonomous, with teachers and principals able to exercise discretionary powers at the building level. This condition —organizational autonomy as well as the nature of the teaching task— argues for a professional mode of school organization, i.e. one based upon technical expertise. Organization based upon such expertise, however, provides the grounds for intergroup conflict. This conflict becomes evident when teachers insist that final decisions must remain in the hands of the professional and that the principal must function strictly in administrative affairs and not in professional matters. The principal can ameliorate the threat to his position only by recognizing the bases of conflict and by working with vigor to protect the autonomy of the school unit of organization and by establishing his leadership role upon professional as well as administrative grounds.

REFERENCES

Allen, Roy B., and Schmid, John, *Collective Negotiations and Educational Administration* (Columbus, Ohio: University Council for Educational Administration, 1968).

American Association of School Administrators, *Imperatives in Education* (Washington, D.C.: the Association, 1966).

12. A team of the Midwest Administration Center, University of Chicago, conducted these interviews in 20 school districts.

Cahill, Robert S., and Stephen P. Hencley, *The Politics of Education* (Danville, Ill.: Interstate, 1964).

Conant, James B., *Shaping Educational Policy* (New York: McGraw-Hill, 1964).

Davis, Donald E., and Neal C. Nickerson, *Critical Issues in School Personnel Administration* (Chicago: Rand McNally & Company, 1968).

Department of Elementary School Principals, *The Elementary School Principalship in 1968* (Washington, D.C.: National Education Association, 1968).

Epstein, Benjamin, *The Principal's Role in Collective Negotiations* (Washington, D.C.: National Association of Secondary School Principals, 1965).

Goslin, David A., *The School in Contemporary Society* (Chicago: Scott Foresman, 1965).

Harrington, M., *The Other America* (New York: Macmillan, 1962).

Hechinger, Fred M., *Pre-School Education Today* (Garden City, N.Y.: Doubleday, 1966).

Jarvis, Oscar T., and Lutian R. Wootan, *The Transitional Elementary School and Its Curriculum* (Dubuque, Iowa: Wm. C. Brown Co., 1966).

Klausmeier, Herbert J., et al., *The Multiunit Organization and Elementary Education in the Decade Ahead* (Washington, D.C.: U.S. Department of Health, Education, and Welfare, Cooperative Research Program OE 5–10154, 1968.)

Myrdal, Gunnar, *Challenge to Affluence* (New York: Pantheon Books, 1962).

National Education Association, *Deciding What to Teach* (Washington, D.C.: the Association, 1963).

———, *The New Elementary School* (Washington, D.C.: the Association, 1968).

National Society for the Study of Education, *The Changing American School, 65th Yearbook,* Part II (Chicago: University of Chicago Press, 1966).

———, *Social Forces Influencing American Education, 60th Yearbook,* Part II (Chicago: University of Chicago Press, 1961).

Rudy, Willis, *Schools in an Age of Mass Culture* (Englewood Cliffs, N.J.: Prentice-Hall, 1965).

Watson, Goodwin, *Concepts of Social Change* (Washington, D.C.: National Training Laboratories of the National Education Association, 1967).

Chapter 3

EMERGENT FORCES AND
NEW DIRECTIONS TO
EDUCATIONAL CHANGE

ACCOUNTS of the accelerated rate of change in educational practices cite as causal factors such events and conditions as World War II, Sputnik, public attention to quality and purposes of education, demands to accommodate special needs not previously considered, money expended for research and development, technological and cultural changes, and the knowledge explosion.[1] These manifestations have not been linked in satisfactory cause and effect relationships between any one of them and a given set of school practices. Even the Sputnik launching, which can be directly linked to the passage of the National Defense Education Act and subsequent activity in mathematics, science, and modern foreign language curriculums, is a precipitating event rather than a cause.

The accounts cited above are only representative of a long list that does, however, solidly document the facts of the occurrence of change. Many, including Carlson, a recognized investigator of educational innovation, believe the changes represent a revolution in education. Carlson writes:

A good many people, reflecting on our times, suggest that we are in the advanced stages of a revolution in education. To support their case, these people point to an accelerated rate of change and consideration of change

1. Glen Heathers, "The Role of Innovation in Education," *National Elementary Principal*, September, 1963; Richard I. Miller, "Some Current Developments in Educational Change," *A Multidisciplinary Approach to Education Change* (Lexington, Ky.: Bureau of School Service, University of Kentucky, 1965), p. 8; and Hilda Taba, *Curriculum Development Theory and Practice* (New York: Harcourt, Brace and World, 1962), p. 3.

in educational practices that have occurred over the past eight or nine years. The evidence is somewhat convincing.[2]

If the changes are revolutionary rather than evolutionary in character, and the authors will attempt to establish that some of the changes do indeed represent revolutions, those who work with elementary programs require a perspective and approaches fundamentally different than would otherwise be the case.

THE STATE OF REVOLUTION IN EDUCATION

The state of affairs that requires a careful examination of emergent forces and directions to educational change can be enumerated briefly. First, "crash" programs have been mounted in practice and in research that bear upon elementary education. They have occurred only because of a recognized need and are made possible by unprecedented support, largely by the federal government. Second, the emergent forces for change are national in character, exerting influences apart from the local and state agencies that traditionally and legally determine the nature of elementary education. These influences, though stemming from groups and individuals both inside and outside of education, see local and state systems as targets for change. Third, the impact of change occurred first in secondary schools and is only now beginning to be felt heavily at the elementary level. The responses of practicing elementary school administrators and teachers are yet to be determined. These conditions argue for the most serious study and consideration by those working in the elementary schools.

The picture is confused on several counts. Revolutionary changes have occurred or are occurring in areas of society that are of fundamental concern to elementary education; they are also occurring within education itself. At the same time, the tempo of evolutionary change has rapidly increased. (Some mistakenly argue that this alone is revolutionary.) To illustrate, one major source of influence new to elementary education—national curriculum projects—is predicated on the assumption that what is taught is shaped primarily, if not exclusively, on academic disciplines. At the same time, other sources are actively urging new attention to characteristics of children and to new conditions in society. These inconsistent, if not opposing, influences are creating pres-

2. Richard O. Carlson, *Adoption of Educational Innovations* (Eugene, Ore.: University of Oregon, 1965), p. 2.

sures upon schools. In this chapter the authors attempt to focus upon selected elements of the conditions noted above: the concept of revolution as that concept applies to elementary education, the fundamental nature of some of the forces having importance for elementary education, and conditions underlying change in the elementary schools.

EVOLUTIONARY DEVELOPMENT: CONVENTIONAL VIEW

The body of principles, theories, and practices that guides the mainstream of educational work today is usually thought of as having developed through an evolutionary process. At some point in time a given condition was studied, and a principle was discovered that was built into the knowledge and technique of the field. Through this process of accumulation, current practice arrived at what it is today—false or less effective methods giving way to others. Apparently this somewhat comfortable notion of normalcy and progress does not account for the manner in which any professional or scientific field develops, including education. A somewhat different explanation seems to fit the facts— one that might be more useful in explaining current developments in elementary education.

A CONCEPTION OF NORMAL PRACTICE

The group of teachers, administrators, professors, leaders of professional associations, and a relatively few others involved in educational affairs came to develop common beliefs about various aspects of educational practice—pupil grouping, instructional modes, school organization, curriculum and its development, in-service training of teachers, and the like. These beliefs are derived from study, observation, and practice and, with these, a *tradition* and a *commitment*. This set of beliefs represents a way of dealing with the problems encountered by the profession, and a considerable element of arbitrariness is included.

Each major function and facet of work becomes regularized into modular, or normal, practice. Normal practice gets written into the texts by which new members of the profession are trained, and most of the professionals spend their lives working out these ideas and refining them. Normal practice functions so that each problem need not be attacked as though it were unique. This condition requires a common way of approaching problems so that basic assumptions are not dredged up and examined each time a problem is encountered. Practice becomes closely aligned to the models and is fitted to the "natural order of things." New ideas and insights add novelty, but they do not get built into practice when they run counter to the models; when they don't "fit," they are termed interesting but not useful.

In the development of a field, the emergence of a given model means that random practice, or practical experimentation outside of the model, largely disappears. Those who cling to one or another of the older views are shunted aside from the mainstream of work and are thereafter ignored by the professional. The emergence of the graded elementary school combined with the self-contained classroom brought on feverish work in the writing of graded textbooks. Curriculum development became primarily an effort to place content into grade-level blocks. Teacher specialization became based upon the grade structure, and many toiled over the rudiments of music, drawing, and other features of the isolated, self-contained classroom. The practical work of the field became that of implementing the accepted model.

To be accepted, a model must *seem* better than alternative models. It need not solve all the problems; even a model competing to replace an established one need not solve all the problems of the model it seeks to replace. However, it must have promise, capture the imagination of the profession, and gain commitment from the profession. Once accepted and put into practice a model is not easily replaced. The graded elementary school and the self-contained classroom successfully competed with a number of models including the platoon school, the Dalton plan, the Winnetka plan (see Chapter 6), and others. These competing models were based upon new knowledge concerning individual differences and learning theory and were successfully demonstrated; yet the profession would not give up its older model. Instead, it incorporated some of the features that fit the old model—specialist teachers to supplement the self-contained classroom, activity periods, even platoon scheduling within the old pattern—and it ignored the rest: those elements that did not fit.

All professions and fields of study seem to evolve in this way—medicine, law, engineering, even the research disciplines operate on the basis of models and paradigms that govern practice, determine the problems to be solved, and guide selection of strategies to solve them. No field can be understood and interpreted in the absence of an *implicit* body of theoretical and methodological belief that serves as a guide to evaluation, criticism, and selection of practice. The acceptance of such models serves to end intradiscipline debate (by making unnecessary constant argument over fundamentals) and provides confidence to get on with the more detailed, precise, and consuming work. In the fields of the precise sciences Kuhn writes:

No part of the aim of normal science is to call forth new sorts of phenomena; indeed those that will not fit the box (paradigm) are often not seen at all. Nor do scientists normally aim to invent new theories, and they are often intolerant of those invented by others. Instead, normal-scientific research is directed to the articulation of those phenomena and theories that the paradigm already supplies.[3]

Normal practice in education, the authors contend, is not that of invention of new models. Evolutionary development, as in all the professional and scientific fields, consists of the refinement and application of established models to the problems encountered in practice. What then is the function of revolution in educational development, how does it occur, and where are the areas of revolutionary development that need to be studied and observed—those that are likely to determine the new directions?

ANATOMY OF EDUCATIONAL REVOLUTION

Educational revolution seems to occur in three fundamental ways. The first cause of change is basically evolutionary but results in minor crises within the domain of the professional community. As indicated above, normal practice or research does not seek to invent new models for practice or to refute an existing one. Normal practice does not seek out new fact or theory and, when successful, finds none. Also noted is the fact that no model is capable of resolving all problems—the program designed for all students is not likely to be maximally effective for all; the program designed to be completely individualized is likely to lose coherence and overall direction. Problems that occur in the application of a model do not cause the model to be discarded. For one thing, no model is likely to be rejected unless another, more promising, is available to take its place. Problems that occur in applying a model in practice result in elaborate adaptations. The need to individualize instruction moved elementary schools to introduce multiple texts which aided in large part to introduce the unit method of teaching. None

3. Thomas S. Kuhn, *The Structure of Scientific Revolutions* (Chicago: University of Chicago Press, 1962), p. 24.

of these were particularly crisis evoking until, through the unit method, fused, core, broad fields, and other curriculum models began to be proposed.

Revolution Through Crisis by Inventive Practice

In the case noted here, adaptations of the model in order to make it function satisfactorily in practice eventually produced the invention of competing models. The fused (social studies, language arts) and the broad fields (particularly, the sciences) replaced the separate subject curriculum in the elementary schools. A second kind of crisis could have arisen in this type of revolution. It is best illustrated, in secondary rather than in elementary education, in the case of the comprehensive high school. In this case attacks upon the problems unresolved by the model of the comprehensive high school resulted in so many minor adjustments that the model became increasingly blurred. Few practitioners could agree about what the comprehensive high school was. Conant wrote his book *The American High School Today* largely to attempt to rally the profession to a common acceptance of his view of the comprehensive high school—an authoritative person was needed to clarify and save the model.

Crises, such as the ones described, are largely internal to the profession. They create considerable insecurity and conflict. Early attacks upon problems unresolved by the model are approached through normal practice—minor adjustments are made until, still unresolved, the problems call for a major transformation or model substitution.

Revolution Through Crisis in Theory Development

A second type of crisis occurs, often producing educational revolution, when able men consciously examine assumptions underlying present practice as a means of freeing the hold of established models. Then, such men focus upon a given problem and attempt to give it structure— perhaps to magnify the breakdown, make the conditions more striking and more suggestive of imaginative solution; finally, a new proposal emerges, and efforts are made to experiment with it. This is perhaps the popular image of the educational researcher or the creative professor. The recent work of Goodlad in his espousal of the nongraded elementary school is an excellent illustration (briefly described in Chapter 6).[4]

4. John I. Goodlad and Robert H. Anderson, *The Nongraded Elementary Schools* (New York: Harcourt, Brace & World, rev., 1963).

This sort of crisis is not a cumulative process as in the first type. It is rather a reconstruction of a major feature of the field from fundamentals, a reconstruction that changes some of the most fundamental generalizations as well as several models, their methods and applications. During the transition (and a transition is definitely underway toward the nongraded elementary school), there will be decisive differences in the modes of solution of problems by the old and the new model, neither being entirely successful. When the transition is complete, the profession will have changed its view of its problems, its methods, and its strategies. The effect upon curriculum construction, instruction, and other features of the elementary school due to the adoption of the nongraded plan is ample evidence of a change similar to the visual gestalt—some things are now seen that were not seen before. This type might well be termed revolution created by new theory. Even so, it is likely to occur only when established practice is felt to have gone badly astray.

Revolution Through Social-Cultural Change

The third type of revolution is created directly by change in the social-cultural environment. The *raison d'être* of education is an external social need. Any significant social or cultural event is likely to have an impact upon the schools. Several significant external forces are noted, but the dynamics of how such events and conditions become forces for educational change are not examined here: first, because such examination is not essential to treatment of the concept of educational revolution and, second, because the manner in which external conditions become influential to educational change seems to be highly particularistic, even to some extent accidental.

Several kinds of conditions in the social-cultural environment may have potential to create educational revolutions—as defined by a state of crisis and replacement of modular practice. Three kinds of conditions, though interrelated, seem to represent categories significant to education. These are: (1) knowledge and the changed view of the function of knowledge, (2) technology, and (3) social perspectives. Each is briefly examined here.

Knowledge and the Uses of Knowledge. The knowledge explosion and the employment of structural and conceptual features of knowledge as different ways of perceiving, integrating, and applying knowledge in fruitful inquiry have important implications for the theory of educational revolution. They are, in fact, emerging models (perhaps more correctly, paradigms) for the organization and presentation of content in the elementary school curriculum. This emphasis is responsible for the movement to reconstruct elementary curriculums more in line with purely intellectual pursuits and away from content based upon immediate, real problems of learners.

The emerging model contains the following elements: (1) discreteness of the academic disciplines, (2) identification of "new" content, (3) preparation of "packaged" instructional materials to be introduced wholesale to the schools rather than developed in the schools, (4) in-service training of teachers in institutes where the package is taught in much the same manner as the teacher is expected to teach it, and (5) attempts to base materials on the "structure" of the discipline and shape instruction to attain "intuitive thinking" and "discovery" of concepts. As with the broad fields and fused curriculums, this model leaves many problems unresolved. Among these problems is the matter of priority among as many as 30 separate disciplines, the tendency to organize content from the top down thus creating serious sequence and time-fit problems, and the loss of spontaneity and creative teaching.

There is no question, however, that the elementary school must deal with the problems of new knowledge and new uses of knowledge. Whether experimental work will produce a model that will resolve the "knowledge crisis" or whether the one broadly outlined above can become a serious contender of current practice remains to be seen.

Technology. Many students of change believe that technology is the basic cause of cultural change. Rapid transportation and communication, automation and cybernetics, increased productivity, and the host of other technological advances that have transformed our lives have also created changes in cultural values, permitted the population explosion, and required population mobility and the urban crush. That same technological advance has invaded education. Closed circuit television, computerized learning centers, language laboratories, teaching machines, overhead projectors, programed texts, and seemingly innumerable other items have become available to elementary schools within the past decade.

At this moment the introduction of technology is viewed as merely another aid to the teacher, an adjunct to the teaching process. Goodlad, writing about the changing American school, comments:

Still another asset in present-day curriculum change is extensive inclusion of materials other than textbooks in the total instructional package: films, filmstrips, programed exercises, living creatures, and realia of many kinds. It often is impossible for teachers to offer the courses without using the new audiovisual media.

He concludes by stating, ". . . the problems now call largely for wise expenditure of funds and improved education of teachers." [5] Goodlad's statement represents the usual response to an invention or an innovation, that it is only another aid to the ongoing work.

If technology works in such revolutionary ways in society at large, is there any reason to believe that it will not have fundamental influences upon the educational establishment and the manner in which education is patterned and its processes carried out? The assimilation of technology under established models for practice means the introduction of novelty, and this is the seed of revolutionary change. If the new technologies are really assimilated into teaching practice, something that did not occur with the motion picture, it is likely that teaching procedures will be fundamentally changed.

Social Perspectives. The reality of social and cultural change need hardly be argued. Values, ideas, and attitudes relative to very important concerns of family relationships, material well-being, minority groups, and a host of other matters that range from individual morality to government responsibility for social problems and international tensions form perspectives within which individuals make decisions. The dilemmas of such choices become sharply focused when one is instantly and dramatically faced—through modern media of travel and communication—with discrepancies between values and practice. The movement to a more open society, to relativity in values, and to objectivity in choice runs counter to practices and values that permitted the growth of poverty and delinquency alongside of affluence, of discrimination in a society committed to freedom, and of routine and drab communities when the human spirit seeks achievement, variety, adventure, and appreciation.

The discrepancies between desire and reality, between practiced values and ideas created the social crisis. As Clifton Fadiman has observed:

It [our times] is marked by the absence of any general, tacit adherence to an agreed-upon system of values. It is in such a crisis period that we live. . . .

5. John I. Goodlad, "The Curriculum," *The Changing American School, 66th Yearbook of the National Society for the Study of Education* (Chicago: University of Chicago Press, 1966), p. 47.

Our present educational system quite properly mirrors this uncertainty. It mirrors our mental chaos. There is nothing else it can do. . . .[6]

If Fadiman's observation has any truth in it, it points to the fact that value crises in society penetrate the schools. Crisis does not always lead to revolution because, in the culture realm, it may lead to a strong reactionary movement—a return to old values. The contending models have appeared; the revolution may be well under way.

THE PROCESS OF REVOLUTIONARY CHANGE

In preceding sections, the authors have attempted to describe normal practice, to explore and illustrate the thesis that revolutionary change does occur and is occurring in education—particularly elementary education —and to identify the types of forces internal and external to education capable of producing revolutionary changes. Here an attempt is made to suggest explicitly the process by which revolutionary change occurs.

Premodel Stage

Until the time when a given model or set of models emerges, no field or discipline, in the true sense, exists. Some individuals work at a given function, usually with a minimum of communication between them; no body of specialists or programs of training appear; and work proceeds pretty much at random, without guides or principles for making choices or evaluating results. Each individual must construct his own notion— of a school, an area of science, or whatever he works upon—starting with basic assumptions and working to propositions upon which he will base his work. In short, without models each individual must begin anew rather than build upon the work of others.

This was the process in elementary education into the 1830's. By then a group of men, including Horace Mann, Caleb Mills, and others, began to search for models to guide practice. Mann went to Germany and then spent the remainder of his life getting an adapted version of the German elementary school accepted in the United States. By 1841, the graded elementary school was successfully introduced and accepted.

6. Clifton Fadiman, "Today's Lost Generation," *Saturday Review*, September, 1959, p. 13.

Emergence of Models

The acceptance of a model requires considerable faith because it obviously will not solve all the problems of a given area of interest, and commitment is necessary because much work remains in putting a given model into practice. However, a model with promise offers the chance to avoid tedious bickering and justification of assumptions and permits serious work to begin. As a given model gains acceptance, the work of the original men becomes recognized, a community (profession) of interest forms with much communication, support, and reinforcement. In mature professions of medicine, law, and education, associations support the model, journals publicize it, and educational programs incorporate it and teach adherence to it. This begins a period of *normal practice,* and evolutionary pursuits usually result in successful, high accomplishment.

Crisis and Emergence of Competing Models

In the course of normal practice various problems resist solution—as that of individual differences in the old model of the elementary school. Also, new problems arise both within the profession and within society which provide the reason for the profession's existence. The prevailing model is patched up and amended to make do. A model is not likely to be given up without a new one to take its place, and then only after resistance.

When a model becomes blurred—as has that of the self-contained classroom—some members of the profession become disenchanted with the model; others become concerned and work harder to support it. When the model does not serve to prescribe practice clearly, it causes erratic practice to occur and other possibilities are tried. *Once a significant group abandons the model, revolution can begin.*

The Revolutionary Phase

At the point that a group of the professional community commits itself to *some concrete proposal* to supplant an existing model, revolution has occurred. It may be a quiet revolution; it may be a small one—affecting only a segment of the total professional community; but it is revolution nonetheless. This is so because the new group must attack the old. It must persuade and force a new institutional arrangement. It must amass supportive data and argument, capture the journals,

training programs, professional associations, and convince visible practitioners to demonstrate the new approach. This has happened, or is
happening, in regard to a host of elements in education.

Once a model is refuted and attacked, each group must establish
within the professional community the premises on which its model is
based or the choice *ipso facto* goes to the other side. There are no
grounds, even in science, for the testing of one model against another;
for evaluative procedures depend in large part upon the model itself.
It is because of this fact that the evolution of a profession or a discipline
depends upon revolution.

The return to normal practice actually is but a beginning in the cycle
of change. The view thus far presented—and it must be studied as a
theory within which emergent forces and new directions can be assessed
—leaves out consideration of change at the level of the school itself.
This aspect must now be examined.

EDUCATIONAL CHANGE AND THE SCHOOL

In periods of educational revolution the school cannot merely go
about its normal business. It is caught up in much of the trauma of
conflict and/or uncertainty. Some schools, for various reasons, leap to
be one of the first to emulate a newly proposed practice. Others hold
back until the new proposal has been demonstrated and the demanding
work of establishing procedures for change, preparing materials, and
whatever is entailed in the change is worked out. Still others resist
change or attempt to ignore it. Those who hold out to the bitter end,
when not located in some isolated area or in a particularly provincial
community, are more or less written off by the profession. Each school
establishes a characteristic mode of approach to change—a stance.

In any specific change process, some schools become the "first introducers." Whether or not a school can function as a first introducer
depends heavily upon the community and the characteristics of the
authority structure in the school and the school system. The findings of
Ross seem to be representative of other studies in describing necessary
community characteristics:

It tends to be high in per capita wealth, per pupil expenditure for education,
percent of eighth grade, high school, and college graduates. A fairly high
median (educational level) has been attained by those who are 25 years of
age and older. A low percentage of the population is foreign born. It has a

high level of understanding of what schools can do. This community is part of a super community which offers many cultural advantages and which contains other schools interested and actively engaged in promoting more adaptable schools. The symbiotic groups in the community are staff-connected with the schools. These groups are interested in the quality of schools in their area. The school makes special effort to work with groups that have a favorable effect upon adaptability.[7]

Certainly all communities with the characteristics noted above do not become first introducers. Communities with these characteristics have produced the vast majority of first introducer schools largely because they sought able administrators and teachers, provided resources, and supported imaginative approaches to improvement.

A critical element in the school setting itself is the administration group and whether or not individuals at key levels become agents for change and/or support individuals within the professional staff who can become agents for the intended change. Brickell writes:

Authority is a critical element in the shaping of institutional decisions. Schools depend heavily upon administrative authority in decision making. Consequently, the control center of the institution, as the schools are managed today, is the administrator. He may not be—and frequently is not—the *original source of interest in a new type of program,* but unless he gives it his attention and actively promotes its use, it will not come into being.[8]

Individuals who are willing to support and lead change (change agents) must occupy key positions in the administration at the central office level, in the principalship, and in the strategic teaching roles involved.

The role of the principal is a key one because he must work at both the policy and implementation levels. He must create an optimum climate within his school and work to achieve understanding and reinforcement for it within both the school system and the community. The principal is faced with four kinds of problems in his role as change agent. He must find the time and resources for analysis and planning both for himself and his staff; he must develop methods of intervening in the operation of normal practice without destroying morale and introducing confusion; he must devise ways to minimize risk to pupils and teachers which do not compromise the practices he wishes to try out;

7. David H. Ross, *Administration for Adaptability* (New York: Metropolitan School Study Council, 1958), p. 14; also see the writings of Henry M. Brickell, Richard O. Carlson, and Matthew Miles.
8. Henry M. Brickell, *Organizing New York State for Educational Change* (Albany, N.Y.: State Education Department, 1961), p. 24.

and he must find ways to recognize and reward the efforts of those who invest themselves in improvement of the school.

The principal's role as change agent is more important than it might at first appear. Considerable evidence is accumulating that neither supervisors nor teachers are effective in the change process. Harris, an apparent spokesman for the professional association for supervisors, writes, "The schools do not have recognized change agents. Supervisors have not been perceived as change agents in most school systems and have rarely functioned as such." [9] If the schools do not have change agents, the principal is at the most critical position in the structure to prepare the organizational arrangements—create roles, and train individuals at the teaching and supervisory levels to function in those roles.

A review of investigations of the teacher's role in change presents a picture of how serious might be the task of the principal as a trainer of teachers and creator of roles for change. Pellegrin, as a result of his own investigations and the analysis of the work of other researchers, concludes:

... existing role expectations both discourage and impede change, but in the main they mitigate against the teacher's serving as a source of innovation ... it is quite evident that there is a lack of institutionalized procedures through which the teacher can play an important role in the innovative process. Given this existing situation, it is unrealistic to expect basic changes to occur as a result of innovativeness by the teachers.[10]

Basic strategies for change depend to some extent upon the specific change being considered, but whether a change is considered at all with the possibility of successful adaptation depends upon creating structure— both roles and processes—within the school.

Whether the school is a first-introducer of change, an early-adopter, or a late-adopter, change is now an inevitable condition of educational life. This does not require that schools assume a "change for change's sake" approach. Rational choice is not excluded from the change process —except as the choice of the local administrator himself. Further, note

9. Ben M. Harris, "Strategies for Instructional Change: Promising Ideas and Perplexing Problems," in James Roth and Robert R. Leeper (eds.), *The Supervisor: Agent for Change in Teaching* (Washington, D.C.: Association for Supervision and Curriculum Development, 1966), p. 93.

10. Rolland J. Pellegrin, *An Analysis of Sources and Processes of Innovation in Education* (Eugene, Ore.: Center for the Advanced Study of Educational Administration, University of Oregon, 1966), pp. 8–9. Matthew Miles, Paul Rodgers, H. M. Clements, and Clifton Clayne provide analyses that are in fundamental agreement with those of Pellegrin.

should be taken that many kinds of change occur from mere drift, to accidental innovation, to total adoption of an already existing practice, to a planned and controlled change that includes adaptation and revision to meet local conditions.

AN APPRAISAL

The conception of educational change as revolution as a normal part of the overall evolutionary development of the field seems to fit the facts of both history and contemporary developments. Unfortunately the lack of machinery—now possibly begun to be provided through large federal expenditures—has made the development of new models a slow process. Rather than "growing" competing models, education has tended to experience crisis through disenchantment with old forms and practices and long periods of agonizing appraisal and uncertainty. Now a period of crisis (as defined by the theory being proposed in this chapter) is upon education. The crisis will be more intense for the elementary schools than the secondary and perhaps greater than for higher education. In fact, it might be argued that the crisis period for secondary education is passing, and the acceptance of newer models is about to begin a long period of normal practice. Not so for elementary education.

Elementary education cannot follow the lead of the secondary schools. The scholars who helped reconstruct the secondary school curriculum have largely failed at the elementary level or have come to see the protracted period that is necessary to make solid progress and have fled. The crisis period, despite the discomforts it brings, means opportunity. The strictures of normal practice are gone and able men can try imaginative proposals and participate in their trial. This is the period—the time when the new directions are set—that may well be the most exciting period of this century in elementary work.

REFERENCES

American Association for Supervision and Curriculum Development, *New Insights and the Curriculum, 1963 Yearbook* (Washington, D.C.: the Association, 1963).

Carlson, Richard O., *Adoption of Educational Innovations* (Eugene, Ore.: University of Oregon, 1965).

Carter, Launor F., *The Impact of Automation and Technology on Education,* SP-282 of System Development Corporation (Santa Monica, Calif.: the Corporation, 1961).

Chase, Francis S., "School Change in Perspective," *The Changing American School, 65th Yearbook of the National Society for the Study of Education* Chicago: University of Chicago Press, 1966).

Ellul, Jacques, *The Technological Society* (New York: Alfred Knopf, 1964).

Miles, Matthew (ed.), *Innovation in Education* (New York: Bureau of Publications, Teachers College, Columbia University, 1964).

National Education Association, *Principals Look at the Schools* (Washington, D.C.: the Association, 1962).

Passow, Harry A. (ed.), *Education in Depressed Areas* (New York: Bureau of Publications, Teachers College, Columbia University, 1963).

Schramm, Wilbur, *Programmed Instruction: Today and Tomorrow* (New York: Fund for the Advancement of Education, 1962).

Williams, Thomas R., "The Study of Change as a Concept in Cultural Anthropology," *Theory into Practice*, February, 1966.

Willower, Donald J., "Barriers to Change in Educational Organizations," *Theory into Practice*, December, 1963, No. 2: pp. 261–264.

Part II

Functions, Leader Behavior, and Organization

Chapter 4

FUNCTIONS OF THE
PRINCIPALSHIP

ADMINISTRATION in elementary schools has existed for more than a century—a period during which the position of elementary school principal has become standard in the administrative organization patterns of American school districts. Yet, far from becoming standardized, the appropriate functional responsibilities of the principalship have been viewed from a variety of standpoints that have produced a great diversity in definitions of the principal's role. These are evident in current school district practices, are reflected in research on the principalship, and are fostered by divergent scholarly viewpoints.

Thus, the principal has been seen variously as an instructional leader; as a guidance person; as a pupil control agent or disciplinarian; as a group dynamics expert who can work with a variety of teacher cliques within a building; as an expert organizer of the school schedule; as a diplomat who can work smoothly with irate parents; as a chief of the building custodians who knows how to keep a building spic and span; as a business man who keeps his budgets, accounts, and supplies in order; as an office manager who prepares accurate records on time; as a mediator of various forces within the community; or as an effective worker with the PTA and other school groups.[1] He is also seen at times as one who assists in policy making; as one who initiates innovations; and as one who is adept at playing many different roles in interaction with diverse school publics.

1. *The Right Principal for the Right School* (Washington, D.C.: American Association of School Administrators, 1967), p. 16.

PRACTICE, RESEARCH, AND SCHOLARLY VIEWPOINTS

Current practice in school districts is simultaneously a witness to instability in definitions of the principal's role and a prime motivator for attempts to formulate more adequate conceptions of his role. That divergent practices reflect differences in role definitions is evident in (1) the varying ways in which principals spend their time, (2) the unstandardized expectations for the principal's participation in policy making and leadership activities, (3) the variation in importance attached to particular administrative duties, and (4) the diversity of expectations for participation in the building of educational programs; in improving teaching and learning; in upgrading the quality of staff and student performance; and in developing sound school management procedures. In identifying these situations, the Illinois Elementary School Principals Association commented as follows:

Although the position is well known, the role of the principal is not always so clearly understood. The reasons for this are numerous, especially at the elementary school level. What is expected of an elementary building principal varies greatly among school districts—in some districts the individual principal has been allowed to determine his or her own role—until very recently educational standards for assignment to the position have not been well defined—in many communities elementary principals have not enjoyed the time and freedom to participate in the conferences and programs of their regional, state, or national professional associations to as great an extent as the high school principals or superintendents—until very recently the large number of very small districts in America was not conducive to the development of well-planned administrative structure and adequate definitions of administrative and supervisory roles.[2]

Results of research on the elementary principalship point to the same kinds of problems regarding role definition. Ranniger, after analyzing doctoral theses, textbooks, and staff handbooks, concluded (1) that there is disagreement about the appropriate duties of elementary school principals, (2) that job descriptions are usually not in written form, (3) that principals characteristically spend much time in duties of a clerical nature, and (4) that there is great variation in the time devoted to curriculum development, supervision, and public relations.[3] Similiar varia-

2. Illinois Elementary School Principals Association, *Raising Standards for Elementary School Principals* (Springfield, Ill.: the Association, 1963), p. 13.
3. Billy J. Ranniger, "A Summary Study of the Job Responsibilities of the Elementary School Principal" (Doctoral dissertation, University of Oregon, 1962).

tions in conceptions of the principal's role are strikingly revealed through analysis of the more than 50 studies on the elementary principalship reported in *Dissertation Abstracts* since 1960.[4] In addition, Gross and Herriott's study of the elementary school principalship showed that there are differences in leadership expectations for the principal, in managerial and social support provided by the principal's superiors, in the extent of involvement of principals in teacher selection procedures, and in expectations for the principal's role as an agent of change.[5]

Scholarly viewpoints regarding the principal's role are both a source and an expression of diversity. They sometimes present conflicting ideals for the principal to emulate, and they often advocate extending the principal's responsibilities beyond current practice in a variety of areas. Thus, although McNally and Dean have noted that "... there are no clearly defined and commonly agreed-upon criteria enabling us to identify with any degree of certainty or unanimity those knowledges, insights, and skills uniquely necessary to the proper functioning of an elementary school principal,"[6] a large portion of the existing textbook literature has stressed a *leadership* conception of the principal's role. Particular emphasis has been placed upon the principal's responsibilities in the following areas: developing expertise in instructional supervision, enhancing teaching-learning climates and situations, improving staff morale, and structuring staff leadership activities. Pronouncements of the national and state associations of elementary school principals have tended to reinforce these emphases.

That scholarly viewpoints sometimes present the principal with con-

4. See, for example, Barbara Ruth Frey, "An Analysis of the Functions of the Elementary School Principal, 1921–1961" (Doctoral dissertation, Indiana University, 1963); John Herbert Crotts, "A Comparison and an Analysis of the Concepts of the Role of the Elementary School Principal" (Doctoral dissertation, University of Missouri, 1963); Harry Seymour, Jr., "A Study of Ideal and Actual Curriculum Role Conceptions of Selected Elementary School Principals from Southern Illinois" (Doctoral dissertation, Southern Illinois University, 1963); Truman Owens, "A Study of the Role of the Elementary Principal as Perceived by Parents" (Doctoral dissertation, University of Michigan, 1963); Elmo Raymond Giulieri, "The Role of the Elementary School Principal as Perceived by PTA Executive Board Members and Principals" (Doctoral dissertation, University of California, Berkeley, 1963); George Joseph Smith, Jr., "A Handbook of the Responsibilities and Functions of the Rural Elementary Principal in Connecticut" (Doctoral dissertation, Columbia University, 1963).

5. Neal Gross and Robert E. Herriott, *Staff Leadership in Public Schools* (New York: John Wiley & Sons, 1965), pp. 106–120.

6. Harold J. McNally and Stuart E. Dean, "The Elementary School Principal," in Donald Leu and Herbert Rudman (eds.), *Preparation Programs for School Administrators* (East Lansing, Mich.: Michigan State University, 1963), p. 114.

flicting ideals is illustrated by views regarding his role in instructional supervision and leadership. Contrary to the idea that principals have an important direct role to play relative to instruction, some critics have maintained that such activities violate the need for autonomy in the work of teachers—that the work of principals should be increasingly oriented toward the administration and strategic coordination of school operations rather than toward central involvement in teaching-learning activities.[7] A succinct statement of this point of view has been offered by Campbell:

... for any principal to assume that he can know all about first grade reading, all about the social studies, all about language arts, all about science, is absurd. Instead of acting as though he were an instructional expert, the principal should be concerned with getting instructional experts, what to do with them when he gets them, and how to relate these experts to each other. If the principal insists on being the math or reading expert, he may fall down on doing some of the things which only *he* can do. He may fail to fulfill his responsibilities for clarification of purpose, for coordination of total effort, and for securing the best possible resources.[8]

Such a diversity in definitions of the elementary principal's role defies summary except in terms broad enough to include school administrators in general. Indeed, definitions of their roles and functions *as a class* have shown significant variation over the years.[9] These can be expressed as types, each of which has had its impact in shaping concepts of the appropriate functional responsibilities of school executives. The *inclusive type* has required school administrators to be competent in the performance of all administrative tasks and duties identifiable in the school setting. The *exclusive* or *restrictive type* has sought to establish a clear separation between policy making and administration—with a resultant emphasis upon the organizational maintenance function of school executives.[10] The *standardized* or *division-of-labor type* has stressed the need for impersonalizing and standardizing administrative procedures through the development of job descriptions, the establish-

7. See Myron Lieberman, *Education as a Profession* (Englewood Cliffs, N.J.: Prentice-Hall, 1956), Ch. XV; and Donald A. Erickson, "Changes in the Principalship," *The National Elementary Principal*, Vol. 44, April, 1965, pp. 16–20.

8. Roald F. Campbell, "Application of Administrative Concepts to the Elementary Principalship," *The National Elementary Principal*, Vol. 44, April, 1965, pp. 21–26.

9. Van Miller, "Four Definitions of Your Job," *Overview*, November, 1960, pp. 60–61.

10. See John Walton, *Administration and Policy Making in Education* (Baltimore, Md.: Johns Hopkins Press, 1959).

ment of bureaucratic working patterns, and the structuring and formalization of work flow procedures in the school setting. A more encompassing definition, the *integrative* or *relational type*, has directed attention to the need for developing, maintaining, and managing decision processes in relation to educational goals and purposes, school operations, and necessary adjustments and interactions (*a*) within the organization and (*b*) between the organization and its environment.[11] Each of these types has grown out of different, though overlapping, bodies of assumptions regarding the purpose, emphases, and character of educational administration. Models of administrative function based on these assumptions have resulted in a diverse array of images for the performance expectations of school principals.

TOWARD A RATIONALE

In today's elementary school an imposing variety of demands confronts the principal. From the exigencies of day-to-day practice, from the conclusions of reputable research, and from the value judgments of scholars, he must derive priorities for the numerous functions of his office. Successful performance of his administrative duties will depend upon his ability to separate the crucial functions from those that are trivial. A conceptual scheme for identifying the significant dimensions of his performance is presented in the rationale underlying the functional view of administration presented in this chapter.

Major Premises

The following major premises lie at the base of the functional view of administration:

1. *The elementary school administrator functions not in isolation but as an important member of an administrative performance system.*

Systems have been defined in many ways, but the two which follow are particularly applicable to school administrative performance systems. One author has visualized a system as consisting of:

...a bounded collection of interdependent parts, devoted to the accomplishment of some goal or goals, with the parts maintained in a steady state in relation to each other and the environment by means of (1) standard

11. Daniel E. Griffiths, *Administrative Theory* (New York: Appleton-Century-Crofts, 1959).

modes of operation, and (2) feedback from the environment about the consequences of system actions.[12]

A second writer has defined a system as:

... any recognized aggregate of dynamic elements that are in some way interconnected and interdependent and that continue to operate together according to certain laws and in such a way as to produce some characteristic total effect. A system, in other words, is something that is concerned with some kind of activity and preserves a kind of integration and unity; and a particular system can be recognized as distinct from other systems to which, however, it may be dynamically related. Systems may be complex; they may be made up of interdependent subsystems, each of which, though less autonomous than the entire aggregate, is nevertheless fairly distinguishable in operation.[13]

It should be recognized that in the school setting administrative systems are complex and extensive. They involve many different positions —from department head to superintendent—which embrace a large number of functions. Functional interdependence of parts—a basic aspect of systems—is highly visible in the educational administrative systems, and effective meshing of various functions is essential to the operation of the system.

2. *A well-rounded concept of administrative function at the elementary school level can best be achieved through comprehensive consideration of the significant functions of school district administrative performance systems, and through intensive analysis of the interrelationships between the functions of elementary school administration and the functions of the total administrative system.* In developing this concept, attention must be focused upon (*a*) the functional emphasis of different positions, (*b*) the context in which the functions are performed, (*c*) the integrative relationships among functions and positions, and (*d*) the processes used to guide interaction within the system and between the system and its environment.

3. *The functions of a school district administrative performance system may be encompassed along four major dimensions.* The descrip-

12. Matthew B. Miles, "Planned Change and Organizational Health," in Richard O. Carlson, *et al., Change Processes in the Public Schools* (Eugene, Ore.: Center for the Advanced Study of Educational Administration, University of Oregon, 1965), p. 15.

13. Floyd H. Allport, *Theories of Perception and the Concept of Structure* (New York: John Wiley & Sons, 1955), p. 469.

tive model of elementary school administration presented in Chapter 1 foreshadowed these four dimensions and indicated some of the important functional responsibilities of the elementary school administrator along each dimension.

Dimension I. *Development and legitimation of broad educational policies relating to the basic ends and purposes of education.* This dimension of administrative activity is essentially political in character. It involves the performance system's responsibility to structure policy that will define the directions and emphases of public education. Effective performance along this dimension requires members of the system to accept responsibility for offering professional advice on issues of public policy affecting education. Moreover, educational administration is seen as being intimately related to public administration: concern is evidenced for defining the interrelationships between education and existing economic and social policies, programs of social reform, and problems associated with race relations, equal educational opportunity, changing occupational structures, the growth of science, and mass society.

Dimension II. *Development and legitimation of operational policies that seek to implement broad educational policies.* Here, the administrative performance system seeks to translate broad educational policies into specific operational policies in each task area of administration: instruction and curriculum development, staff personnel, pupil personnel, finance and business management, school plant and services, school-community relations, and relations with local, state, and federal agencies.

Dimension III. *Technical-managerial implementation of legitimized educational policies.* The implementation of legitimized policies proceeds through several steps: (*a*) determination of the specific functions required in each task area if organizational goals are to be achieved, (*b*) allocation of functions to positions through a logical system of task division, (*c*) formalization and integration of decision making, communication, and work-flow patterns, and (*d*) definition of authority and responsibility relationships within the organization.

Dimension IV. *Sophisticated use of administrative processes in each phase of administrative activity.* Effective school leaders and managers are characterized by skill and competence in decision making, programing, communicating, directing change, appraising, and improving morale. Competence in the use of these processes is essential in both organizational and community settings if the first three dimensions of administrative function are to be mounted in effective fashion.

DEVELOPING BASIC EDUCATIONAL POLICIES

The practice of democracy as it evolved in America showed concern for the free expression of the governed regarding governmental jurisdiction. This concern led to a separation of functions in both public and private sectors of the society between constituencies or their representatives and agencies for operating society's institutions. Thus, an underlying assumption of administration, as pronounced by Goodnow, has been that government consists of two separate functions: politics and administration.[14] Ideally, the constituents (or their representatives) are responsible for making policies while the administrators of their institutions are responsible for carrying the policies into effect. However, increasing complexity of institutions and growing professionalism on the part of administrators have led to criticisms of this view. Respecting the public sector, for example, Price has stated that

... the great failure in our political vision is our not seeing that the main function of the top career administrators is to develop policy. If the career administrators above the level of the specialized bureaus do not provide strong support for their political superiors in the development of policy, our system of political responsibility suffers.[15]

In the school setting, the classical view has dictated that the school board, as representative of the people, should make policies, and that the administrator should implement the policies. This view has also come under criticism in recent years.[16] There is evidence that in actual practice the activities of school boards and superintendents are not clearly separated. Griffiths, after studying boards and their superintendents, concluded that

... there was no real dichotomy of board and superintendent functions. As far as could be determined ... they worked as a team, with considerable overlap in functions. The generally accepted notion that the board establishes

14. Frank J. Goodnow, *Politics and Administration* (New York: Macmillan, 1900).
15. Don K. Price, "Administrative Leadership," *Daedalus*, Fall, 1961, p. 8.
16. See for example, Paul H. Appleby, *Policy and Administration* (University, Ala.: University of Alabama Press, 1959); Jack Culbertson, "Essay-Review: The School Administrator and Policy-Making Function," *School Review*, Spring, 1961, pp. 98–111; Philip Selznick, *Leadership in Administration* (Evanston, Ill.: Row, Peterson & Co., 1957); James G. Harlow, "Purpose Defining: The Central Function of the School Administrator," in Jack A. Culbertson and Stephen P. Hencley (eds.), *Preparing Administrators: New Perspectives* (Columbus, Ohio: University Council for Educational Administration, 1962), pp. 61–71.

policy and the superintendent administers the policy would seem to be an oversimplification of what is actually a rather complex relationship.[17]

Certainly, the nature of this relationship draws the superintendent inevitably into policy-making activities. He is a participant in deliberations which precede policy decisions and is thus in a strategic position to influence their outcome. His ideas and advice are sought by the school board as guides to its policy making. And finally, his responsibilities to the board frequently make him the initiator of new policies.

Focusing on the relationship that exists in practice between school boards and superintendents provides an example of the interdependence in interaction of two elements of the administrative performance system. For successful operation, the relationship should be characterized by cooperation and coordination that will enhance both functions of policy making and policy administration. Indeed, the emphasis upon system dynamics is well placed by Griffiths when he states,

The strength of the governance of the American public school resides in this interplay between the superintendent and the board. The relationship between the board and the superintendent can best be described as one of *teamwork*. One cannot function effectively without the other. Good policies cannot be made without the help of the superintendent, and good administration is impossible without the support and encouragement of the board.[18]

This statement is no less true when applied to the entire administrative system of which the board and superintendent are inseparable parts. It is the system as a whole that must meet the challenge of formulating good basic policy, and meeting the challenge requires attention to both the system's environment and its internal operations. This requires keen perception of education as part of the whole society—political, social, and economic. It demands sensitivity in this context to educational implications of current trends. It calls for skills not only in advocating alternatives for serving social purposes, but also in utilizing properly all components of the system in determining and legitimizing educational purposes.

The Principal and Broad Policy Development

As the administrative performance system functions to formulate broad policy, the central functions are performed by the superintendent

17. Daniel E. Griffiths, *The School Superintendent* (Albany, N.Y.: Center for Applied Research in Education, 1966), p. 93.
18. *Ibid.*, p. 94.

and those administrators who work closely with him—his "cabinet."
Elementary principals may actually be members of this group, as in
small and medium-sized school districts, or the cabinet may consist of
various central-office personnel such as directors of program, staff personnel, pupil personnel, business affairs, and research. Nevertheless, the
nature of tasks related to policy making demands that principals work
closely with these people.

Principals in the modern social context characterized by rapid change,
are often in the most strategic positions to appraise the educational
implications of changes taking place. They stand as heads of operating
units of the school system where the impact of social movements is felt.
If school principals can develop insights into the relationships between
educational policy and social trends and can visualize ways for education to help meet cultural ends, they will be in a position to function in
the policy-making dimension within their administrative systems.

The principal should expect to cooperate with other cabinet members
to develop broad educational policies for legitimation by the board of
education and the broader community. His capacity will be to assist, to
advise, and to create meaningful educational propositions for consideration by the administrative cabinet. With them, he has a responsibility to
find a stance on policy issues that may be tested with community groups
and opinion leaders as well as advocated by the board of education.

The interrelationships that exist between members of a typical administrative performance system in the policy-making dimension are indicated in Table 4–1. The functioning of elementary principals in this
matrix may be clarified by discussing some of the indicated problem
areas. For example, population growth and metropolitanism in a growing industrial community produce continual population shifts and con-
centrations which have impact particularly on the elementary schools.
The situation is often complicated by difficult race relations, and serious
questions arise regarding equal educational opportunity and quality of
programs. When the administrative system is faced with the need for
basic policy in problems such as this, the elementary principal functions
to assist the superintendent (position indicated by 3 in Table 4–1), who
coordinates the efforts of his cabinet and advocates their policy stance
with the school board (depicted by 2). The system also draws upon
its other members functioning at different levels (depicted by 4 and 5)
to bring all its resources to bear on the problem.

The system pictured in Table 4–1 may be more or less like various

Table 4-1. Suggested Interrelationships Among Positions in the Determination of Broad Educational Policies

Position	Rating
Superintendent	2
Secondary School Principal	3
Asst. Sec. School Prin.	5
Department Head	4
Elem. School Principal	3
Director of Program	3
Coord. of Adult Education	4
Coord. of Sec. Education	4
Coord. of Elem. Educ.	4
Instructional Supv. and/or Consultant	5
Dir. of Pupil Personnel	3
Coordinator of Guidance	4
Attendance Officer	
Dir. of Staff Personnel	3
Dir. of Research	3
Dir. of Business Affairs	3
Coord. of Bldgs. & Grounds	5
Coord. of Transport	5
Coord. of Cafeteria	4
Business Manager	5
Teachers	4
Community Leaders & Groups	5
Lay Advisory Boards	4
Board of Education	1

Function: Relating educational policy to broad societal movements and determining ways in which education can implement the purposes of the broader culture

LEGEND

1 = Enact policy
2 = Advocate policy, consult, coordinate
3 = Assist supt. in determining policy to be advocated
4 = Advise on matters specifically submitted
5 = Provide exchange of views

Sample problem areas:

1. Equal educational opportunity
2. Excellence in education
3. Population growth and mobility
4. Allocation of societal resources
5. Automation, science, technology
6. Changing occupational structure
7. Race relations and cultural deprivation
8. Conflicting world ideologies
9. Public-private interest conflicts
10. Metropolitanism

actual systems depending on their size and location. The functions of elementary principals in various systems may differ in particulars, but the nature of this function will remain essentially the same in developing broad educational policies. They should assist and advise at the cabinet level, structure meaningful educational propositions, and communicate freely with teachers and the community in testing them.

DEVELOPING OPERATIONAL POLICIES

Enactment of broad educational policies by the board of education establishes ends to be met by the operation of the school system. Stating desirable ends, however, does not guarantee that they will be met, because there is always a multiplicity of means through which a given goal may be realized. The administrative performance system is faced with the problem of outlining the best methods for achieving its purposes. These decisions are expressed in the form of operational policies which serve to translate broad policies into more specific workable terms that will guide the functions of the system in each of its administrative tasks. In this dimension, the system is primarily occupied with the allocation of its own resources, the exercise of its own skills, and the employment of its own means toward achieving its purposes. The professional abilities of its members are drawn upon for devising intelligent guidelines to implement general policies set by the board of education. Since general policies represent value decisions already made, the formulation of operational policy involves technological-managerial decision making rather than political decision making. Decisions made will be based primarily on *knowledge* rather than on *values,* as is indicated in Figure 4–1.

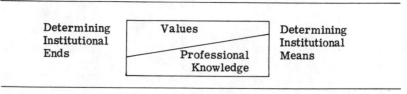

Figure 4-1. Values and Knowledge in Decision Making

Figure 4–1 suggests that decisions relating to institutional ends or purposes will be based more heavily on values than on professional knowledge—although both components will enter into decision delibera- tions. Contrariwise, the determination of means for attaining ends or purposes will ordinarily be based more heavily on professional knowl- edge than on values. Thus, values and professional knowledge enter into both kinds of decision making, but with a shift in emphasis from one to the other depending on whether the deliberations encompass institutional "ends," or institutional "means."

In education the basic purposes must be met through operational policies in the following areas: (a) educational programs and instruc- tional procedures; (b) pupil personnel, staff personnel, and finance and business policies; (c) environmental conditions that will optimize the teaching-learning process; (d) school-community relations and interac- tions; (e) emphasis to be placed on research in the improvement of knowledge and practice; and (f) attitude toward local, state, and federal agencies. The administrative system will also have to decide how poten- tial means of operation such as ETV, learning machines, packaged courses, team teaching, and teacher aides are to be used.

Developing operational policies, as an intraorganizational process, requires the involvement of all types of personnel within the admin- istrative system. Both generalists and specialists, both those with line authority and those with specialized technical knowledge have inter- dependent functions in this dimension of performance. Table 4–2 indi- cates the interrelated functions of members in a performance system for developing operational policies. In the area of pupil personnel, for ex- ample, major responsibility for developing policy falls on the line officer —the principal—and the staff personnel—the director of pupil per- sonnel and director of program—whose authority and special technical competencies are most directly related to the task area. Other line and staff personnel are consulted when their specialties are relevant to par- ticular problems (indicated by 4), and still other members of the system provide exchange of views or advice that may affect the policy (indicated by 5 and 6).

It is advantageous in addition, for the administrative system to main- tain open communications with interested external groups such as com- munity leaders or lay advisory groups. Their views along with those of members of the administrative system at all levels are helpful in review- ing and assessing initial policy statements. Their suggestions should be given careful attention prior to the final legitimation of operational policies by the board.

Table 4-2. Suggested Interrelationships Among Positions in Developing Operational Policies

LEGEND

1 = Enact policy
2 = Advocate policy, consult, coordinate
3 = Major responsibility for policy development in this area
4 = Moderate responsibility for policy development in this area
5 = Advise on points specifically submitted
6 = Provide exchange of views

Developing operational policies	Superintendent	Secondary School Principal	Asst. Sec. School Prin.	Department Head	Elem. School Principal	Director of Program	Coord. of Adult Education	Coord. of Sec. Education	Coord. of Elem. Educ.	Instructional Supv. and/or Consultant	Dir. of Pupil Personnel	Coordinator of Guidance	Attendance Officer	Dir. of Staff Personnel	Dir. of Research	Dir. of Business Affairs	Coord. of Bldgs. & Grounds	Coord. of Transport	Coord. of Cafeteria	Business Manager	Teachers		Community Leaders & Groups	Lay Advisory Boards	Board of Education
1. Instruction and curriculum policies	2	3	6	5	3	3	3	3	3	4	3	5		4	4	4	6	6	5	5	4		6	6	1
2. Pupil personnel policies	2	3	4	5	3	3	4	4	4	5	3	6	5	4	4	4	6	6	5	6	4		6	6	1
3. Staff personnel policies	2	3	5	5	3	4	5	5	5	6	4	6		3	4	3	4	4	4	4	4		6	6	1
4. Finance and business policies	2	4	6	6	4	4	5	5	5	6	4	5		4	4	3	4	4	4	3	6		6	6	1
5. School plant and services policies	2	3	5		3	4	5	5	5	6	4	6		4	6	3	3	3	3	3	5		6	6	1
6. Community relations policies	2	3	5	5	3	3	4	4	4	6	3	5	5	3	3	3	4	4	4	4	5		6	6	1
7. Policies in relation to local, state, and federal agencies	2	3	6		3	3	5	5	5	6	3	5		3	4	3	5	5	5	3	6		6	6	1

The Principal's Role in Developing Operational Policies

The principal as head of the operating unit has the responsibility of seeing that the operational policies developed in his school are in keeping with the basic policies of the school system. If he operates as a functional part of his administrative system, his activities will coordinate not only with those of central office personnel and other principals, but also with those of his teachers. The time is past when teachers and other staff members are willing to accept policies and regulations handed down from their superordinates without representation from among their own members. Most teachers today have been taught aspects of democratic administration which cause them to object to dictatorial policy making.[19]

In formulating operational policies, the elementary school principal has one advantage. Unlike secondary teachers, his faculty members are not already committed to a specific department or curricular area. Similarity of their assignments often facilitates agreement upon operational policies. The effective elementary school administrator will use his influence to see that operational policies developed will allow for necessary changes in the instructional program. In addition, he needs to be aware of new ideas and innovations in education and to direct the skills of his staff members toward using them in this dimension of administrative function.

TECHNICAL-MANAGERIAL IMPLEMENTATION

Following legitimation of broad and operational policies, the administrative performance system is faced with the necessity of carrying them out. Indeed, the importance of this dimension of performance cannot be understated. As Price has pointed out: ". . . the administrator of the future, for all his concern for policy, can never forget the other aspect of his job, which is to organize and coordinate a complex and dynamic system to carry out policy decisions. . . ."[20] In a system composed of dynamically interrelated parts, this involves not only identifying specific functions that fit into the operational scheme and allocating those functions to positions in the system, but it also requires structuring and coordinating functional interrelationships.

19. Paul J. Misner, Frederick W. Schneider, and Lowell G. Smith, *Elementary School Administration* (Columbus, Ohio: Charles E. Merrill Books, 1963), p. 33.
20. *Price, op. cit.,* p. 9.

Table 4-3. Suggested Interrelationships Among Positions in the Technical Areas of Administration[1]

LEGEND

X = Work is done
1 = General supervision
2 = Direct supervision over work done
3 = Supervision & coordination
4 = Decision on points specifically submitted
5 = Person must be consulted
6 = Person must be notified
7 = Person may be called in for exchange of views

	Superintendent	Secondary School Prin.	Asst, Sec. School Prin.	Department Head	Elem. School Prin.	Director of Program	Coord. of Adult Educ.	Coord. of Sec. Educ.	Coord. of Elem. Educ.	Instructional Supv. and/or Consultant	Dir. of Pupil Personnel	Coord. of Guidance	Attendance Officer	Dir. of Staff Personnel	Dir. of Research	Dir. of Business Affairs	Coord., Bldgs. & Grounds	Coord. of Transport	Coord. of Cafeteria	Business Manager
A. Instruction and curriculum development																				
1. Revising curriculum content and organization	1	2	7	5	2	3	X		X	5	7	7								
2. Selecting curricular materials	1	2	7	5	2	3	X	X	X	X	7	7							7	
3. Relating curriculum to time, facilities, personnel	1	2	X	5	X	7	X	7	7	7						7	6			
4. Articulating elementary and secondary program	1	2			2	3			X	5										
5. Directing program for exceptional children	1	X	4	X	X	3		7	7	7	7	7								
6. Planning and directing remedial instruction	1	2	4	X	2	3		7	7	X	5	7								
7. Directing school testing program	1	2	4	X	2	3		X	X			4			7					
8. Assisting teachers in instructional improvement	1	2	4	4	2	3	X	X	X	X	7	6			5					

[1] See Daniel E. Griffiths, et al., Organizing Schools for Effective Education (Danville, Ill.: The Interstate Printers and Publishers, 1962), p. 320.

Function	1	2	3	4	5	6	7	8	9	10	11	12	13	14	15	16	17
9. Assisting in diagnosis of pupil learning difficulties	1	2	4	4		3	X	X	X	3	X		7	7			
10. Directing adult education program	1	4	7	7	2	3	X						7	7			
11. Coordinating use of instructional equipment	1	2	7	7	2	3	X	X	X	X	7	X	7	7	5	4	5
12. Directing research and experimentation	1	5	7	7	5	5	5	5	7	7	7	X					
B. Staff personnel																	
1. Recruitment of professional staff personnel	2	5	7	7	5	5	7	7		5	5	X	7	5	5	4	5
2. Recruitment of nonprofessional staff personnel	2	5	5	5		7						X	3	5			
3. Selection of professional staff personnel	2	5	7	7	5	5	7	7		5	5	X	7				
4. Selection of nonprofessional staff personnel	2	5	5	5		7						X	3	5	5	4	5
5. Induction and orientation of professional staff personnel	1	X	3	3	X	3	X	X	3	3		5	4				
6. Induction and orientation of nonprofessional staff personnel	1	3	3	3								5	2	X	X	X	X
7. Scheduling of professional staff personnel	1	2	X	5	X	3	X	X		X	X	6					
8. Scheduling of nonprofessional staff personnel	1	3		3	3	3			3	X		6	2	X	X	X	X
9. Supervision of professional staff personnel	1	X	7	3	X	3	X	X	3	X	X	7	2	X	X	X	X
10. Supervision of nonprofessional staff personnel	1	3	3	3	3	3	3		3	3	X	7	2	X	X	4	X
11. Evaluation, recommendation to board of promotion, and retention of professional staff personnel	X	X	7	7	X	5	7	7	7	5	5	5					

(cont.)

Table 4-3. Suggested Interrelationships Among Positions in the Technical Areas of Administration (cont.)

LEGEND

X = Work is done
1 = General supervision
2 = Direct supervision over work done
3 = Supervision & coordination
4 = Decision on points specifically submitted
5 = Person must be consulted
6 = Person must be notified
7 = Person may be called in for exchange of views

	Superintendent	Secondary School Prin.	Asst. Sec. School Prin.	Department Head	Elem. School Prin.	Director of Program	Coord. of Adult Educ.	Coord. of Sec. Educ.	Coord. of Elem. Educ.	Instructional Supv. and/or Consultant	Dir. of Pupil Personnel	Coord. of Guidance	Attendance Officer	Dir. of Staff Personnel	Dir. of Research	Dir. of Business Affairs	Coord. Bldgs. & Grounds	Coord. of Transport	Coord. of Cafeteria	Business Manager
12. Evaluation, recommendation to board of promotion, and retention of nonprofessional staff personnel	X	5			5									5		X	5	5	5	5
13. Maintaining staff personnel records	1	5	X		5	5					5			X		X				
14. Obtaining and scheduling substitute teachers	1	2	5	X	X															
15. In-service education of professional personnel	1	3		X	3	3	X	X	X	X	X	7		5		3		X	X	X
16. In-service education of non-professional personnel	1							X	X	X	X			5	X		X	X	X	X
17. Directing research and experimentation	1	5			5	5					5			5	X	5				
C. Pupil personnel																				
1. Providing orientation for students	1	2	X	X	2		X	7	7		7	X								

2. Scheduling pupils	1	2	X	4	2	7	X	4	4	4	4		7	X			
3. Providing student counseling services	1	2	X	4	2								3	X			
4. Scheduling student health services	1	2	7	X		7		7	7				3				
5. Providing stud. placement & follow-up	1	2	7	7									3	X			
6. Maintaining indiv. stud. records	1	2	2	4	2	7	2	5	5								
7. Providing occupational & educational information services	1	2	X	7		7		7					3	X			
8. Assessing and interpreting student growth	1	2	X	X	2		2	4	4	5				X			
9. Dealing with pupil irregularities	1	2	X		X								7	4			
10. Applying extreme measures under dealing with pupil irregularities	X	4	5		4								7	6			
11. Directing and supervising activity programs	1	2	X	7	2	7		7	7								
12. Maintaining student accounting (attendance and census)	1	2	3		2		2							X	X	3	
13. Directing the guidance program	1	2	7	7	2	3								X			
14. Directing research & experimentation	1	5		7	5	5						5			X		
D. Finance and business management																	
1. Construction of the budget	2	X	7	6	X	X	4	4	4	6		X	X	4	X	4	4
2. Control of the budget	X	6			6	6						6		6	1		5
3. Administration of the budget	1													X	X		5
4. Debt service administration	1														2		X

(cont.)

Table 4-3. Suggested Interrelationships Among Positions in the Technical Areas of Administration (cont.)

LEGEND

- X = Work is done
- 1 = General supervision
- 2 = Direct supervision over work done
- 3 = Supervision & coordination
- 4 = Decision on points specifically submitted
- 5 = Person must be consulted
- 6 = Person must be notified
- 7 = Person may be called in for exchange of views

	Superintendent	Secondary School Prin.	Asst. Sec. School Prin.	Department Head	Elem. School Prin.	Director of Program	Coord. of Adult Educ.	Coord. of Sec. Educ.	Coord. of Elem. Educ.	Instructional Supv. and/or Consultant	Dir. of Pupil Personnel	Coord. of Guidance	Attendance Officer	Dir. of Staff Personnel	Dir. of Research	Dir. of Business Affairs	Coord., Bldgs. & Grounds	Coord. of Transport	Coord. of Cafeteria	Business Manager
5. Administration of payroll	1															2				X
6. Supervising and auditing internal accounts	1															2				X
7. Administering insurance program	1															2				X
8. Determining specifications for equipment and supplies	1	2	7	X	2	5	5	5	5	5	5	X		5	5	2	X	X	X	X
9. Writing specifications for equipment and supplies	1															2	X	X	X	X
10. Purchasing equipment & supplies	1															2		3	X	X
11. Distributing equipment & supplies	1	6		X	6	3	X			X		6		6		2	3	3	3	X
12. Inventorying equipment & supplies	1	2	3	X	2	3		X	X	X	3	X				2	X	X	X	X
13. Administering programs such as NDEA	1	2	7	7	2	3	X	X	X	X	3	X		3	3	2				X
14. Directing research and experimentation	1	5			5										X	5				

Function																		
E. School plant and services																		
1. Plant planning	1	X	7	5	X	7	5	5	5	5	7	5	7	X	5	7	X	
2. Plant construction	1																	
3. Plant operation & maintenance	1	3	7	3	3	3							X	2	2	X	7	
4. Grounds maintenance	1	3	7	3	3								X	2	2	X		
5. Scheduling bus operations	1	3	7	3	3								2	2	X			
6. Directing bus maintenance program	1												2	2	X	X	7	
7. Directing plant safety program	1	3	7	3	3								2	2	X X	X X		
8. Directing transportation safety program	1	3	7	3	3								2	2	X X	X X		
9. Coordinating and directing school lunch program	1	2	5	2	2								3	X	X			
10. Directing research & experimentation	1	5		5	5					X	X	5	5					
F. School-community relations																		
1. Preparing reports and bulletins for community distribution	1	2	X	7	5	3	X	X	X	X	7	3	X	3	5	5	X	
2. Conferring with parents and citizens	X	X	X	X	X	X	X	X	X	X	X	X	7	X	7	7	7	
3. Developing and coordinating the program	X	X	7	7	X	7	7	7	7	7	7	7	7	X	7	7	7	
4. Preparing releases for communications media	1	X	7	7	X	X	X	X	X	X	X	X	X	X	7	7	7	
5. Improving means for reporting to parents on pupil progress	2	X	5	7	X	3	5	5	5	3	7			7	7	7		
6. Direction of program for use of school facilities by nonschool groups	1	5	5	5	X	5							3	3	X		5	

In systems of public education, basic purposes point to a large number of functions, many of which will be common to all school districts. These can be grouped conceptually into task areas such as those in Table 4–2. It should be clear that there is no unique pattern for allocating these numerous functions among positions within the system. Instead, the pattern will vary from one system to another depending on fundamental assumptions sanctioned within the system concerning various positional roles and their interrelationships. Administrators, though not powerless to influence the nature of these assumptions, should certainly take them into account when allocating functions to positions.

Table 4–3 represents a scheme for allocating functions within an educational administrative performance system. The functions included are those expected to be common in most school districts, and they are classified according to the categories represented in Table 4–2. An attempt has been made to structure interrelationships in a manner adaptable to varying fundamental assumptions regarding the roles of various positions. In doing this, the following considerations were used as guides: (a) the basic task of the system in this performance dimension was taken to be that of maintaining, facilitating, and improving educational opportunity; (b) for proper functioning of the system as an integrated whole, the necessity for extensive communication and cooperation among its members was granted; (c) a decentralized pattern of operation (emphasizing the principal's role and increasing the autonomy of building units) was conceived as most compatible with this approach; (d) the concept of organization was followed which places primary responsibility for maintaining and improving teaching-learning opportunity upon the operating line extending from the superintendent to principals to teachers.

Two aspects of this last item should be mentioned. First, acceptance of this organizational principle grants authority of knowledge but denies line authority to staff personnel, making their capacity in the system an advisory one in this dimension of performance. Staff personnel function as advisors at both the central office level, where they advise the superintendent, and at the attendance-unit level, where they advise principals and teachers. Secondly, it should be recognized that in this scheme, though the superintendent has general supervisory responsibilities for functions in this dimension, the responsibility for direct supervision falls in greatest measure upon the building principals.

To illustrate how Table 4–3 may be interpreted, the first function listed (that is, revising curriculum content and organization) may be considered. For this function, major responsibility falls upon the coordinators of elementary, secondary, and adult education. The Director of Program acts in the staff capacity, while general and direct supervision of the function follows the line channel, involving the superintendent and principals, respectively.

The Principal's Role in Technical-Managerial Implementation

Technical-managerial implementation imposes a wide variety of functions upon the administrative performance system, and the elementary school principal must assume a vital position relative to nearly all of them. He is called upon to interact with a large number of the members of the system in a variety of ways. Thus, he finds himself involved in a complex role. His position as the head of an operating unit involves him crucially in work-flow patterns and requires key decisions of him relative to the total functional matrix. Thus, he is a significant person in nearly every task category.

The extent and nature of the elementary principal's involvement may be gauged by examining Table 4–3. For example, in instruction and curriculum development his responsibility encompasses either doing the work or exercising direct supervision over the work being done. On the other hand, in staff personnel, when he isn't called upon to perform tasks such as orienting and scheduling professional personnel, he performs the staff function of coordinating or advising relative to personnel selection and recruitment.

As might be expected, the elementary principal is extensively involved in the area of pupil personnel. His responsibility for nearly all functions in this category is direct supervision. That this is not done in isolation, however, is illustrated by the functional interrelationships shown in Table 4–3.

Even in finance and business management, where the principal is not generally intensively involved, he has some significant responsibilities associated with budget and school equipment and supplies.

Another major responsibility for the elementary school principal lies in school plant and services. He is involved in and exercises some degree of supervision over plant operations and maintenance, bus operations, and plant planning. Moreover, he supervises the coordination of the school lunch program.

Finally, the principal is the one who performs many of the functions relating to school-community relations. He is the one who confers with parents and citizens, who develops and coordinates the community relations program, who prepares releases for the communications media— in addition to other important responsibilities in this task category.

All of the responsibilities indicated in Table 4–3 for the elementary principal form a significant part of the administrative system's operation in implementing its policies. To function adequately as an integrated part of the system, the principal will need broad preparation in a variety of technical competencies.

PROCESSES OF ADMINISTRATION

Performance of the administrative system in each of the functional dimensions occurs through the operation of various administrative processes. The employment of processes such as organizing, coordinating, appraising, and the like marks the final dimension of performance within the administrative system; and, while an exhaustive description of all administrative processes cannot be given here, there are two aspects of administrative systems which point up certain fundamental processes that cannot be overlooked.

To begin with, the administrative performance system must be recognized as an open system. This means that it interacts with its environment, receiving (inputs) from and delivering (outputs) to it, and that it possesses the ability to recognize the effect of its outputs in the environment (feedback). For administrative performance systems in education, the system-environment interchange is complicated by the intricate sociopolitical context within which it occurs, as is represented in simplified form in Figure 4–2.

Figure 4–2 suggests that members of the administrative performance

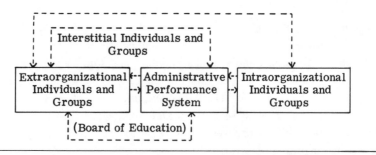

Figure 4-2. The Administrative Performance System
as an Open System

system interact with, and receive inputs from, several types of individuals and groups:

1. From *extraorganizational* individuals and groups such as citizens tax groups, the chamber of commerce, the Labor Council, NAACP, CORE, and the like.

2. From *interstitial* individuals and groups such as the Board of Education, the PTA, various "booster clubs," and the like.

3. From *intraorganizational* individuals and groups such as teachers, administrators, custodial personnel, and the like.

Moreover, the administrative performance system delivers communications (outputs) to each of the above individuals and groups and recognizes the impact of such outputs in the sociopolitical environment in which it functions. Most importantly, the system is "open" rather than "closed." Much of what goes on is determined by the nature of the inputs generated in the environment of the system and by the nature and quality of the system's responses to these inputs.

It is important to note that administrative systems have human individuals and groups as components. This means that standardized response patterns cannot be permanently programed into the system (as they can be in a purely mechanical system), and that exchanges within system components, and between components and the environment (indicated by arrows), are essentially human interactions.

These aspects of administrative performance systems focus on four fundamental processes which are essential to the system's survival: (*a*) effective communications both within and outside the system to facilitate interpretation of both inputs and outputs, promote effective meshing of functional components, and assure reliable response of the system to the environment; (*b*) realistic change of the system in response to feedback, to establish dynamic equilibrium with the environment; (*c*) intelligent decision making which will regulate response patterns of system components for optimum performance; and (*d*) careful morale building that will promote group solidarity, to achieve system integrity. Administrators must achieve competence in these essential processes which become operative at the total school district level as well as the attendance unit level.

Administrative Process in the Principal's Role

For the elementary principal, the primary sphere of operation of the administrative process is the attendance unit. The nature of an individual attendance unit, located as it is in a more or less interested community, draws the principal into contacts not only within his organization, but also between it and the outside. Thus, demands for his competencies in using the processes of administration, while not as heavy at the total school district-community level as at the attendance unit level, will be twofold at all levels: intraorganizational and extraorganizational.

For example, the process of communication, which is essential for maintaining the administrative system in relation to its environment, requires the elementary principal to confront teachers, pupils, and other personnel within his operating unit, but it also requires him to face parents, civic-minded citizens, and others outside his organization. The pattern of involvement in communications for various positions of an administrative system is indicated in Table 4–4. In this scheme, the elementary school principal has significant responsibility for all types of communications, two-person, small group, large group, and written, in both intra- and extraorganizational spheres at the attendance unit level. Demands at the community-school district level are present, but not as heavy.

Equally important to direct channels of communication are the feedback loops indicated in Figure 4–2. The administrative performance system will perceive (more or less effectively) the impact of its outputs in the environment. This provides the system with an opportunity to modify itself for better adaptation to the environment: for an effective system, the feedback loops form the basis of systemic change. In the school setting, new patterns of organization seem to be called for if the process of change is to operate properly,[21] and the elementary principal who does not take an active role as change agent [22] may have to revise his role perception in this respect.

Table 4–5, which represents the involvement pattern for systemic change in an administrative performance system, indicates that the elementary principal has significant responsibility in the process. This is true not only for directing change but also for *initiating* change, particularly at the attendance-unit level. Once again, his competencies in this

21. See Matthew B. Miles, "Education and Innovation: The Organization as Context," in Max G. Abbott and John T. Lovell (eds.), *Change Perspectives in Educational Administration* (Montgomery, Ala.: Paragon Press, 1965).
22. Daniel E. Griffiths, "The Elementary School Principal and Change in the School System," *Theory into Practice*, Vol. II, December, 1963, pp. 278–284.

Table 4-4. Communication Demands for Selected Positions

LEGEND
1 = Major demand
2 = Moderate demand
3 = Occasional demand
4 = Rare demand

	Superintendent I*	Superintendent E†	Sec. School Principal I	Sec. School Principal E	Elem. School Principal I	Elem. School Principal E	Director of Program I	Director of Program E	Instructional Supv. and Consultant I	Instructional Supv. and Consultant E	Dir. of Pupil Personnel I	Dir. of Pupil Personnel E	Dir. of Staff Personnel I	Dir. of Staff Personnel E	Director of Research I	Director of Research E	Director of Business Affairs I	Director of Business Affairs E
A. Total community-school district context‡																		
1. Two-person	1	1	3	3	3	3	1	3	3	4	2	2	1	3	2	4	2	3
2. Small-group	1	1	3	3	3	3	1	3	2	4	2	3	2	3	3	4	2	3
3. Large-group	1	1	3	3	3	4	2	2	3	3	3	3	2	3	4	4	2	3
4. Written	1	1	3	3	4	4	1	2	2	3	2	2	1	4	2	3	1	3
B. Attendance unit context**																		
1. Two-person	3	3	1	1	1	1	3	4	1	4	2	2	3	4	2	4	3	3
2. Small-group	4	4	1	1	1	1	3	4	2	4	3	3	3	4	2	4	3	3
3. Large-group	3	3	1	2	2	2	3	4	4	3	4	4	3	4	3	4	3	3
4. Written	2	1	1	2	2	2	3	4	3	4	2	2	2	4	2	4	2	4

* I = intraorganizational demands.
† E = extraorganizational demands.
‡ Refers to the total school district and its community environment.
** Refers to attendance units and their immediate community environments.

Table 4-5. Demands upon Selected Positions for Initiating and Directing Change

LEGEND
1 = Major demand
2 = Moderate demand
3 = Occasional demand
4 = Rare demand

	Superintendent		Sec. School Principal		Elem. School Principal		Director of Program		Instructional Supv. and Consultant		Dir. of Pupil Personnel		Dir. of Staff Personnel		Director of Research		Director of Business Affairs	
	I*	E†	I	E	I	E	I	E	I	E	I	E	I	E	I	E	I	E
A. Total community-school district context‡																		
1. Individual	1	1	3	3	3	3	1	3	3	4	2	3	3	3	2	4	2	3
2. Small-group	1	1	3	3	3	3	1	2	2	4	2	3	2	3	3	4	2	3
3. Large-group	1	1	4	4	4	4	2	3	3	4	3	4	3	3	4	4	2	3
B. Attendance unit context**																		
1. Individual	3	3	1	1	1	1	3	4	1	3	3	3	2	4	3	4	3	3
2. Small group	3	3	1	1	1	1	3	4	1	3	3	3	2	4	3	4	3	3
3. Large group	3	3	2	2	2	2	3	4	4	4	4	4	3	4	3	4	3	3

* I = intraorganizational demands.

† E = extraorganizational demands.

‡ Refers to the total school district and its community environment.

**Refers to attendance units and their immediate community environments.

process must include individual, small group, and large group inter-personal skills.

Demands upon the elementary school principal as an element of the administrative system regarding the decision-making process and the morale-building process are expressed in Table 4–6 and 4–7 respectively. In these areas also the principal must command individual, small group, and large group skills.

An increasing amount of information is available as a product of research in the behavioral sciences that relates to the processes of administration.[23] Studies in disciplines such as sociology and social psychology have shed light on the processes of morale building, change, and communications; research in industry and government has examined the decision-making process. Recent work in the field of education has focused on aspects of these processes related to organizational variables peculiar to educational institutions.

Competent use of the administrative processes requires an under-standing of the organizational context within which they operate. Elementary school principals become closely involved in the dynamics of organizational subsystems as they seek to employ administrative processes toward achievement of institutional goals. They need to identify and comprehend subsystems such as those outlined by Stogdill:

1. The structure of positions which is given formal definition and sanction by the differentiation of function and status.
2. The operative role system which is defined by the different degrees of responsibility, authority, and delegation exhibited by the occupants of the various positions.
3. The formal interaction system which tends to parallel the formal structure of positions but is subject to deviation in response to changing demands for coordination of individual performance and subgroup operations.

23. See, for example, Ronald Lippit, Jeanne Watson, and Bruce Westley, *The Dynamics of Planned Change* (New York: Harcourt, Brace & Co., 1958); Edgar L. Morphet and Charles O. Ryan (eds.), *Planning and Effecting Needed Changes in Education* (Denver, Colo.: Publishers Press, 1967); Carl Hovland, Irving Janis, and Harold Kelley, *Communication and Persuasion* (New Haven, Conn.: Yale University Press, 1953); Alfred G. Smith, *Communication and Status: The Dynamics of a Research Center* (Eugene, Ore.: Center for the Advanced Study of Educational Administration, 1966); Herbert A. Simon, *Administrative Behavior* (New York: Macmillan, 1959); Morris Viteles, *Motivation and Morale in Industry* (New York: W. W. Norton & Co., 1953); and Edgar L. Morphet and Charles O. Ryan, *Planning and Effecting Needed Changes in Education* (Denver, Colo.: Publishers Press, Inc., 1967).

Table 4-6. Decision-making Demands for Selected Positions

LEGEND

1 = Major demand
2 = Moderate demand
3 = Occasional demand
4 = Rare demand

* C = critical decision making (general purposes and objectives).

† R = routine decision making (specific operational objectives).

‡ Refers to total school district and its community environment.

** Refers to attendance units and their immediate community environments.

	Superintendent C*	Superintendent R†	Sec. School Principal C	Sec. School Principal R	Elem. School Principal C	Elem. School Principal R	Director of Program C	Director of Program R	Instructional Supv. and Consultant C	Instructional Supv. and Consultant R	Dir. of Pupil Personnel C	Dir. of Pupil Personnel R	Dir. of Staff Personnel C	Dir. of Staff Personnel R	Director of Research C	Director of Research R	Director of Business Affairs C	Director of Business Affairs R
A. Total community-school district context ‡																		
1. Individual decision making	1	1	4	4	4	4	2	2	3	3	2	2	2	2	3	2	2	2
2. Individual decision making with intragroup consultation	1	1	4	3	4	4	1	2	3	3	2	2	2	2	4	3	2	1
3. Individual decision making with extragroup consultation	2	1	4	4	4	4	1	2	3	4	3	4	3	4	4	4	3	3
4. Small-group decision making	1	1	3	3	3	3	1	2	3	3	2	2	2	2	2	2	1	2
5. Large-group decision making	1	2	3	3	3	3	2	3	4	4	3	4	3	4	4	4	3	3
B. Attendance-unit context **																		
1. Individual decision making	3	3	1	1	1	1	3	4	3	2	3	4	3	4	4	4	3	3
2. Individual decision making with intragroup consultation	3	3	1	1	1	1	3	4	3	3	3	4	3	4	3	4	3	4
3. Individual decision making with extragroup consultation	3	3	1	2	1	2	3	4	4	4	4	4	4	4	4	4	4	4
4. Small-group decision making	3	3	1	2	1	2	3	4	3	2	3	3	3	3	3	3	3	3
5. Large-group decision making	3	3	1	3	1	3	4	4	4	4	4	4	4	4	4	4	4	4

Table 4-7. Demands upon Selected Positions for Maintaining and Improving Morale

LEGEND

1 = Major demand
2 = Moderate demand
3 = Occasional demand
4 = Rare demand

	Superintendent	Sec. School Principal	Elem. School Principal	Director of Program	Instructional Supv. and Consultant	Dir. of Pupil Personnel	Dir. of Staff Personnel	Director of Research	Director of Business Affairs
A. Total school district context*									
1. Individual	1	3	3	1	2	1	1	2	1
2. Small-group	1	3	3	1	3	2	2	3	1
3. Large-group	1	3	3	2	4	4	4	4	2
B. Attendance unit context†									
1. Individual	3	1	1	3	1	3	3	3	3
2. Small-group	3	1	1	3	2	3	3	3	3
3. Large-group	3	1	1	4	4	4	4	4	4

* Intraorganizational.
† Also intraorganizational.

4. The norm system of the group and of its subgroups which, through sanction and prescription, defines acceptable conduct for group members.
5. The system of member performances which describes the operation of the group and changes in response to variations of the group task.
6. The system of informal interactions which brings together group members on the basis of propinquity, mutual liking, and similarity of interests.
7. The system of covert interactions, if present, which brings together persons who challenge the legitimacy of the operative role structure and differential sanctions associated with it.[24]

Additional organizational variables also demand consideration:

1. All administrative systems function in a milieu of power. Principals require competence in identifying and working with formal and informal power systems in both school and community settings.

2. Motivation toward action and accomplishment in organizations and communities is affected not only by prevailing value patterns but by important psychological, economic, political, and sociological factors. Principals require sophistication in (a) identifying existing systems of belief and thought, and (b) utilizing available motivational bases to generate activity and support for the betterment of schools.

3. The leadership potential available in administrative performance systems can significantly affect organizational effectiveness and efficiency. Principals must clearly define their leadership roles in policy formation and legitimation, in decision making, in initiating and directing change, in morale building, in conflict resolution, in building functional organizations and unified work-flow patterns, and in improving the organizational-environmental exchange system.

REFERENCES

Appleby, Paul H., *Policy and Administration* (University, Ala.: University of Alabama Press, 1949).

Bailey, Stephen, *et al., Schoolmen and Politics* (Syracuse, N.Y.: Syracuse University Press, 1962).

Bertalanffy, Ludwig, and Anatol Rapaport (eds.), *General Systems—Yearbook of the Society for the Advancement of General Systems Theory* (Ann Arbor, Mich.: Braun-Brumfield, 1956).

24. Ralph M. Stogdill, *Individual Behavior and Group Achievement* (New York: Oxford University Press, 1959), pp. 147–148.

Cahill, Robert S., and Stephen P. Hencley, *The Politics of Education in the Local Community* (Danville, Ill.: Interstate Printers and Publishers, 1964).

Carlson, Richard O., *et al., Change Processes in the Public Schools* (Eugene, Ore.: Center for the Advanced Study of Educational Administration, University of Oregon, 1965).

Culbertson, Jack A., and Stephen P. Hencley (eds.), *Preparing Administrators: New Perspectives* (Columbus, Ohio: University Council for Educational Administration, 1962).

Foskett, John M., *The Normative World of the Elementary School Principal* (Eugene, Ore.: Center for Advanced Study of Educational Administration, 1967).

Griffiths, Daniel E. (ed.), *Behavioral Science and Educational Administration, Sixty-Third Yearbook,* Part II, National Society for the Study of Education (Chicago: University of Chicago Press, 1964).

Griffiths, Daniel E. (ed.), *Developing Taxonomies of Organizational Behavior in Education Administration* (Chicago: Rand McNally & Company, 1969).

Griffiths, Daniel E., *et al., Organizing Schools for Effective Education* (Danville, Ill.: Interstate Printers and Publishers, 1962).

Gross, Neal, and Robert E. Herriott, *Staff Leadership in Public Schools* (New York: John Wiley & Sons, 1965).

Harris, Ben M., *Supervisory Behavior in Education* (Englewood Cliffs, N.J.: Prentice-Hall, 1963).

Kimbrough, Ralph B., *Political Power and Educational Decision-Making* (Chicago: Rand McNally, 1964).

Leu, Donald J., and Herbert C. Rudman, *Preparation Programs for School Administrators* (East Lansing, Mich.: Michigan State University, 1963).

Likert, Rensis, *New Patterns of Management* (New York: McGraw-Hill, 1969).

Walton, John, *Administration and Policy Making in Education* (Baltimore, Md.: Johns Hopkins Press, 1959).

Chapter 5

LEADER BEHAVIOR
IN THE PRINCIPALSHIP

LEADER-STATESMEN are distinguished from manager-executives in elementary school administration by a most important characteristic: the statesmen have effected the transition from administrative management to institutional leadership. Although the increasing sophistication of American school systems is requiring much greater increments of institutional leadership from all school administrators, elementary school principals have experienced difficulty in making the significant transition demanded by this new role model.

From the time of the first "principal teachers," the image of the elementary school principal has developed in many communities as a person who is competent in managing facilities, equipment, and supplies; allocating teaching functions; promoting, guiding, and disciplining pupils; scheduling school buses, classes, and PTA meetings. All of these tasks focus primarily on technical management and have tended to project a low-level image for elementary administration. Many principals, anxious to fill these expectations adequately, have been satisfied to limit themselves to executive details and "administrivia." They have allowed themselves to become so enmeshed in the immediate problems of heading a school organization that they have failed to consider the more fundamental problems of institutional leadership.

Institutional leaders are concerned with effecting organizational change, defining organizational goals and purposes, and determining the basic character of the educational enterprise through critical choice making. These tasks are related to the purposes or ends of organizations. Through excessive preoccupation with educational means rather than educational ends, professional educators and training institutions have tended to promote a manager-executive image for the elementary school administrator. Such an emphasis and orientation, however, has shed little light upon his role as an educational statesman.

The tendency to emphasize means rather than ends has been reinforced in the past by the acceptance of leader images that have evolved in government, industry, and business. In these fields, techniques have been developed for meeting predetermined ends through building efficient organizations, and emphasis has been placed on routine decision-making skills aimed primarily at organizational maintenance. Thus, the scientific management and human relations movements; the intensive study of organization; the emphasis on social roles and organization-individual interaction; the cult of the administrative process; the study in depth of communication, decision making, conflict, and morale; and the emphasis on efficiency have been primarily concerned with organizational means rather than organizational ends. Their impact on education has been to create an additional number of models for the school administrator that focus attention on educational means. Several of these models have had a major impact upon leader behavior in elementary education; others will undoubtedly continue to influence such behavior as the profession moves toward greater responsibility for institutional leadership.

IMAGES OF THE LEADER

In this country several leader images have emerged that have had implications for the elementary school administrator. They have reflected the historical phases of economic and social development that have occurred since colonial times. The first of these originated with the Dame Schools of the New England Colonies and the private tutors of the Middle and Southern Colonies. This was followed by a second image, the principal/teacher, begun in 1847 with the establishment of the New Quincy School in Boston and developed with the rapid growth of graded elementary schools.[1]

The Industrial Revolution of the nineteenth century spawned two conceptualizations of leadership based on mechanical and structural efficiency. The first of these grew out of Frederick W. Taylor's scientific

1. Edward A. Krug, *Salient Dates in American Education, 1635–1964* (New York: Harper & Row, 1966).

management theory at the turn of the century,[2] and it was followed from the 1920's to the 1940's by an image, described by Urwick, which stressed the leader's role in conceptualizing design and structure in formal organizations.[3] A trend away from the mechanical, toward a more sophisticated behavioral approach began with the work of Mary Parker Follett and others, who viewed leadership and administration as a science, an art, and an ethical practice.[4] It formed the beginning of a trend that culminated in the work of the Harvard Group which stressed human relations in its conceptualization of the leader as a "social engineer." More recently, a view of the leader as clinician has been popular.[5] Each of the above leader images has affected conceptions of the role of leadership; each should be understood if one is to grasp the full significance of mature institutional leadership.

The Teacher/Principal

The earliest image of elementary school leadership grew around the teacher/principal, a model made available during the 200 years from the establishment of the American colonies to the middle of the nineteenth century. It was characterized by autonomy and the primacy of the teaching function. Both the proprietors of the Dame Schools and the private tutors controlled the content and method of instruction to be offered their pupils. No authority existed beyond them except the sanctions patrons might exert by giving or withholding patronage.

The established teacher/principal image persisted even after the colonies began enacting compulsory school attendance laws and setting up agencies for external control of the schools. The teacher/principal was still selected on the basis of teaching ability, and he continued to decide what to teach and how to teach it. It has taken increased urbanization and population growth, which have made the one-room school obsolete and created complex, consolidated school districts, to eradicate the teacher/principal image. Even though there are small nongraded elementary schools today, the decision-making powers of their administrators are encompassed within a larger system.

2. Frederick W. Taylor, *Principles of Scientific Management* (New York: Harper & Bros., 1911).

3. W. Edgar Vinacke, Warner R. Wilson, and Gerald M. Meredith (eds.), *Dimensions of Social Psychology* (Chicago: Scott, Foresman and Co., 1964).

4. Henry C. Metcalf and L. Urwick (eds.), *Dynamic Administration: The Collected Papers of Mary Parker Follett* (New York: Harper & Bros., 1940).

5. W. D. Schutz, "The Interpersonal Underworld," *Harvard Business Review,* July-August, 1958, pp. 123–135.

The Principal/Teacher

Though the establishment of the Boston Quincy School in 1847 provided the setting for a change in the elementary administrator's role, the transition from the traditional image was slow in coming. "By 1860, the grading of elementary schools in the larger cities was well under way, but it should be remembered that at this date less than one-sixth of the population lived in cities. Most of the nation's children continued to be educated in primitive, ungraded, one-room rural schools." [6]

The new image, principal/teacher, as it evolved, retained emphasis on the teaching function. The position was given to some "best" teacher —to be filled in addition to teaching duties for extra compensation. But, for the first time, it involved organization and direction of the efforts of other teachers in the same building.

The autonomy characteristic of the teacher/principal, of course, did not accompany the principal/teacher. Rather, the latter was a counter of supplies and a dispenser of textbooks. His role was managerial in nature, with an emphasis on accountability. He bore no responsibility for educational change or determination of objectives.

The Efficiency Expert

Tasks performed by the elementary school principal as the twentieth century began lent themselves readily to scrutiny by thinkers who followed the early exponents of scientific management such as Taylor, Gantt, and Gilbreth. Their philosophy, in keeping with the industrial culture of the time, was oriented toward examining the worker as a production unit not basically different from a machine. The tasks he performed were analyzed—each operation broken down into its fundamental motions—in an attempt to make him a smoother functioning part of the production process. The idea was to adapt the man to the tools and processes so perfectly that he could perform his task without thinking. Thinking was done by his leaders, whose responsibility it was to fit him to the task through scientific analysis of his mechanical abilities.[7] The scientific managers sought to create a smoothly functioning organization of men ideally adapted to their jobs, who would be

6. Newton Edwards and Herman G. Richey, *The School in the American Social Order* (Boston: Houghton Mifflin Co., 1963).
7. James G. March and Herbert A. Simon, *Organizations* (New York: John Wiley and Sons, 1958), p. 13.

capable of ever-improving production rates. Their ultimate objective was a greater degree of efficiency.

The impact of this "scientific management" approach on educational thought produced an image of the school administrator as an efficiency expert. This industrially oriented philosophy was well expressed in Cubberley's statement:

Our schools are, in a sense, factories in which the raw products (children) are to be shaped and fashioned into products to meet the various demands of life. The specifications for manufacturing come from the demands of the Twentieth Century civilization, and it is the business of the school to build its pupils according to the specifications laid down. This demands good goals, specialized machinery, continuous measurement of production to see if it is according to specifications, the elimination of waste in manufacture, and a large variety in the output.[8]

To fit the student to twentieth-century specifications and to avoid waste in manufacture may well have been among the objectives of the "platoon," or "work-study-play" school as it was called by its founder, William Wirt. Mr. Wirt claimed that the school must offer a rounded program involving work, study, and play if its pupils were to be properly prepared for their societal roles.[9] Furthermore, the greatest benefit for the student could be derived by the greatest efficiency of school plant utilization. The principle of efficiency as stated by Wirt is: "Each child can be in only one of the four places (provided in the school plant) at the same time. The new school so arranges the classes that different sets of children are in the four departments all of the time." [10] This principle, utilizing every student station every hour of the day, made it possible to handle double and sometimes triple the usual number of students in a given facility.

Although this efficiency device, as well as numerous others, has persisted in schools to the present time, the management philosophy upon which it is based demands of the leader only those skills necessary to devise and maintain smoothly running organizations. Since it tends to stress the mechanical aspects of organizational production, it is more or less blind to the psychological forces that complicate human enterprise.

8. Ellwood Cubberley, *Public School Administration* (Boston: Houghton Mifflin Co., 1916), p. 33.
9. Roscoe David Case, *The Platoon School in America* (Stanford, Calif.: Stanford University Press, 1931), pp. 4–6.
10. Charles L. Spain, *The Platoon School, A Study of the Adaptation of the Elementary School Organization to the Curriculum* (New York: Macmillan, 1929), p. 41.

The Organizational Engineer

Focused attention on efficient organizations led, between 1920 and 1950, to a leader image centered around organizational structure. Given a purpose, the job of the leader was to specify carefully the nature and form of relationships within the organization which would serve the purpose. The essential task of the leader was to outline tasks to be performed, as Gulick has stated, in terms of purpose, process, clientele, and place.[11] Through this approach, the leader became concerned with the uses of authority. His tasks were to delineate the relationship between authority and responsibility, to facilitate the exercise of authority by maintaining unity of command and a proper span of control, and to promote the flow of authority by separating line and staff. Devices such as departmentalization and decentralization of control were found to be effective.

All of these things could be expressed with an organizational chart and job descriptions. These tools provided a perfectly clear picture of the organization's structure and the functional relationships between its parts; it remained for the leader, the organizational engineer, to keep the organization functioning smoothly. This he could do by mastering the administrative processes outlined by Urwick's mnemonic, POSDCORB: planning, organizing, staffing, directing, coordinating, reporting, and budgeting. (See Chapters 1, 10, and 11.)

Such a picture of administration, as Gulick has admitted, is cast from the "standpoint of organization" and neglects "political life and leadership"; but as it emerged in education this qualification was obscured. Contemporary proposals to revamp elementary school organization in favor of departmentalized instruction to cope with the knowledge explosion; to form hierarchical teaching staffs with teacher's aides; to organize a variety of teaching teams—these and other schemes for streamlining the educative process are witness to the impact of the organizational engineering concept on elementary school leadership.

A school, however, is an organization dedicated to unique values. Learning is much more a social than a mechanical process. It is not likely that an intricate organizational chart depicting interpersonnel relationships will establish group loyalty or commitment sufficient to create

11. Luther Gulick, "Notes on the Theory of Organization," in Luther Gulick and L. Urwick (eds.), *Papers on the Science of Administration* (New York: Institute of Public Administration, 1937), p. 1.

the kinds of interpersonal relationships that will help children learn. The skills of the organizational engineer are insufficient; the school administrator needs the maturity and vision of institutional leadership.

The Social Engineer

A new and exciting dimension of the leader's role was opened up by work begun in the late 1920's and given impetus by studies of industrial fatigue done by Mayo and Henderson. It directed the attention of theorists in many fields away from the impersonal, mechanistic aspects of organizational functioning and focused on the human relationships that affect organizational efficiency. The importance of social psychological factors such as primary group relations and self-images was demonstrated in startling fashion by the work of the Harvard Group (Mayo,[12] Henderson, Roethlisberger,[13] Homans,[14] and Lombard). Their results, bolstered by the work of others such as Chester Barnard,[15] helped to create the image of the leader who is not only cognizant of human relations but who cultivates and even exploits them for the benefit of the organization. This type of leader may appropriately be called the social engineer.

The monumental work done in building this leader image is the research of the Harvard Group which began as a routine efficiency study at Western Electric's Hawthorne Plant. The research group was able to demonstrate that social and psychological variables were as important as most other organizational variables in determining organizational production rates. Thus, the researchers found that workers responded with increasing output (regardless of changing physical environment) primarily because they felt that management had taken a personal interest in them. The act of singling them out for special study gave them recognition—filling a psychological need—that boosted their morale and increased productivity. This result has since come to be known as the "Hawthorne Effect."

A second important finding of the Harvard Group studies was the significance of a worker's primary group on the job. Production and

12. Elton Mayo, *The Social Problems of an Industrial Civilization* (Cambridge, Mass.: Graduate School of Business Administration, Harvard University, 1945).

13. F. J. Roethlisberger, *Management and Morale* (Cambridge, Mass.: Harvard University Press, 1941).

14. George C. Homans, *The Human Group* (New York: Harcourt, Brace and Co., 1950).

15. Chester I. Barnard, *Functions of the Executive* (Cambridge, Mass.: Harvard University Press, 1938).

output standards were informally set within this group. A worker's loyalty and standing in the informal group proved to be a more important predictor of behavior than economic incentives offered by management in attempts to exceed the group's production standards. Acceptance and recognition by fellow workers were shown to be as important in motivating worker behavior as the time-honored mechanism of increased financial compensation. Moreover, job situations that afforded no opportunity for workers to associate with an informal group were characterized by high turnover and absenteeism.

The implications for leaders were obvious. The leader needed to recognize the importance of a person's need for a feeling of personal worth and for status among his associates. If tacit, even subconscious, arrangements based on social-psychological motivations could be made by workers to thwart management's leadership, such factors could equally well be used to promote organizational goals. The assumption that employees would automatically accept management's decisions would have to be set aside in favor of opening channels for communicating and cooperating with workers concerning changes that would affect their work. Leader behavior would need to be tailored (a) to developing respect for others, accepting individual differences, sharpening sensitivity to the feelings of others, and recognizing that kindness is not a weakness; and (b) to developing awareness of the importance of a clinical approach to human relations problems.

In educational administration, the social engineer image of the leader has become widespread. It has added a refreshing ingredient to the impersonal-mechanical manipulator idealized by the efficiency expert and organizational engineer images. However, the concern for healthy human relations was sometimes carried to an extreme in the name of "democratic" administration. The elementary school principal often came to be pictured as a type of social catalytic agent who stimulated interpersonal relationships among students and teachers without exercising prerogatives over the directions to be taken by the educational enterprise. That authority in organizations must be exercised and that leaders in organizations must lead were administrative axioms that appeared expendable to certain extreme groups.

The Clinician

Awareness of the importance of human relations has focused attention on the individual as he interacts with other individuals and groups.

Work done by Moreno and Lewin in group dynamics has shown the power of activities such as psychodrama and role playing in making an individual aware of how he is viewed by others in his associations. This awareness, or sensitivity, to the feelings and perceptions of others facilitates healthy operation of interpersonal relationships—the important goal for the leader as clinician.

The mechanism for developing this awareness is the "sensitivity training workshop," [16] which originated at the National Training Laboratory in Group Development in Bethel, Maine. Sensitivity training is not only offered by universities but has also been used by companies such as International Business Machines, Western Electric, and Standard Oil of New Jersey to improve relations among their personnel. The technique aims at uncovering dissatisfactions, hostilities, and internal power struggles that underlie human interactions within the organization. Focus is on interpersonal relationships, structured theoretically by Schutz as follows:

There are three interpersonal need areas—inclusion, control and affection—sufficient for the prediction of interpersonal behavior. Orientations which an individual acquires toward behavior in the areas are relatively invariant over time. Compatibility of two or more persons depends on (a) their ability to satisfy reciprocally each other's interpersonal needs; (b) their complementarity with respect to originating and receiving behavior in each need need area; and (c) their similarity with respect to the amount of interchange they desire with other people in each need area. . . .

Every interpersonal relation follows the same general development sequence. It starts with inclusion behavior, is followed by control behavior, and finally affection behavior. This cycle may recur. When the relation approaches termination, it reverses direction, and investment in the relation is withdrawn in the order affection, control, and inclusion.[17]

Whether sensitivity training is effective has not been settled; both claims in its behalf and criticisms of its alleged weaknesses are voiced. Whether it awakens insights into human behavior or magnifies injurious self-criticism; whether it improves capacities to participate in interper-

    16. Also referred to as "T-group training," "awareness training," "laboratory training," and "diagnostic skill training." See, for instance, John H. Suchr, "Awareness Training for School People?" *Phi Delta Kappan,* Vol. XLIII, No. 6, March 1962, pp. 263–265; and Max Birnbaum, "Sense about Sensitivity Training," *Saturday Review,* November 15, 1969, p. 82 ff.
    17. William C. Schutz, "The FIRO Theory of Interpersonal Behavior," in Stephen P. Hencley (ed.), *Research in Educational Administration,* Report of Cooperative Research Project No. F-2 (Columbus, Ohio: University Council for Educational Administration, 1962), pp. 150–151.

sonal relations for everyone or only for those originally capable; or whether it stimulates group solidarity or aggravates the sores of group hostility are matters yet to be determined. Nevertheless, its implications for leadership will grow in coming years, and their projections into educational administration, as with the other movements, will add new images to the leadership role.

LEADER BEHAVIOR STUDIES

The virility of American culture, attributed by people at large to a democratic philosophy and folklore such as that which supports the theory of rugged individualism, has produced a great deal of speculation about leadership and *a posteriori* study of "great" leaders. As a consequence, leadership has been represented as a mysterious quality bestowed upon select men from sources unknown. The preponderance of this theme permeating many volumes written on the subject has led one writer to deplore the view that "leaders are indeed mystery men, born in paradise or in some Devil's pit, but that they never must have become leaders through the study of books on management or of treatises on the making of higher executives." [18]

Such representations are based on "common sense" opinions; they have little support from empirical fact. However, an increasing number of studies have been conducted in recent years by governmental, business, and educational agencies which have produced valuable concepts and knowledge relating leader behavior to human interrelationships in organizations.

Indeed, one inquiry seeking to identify leaders in community and public life concluded that, far from being ethereal beings, leaders in most communities were readily identifiable. Some held status positions. Others were members of informal community power structures. Still others were (*a*) latent leaders who held no office, (*b*) community service volunteers, and (*c*) individuals who exercised initiative in particularly unusual circumstances. [19]

Investigations vary in estimates of how concentrated leadership is. Floyd Hunter has estimated that fewer than 300 people exercise effec-

18. Henri Peyre, "Excellence and Leadership: Has Western Europe Any Lessons for Us?" *Daedalus,* Vol. 90, No. 4, Fall, 1961, p. 629.
19. Wendell Bell, Richard J. Hill, and Charles R. Wright, *Public Leadership* (San Francisco: Chandler Publishing Co., 1961), Chapter II.

tive power at the national level.[20] Other studies have made estimates of several thousand.

Traits Approach

Early studies sought to identify common characteristics or personality traits that would distinguish leaders from nonleaders. For the most part, such inquiries were unproductive. Attempts to identify inherent qualities subject to conflicting definition and dubious measurability fell short of providing useful knowledge about leadership. However, much effort was expended in this direction before investigators became conscious of the need to base their studies on more concrete formulations. The shift from the study of traits to a study of leader behavior has produced more fruitful results, and has shifted factors of leadership success from inherent traits to characteristics attainable through human endeavor.

Several criticisms have been leveled at the trait approach to the study of leadership. It has been pointed out that such studies have been unable to distinguish between traits necessary for leadership and those required to attain leadership positions. Moreover, the studies have not been able to determine the relative importance of different traits; they have not proved various traits to be mutually exclusive; and they have produced contradictory evidence showing that leaders who possessed strikingly dissimilar traits have been equally successful.[21] A consideration of attempts to single out leadership traits has led to the following conclusions:

The early work of psychologists sought to find the characteristic traits of the effective leader. The only trait which was found almost universally among leaders of business, education, politics, and the military was a higher-than-average level of energy. No traits of personality or of intellectual functioning were identified. Efforts to discover other traits which might be common to effective leaders in a single field were not successful.[22]

20. Floyd Hunter, *Top Leadership U.S.A.* (Chapel Hill, N.C.: University of North Carolina Press, 1959); *See also:* Marilyn Gittell and Alan G. Hevesi, *The Politics of Urban Education* (New York: Frederick A. Praeger, 1969).

21. See R. M. Stogdill, "Personal Factors Associated with Leadership: A Survey of the Literature," *Journal of Psychology,* January, 1948; and C. A. Weber and M. E. Weber, *Fundamentals of Educational Leadership* (New York: McGraw-Hill, 1955).

22. Ralph W. Tyler, "The Behavioral Sciences and the Schools," in *The Changing American School,* John I. Goodlad (ed.), *Sixty-fifth Yearbook of the National Society for the Study of Education* (Chicago, Ill.: University of Chicago Press, 1966), p. 213.

This conclusion is borne out by Stogdill who has claimed that no combination of personal traits produces leaders. However, he has cited studies indicating that leaders are characterized by good intelligence, dependability, social activity, scholarship, and socioeconomic status [23]— behavior-oriented, attainable factors.

Recent emphasis in a number of studies has shifted to identifying leaders in terms of types of observable behavior as judged by competent people. Malo, for example, identified promotable and nonpromotable insurance underwriters by judgments of their superiors and found that those judged promotable were characterized by the following personality variables: intensity, conjunctivity, social ability, reality orientation, achievement drive, and superego orientation.[24] In the school setting, principals judged to be competent by their superiors have been gauged by various personality scales. Lipham used the Edwards Personal Preference Schedule in combination with a projective test, a self-report inventory, and a personal interview. He found little difference between effective and ineffective principals in extent of training, job experience, intelligence, sex, or marital status. Effective principals, however, exceeded ineffective principals in engaging in purposeful activity, striving for upward professional mobility, associating with others to solve problems, feeling secure in family and work environments, and achieving a greater degree of emotional control in frustrating situations.[25] Boyce reported studies showing a positive correlation between judged effectiveness and the Aesthetic and Religious Scales of the Allport-Vernon-Lindzey Scale of Values, as well as the Abasement and Nurturance Factors of the Edwards Personal Preference Schedule.[26]

Gross and Herriott formulated a behavioral definition of "Executive Professional Leadership" which allowed them to identify elementary principals who were effective leaders as judged by their teachers rather than by their superordinates. With respect to personal characteristics, their conclusions bear out those cited above:

... if Executive Professional Leadership is to be the criterion, many school systems are selecting principals on grounds that appear to have little em-

23. Stogdill, *op. cit.*
24. Albert H. Malo, "Personality Variables Related to Administrative Potential" (Doctoral dissertation, University of Chicago, 1959), p. 185.
25. James M. Lipham, "Personal Variables of Effective Administrators," *Administrator's Notebook,* Vol. IX, No. 1, September, 1960, pp. 1–4.
26. R. D. Boyce, "An Empirical Evaluation of Five Tests for Administrator Selection: The Composite Study" (Doctoral dissertation, Stanford University, 1960).

pirical justification: type or amount of teaching experience, experience as an assistant or vice principal, number of undergraduate and graduate courses in educational administration, sex, and marital status. On the other hand, characteristics that should be preferred in appointing elementary principals are: a high level of academic performance in college, a high order of interpersonal skill, the motive of service, and relatively little seniority as teachers.[27]

Situations Approach

A further step in the trend of leadership research has been based on sociological theories of roles and relationships of people within organizations as behavioral determinants.[28] The study of Executive Professional Leadership (EPL) by Gross and Herriott is an example of this approach. It is cast in a theoretical framework that assumes an elementary school principal will be influenced in his performance by his conception of his role in the school and by the behaviors of the teachers under him and the administrators over him.[29]

Hypotheses substantiated by Gross and Herriott indicate that greater professional leadership and more social support by immediate superiors are associated with greater EPL on the part of principals. Moreover, when a principal allows teachers to share in his decisions; when he supports them socially, managerially, and in conflicts with students; and when he promotes egalitarian relationships with them—all such behaviors are associated with a higher degree of EPL.[30] The sociological viewpoint would predict that an elementary principal finding himself in situations with these qualities would exhibit more professional leadership than if he found them lacking.

Results of individual studies examining both traits and situations may be encouraging, but the broad overview pinpoints their weakness as bases for leadership theory. While formal leaders of the same type of organization may exhibit traits and may respond to situations that are associated with variations in their leadership, the commonality among significant traits and situations is lost when a variety of organizations is considered. For a broad base in leadership theory, a fresh approach must be sought.

27. Neal Gross and Robert E. Herriott, *Staff Leadership in Public Schools: A Sociological Inquiry* (New York: John Wiley & Sons, 1965), p. 157.

28. Fred Massarick, Robert Tannenbaum, and Irving R. Wechsler, *Leadership and Organization: A Behavioral Science Approach* (McGraw-Hill, 1961), p. 23.

29. Gross and Herriott, *op. cit.*, Chapter 5. For a critique of this study see Donald A. Erickson, "Some Misgivings Concerning a Study of Leadership," *Educational Administration Quarterly*, Vol. 1, No. 3, Autumn, 1965, pp. 52–59.

30. Gross and Herriott, *op. cit.*

CURRENT EMPHASES IN LEADERSHIP THEORIES

Perhaps the most significant aspect of the trend in leadership research has been its focusing on behavioral definitions of leadership. Behavioral definitions form a basis for empirical observations that can be used to clarify and refine ideas. In this way, definitions of leadership themselves become more concrete. Thus, an early behavior-oriented definition states that "leadership is a man's ability to take the initiative in social situations, to plan and organize actions, and in so doing evoke cooperation." [31] A more recent definition for educational leadership is: "That action or behavior among individuals or groups which causes both the individual and the groups to move toward educational goals that are increasingly mutually acceptable to them." [32]

The elements expressed by both of these definitions are represented with remarkable consistency in the results of current research regarding organizational behavior as it applies to leaders. They are suggested in Barnard's criteria of effectiveness and efficiency: an organization is effective if its common purposes are being achieved; it is efficient if cooperation among individuals exists and their motives are satisfied.

Cartwright and Zander, in describing how groups function, have delineated two types of activities: (1) activities directed toward the attainment of stated group goals, promoted by such member behaviors as "initiates action," "keeps members' attention on the goal," "clarifies the issue," "develops a procedural plan," "evaluates the quality of work done," and "makes expert information available"; (2) activities directed toward maintaining or strengthening the work group, promoted by such behaviors as "keeps interpersonal relations pleasant," "arbitrates disputes," "provides encouragement," "gives the minority a chance to be heard," "stimulates self direction," and "increases the interdependence among members." [33] Similarly, Kahn and Katz have observed two types of behavior exhibited by supervisors: production-oriented and employee-oriented.[34] The employee-oriented supervisors appeared interested in

31. Offices of Strategic Services Assessment Staff, *The Assessment of Men* (New York: Rinehart & Co., 1948), p. 301.
32. John A. Ramseyer, "A Concept of Educational Leadership," *Leadership for Improving Instruction* (Washington, D.C.: Association for Supervision and Curriculum Development, National Education Association, 1960), p. 27.
33. Dorwin Cartwright and Alvin Zander, *Group Dynamics: Research and Theory* (Evanston, Ill.: Row, Peterson & Co., 1953), p. 541.
34. Robert L. Kahn and Daniel Katz, "Leadership Practices in Relation to Productivity and Morale," in Cartwright and Zander, *op. cit.,* pp. 554–570.

motivating employees, satisfying their needs, and building their morale. Production-oriented supervisors concentrated on increasing efficiency and production, and attaining institutional goals.

A significant step in behavior-oriented research was made by members of the Personnel Research Board, Ohio State University, when they reformulated the object of study into "leader behavior" rather than leadership. Leader behavior was a more concrete concept subject to observation, job analysis, R-A-D Scales, and a Leader Behavior Description Questionnaire (LBDQ), devised by the Ohio State group. They were able to factor analyze data collected by these methods. Two major dimensions of leader behavior emerged:

1. *Initiating Structure in Interaction,* that is, the leader's behavior in relation to (*a*) outlining, clarifying, and delineating leader-follower relationships, and (*b*) establishing clear organizational patterns, communication channels, and procedures for accomplishing organizational tasks.
2. *Consideration,* that is, the leader's behavior in indicating friendship, respect, trust, and warmth in relationships between himself and group members.[35]

More recently, Getzels and Guba have delineated several styles of leader behavior derived from their study of administration as a social process. These men have stated that administration occurs, structurally, as a hierarchy of subordinate-superordinate relationships within a social system. Functionally, the administrative process consists of the allocation and integration of roles and facilities for the achievement of the goals of the system with reference to a broader cultural framework. Operationally, administration takes place in an interpersonal setting and is invariably concerned with social relationships. Social behavior is conceived of as a function of interactions among elements of the nomothetic dimension (institution, role, expectation) and elements of the idiographic dimension (individual, personality, need-disposition) which are ongoing in social systems.[36] Figure 5–1 shows the model expressing interrelationships between the two dimensions.

Thus, the institutional dimension of the model indicates that within social systems there exist institutions (such as those for governing, educating, and maintaining order) which are defined by the roles performed

35. Andrew W. Halpin, *The Leadership Behavior of School Superintendents* (Chicago: Midwest Administration Center, University of Chicago, 1959), p. 4.
36. J. W. Getzels and E. G. Guba, "Social Behavior and the Administrative Process," *School Review,* Vol. LXV, No. 4, Winter, 1957, pp. 423–441.

by position holders. The roles themselves are defined by the expectations attached to them. The school, then, is an institution defined by roles such as superintendent, teacher, principal, custodian, and teaching aide. The roles are defined by what is "expected" of position holders in the various categories. These "expectations," then, if followed by position holders will lead to certain generalized, normative behavior typical of the "teacher role," "superintendent role," and so forth. The principal who relies entirely on the nomothetic dimension as a guide for monitoring his behavior will tend to do things "by the book" and will likely stress similar behavior for others. The meeting of role expectations will become very important even if they must be met at great personal cost.

The personal or psychological dimension of the model indicates, however, that social systems are peopled by individuals who possess unique personalities defined by varying need-dispositions. Behavior within a social system, then, is guided not only by expectations attached to a generalized role, but also by the needs of the individual occupying the role. The principal who stresses the idiographic dimension as a behavior guide will tend to emphasize the meeting of personal needs—even if these run counter to normative role-expectations.

There is, of course, a third possibility. The principal may, at times, stress the nomothetic dimension while at other times he may stress the idiographic dimension—depending, of course, upon his considered judgment as to what will be best for both the school and the position. Many principals do, in fact, behave in just such a fashion. Such behavior has been characterized by Getzels as "transactional."

Thus, leader behavior, as dimensionalized in this model, could be characterized by an emphasis on nomothetic considerations, an emphasis on idiographic considerations, or a judicious combination of the two.

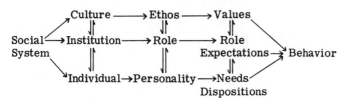

Figure 5-1. Behavior in Social Systems:
The Getzels-Guba Model

Results of other work, such as that of Bass,[37] Argyris,[38] and Etzioni,[39] provide similar two-dimensional characterizations of leader behavior. While it could not be claimed that different studies have isolated exactly the same variables, they do seem to indicate that leaders are involved with activities related to the establishment of clear goals, work plans, and the initiation of productive action on the one hand; and with activities related to the establishment of warm relationships, and cooperation with group members on the other. The terminology used to describe these activities varies, but the form of their results is strikingly similar, as is indicated by the summary in Table 5–1.

Table 5-1. Summary of Some Major Concepts Relating to
Leader Behavior

Author	Behavior Dimensions	
Barnard	effectiveness	- efficiency
Cartwright & Zander	group locomotion	- group maintenance
Halpin	initiating structure	- consideration*
Kahn & Katz	production-oriented	- employee-oriented
Getzels-Guba	nomothetic	- idiographic
Argyris	formal behavior	- individual behavior
Bass	task effectiveness	- interaction effectiveness
Schachter	induction	- cohesion

*For a report of a study which utilizes Stogdill's new Leader Behavior Description Questionnaire.Form XII (LBDQ-12), see Alan F. Brown, "Reactions to Leadership," Educational Administration Quarterly, Vol. III, No. 1, Winter, 1967, pp. 62-73.

LEADER BEHAVIOR GENERALIZATIONS

Application of theoretical frameworks to specific problems has produced knowledge that will help elementary school administrators better understand their leadership roles. The following are a number of generalizations about leadership that are supported by research in various fields:

1. *Public School Leaders Exhibit Different But Characteristic Leader Behavior Styles.* By conceiving of the Initiating Structure and Considera-

37. Bernard M. Bass, *Leadership, Psychology, and Organizational Behavior* (New York: Harper & Row, 1960).
38. Chris Argyris, *Personality and Organization, the Conflict Between System and the Individual* (New York, Harper & Row, 1957).
39. Amitai Etzioni, *Modern Organizations* (Englewood Cliffs, N.J.: Prentice-Hall, 1964).

tion dimensions as independent, Halpin was able to arrange the possible combinations of high and low status on each dimension to express four leadership styles. His study indicated that some leaders were perceived to be high on both dimensions; others were perceived to be low on both dimensions; still others were perceived to be above average on one dimension but below average on the other.[40] These relationships are diagramed in the quadrant scheme depicted in Figure 5–2.

C– S+ (IV)	C+ S+ (I)
C– S– (III)	C+ S– (II)

Figure 5-2. A Quadrant Scheme for Describing Leader Behavior on the Initiating Structure and Consideration Dimensions

In Quadrant I, S+ C+ (high initiating structure and high consideration), leaders were perceived by reference groups as being highly effective. In Quadrant III, S– C–, leaders were perceived as least effective, their leadership resulting in confusion. Leaders in Quadrants II and IV exhibited behavior typical of some leader images discussed earlier. For example, the social engineer, whose concern for "democratic" leadership overrides other considerations, would fall in Quadrant II, S– C+. Emphasis by leaders in this category upon *consideration* and neglect of *initiating structure* led to ineffectiveness: they lost sight of their obligation as leaders to lead. At the other extreme, S+ C–, preoccupation with *initiating structure* caused leaders to exhibit characteristics of the

40. Andrew W. Halpin, *op. cit.* See also Halpin's *Theory and Research in Administration* (New York: Macmillan, 1966), pp. 81–130.

efficiency expert. They treated people more like machines in "getting the job done."

The study of Executive Professional Leadership among elementary principals produced similar results. Data showed that, while concern for managerial tasks was negatively related to EPL, there was a point beyond which neglecting managerial tasks in favor of professional relations with staff resulted in a decline of EPL.[41] Thus, optimum professional leadership is characterized by the operation of both factors.

The model of Getzels and Guba was also used to generate three leader behavior styles for characterizing superintendent-principal relationships. The nomothetic style demanded behaviors of the leader which would lead to achieving school goals. It gave precedence to centralized authority and rules and regulations over the needs of organizational members. The idiographic style deemphasized rules and regulations, reinforced individualistic relationships between superior and subordinate, and elevated the value of people as individuals. The transactional style made judicious use of both nomothetic and idiographic behavior as the occasion demanded.[42]

2. *Reference Groups Express Conflicting Expectations and Preferences Concerning Leader Behavior.* Gross and Herriott postulated that behaviors of both a principal's superior and his teachers would provide barriers to his exercise of professional leadership.[43] The nature of these barriers has been revealed by a number of studies to stem from variations in the expectations of reference groups for the behavior of leaders. Halpin found that school boards preferred structure-initiating behavior while school staffs preferred consideration from their leaders.[44] His study of leader behavior in the Air Force showed that superiors viewed initiating structure as fundamental to leader behavior.[45] Guetzkow found that authoritarian leader behavior was "rejected by relatively many followers and accepted by relatively many superiors," while nonauthoritarian behavior was "accepted by relatively many followers and rejected by

41. Neal Gross and Robert E. Herriott, "The EPL of Elementary Principals— A Study of Executive Professional Leadership," *The National Elementary Principal,* Vol. XLV, No. 5, April, 1966, pp. 70–71.

42. Robert P. Moser, "The Leadership Patterns of School Superintendents and School Principals," *Administrator's Notebook,* Vol. VI, No. 1, September, 1957, pp. 1–4.

43. Gross and Herriott, *op. cit.*

44. Halpin, *op. cit.,* p. 78.

45. Andrew W. Halpin, "The Leadership and Combat Performance of Airplane Commanders," *Journal of Abnormal and Social Psychology,* Vol. XLIX, No. 1, January, 1954, pp. 19–22.

relatively many superiors." [46] Moser's study indicated that a principal, subject to different expectations from his superintendent and his teachers, behaves in one way with his superiors and another way with his subordinates. Furthermore, superintendents were found to prefer principals who were transactional, with some emphasis on nomothetic behavior.[47] A study by Seeman involving 77 school leaders and 1,065 teachers showed that conflicting expectations of reference groups led to ambivalence among leaders with regard to (a) the status dimension, (b) the authority dimension, (c) the institutional dimension, and (d) the means-ends dimension.[48]

The conflicting expectations impinging on a school leader are not limited to the formal structure of the school system. Hencley has reported wide divergences in the expectations toward superintendents from business groups, parent groups, and labor groups.[49] For the principal's role, similar conflicting expectations have been reported by Buffington [50] and Medsker.[51]

3. *Incongruence in Expectations for Leader Behavior Influences Satisfaction, Effectiveness, Confidence in Leadership and Attitudes Toward the Work Situation.* In a study of teachers' attitudes and expectations, Moyer found that the more alike members of a teaching group were in terms of their attitudes toward leadership, the more alike they were in amount of satisfaction derived from working in the school situation.[52] Brown and Neitzel have reported a parallel finding: morale tended to suffer if there were disagreements among leaders and their reference groups in defining the leaders' role.[53] Campbell, in studying

46. Harold Guetzkow, *Groups, Leaders, and Men* (New Brunswick, N.J.: Carnegie Press, 1951), p. 171.

47. Moser, *op. cit.*, pp. 1–4.

48. Melvin Seeman, "Role Conflict and Ambivalence in Leadership," *American Sociological Review*, Vol. XVIII, No. 4, August, 1953, pp. 373–380.

49. Stephen P. Hencley, "A Typology of Conflict Between School Superintendents and Their Reference Groups," (Doctoral dissertation, Department of Education, University of Chicago, 1960).

50. Reed L. Buffington, "The Job of the Elementary School Principal as Viewed by Parents," *Dissertation Abstracts* (Ed. D. dissertation, Stanford University, 1954), Vol. 14, No. 6, pp. 943–944.

51. Leland L. Medsker, "The Job of Elementary Principals as Viewed by Teachers," *Dissertation Abstracts* (Ed. D. dissertation, Stanford University, 1954), Vol. 16, No. 6, pp. 946–947.

52. Donald C. Moyer, "Teachers' Attitudes Toward Leadership as They Relate to Teacher Satisfaction" (Doctoral dissertation, University of Chicago, 1954).

53. C. G. Brown and Betty J. Neitzel, "Communication, Supervision, and Morale," *Journal of Applied Psychology*, Vol. XXXVI, No. 10, April, 1952, pp. 86–91.

role conflict among teachers, also found that (*a*) teachers whose wants and needs agreed with their principals' expectations expressed more confidence in the leadership of their principals; (*b*) teachers whose desires and needs approached their principals' expectations expressed significantly higher job satisfaction than did teachers whose desires were in conflict with their principals' definitions of their roles; and (*c*) when principals designated the effectiveness of teachers, the effective teachers were those whose desires and needs were similar to the principals' expectations.[54]

These findings are also supported by Moser's study of principal-superintendent relationships, which concluded, "high mutual ratings of effectiveness and confidence by superintendents and principals were accompanied by similarities in leadership style, feelings of security, general satisfaction with the relationships, desire to consult one another on important matters, and clear delineation of duties and authority for decision making." The absence of high mutual ratings corresponded to relationships characterized by "confusion, lack of security, general dissatisfaction with the relationship, poorly defined duties, and poor delineation of authority for decision making." [55]

4. *Misconceptions and Value Differences Interfere with the Effectiveness of Leaders in Interpersonal Relations.* Getzels has suggested that difficulties in interpersonal relationships arise not so much from complexities and differences in values that are in the open and understood as from complexities and differences that are underground and misunderstood.[56] Several studies appear to have corroborated this view. Sletten has reported that attitude and value differences account for many conflicts between school leaders and boards of education.[57] McPhee found that congruence in educational viewpoint between community residents and school teachers was related to the degree of school support manifested by the citizens.[58] In examining the influence of values upon relationships between school leaders and boards of education, Abbott

54. Merton V. Campbell, "Self-Role Conflict Among Teachers and Its Relationship to Satisfaction, Effectiveness, and Confidence in Leadership" (Doctoral dissertation, University of Chicago, 1958).

55. Moser, *op. cit.*, pp. 1–4.

56. J. W. Getzels, "Changing Values Challenge the Schools," *School Review*, Vol. LXV, No. 1, Spring, 1957, p. 1.

57. Vernon Sletten, "A Related Study of the Opinions of Montana School Board Members and Superintendents on Selected Board Policy Practices" (Doctoral dissertation, University of Oregon, 1954).

58. R. F. McPhee, "Individual Values, Educational Viewpoint, and Local School Approval," *Administrator's Notebook*, Vol. VII, No. 8, April, 1959.

noted that these relationships are influenced not only by differences of viewpoint on basic issues but by accuracy or inaccuracy characterizing individual perceptions of others' positions in relation to these issues.[59]

5. *Leader Behavior Affects Organizational Achievement.* Stogdill's "middle-range" theory of organizational achievement has supported the view that organized groups are input-output systems that are maintained in unstable balance. The components of his theory, as shown in Table 5–2, indicate that group outputs are determined not only by member inputs but also by a number of mediating variables normally present in all organizations.[60]

Table 5-2. Stogdill's Theory of Organizational Achievement

Member Inputs	Mediating Variables		Group Outputs
Behavior	Formal Structure	Role Structure	Achievement
Performance	Function	Responsibility	Productivity
Interactions	Status	Authority	Morale
Expectations	Purpose	Operations	Integration
	Group Structure and Operations		Effects

In addition to the generalizations stated above, research studies on leadership in various fields lend support to the following propositions:

1. Leader behavior evolves from group interaction; it is not a product of formal group structure. Status may enhance, but it does not create, leadership capacity, which emerges, under the right circumstances, during group interaction.

2. Leader behavior is not a function of static qualities or personal characteristics of individuals. Leaders with markedly dissimilar traits have been successful in a variety of situations, and success in one group situation does not guarantee success in all situations.

3. Power and leadership are not synonymous. The authoritarian use of power derived from status cannot be equated with leadership.

4. Regardless of opinions about what leader behavior *should* be, in actual practice it is characterized by two types of activities: initiating

59. Max G. Abbott, "Values and Value-Perceptions in Superintendent–School Board Relationships," *Administrator's Notebook,* Vol. IX, No. 4, December, 1960.

60. Ralph M. Stogdill, *Individual Behavior and Group Achievement* (New York: Oxford University Press, 1959).

group action toward acceptable goals and maintaining group cohesion, cooperation, and commitment.

5. Values play an important role in the leadership process. Effective leaders accurately perceive the value orientations of those with whom they interact and seek to modify values that appear inconsistent with organizational objectives.

INSTITUTIONAL LEADERSHIP

Elementary school administrators undergo a period of preprofessional experience during which their future roles are represented to them as leadership roles. Evidence indicates that they internalize this conceptualization to large degree.[61] Its nature, however, is based on trends which depict leadership in terms of means and processes. Certainly, it is essential for elementary principals to master the decision-making and communications skills which are the means to achieving organizational effectiveness and efficiency. Facility in the use of means and processes, however, will not provide them with the foundation they need to exercise institutional leadership. Nor will facility in the use of means and processes provide an adequate foundation for educational statesmanship.

The statesman is distinguished from the organizational manager by his involvement with policy and purpose. His interests extend beyond means and processes to ends and purposes. His competencies encompass organizational maintenance, interpersonal leadership, and matters pertaining to policy implementation. But they also include the creation and development of policy. The institutional leader in education has a grasp of significant educational goals to be achieved in our time, and he understands how his institution relates to them. Thus, he seeks to define and to interpret the aims of the schools, to conceptualize necessary roles, and to build value-infused social structures for achieving its goals.

There can be little doubt that some elementary school administrators have been kept from serving their field as professional leaders and educational statesmen because they have not understood that *the attainment of complete institutional leadership requires a political orientation. The primary concern of institutional leaders is policy; their profession is*

61. Ninety-five percent of one group of 2,410 elementary principals perceived their role to be a leader's role. See *The Elementary School Principalship—A Research Study, Thirty-Seventh Yearbook of the Department of Elementary School Principals* (Washington, D.C.: National Education Association, 1958), p. 39.

politics. School administrators who feel impelled to serve their communities as leaders must realize that supplanting administrative management with institutional leadership will require a broadening of their professional responsibilities.

Responsibilities of Institutional Leaders

Many of the tasks of elementary school administrators, as indicated in Chapter 4, center around organizational maintenance. Such tasks involve routine activities at the level of policy implementation; they do not require the depth in decision making employed by institutional leaders.

There are many areas, however, within the realm of elementary school administration that focus on basic institutional values and goals. In these areas, as Selznick says, "leadership creates and molds an organization embodying—in thought and feeling and habit—the value premises of policy." [62] To mold thoughts, feelings, and habits requires *change* in people. In the school setting, a great many individuals and groups within and outside the formal educational organization are involved. To effect their cooperation for policy formulation in the several areas discussed below will demand institutional leadership of elementary school administrators.

Development of Goals and Purposes

The technological and social demands of today's society continually magnify the recognition of education's essential role in the lives of people. The concern for better ways to educate America's children has created many opportunities for administrators to advocate policies and programs in the public forum. Too often, however, school administrators have avoided rather than seized these opportunities.

The disposition of school leaders to regard activities in the political arena as inconsistent with educational ideals has caused them to leave to others the formulation of important educational policy. Failure of educators to meet significant issues at community and national levels has left them exposed to outside pressures. They have found themselves, at times, in the embarrassing position of having to answer to proposals put forth by scientists, lawyers, and admirals. Educators, by their reticence, have tended to place themselves outside the mainstream of activ-

62. Philip Selznick, *Leadership in Administration* (Evanston, Ill.: Row, Peterson & Co., 1957), p. 62.

ities related to the creation and development of fundamental educational policies.

Institutional leadership requires elementary school administrators, superintendents, and other professionals to play a vital role in forging common agreements relating to educational goals and purposes among citizens, teaching staffs, and boards of education. The responsibility to be assumed by administrators as part of institutional leadership has been outlined by Keppel as follows:

1. Educational administration . . . must feel a corporate sense of responsibility as a professional adviser on issues of public policy that affect education and on which education has an effect. Rather than make more difficult the present role conflicts of the school administrator in his local community, such a change will, in my opinion, make his local task easier. He will be seen as a participant in a larger movement, as a man of standing in a larger community.
2. Educational administration . . . having reached this self-view, must relate itself to other aspects of public administration, and particularly to economic policy, programs of social reform, and foreign affairs. . . .
3. After having taken these two steps, school administration would be ready to become an active participant in the formulation and execution of national policy. Its statements would be heeded in the halls of Congress, in the executive branch of the government, and in the judiciary. Even the fourth estate might be impressed.[63]

Increasing Teaching-Learning Potentials

To the outline of broad responsibilities for the principal as institutional leader should be added a number of specifics related to the improvement of teaching-learning potential in schools. It is the authors' view that the improvement of teaching-learning environments in elementary schools will require the following leadership activities on the part of principals:

1. The principal, as leader, will provide opportunities for continuous clarification and redefinition of educational goals and aims to guide the instructional process toward worthy purposes accepted by both citizens and professional staff members.
2. The principal will strive to provide opportunities in the elementary school for the development of the variety of student abilities as

63. Francis Keppel, *Public Policy and School Administration* (Cambridge, Mass.: The New England School Development Council, 1961), pp. 21–22. See also Seymour E. Harris, *Education and Public Policy* (Berkeley, Calif.: McCutchan Publishing Corp., 1965).

they emerge. He will develop with his staff learning opportunities that will ensure the acquisition of basic skills and knowledge and create individual responsibility and citizenship. He will understand that effectiveness of the school as an organization will be maximized when individual and organizational values reinforce one another. To this end, he will work to establish congruent values among his staff and common conceptions of the role and purpose of the elementary school in the educational scheme.

3. The principal will assume responsibility for reaching agreement regarding the effectiveness of various resources, both mechanical and human, which may facilitate the instructional process. These include new building designs and utilization of technological media such as ETV, teaching machines, and "systems" approaches to instruction on the one hand, and, on the other, new staffing patterns including team teaching and teacher aides, and new pupil deployment patterns for large and small groups, as well as individualized instruction. Maximum effectiveness of resource utilization calls for reexamination of traditional ideas regarding educational practice. Among these are the notion that all teachers are fundamentally alike and should therefore perform similar instructional roles; the assumption that learning takes place only if classes are small; and the assumption that teachers must take responsibility not only for professional tasks involved in the teaching-learning process but for tasks of a clerical, custodial, and police nature. Intelligent leaders will take the responsibility for testing the validity of these and other "sacred cows" in education.[64]

4. The principal will create opportunities for members of his teaching staff to improve their instructional effectiveness. Effective instruction cannot be achieved without effective teachers, and if the administrator is exercising creative leadership, his school will be the best place for his staff to learn how to improve. Barriers to his guidance in this area constitute some of the most stimulating challenges to be met by the elementary school principal.

Leadership in instructional improvement becomes evident in (a) the nature of questions and hypotheses used to promote instructional improvement, (b) the encouragement of creativity, exploration, and experimentation in instruction, (c) the opportunities made available for the acquisition of new skills and the use of new resources in the teach-

64. See Lester W. Nelson, "New Ideas in Education," *Harvard Graduate School of Education Association Bulletin,* September, 1959.

ing-learning process, and (*d*) the use of valid concepts for evaluating teaching effectiveness.[65] As principals assume responsibility for promoting revolutionary techniques in instructional media and staff deployment, new degrees of freedom will present themselves for in-service education of teachers.

5. In the past in many communities, educational innovations based on sound theory have failed to become a functioning part of the instructional program because they have not gained support of the school's community. The principal must assume responsibility for making his community aware of the need for continually upgrading the quality of resources, both human and mechanical, utilized in his school. This means that he will prepare them to understand the nature and role of new developments in media, curriculum, and facilities. He will also see that the community develops appreciation of the need to keep the school's human resources abreast of changes in these areas.

6. The principal will provide the energy and stimulation for creating a wholesome climate for growth, leadership development, and administrative teamwork. Premium will be placed upon creativity. Questioning and the seeking of answers will be encouraged. Emergent leadership will receive recognition and credit. Staff members who request assistance in overcoming professional weaknesses will be encouraged rather than censured. The administrator who accepts his responsibility for establishing a healthy organizational climate will promote the professional stature of his entire staff.

7. The principal will provide a framework for pursuing research to improve the instructional process. Careful and rigorous testing of new ideas will provide a solid basis for improved curricular organizations, more effective utilization of new media, more efficient functioning of staffs, and other improvements in teaching-learning opportunities.

In all ways possible, the leader will seek to build a productive organization where goals and purposes are jointly formulated and mutually accepted, where common values prevail, where organizational roles and relationships are cooperatively defined, where communication is facilitated, where destructive conflict is minimized, and where role achievement and role satisfaction are optimized.

65. Ramseyer, *op. cit.*, p. 35.

REFERENCES

Association for Supervision and Curriculum Development, *Leadership for Improving Instruction, 1960 Yearbook* (Washington, D.C.: the Association, 1960).

Bass, Bernard M., *Leadership, Psychology, and Organizational Behavior* (New York: Harper & Bros., 1960).

Gross, Neal, and Robert E. Herriott, *Staff Leadership in Public Schools: A Sociological Inquiry* (New York: John Wiley & Sons, 1965).

Halpin, Andrew W., *Theory and Research in Administration* (New York: Macmillan, 1966).

Harris, Seymour E., *Education and Public Policy* (Berkeley, Calif.: McCutchan Publishing Corp., 1965).

Jennings, Eugene E., *An Anatomy of Leadership* (New York: Harper & Bros., 1960).

Leu, Donald, and Herbert Rudman, *Preparation Programs for School Administrators* (East Lansing, Mich.: College of Education, Michigan State University, 1963).

Likert, Rensis, *New Patterns of Management* (New York: McGraw-Hill, 1961).

Moore, Hollis A., *Studies in School Administration* (Washington, D.C.: American Association of School Administrators, 1957).

National Education Association, *The Changing World of the Elementary School Principal,* Parts I and II (Washington, D.C.: the Association, 1968).

National Society for the Study of Education, *Behavorial Science and Educational Administration, Sixty-third Yearbook,* Part II (Chicago: University of Chicago Press, 1964).

Selznick, Philip, *Leadership in Administration* (Evanston, Ill.: Row, Peterson & Co., 1957).

Stogdill, Ralph M., *Individual Behavior and Group Achievement* (New York: Oxford University Press, 1959).

Tannenbaum, Robert, Irving R. Wechsler, and Fred Massarick, *Leadership and Organization* (New York: McGraw-Hill, 1961).

Chapter 6

ORGANIZATION AND THE ELEMENTARY SCHOOL

ORGANIZATIONAL considerations have many implications for the program of the elementary school and its improvement. Organization refers to patterns of activity, working relationships, systems of control and development, and other arrangements by which a group of individuals is brought together to accomplish prescribed purposes. Although sound organization does not in itself guarantee an effective program, it is an essential element in maximizing effectiveness; and worthwhile programs can be seriously affected, even destroyed, by poor organization. The design or plan which gives substance and meaning to ongoing activity is a central concern of the administrator's attention— well-conceived purposes and tasks, clearly defined responsibilities, stimulating and productive relationships, and a continuously developing design of operation geared to imaginative use of staff, facilities, and resources.

Since the school is the operational unit for education, it becomes the focus of attention in matters relating to organization. No single teacher or educational specialist can function adequately in an isolated or autonomous fashion in the modern elementary school. At the same time, district level plans and actions are not capable of coordinating and directing educational programs at the operational level—they can, at best, only facilitate the work within each school. The major responsibility for organization rests with the school principal.

Functional interrelationships of positions within school district organization are presented in Chapter 4. They represent an attempt by the authors to present a clear definition of administrative tasks and their assignment to positions within the total administrative structure. The scheme can be used as a device for the analysis of existing administrative structures within actual school settings or as a model for study. In this chapter the presentation is directed toward concepts and points of view that seem most fruitful for an understanding of the internal organization of elementary schools.

NATURE OF ORGANIZATION

Organizations are a prominent, many believe dominant, characteristic of modern life. S. S. Wolin writes, "Everywhere there is organization, everywhere bureaucratization; like the world of feudalism, the modern world is broken up into areas dominated by castles . . . the castles of Kafka." [1] The school is certainly one of the castles to which Wolin refers. The administrator needs to concern himself seriously with the kind of "castle" his school has become in terms of learning, growth, individual development, opportunities for creative expression, wholesome relationships, and meaningful, joyful living. Organization is a necessary means to productive group effort, but it must be rationally controlled to ensure that it is facilitative rather than inhibitive of group effort and that individuals, especially the administrators, do not use it to achieve purely personal ends.

THE CONCEPT OF ORGANIZATION

Most students of current organizational problems base their study, in one way or another, upon the conceptual work of Max Weber and of Chester I. Barnard. Weber began with the definition of the corporate group as dependent upon three criteria: (1) Definite membership requirements are established and individuals participate subject to specified conditions (roles). (2) A legitimate order is created through rules and norms that define conduct. (3) A differentiation of power is made through a "legal" structure so that control can be exercised and sanctions administered. To be an organization two additional criteria were proposed by Weber: (4) The group becomes "associative" rather than "communal." Members do not participate *totally,* sharing feelings of sentiment, tradition, belongingness, and the like, as a family would or even as a nation does. Rather, they participate primarily through their expertise to pursue common interests and values. (5) Organizational

1. S. S. Wolin, *Politics and Vision* (Boston: Little, Brown & Co., 1960), p. 354.

activities are continuous, a process, and the objectives are limited and specific.[2]

In Weber's definition an organization, such as a school, would differentiate itself, in terms of purposes, from other organizations and corporate groups. The reader might wish to return to Chapter 2 to the treatment of the school's overall purposes and review attempts to differentiate the school's purposes from those of the family and other community agencies.

Barnard, on the other hand, defined organization as a "system of consciously coordinated activities . . ."[3] The necessary conditions of organization, according to Barnard, are to have a specific group of people (1) willing to cooperate together and contribute their talents, (2) to attain a common purpose(s), and (3) a system of communication to direct and coordinate their efforts.

Barnard emphasizes rational self-interest focusing upon a communication system that allows organizational members to work together effectively. Weber emphasizes shared moral commitments with the allocation of legitimatized power sufficient to accomplish purposes. From these two formulations has come the notion that organizations are both communications and power structures and that members of organizations are motivated both by shared values and by self-interest.

The details of each point of view are further developed in this chapter. The premises for educational organization to be examined here are: (1) The approaches, as illustrated by the definitions, represent two orientations that are being followed in school organization today. (2) Although not in direct opposition, the two orientations are not completely complementary, and at certain points, create serious conflict—particularly when administrators are not insightful about the consequences of organizational processes. (3) Organizational forms and procedures that establish the norm, or model, for elementary school organization do not permit maximal attainment of desired results. (4) Elementary school administrators need to give serious attention to the ongoing study of conditions of organization in their schools and exercise far more initiative than is currently in evidence to build effective organizational designs.

Conventional Versus Professional Bureaucracy. The most common form of organization in modern society is the bureaucratic, and schools

2. Max Weber, *The Theory of Social and Economic Organization,* translated by A. M. Henderson and Talcott Parsons (Glencoe, Ill.: Free Press, 1947).

3. Chester Barnard, *Functions of the Executive* (Cambridge, Mass.: Harvard University Press, 1938), p. 73.

tend to follow this form. Two basic tenets of bureaucratic organization are rationality and legitimacy. All behavior, while one is participating as an organizational member, is expected to be rationally determined by the prescribed goals, procedures, and operations as established *or sanctioned* by constituted authority. The conventional bureaucracy—that is the commonly held image of government or corporate bureaucracy— is one in which a large amount of routine is to be handled. Lower officials handle almost all of the work by simply following regular procedures. Supervisors and administrators deal with decisions about exceptional cases, adjustment of procedures to new situations, overall management and planning, evaluation of results, and the like.

The point to be made here is that conventional bureaucracy provided the model for educational organization.[4] Unfortunately the largest profession and the one that most pervades the society, by following this model uncritically, has exhibited the least creative study of organizational problems and conditions. This is regrettable because the schools, of all the agencies of society, should be most concerned about human factors associated with organizational life and should be providing models that mitigate against the debasing of the individual in a bureaucratically structured society that has come to receive the epitaphs of the "faceless society" and the "organization man." [5]

Conflicts in Current Conceptions of Organization. Examination of several important features of organization bring to light the conflicts and dilemmas within present conceptions of organization (illustrated briefly in the Weber and Barnard definitions in the previous section), but also between the conditions of organization required by the nature of the educational task and that represented by conventional bureaucracy. Each of the organizational features dealt with here are present in the elementary school. Points of view relative to each feature are held by parents, staff members, the principal, superiors in the administrative hierarchy, and policy-making bodies. Since the position of the principal is the focal point of implementation, differences in perceptions and

---

4. For a thorough study of this condition the reader is encouraged to refer to Raymond E. Callahan, *Education and the Cult of Efficiency* (Chicago: University of Chicago Press, 1962); and Rafael Lewy, *The Secondary School Principal in Theory: An Examination of Major Theoretical Trends of the Principalship* (Urbana, Ill.: Unpublished doctoral dissertation, 1965).

5. Martin Mayer, noted student of and writer on educational problems and conditions, provides a case study of his own experience with bureaucratic organization while serving as a school board member in: "What's Wrong With Our Big City Schools," *Saturday Evening Post,* September 9, 1967, pp. 21–23, 66–68.

points of view regarding them are certain to center upon the principal. Unless he is sufficiently knowledgeable, as well as skilled in dealing with conflicting viewpoints, he is not likely to deal effectively with organizational concerns.

1. *Specification of tasks.* The means of attaining rationality in conventional bureaucracy is the specification of tasks through general rules and procedures. This method is frequently resorted to by administrators and teachers in the regulation of pupil behavior and by administrators in the regulation of teacher behavior. The extent to which tasks are to be detailed and formalized in rule-following behavior needs to be carefully considered in the school.

If teaching and learning are to be reasonably creative and flexible in terms of the needs of pupils and teachers, overly formal arrangements are likely to interfere with organizational effectiveness. Further, the authors contend that, at the present time, institutional leadership itself must be imaginative in character. Undue restraints upon the school by higher authority are likely to be detrimental—imaginative leadership, particularly in organizational matters is now a necessity not a luxury.

2. *Purpose-task relationship.* The purpose-task dimension of organization is treated in detail in a later section of this chapter. However, the abuse of school organization at the hands of public figures and laymen in terms of demanding "a businesslike approach" to the management of schools needs to be noted at this point. Organizations that have limited and specific objectives are found to have more centralized authority structures, are less concerned with involvement of members in planning and decision making, and do not expend the effort upon internal communications exerted by organizations with multiple purposes.[6] The school represents an institution with purposes that are diffuse and often lacking in clarity—sometimes even in conflict with each other—largely because of the lack of a clear, consistent public policy, but also due to the requirements of a comprehensive program. In the educational institution, time and resources must be allocated to the study of purposes and the design of tasks to meet them. In the process, lack of clarity, conflicts between purposes, and their causes need to be investigated. However, multiple purposes, the lack of clarity of some, and even conflicting purposes are a reality of educational organization.

6. R. L. Simpson and W. H. Gulley, "Goals, Environmental Pressures, and Organizational Characteristics," *American Sociological Review,* Vol. 27, 1962, pp. 344–351.

3. *Human versus technological products.* Schools, hospitals, churches, and various social agencies represent organizations in which a client rather than a product is involved. Student unrest and demonstrations in the universities amply demonstrate the consequences to institutions that are treating clients as products. Pupils are members of school organization and the organization must provide suitable means for their participation. One theory relating to the nonlearner, particularly the culturally deprived, is that he does not find identity in the institutional makeup of the school. Much has been written about the "unattached," the "cool generation," and the "hippies." A large part of the responsibility for this condition rests upon the fact that conventional bureaucratic models require the member to adapt to objective, depersonalized procedures.

Organization in the conventional bureaucracy is based upon simplifying and routinizing procedures predicated upon a measure of the "average person." School administrators who permit organization to function in this way are guilty of defeating the most basic purpose of education— to foster maximum development of each individual's talents.

In regard to this point, note must be taken of the slow recognition of educational institutions that the educational values desired for learners are not likely to be realized unless they apply to the professional staff as well. Challenging in-service training programs, a stimulating intellectual environment, opportunities for continued study, and provision of the means to pursue varied interests are necessary if teachers are to exemplify the values these activities imply.

4. *Bases of authority.* Perhaps the primary feature of organization is the hierarchical structure of authority. Many theorists—some in educational theory—have attempted to define the manner in which authority is exercised. First, authority is limited in scope, and the procedures for its exercise are identified. Individuals in subordinate positions may disregard directives if they are beyond the prescribed areas in which authority is to be exercised or if proper procedures are violated. In this sense, each directive is legitimated by the person receiving direction. Second, authority does not mean influence. The recipient of a directive is not to demand reasons or expect each directive to be justified before he obeys—providing the directive meets the two criteria of legitimacy. Third, the basis of legitimacy is the acceptance among the members of the organization that the authority figures should control, direct, and supervise.

This simple, straightforward view does not account for the complex authority relationships and the dynamics of organizational control even in conventional bureaucracy. The fact is that the role of the principal in the authority hierarchy is undergoing steady attrition, and this condition is likely to become of central concern in school organization during the next decade. This problem is examined in the following section as part of the analysis of administration of organization.

ADMINISTRATION OF ORGANIZATION

Administration and organization are two interrelated concepts. Organization is not possible until individuals find the need to cooperate together and surrender some of their autonomy in the process, in order to achieve purposes not otherwise possible. In doing this they must see the organizational purposes to be worthwhile and see values to themselves in their participation. The first requirement of this kind of group effort is the establishment of procedures for coordinating the efforts of the various organizational members so that work can proceed effectively and efficiently. To accomplish coordination, administrative processes are required. In this sense, administration is the *art and science of coordination* within organization.

In simple organizations—the small elementary school, for example— the administrative function may be handled informally or delegated to one member. The teaching principal is still common in the elementary schools; in fact, the term has only appeared in the literature in this reversed form since the 1920's. Prior to that time the administrator was commonly referred to as the "principal teacher." As complexity of function occurred, administration became a specialty within elementary school organization. However, it differs in important ways from other specialties in that it is the function of overseeing the work of the other specialties and of determining the extent and timing of their contribution to the total effort.

Administration is not superimposed upon organization, and it is not separated from it—administration, while a part of organization, is that part responsible for creating, developing, and directing it. During the period in which bureaucratic organization was becoming dominant in American society, Brooks Adams referred to administration as: "the power of organizing a series of relations between special interests, with all of which no single man can be intimately acquainted . . . yet administration or generalization is not only the faculty upon which social stability rests, but is probably the highest faculty of the human mind." [7]

Need for Administration. The need for the specialty of administration as a distinct part of elementary school organization occurs because of three factors: size of organization, complexity of purposes, and specialization of functions. Until the factors of size, purposes, and specialization of staff begin to produce conditions requiring close, continuous coordination at the building level, administration is nominal and is managerial in character.

The one room school with a single teacher handling all grades required only the managerial concerns for business affairs, building maintenance, and general oversight to see that the teacher was performing his job. As size became a factor, an additional room or rooms were provided duplicating the first. At some point, efficiency in teaching called for a specialization of the staff into primary and intermediate levels or into single grades. The problem of coordination then began to appear with some persistence, and supervision through general oversight by a lay committee or a county superintendent became inadequate. Add to this condition demands for special services—health, food service, activities, and increased teaching specializations—remedial reading, music, speech correction, and the like. Thus, the need for specialized administrative service at the building level was created.

The story does not end with the creation of the specialty of administration. It does indicate the basis of conceptualizing of administration at the building level as the "art and science of coordination." It also provides a basis for understanding the most basic dilemma in the administrator's role—a dilemma about which the elementary principal is too frequently unaware.

Basic Dilemma of Administrator's Role. The brief, and incomplete, story of the historical evolution of the specialty of administration can provide one entrée to the further analysis of the nature of organization and of the administrative function. As indicated above, one facet of administration derived from constituted authority—that is, the need to provide a building and a teacher, establish overall purposes, control through general oversight or inspection, and the like. Another facet of administration derived from the nature of teaching and the needs of the organizational unit itself.

Returning to the two definitions of organization, given in the opening

7. Brooks Adams, *The Theory of Social Revolutions* (New York: Macmillan, 1913), p. 19.

section of this chapter, one facet of administrative authority is power; the other is cooperation and consent. Barnard would argue that authority comes from below—from those being directed. As the administrator, through a communication system, builds understanding of the tasks at hand, individuals in the organization consent to his authority to direct them. Weber would argue that as long as the authority was within the legitimate bounds direction should not be questioned. Under the Weber definition, the authority to lead comes from above and is conditioned only by the members' shared values concerning legitimacy.

Each position is stated here in its most extreme form in order to bring out the dilemma involved, but the differences in orientation lie at the root of very practical organizational problems. The practical division is clear when presented in statements such as that of Stuart Dean:

On the one hand, there is organization for strictly administrative purposes, relating to the operational management of large numbers of children and staff, building maintenance, business responsibilities and ancillary services. On the other hand, there is organization, quite apart from the operational, which relates to the instructional responsibilities of the school.[8]

Unfortunately, such a division between organization for management purposes and organization for program purposes is untenable as a solution to the dilemma. It separates management from program concerns when management should be shaped by the requirements of the program.

Several influences are operating to maintain the division between program organization and operational management. Some of the major influences can be listed:

1. Professionalization of the teacher has developed pressures for autonomy for the teacher in decisions relating to instruction. The advent of teachers' unions is a manifestation of this influence.

2. Centralization of the educational hierarchy in district central offices in which staff positions (business manager, curriculum director, pupil personnel director, and the like) tend to function in a "line" rather than "staff" relationship to the principal. The central office tends to shape a power relationship to the principal.

3. Supervision has been set up as a separate function outside of administrative authority with supervisors and coordinators attempting to work directly with teachers but without authority to make changes.

4. The inability to evaluate objectively the effects of the program,

8. Stuart E. Dean, *Elementary School Organization and Administration* (Washington, D.C.: U.S. Department of Health, Education, and Welfare, 1960), p. 28.

particularly instruction, in terms of the overall goals of the school weakens the authority of the principal. Evaluation is essential to planning and to decision making relating to change. Without the benefit of sound evaluation, the principal must rely upon other means of influence.

Some districts have made imaginative efforts to minimize the effects of these influences. Others are trapped by them, and the effectiveness of the principal has suffered accordingly. In a study of the school principalship in various types of communities one of these authors has found that the role of the principal is being reduced to management tasks at the expense of program leadership.[9] Apparently, as school size increases, organization structures become more complex, and specialization of staff intensifies, the principal has responded purely to the administrative-managerial tasks to the neglect of developmental and leadership aspects of his job.

Characteristics of Participation—A Key to Understanding Organizational Conditions

One approach to understanding a wide range of problems relating to organizational conditions—administrative function, productivity, staff commitment, conflict, and the like—centers upon the conditions under which an organization attracts and sustains individual participation and effort. The basic postulate of such a theory is that: whether an individual joins, remains in, or leaves an organization depends upon his *perception* of the inducements afforded by the organization in relation to the contributions required of him, measured in terms of his "utilities." [10] Inducement utilities are measured in terms of the values the individual sees by his participation—rewards, status, security, recognition, and the like. Contribution utilities can be defined in more than one way, but useful measures can be attained when they are defined as the individual's perception of the value of alternatives available—that is, what he forgoes in order to contribute.

A definition of inducements and contributions in terms of utility values permits the administrator to observe and/or discuss with staff

9. Lloyd E. McCleary, *An Essay on Role Attrition: Three Studies of the Job of the Principal* (Unpublished paper, University of Illinois, 1969).

10. First proposed as the Barnard-Simon theory of organizational equilibrium, the postulates are stated in Herbert Simon, D. W. Smithburg, and V. A. Thompson, *Public Administration* (New York: John Wiley & Sons, 1950), pp. 381–382, and in an expanded form including testable propositions in James March and Herbert Simon, *Organizations* (New York: John Wiley & Sons, 1958), pp. 84–111.

members (1) the "utility balance" and (2) predict contributions, including extent and quality, in terms of inducements. The administrator can conceive of an inducement-contribution utility scale for each individual or group and make certain assumptions about their responses to changes in inducements, changes in the contributions demanded of them, or changes in organizational activity that will likely affect them. In any situation, the administrator can identify the specific utility values and predict the effect of a change on the extent and quality of participation.

From the discussion above, the general postulate can now be stated in other terms: increases in the balance of inducement utilities over contribution utilities, as perceived by the individual, provide the motivation to participate in organizational activity both in terms of quantity and quality of contribution. There is substantial research to indicate that factors in the job situation that provide inducements to teachers operate as two separate mechanisms. Factors such as feelings of achievement, feelings of recognition, and feelings about advancement function to motivate teachers positively; however, absence or decrease of these factors does not lessen such motivation. Moreover, factors such as interpersonal relations with students, parents, and administrators; school policies; supervisory practices; and restraints on personal life operate to motivate teachers negatively only, and the absence or decrease of these factors does not operate positively.[11] One can make the assumption that the positive motivators for teachers in a given situation will be the *intrinsic* factors; whereas, the negative motivators will be the *extrinsic* factors.

A more fully delineated theory of organization in terms of personnel is undertaken in Chapter 10. In the remainder of this chapter, specific features of organization are described and examined.

TYPES OF ELEMENTARY SCHOOL PROGRAM ORGANIZATION

Where elementary school organization has been consciously designed, hard choices have had to be made concerning emphasis. If the emphasis is placed upon content and skills—that is, upon the curriculum—the decision must first be made about the organization of the curriculum. This

11. Thomas Sergiovanni, "Factors Which Affect Satisfaction and Dissatisfaction of Teachers," *Journal of Educational Administration,* Vol. 5, No. 1, May, 1967, pp. 66–82, and "New Evidence on Teacher Morale—A Proposal for Staff Differentiation," *North Central Association Quarterly,* Winter, 1968.

can be by separate subjects, core, broad fields, fused, or some combination in terms of the instruction to be carried out. If the organization is to emphasize the teacher and teacher competencies and specializations, the decision involves choices between the self-contained classroom, teaming, departmentalization, or some mixture of them. If the emphasis is to be placed upon the pupil, considerations of homogeneous versus plans for heterogeneous grouping are indicated.

Two dimensions of organization are always involved—*horizontal* and *vertical*. Horizontal dimension refers to the manner in which pupils are organized among teachers. The choices include: self-contained or departmentalized classes, homogeneous or heterogeneous grouping, separate subjects or a mix of separate subjects, and core or some other subject arrangement, or teaming with the various options it affords. Vertical dimension refers to upward movement of pupils through the program. Basically the choices in this dimension are limited to a graded scheme by age grouping and a variation called multigrading or to a nongraded plan.

The elementary school has been creative in the development of organizational schemes, and this activity is increasing and likely to continue. At the same time it is necessary to point out that the graded plan organized horizontally by the self-contained homeroom is the dominant type of elementary school organization. This plan, placed in effect in 1847 in the Quincy Grammar School in Boston, became universal and, with some modification of the self-contained concept, is the type of organization employed in more than 80 percent of the nation's elementary schools today.

The graded elementary school provides an illustration of the relationship of the program of the school, allocation of staff and resources, employment of pupil services, and other organizational concerns to the type of organization chosen. The curriculum of the graded elementary school is defined in terms of this type of organization so that the content of each subject must be "graded." The graded placement of content is an overriding concern of curriculum development and certain topics and skills have come to be labeled as "first grade work" or some other grade level. Large amounts of staff time, the materials of instruction, student activities, work with parents, and most other organizational matters are shaped in one way or another by this structure. So it is with the other organizational types; each type has implications for almost all other aspects of the school.

Early Departures from Graded Self-contained
Type of Organization

By 1900 plans began to appear that would break the rigidity of the graded self-contained homeroom plan. From the first, of course, the graded arrangement was modified in many places by *multigrading* where several grades were combined in one room with one teacher. This arrangement was never intended to achieve better instruction or to meet individual needs; it was strictly a practical matter, and pupils were expected to study the same subjects in the same way as in a graded plan. The first organizational plan brought about by fundamental curriculum changes was the *platoon* school.

The *platoon* school curriculum was to emphasize social living in a work-study-play environment that would provide experiences important to the pupil rather than experiences necessary to adult life. This curriculum, initiated at Bluffton, Indiana, in 1900, brought the platoon plan into significance. The school was to operate two half-day schedules: traditional subjects occupied one-half day; library work, gym, art, music, and assembly (auditorium) the other half. Pupils were divided into groups or platoons and broken down into classes by grades. One platoon was studying fundamental subjects while the other platoon was scheduled into the special rooms with special teachers.

Platoon scheduling became important to the *departmentalized* plan, which appeared about the same time, as pupils were kept in classroom-sized platoons and moved through courses taught by teachers considered to be subject specialists. Departmental plans are used *in toto* or in some mixed arrangement with self-contained homerooms at the intermediate and junior high school levels.

In the 1920's two other types of organizational plans came into prominence: the *Dalton* or "contract" plan and the *Winnetka* plan. The curriculum of the *Dalton* plan included English, history, geography, mathematics, and science in one segment of the program and nonacademic subjects in another. Each subject was divided into lesson-sized segments called units. These units were grouped into contracts that represented approximately one month's study. The student entered into contracts with each teacher of an academic subject. Teaching stations, called laboratories, manned by a subject specialist were available to a pupil for approximately one-half day, and the pupil could choose each day the laboratory in which he wished to work. Pupils worked individually or in groups in the laboratory regardless of age.[12] Individualization was provided both by the arrangement of the units in the contract and by the time in which contracts were completed. A more able pupil might require fewer units in a given subject or complete an allotted number faster than average or slow pupils. Each month represented a contract period, however, and a pupil could not move ahead until contracts in each of the five subjects were completed.

The *Winnetka* plan, and a parallel plan employed in Chicago called the *McDade* plan, provided flexible time segments for the mastery of "common essentials" and provided for self-expression and group activities in which no specific skill or knowledge outcome was sought. The common essentials were identified in units of work that were to be highly individualized for each student, but nonetheless they were to be mastered—instead of quality varying, time was varied. A child could take all the time he wished but he must master the segment of the program defined as the common essentials. In the self-expression and group-activities segment the school provided opportunities; the child could get from them what he wished. The plan called for one common essentials block of time and one activities block of time in each half-day.

Organizational concerns were secondary in both the *Dalton* and *Winnetka* plans; yet, each introduced a concept of flexible progress, pupil grouping, teacher role, and time blocks that broke with conventional organizational arrangements. Each retained the vertical grade structure but broke sharply with established patterns of horizontal structure.

New Departures in Program Organization

Three departures in program organization have achieved wide recognition since 1960. Two plans, dual progress and nongraded, represent innovations in vertical organization; the third, team teaching, is an innovation in horizontal organization. Whereas team teaching and nongraded concepts are primarily organizational schemes, they have provided many opportunities for curricular and instructional changes. Dual progress is basically a curriculum plan that holds significant organizational implications. Examination of each is restricted, in this chapter, to matters of organization.

Dual progress, in its organizational characteristics, is almost identical

12. The *Dalton* plan was restricted to Grades 4 and above and was never recommended for primary grades.

with the original platoon concept. Pupils are assigned for one-half day with a "home teacher" who is responsible for instruction in reading and social studies and who serves as counselor. Each home teacher handles two groups of pupils per day. Pupils are assigned to homerooms on a grade-level basis. All remaining instruction is provided by specialist teachers—mathematics, science, music, arts and crafts, health and recreation, and foreign languages as an elective beginning in the intermediate grades. This instruction is in homogeneous groupings on a longitudinal basis. It thus allows for heterogeneous grouping by age with attention to personal problems and homogeneous grouping for maximum development in special subjects. In the special-subjects segment it represents an excellent illustration of multigrading.

Neither *team teaching* nor *nongrading* is explicitly defined because each can be structured in a variety of ways. Both, however, have been amply discussed in the literature and illustrated in practice. Brownell and Taylor provide models of the significant variations of team teaching; see Figure 6–1.

Team teaching offers the possibility, for the first time, of accounting for curriculum considerations, teacher strengths, and pupil needs within one structural plan. In effect, the team concept permits the grouping of pupils in flexible arrangements—from the individual to very large groups, by a group of teachers and various assistants. The following list of essential and optional characteristics provides useful information for understanding the structural and functional possibilities of team teaching.

Essential characteristics of team teaching:

1. Three or more, sometimes as many as eight, teachers assume the instruction of 75–250 children.
2. The area of instruction may be in all subjects for one grade or age grouping; or for only one or two areas (language arts, social studies, science and mathematics, and the like) and encompass several age or grade levels.
3. The team has some organizational structure of its own with status and pay differentials within the group—at least a team leader or leaders and frequently teacher interns, teacher aides, and the like.
4. The team operation is aimed at utilizing the strengths of each member in a jointly planned situation—with specified planning, instruction, study, evaluation cycles. Teachers observe each other in teaching; often the senior team members have assigned supervisory and training responsibilities for the junior team members and the nonprofessional staff.

Model I

At one end of the continuum, a team consists of all classes of a particular grade level. Such a team can be formed for each grade. In a very large school, more than one team per grade could be organized.

grades	1	2	3	4	5	6
classes			team			

Model II

At the other extreme, a team comprises one class from all grade levels. As many teams can be formed as there are vertical arrangements of classes.

grades	1	2	3	4	5	6
classes		team				

Model III

In a middle position, a team contains classes from two grade levels. In a six-grade school, three teams can be formed; in a very large school, more than one team per pair of grades could be organized.

grades	1	2	3	4	5	6
classes					team	

Model Ic

At one extreme, a team consists of one content area and pupils from one grade level. As many teams can be formed as there are major content areas in the curriculum.

grade	6				
classes	A	B	C	D	E
language arts	team				
science	team				

Model IIIc

At the other extreme, a team comprises one content area and pupils from all grade levels. As many teams can be formed as there are similar content areas at all grade levels.

grades	1	2	3	4	5	6
language arts	team					
social studies	team					
mathematics	team					

Model IIc

In a middle position, a team comprises one content area and pupils from two or three grade levels. A team can be formed for each major subject area.

grades	1	2	3	4	5	6
science					team	
language arts		team				

SOURCE: John A. Brownell and Harris T. Taylor, "Theoretical Perspectives for Teaching Teams", Phi Delta Kappan, January, 1962, Vol. 43, No. 4, pp. 152-153.

Figure 6-1. Models of Team Teaching as Organizational Patterns

Optional characteristics of team teaching:

1. Team teaching tends to emphasize experimentation in size of group, time periods, and instructional content and methods. Often the need for these features has led to the team concept so that they are often thought of as essential characteristics.
2. Team teaching facilitates use of nonprofessional personnel because of the differential functions assigned to team members—no one individual is expected to do everything relating to the instruction of a group of children.
3. Team teaching increases the use of mechanical teaching aids and instructional media because these aids tend to be more effective with larger groupings of learners and because one or more team members can be assigned specific responsibility for materials production.
4. Team teaching has promoted the use of nongraded and continuous progress concepts in the classification and promotion of learners.

The reader should be made aware of the fact, however, that few if any teams are likely to exhibit all the characteristics listed. In addition various organizational arrangements must be provided. These include scheduling provisions for varying period lengths, staff time specifically allocated to team planning and instructional preparation, machinery to execute rapid changes in schedules and pupil assignment to groups, and careful selection and assignment of faculty and aides to teams.

Nongrading practices began in the 1940's but virtually disappeared until the work of John Goodlad and Robert Anderson.[13] They attacked the concept of graded elementary schools after surveying the evidence relating to individual differences among children of a given age as grouped in the graded school. They were particularly concerned with the failure of the concept of individualized instruction within the self-contained classroom and the provision of the graded structure that moves pupils through several curriculum areas at an even pace.

Typically, sequences of levels of instruction are organized, and pupils follow these sequences at different rates. Pupils may take two, three, or four years to complete grades one to three. Year-to-year promotion and nonpromotion are eliminated in this plan. In some schools, groups are set up on an age basis with nongraded instruction carried out on an intraclass plan. Some schools form groups on the basis of achievement level by curriculum areas. Grouping, however, is not the primary concern, for it is a horizontal organizational feature whereas nongrading is a *vertical* feature. Also, many specific cases of nongrading exist within

13. Their work resulted in the publication: *The Nongraded Elementary School* (New York: Harcourt, Brace & World, 1963).

a graded system—notably in reading plans in which the graded structure is ignored. As can be seen by an examination of Table 6–1, the
dominant pattern of organization is the self-contained classroom. Some
departmentalization, in significant number, occurs beginning at Grade
four. Team teaching has not gained widespread use, but the relatively
small percents for this pattern indicate that it is most likely used in
Grades four through six.

Table 6-1. Horizontal Patterns in the Six Grade Levels of
Elementary Schools

Types of patterns	Grade Level					
	1	2	3	4	5	6
Self-contained	96.6%	96.1%	95.2%	88.3%	78.9%	71.3%
Departmentalized	.9	1.2	2.1	8.5	16.4	23.0
Team teaching	2.5	2.7	2.6	3.3	4.7	5.7
Number surveyed	2,067	2,063	2,057	2,056	2,040	1,927

SOURCE: The Elementary School Principalship, Department of Elementary
School Principals, National Education Association, 1968, p. 66.

DIMENSIONS OF ORGANIZATION: PURPOSE-TASK, STRUCTURE, CLIMATE

Of central concern to the administrator is the manner in which pupils
and staff are brought together and the provisions by which this is done.
The principal, with his staff, has the opportunity to shape these arrangements and should do so in a deliberate, conscious fashion. However, in
addition to the organizational arrangements, devoted specifically to bringing pupils and teachers together for the purpose of instruction, is the
shaping of the total organizational plan for the school. Three primary
dimensions that comprise the totality of organization for the elementary
school are: purpose-task, structure, and climate.

Purpose-task Dimension

Purposes ascribed to elementary education are examined in Chapter 2. Statements of purposes are useful for delineating broad functions
schools are to serve, but they are not useful guides for directing organizational accomplishment, and they are inappropriate as criteria for
evaluating effectiveness. If schools are to reflect social demands, clear
mandates must be established and legitimatized through policies of

governing agencies *external* to the school. From them, schools, through the technical knowledge available, may identify tasks that might realize purposes most efficiently.

Purposes can be translated into tasks in several ways. The grid method and the taxonomic structure, described in Chapter 2, are means for doing this. Most schools attempt to write curriculum guides directly from statements of general purposes. This procedure is being challenged by those who would like to make schools more directly accountable for the results of instruction.[14]

Care must be taken in using the purpose-task concept that it not be restricted to program considerations alone. The school organization must encompass tasks other than these, although program considerations are the primary ones. The school must also devote staff and resources to: (1) study purposes, clarify tasks, design programs, and assess the results of its work, (2) articulate educational needs and activities to its patrons —citizens—and to related organizations, (3) respond to legitimate requests and directions from higher authority, and (4) provide for the maintenance and improvement of the organization itself, as through in-service training programs. The systems model, described in Chapter 4, encompasses these tasks and is compatible with the treatment followed in this chapter.

Structure of Organization

The emphasis given in this chapter to the ways in which elementary schools organize for instruction indicates the view of the authors that program considerations should determine the basic organizational structure for the school. A second view of the authors, often violated in practice, is that each school should determine, within limits, its own internal structure and arrangements, subject to review through planned evaluation procedures. In order to coordinate work within the district, ensure adequate control and accountability, and provide for stability, district-level designations of positions to be established and supported and guidelines for functions best coordinated at the district level are in order. However, unless the principal becomes knowledgeable about internal organization and skilled in designing structure he is not likely to exercise either program or organizational leadership.

A school organization has identity in terms of location and time,

14. John McNeil, "Antidote to a School Scandal," *The Educational Forum,* November, 1966, pp. 69–77.

pupils being served, processes to be initiated and maintained, and tasks to be accomplished. Pupils, teachers, other professional and nonprofessional staff, and administrators arrange their work within requirements imposed by these four conditions. Organization is determined by the patterning of relationships such that regularized, planned activities can take place with a minimum of confusion and wasted effort. To be "organized" implies that individuals understand what they are to do and when they are to do it, the latitude in the work that is left to their discretion, the person to whom problems are to be referred and directions taken, and the like.

The formal structure of elementary school organization typically is composed of two interrelated forms. One is that of the permanently defined positions such as teacher, librarian, nurse, secretary, counselor, assistant principal, principal, and the like. The other is a group of positions, filled more or less temporarily, by individuals holding permanently defined positions. This latter category includes individuals and groups who perform both service and operational tasks, for example, chairman or member of a curriculum committee, drama coach, safety chairman, audiovisual coordinator, and the like. The "doubling up" of positions and duties is typical of elementary school organization.

Authority Hierarchy: Skeletal Structure. Except in the very large elementary schools two and, at the most, three levels of authority are established. Typically all teachers relate directly to the principal. Some schools employ team leaders, department chairmen, or assistant principals as an intermediate level of authority between teachers and the principal, but this is usually in regard to only one function; in other matters teachers report directly to the principal. Whether in two or three levels, however, an authority hierarchy does exist. It is necessary to decision making, formal communications, proper division of work and responsibility, and to coordination. The definition of *positions* and the *authority hierarchy* represent the skeletal structure of the organization. The official channels defined by the authority hierarchy do little more than monitor the day-by-day work under relatively unchanging conditions. They are used to confirm and record organizational activity. However, in periods of change or crisis the authority structure comes strongly into play—assessment of new conditions, planning, reassigning, and programing change may result in major reorganization of individual and group assignments and of the authority relationships themselves.

Work Group Structure. Individuals and groups that perform the ongoing work of the school are formed and keyed into the authority hierarchy. Work groups may be loosely identified as either *operational* or *service*. At the operational level, they are teacher teams, individual specialists—counselor, speech correctionist, librarian, grade-level groupings of teachers, subject department, or other type. Service work groups may be study committees, action research teams, planning groups, production units preparing instructional materials, or one of a number of kinds of groups performing deliberative and consultative functions. Operational work groups are production units; they perform duties and functions that have been specified by policies and procedures. Service work groups aid the decision-making process, perform planning and evaluation functions, upgrade staff through study, and program changes to be made.

Structure for both service and operational work groups is usually provided function by function. Often a teacher's handbook is prepared that describes the operational tasks to be performed and the necessary instructions. This is activated by the principal in the designation of an individual or group to assume responsibility for the task. Service work groups are usually given a concise "charge" indicating the task, type of result expected, time deadlines, and resources available.

Elementary schools tend to function in a more informal fashion than do junior and senior high schools. This is due largely to the factor of size and to some extent to the absence of sharply delineated specialties that require coordination. Principals operate in face-to-face relationships with pupils and staff and much of the communication is verbal or by informal notes and memoranda. The use of organizational charts, detailed job descriptions, and codified policy manuals are almost totally absent except in the large cities, and here they are usually prepared by the central office rather than by the school. As enrollments increase, as more specialists are added to the elementary schools, and as alterations in program organization occur to create varied groupings of teachers, the elementary school principal will likely find it necessary to turn to more formal means of creating and maintaining organizational structure.

Organizational Climate

Each organization is a goal-oriented, purposive unit, a structure that is rationally ordered, and a social system. It is this latter aspect of organization that is treated here. Almost as soon as an individual seeks employment in an organization he begins to affect it and to be affected by it. He wants his relationships to be warm and friendly as well as businesslike; he wishes others to accept him and enjoy his association; he desires to know about the attitudes, values, and interests of other members beyond those that relate simply to the job he is to do. Those who administer schools understand that provision must be made to see that staff as well as pupils enjoy their working relationships and develop supportive associations in the process of performing their professional tasks.

The presentation in the previous section of this chapter made reference to formal relationships and formal structures. Almost all formal relationships (prescribed) have informal components (unprescribed). Individuals seek personal satisfaction and enjoyment from interpersonal contacts required by the work situation. In addition, they seek out associations not necessarily prescribed by organizational requirements. Within these associations individuals form attitudes about their work, about the worth of the organization and its leaders, and about other individuals and organizations related to the work of the school. These attitudes and values become characteristic of subgroups within a school and of the school itself, and they influence both the behavior and feelings of individual members.

Studies have been made of various aspects of individual and group interaction in constructing what can be called the organizational climate and its effects upon the organization. From studies of organizations other than schools the findings are clear that individuals are influenced considerably by group attitudes and the resulting climate quite apart from their own attitudes and values,[15] that groups within organizations determine the work standards and emphasis to be given tasks often to a greater extent than do the expectations held by formal authorities,[16] and that the more attractive the organization is to its members (termed cohesiveness) the greater is the influence of the dominant values and attitudes upon individuals.[17]

15. P. M. Blau and W. R. Scott, *Formal Organizations* (San Francisco, Calif.: Chandler, 1962), pp. 100–104.
16. H. S. Becker, *et al., Boys in White* (Chicago: University of Chicago Press, 1961).
17. Leon Festinger, *et al., Social Pressures in Informal Groups* (New York: Harper & Bros., 1950).

William Schutz in a study of leadership in groups identified three factors of interpersonal needs that have been substantiated in research and used in studies of school organization. The factors are:

Affection—need to seek interpersonal expressions of friendship, emotional acceptance, close personal attachment, etc. (contrary behaviors would be dislike, emotional distance, and coolness).
Control—need for dominance, rules, authority, etc. (contrary behaviors would be resistance, rebellion, and submission).
Inclusion—need for belonging, communicating, identification (contrary behaviors would be isolated, lonely, ignored, excluded).[18]

The principal can influence climate more than any other individual in the school. He can establish friendly relations, behave so that members feel they are accepted and included, and facilitate informal associations (the Affection factor). He can maintain integrity in his relationships so that what he says and does are consistent, create the feeling that the school is "going somewhere," and express the belief that what is being done is important (the Inclusion factor). He can consult with staff and plan the direction and control of activities so that individuals know what is going on and have confidence in his leadership and can identify with it (the factor of Social Control).

Halpin and Croft developed an instrument (the Organizational Climate Description Questionnaire) to measure the climate of a school. They found three factors that paralleled those identified by Schutz which they labeled: Social Needs, Esprit, and Social Control. Halpin and Croft were able to construct a profile for each school quite like a personality profile for an individual and described six types of climates: Open, Autonomous, Controlled, Familiar, Paternal, and Closed.[19] Halpin's data in the study of a group of 71 schools led him to conclude that openness to closedness were two ends of a continuum that is a measure of "authenticity."

In the open climate schools the behavior of the principal and the

18. William C. Schutz, "The FIRO Theory of Interpersonal Behavior," in Stephen P. Hencley (ed.), *Research in Educational Administration,* Report of Cooperative Research Project No. F-2 (Columbus, Ohio: University Council for Educational Administration, 1962).

19. Andrew Halpin and Don B. Croft, *The Organizational Climate of Schools* (Chicago: Midwest Administration Center, 1963). Halpin has since published a volume containing his complete studies relating to organization and the theoretical basis of them: *Theory and Research in Administration* (New York: Macmillan, 1966).

teachers seemed to be genuine, or authentic. Professional roles were secondary to what the individuals were as human beings—they were free to experiment with their roles and bring their own individual styles to their jobs and their relationships. The "closed" schools lacked this authenticity, and individuals seemed to be acting out someone else's role descriptions—they were "not for real."

For the principal, Halpin writes:

The principal who scores high on thrust is not enslaved by a narrow definition of his role, nor does he seem to be pre-occupied with his status. He is more intent on task-accomplishment, on getting the job done, and on moving the organization toward its goals. [Note, however, that he does this without sacrificing *Consideration*.] In a sense, he is willing to "unfreeze" the organization from one stage of its development—even if that stage be highly satisfying to the group members . . . and to take the risk of change, confident that such change will result in a higher order of organizational development . . . To take this risk . . . the principal "must stand for something." He must also be open in letting his teachers and the school's patrons know what indeed, he does stand for. In short, he must be authentic.[20]

Halpin has prepared an excellent description of the principal's role as it relates to the climate dimension of organization. Eight dimensions of organizational activity were identified as determinants of a school's climate: 1) disengagement, 2) hindrance, 3) esprit, 4) intimacy, 5) aloofness, 6) production emphasis, 7) thrust, and 8) consideration. These dimensions were assigned to a quadrant arrangement to facilitate evaluation. Halpin and Croft have commented as follows on the dimensions encompassed in the four quadrants:

	GROUP	LEADER
Dimensions Associated Primarily with Social- Needs Satisfaction	IV Esprit Intimacy	I Thrust Consideration
Dimensions Associated Primarily with Aspects of Social Control	III Disengagement Hindrance	II Production Emphasis Aloofness

Figure 6-2. Eight Dimensions of the Organizational Climate Description Questionnaire, Form III.

Quadrant I defines a "good" situation in that the group members secure adequate satisfaction of social needs and also feel a sense of task accomplishment. Contrariwise, Quadrant III represents a situation in which the

20. Halpin and Croft, *op. cit.*, p. 79.

group experience is neither an adequate satisfaction of social needs nor a sense of task accomplishment. Quadrants II and IV both provide for only a portion of what one would hope for in an ideal organization. Quadrant II denotes high task-orientation, but with insufficient attention to satisfying the social needs of the group members. Conversely, Quadrant IV defines a situation in which the group members receive a high satisfaction of social needs but also enjoy little sense of task accomplishment.[21]

The approach described above is not prescriptive. It does not provide principles to be followed for attaining a climate conducive to efficiency. Rather, it highlights areas of behavior which contribute to climate. Such dimensions will serve elementary school principals as means for making their own analyses of organizational climate more systematic.

21. Halpin and Croft, *op. cit.*, p. 27.

REFERENCES

Etzioni, Amitai, *A Comparative Analysis of Complex Organizations* (New York: The Free Press, 1963).

Goodlad, John I., and R. H. Anderson, *The Nongraded Elementary School* (New York: Harcourt, Brace & World, revised, 1963).

Guest, R. H., *Organizational Change* (Homewood, Ill.: Dorsey Press, 1962).

Griffiths, Daniel E. (ed.), *Developing Taxonomies of Organizational Behavior in Education Administration* (Chicago: Rand McNally, 1969).

Halpin, Andrew W., *Theory and Research in Administration* (New York: Macmillan, 1966).

Likert, R., *New Patterns of Management* (New York: McGraw-Hill, 1969).

National Education Association, *The New Elementary School* (Washington, D.C.: the Association, 1968).

National Education Association, *The Nongraded School* (Washington, D.C.: the Association, 1968).

National Education Association, *Planning and Organizing for Teaching* (Washington, D.C.: the Association, 1963).

National Society for the Study of Education, *Sixty-Fifth Yearbook*, Part II: *The Changing American School* (Chicago: University of Chicago Press, 1966).

Stoddard, George D., *The Dual Progress Plan* (New York: Harper & Row, 1961).

Part III

Educational Programs and Personnel

Chapter 7

THE PRINCIPAL AND THE
EDUCATIONAL PROGRAM

URRICULUM, instruction, in-service education of staff, and
supervision are complex aspects of the formulation of the total
educational program of the school. They are also interrelated concepts
in educational administration. When the educational program is conceived as the total educative activity of the school, the curriculum
becomes a central concern of the principal with instruction as the vehicle
for its implementation and in-service education and supervision as means
to its evaluation and development.

Although each of the four aspects can be isolated for analysis and
study, as they are in sections of this book, the effectiveness of the school's
program depends upon its curriculum—how it is conceived; how it is
organized; how it is implemented; and how it is continuously developed.
No other task is more important in the principalship, if the principal is
to exercise educational leadership and enhance his role. Nothing could
be more dangerous to education than for this task to be removed from
the principal's purview or responsibility or for it to be abdicated by him
through a lack of understanding of its importance or the ability to perform in this phase of his role.

Major dimensions of the principal's role in relation to the educational
program are examined in this chapter. Before proceeding, however, it is
well to point out that the role is not a static one, nor can an idealized
role be specified in detail that can serve as a model for every school.
Diversity of conditions makes this impossible; but more important, the
dynamic nature of the concepts introduced above make such a task
undesirable. Curriculum, instruction, in-service education, and supervision are constantly evolving concepts as new knowledge about them

becomes available and as experience brings understanding about their applications in practice.

INFLUENCES ON THE EDUCATIONAL PROGRAM

In order to provide perspective and to establish the point of view to be developed, levels of influence that operate to shape the educational program need to be indicated; and certain assumptions about the exercise of that influence need to be expressed.

Four Levels of Influence

The first level of influence, and of first importance, is the teacher. Regardless of how sound the plan, or how enlightened the conceptualization of learning at other levels, it can only be facilitative of the processes initiated and carried out by the teacher with learners. The teacher makes many decisions and shapes the learning situation regardless of how detailed the plan or how carefully designed the materials might be. This condition has led some curriculum specialists to seek the *cibola* of the "teacher free" curriculum and others to opine that nothing else makes any difference "after the teacher closes his door." Empirical evidence indicates that neither of these positions is tenable.

Between those who would design programs of instruction as though the teacher was an automaton and those who would give the teacher complete license many other alternatives are advanced. A flexible curriculum plan, varied materials, careful evaluation of the effects of teaching *with* the participation of the teacher, and continuous improvement of teacher competence are the ingredients of a realistic approach to program development.

The second level of influence is the school unit. The school faculty, with parent and pupil participation at appropriate points, is responsible for planning a coherent, integrated program. This is the level at which the *program* takes shape, for the teacher in isolation, or even in a team organization, cannot provide the coordination the learning environment requires. The contribution of special teachers, of the librarian and materials center personnel, nurse, therapist, counselor, social worker, aides, and other specialists that are available in the modern elementary school requires that the school operate as a fully-functional educative unit. Unless the principal understands this and can exercise the leadership and administrative skills necessary to fulfill this coordinating function the program cannot be as effective as it might otherwise be.

A third level of influence is the system or district level. Universally, some type of formally constituted, local level of administrative authority is established to operate schools. In the United States the concept of the semiautonomous political unit is common practice. Professional status-leadership is provided to carry out the policy of a representative body, a board of education. At this level specialized personnel are often made responsible for personnel, curriculum planning, special services, and the like. The philosophy of administration and the exercise of control at this level largely determine the role of the principal and other school personnel in shaping the educational program at the building level. Considerable responsibility may be delegated to schools within a flexible district plan. Principals and school faculties may participate heavily in planning at the district level. On the other hand, participation can be limited and central staff operate in a highly directive relationship to individual schools.

In addition to the district level of influence there are intermediate and state agencies and officials who function to influence the educational program and to provide services, aid planning, allocate resources, and the like. State laws, regulations of the state office, and state boards of education affect planning at the district level. Also some programs of the federal government require a district plan and other arrangements which place local districts in a direct relationship to the federal government.

A sphere of influence also exists that is external to the school and school system having no legal or administrative relationship to a school or school district. Professional associations—for example, the Association for Supervision and Curriculum Development, the Department of Elementary School Teachers, the Department of Elementary School Principals, the National Society for the Study of Education, the American Educational Research Association—through publications, curriculum materials, research studies, and meetings contribute directly to local planning groups and individuals. Special interest groups seek to influence what is taught, often providing materials directly to schools, but also through pressure on legislatures, boards of education, and local planning groups. Textbook writers, publishers, and more recently foundation-supported curriculum projects have a very direct influence upon the local school program.

DYNAMICS OF INFLUENCE

The traditional approach to program design was strongly influenced by the concept of democracy and of the individual in his relation to group life—particularly that of the state. Education as the bastion of grass roots democracy was conceived as a local enterprise closely tuned to community life. The concept of local control of education was an expression of this belief, and governmental controls and supervision of education reflected this concern. The individual was seen as developing apart from, even to some extent threatened by, impersonalized organization as represented by government and corporate enterprise. The individual (and therefore also, the school) was to be shielded from such influences.

Without going into detail to document the creed of the locally oriented educational program, it produced a model of program planning that depended primarily, if not exclusively, upon local consensus. Citizens and local school authorities often took the view that outside influences were threatening to the values inherent in their concept of democratic process and of individual self-determination.

Traditional Model of Program Planning

The mechanisms for planning and executing program decisions, in what shall be called a traditional model of program planning, were based upon a model that included the following elements:

1. A policy statement by the board of education that permitted the establishment of a curriculum committee or council of citizens and professionals, a coordinating administrative officer, and ad hoc committees by level and/or subject areas
2. Development of a general plan and timetable for the preparation of statements of objectives and curriculum guides
3. Preparation of objectives and guides and the designation of resource units or courses of study by additionally appointed task forces or work committees
4. Accumulation of materials and writing of resource units
5. Publication and reporting of guides and resource units to teachers and their implementation through in-service training

There is nothing inherently wrong with the model as a model, and many worthwhile curriculum activities were undertaken within schools across the country where leadership was competent and adequate resources were made available. The wealthy suburban and smaller communities with skilled consultant help and access to the latest materials and equipment moved ahead rapidly. Some aspects of this model are proposed later in this chapter for use by the principal.

From the beginning, however, several conditions requiring adjustment of the model were not corrected. In the large cities the model produced a curriculum that was not sufficiently flexible to account for the wide variety of differences in school populations and in neighborhoods. In the less well supported schools, particularly in rural areas, resources both in personnel and materials were never made available and a flaccid, book-oriented program was the result—the textbook became the curriculum. Further, the local community often did not make the effort to look beyond its own borders to the rapid changes in content, methods, technology, and the social conditions of the broader, national community—the model was misapplied to foster the values of a naïve concept of democracy and self-determination. Finally, the model was "locked-in" so that specification of objectives did not permit the kind of evaluation that could power change. Evaluation was seen as a review of procedures and an updating of materials in order to do better what was already being done.

Introduction of Competing Models

Following the dynamics of educational change as analyzed in Chapter 3, the advent of new conditions in the form of social-cultural changes, new knowledge and the changed application of knowledge, and technological advance, produced competing models for program formulation and implementation.

Program Formulation by Federal Government. The first model substitution can be linked directly to the enactment of the National Defense Education Act (1958) and subsequently the Elementary and Secondary Education Act (1965). It is outlined in the chart below and reveals how external forces channel influence to local educational programs.

To apply the model to the influence of the federal government under the National Defense Education Act, one might reason as follows: The Soviet success in launching a man-made satellite, Sputnik, into orbit around the earth, an event, brought about concern (awareness) that science was becoming more and more crucial to our national safety, a condition. Opinion-forming agents; experts—in this case, scientists, educators, and military leaders; and politicians deliberated (negotiation). After study, the decision makers—in this case, power figures in the

Model of Educational Program Change

Phase	Some Determinants	Dynamic Elements
Awareness	Problems, issues, trends, conditions	Events
Conceptual- ization	Assessment of educational potential to effect change, resources needed, willingness to expand resources	Negotiation: transactional relations among experts (knowledge), opinion- forming agencies (propaganda), and government (power)
Formulation	Educational results desired, nature of content to be trans- mitted, knowledge of target learners	Interaction: professionals with government agen- cies; clearance by board of education
Implementation	Personnel, institutional structures and con- trols, organizational climate	Action: internal district and school activities
Evaluation	Degree of sustained attention, level of satisfaction with re- sults	Reconceptualization or return to awareness phase

federal government, approved a plan (conceptualization) called the National Defense Education Act. At the local level, plans (formulation) were prepared within the framework of the legislation. To follow the flow of external influence, assume that the remainder of the model illustrates in some form what transpired.

The model suggests the idea that an assessment of data relative to the categories in the column labeled "Dynamic Elements" will reveal the identity of determinants of influence upon the local program and the phase of its development. If determinants persist and maintain sufficient strength, program development will move through the phases indicated. The important point, however, is that decision making and planning at the district and building levels were short-circuited in terms of the pre- vailing model. Although originally referred to as crash programs and justified as temporary expedients, this pattern of activity established program priorities for schools, modes of decision making, and admin- istrative controls that have produced a new model for creating and im- plementing educational programs.

Effects of Federal Government Model. By the time the Elementary and Secondary Education Act (1965) was enacted the model of federal operation in program development was fully worked out. Guidelines concerning what would be funded were made available and local districts could apply; funds were allocated upon the basis of proposals submitted, and further funding was dependent upon approval granted on the basis of annual reports of the uses made of previous funding. No systematic evaluation of either qualitative or quantitative effects has been made, and no alternative patterns—such as the use of equal funding for support of a specified foundation level program, or outright general aid to schools, and the like—have been attempted.

Certain observations can be made, however, about the way in which this model of program development functions. First, it is capable of producing rapid diffusion of specific practices and technologies. Second, it is capable of broadening programs that have become purely local in orientation. Third, it permits national influence to be exerted directly upon local schools. The greatest cause for concern relates to by-products of this latter point.

Effects of influence through federal activity, operating within the model presented above, have produced several consequences that have not as yet been seriously studied by the profession or presented in any articulate fashion to the public. First, the processes of program planning have been disrupted at the local level. The effects of centralization and bureaucratic procedures in decision making have compromised sound principles of program development by (1) removing decision making far from the operational level, and (2) by-passing mechanisms (curriculum councils, area committees, and the like) that ensure representation in planning. Second, the result of specialized emphases upon reforms has created a piece-meal approach with many secondary consequences. Materials have been made available that have not been integrated into the instructional program; language labs and science equipment have been provided without arrangements for in-service training; and meaningful evaluation has been jeopardized because objectives have not been specified, nor data collected relating to them, so that meaningful inferences can not be drawn about the extent to which progress has been made.

Whether or not some redress of the conditions created by this model of operation can be effected will largely depend upon study and criticism by the profession. To this point, however, action has been valued over representation, efficiency in innovation over concern for the individual, and a centralization and bureaucratization of the machinery of program planning has resulted from the model's use.

Model of Curriculum Change Through Large-Scale Projects. Almost concurrently with the introduction of the model for federal involvement in educational program development, a second model for accomplishing curriculum change on a national scale appeared. It represents an effort to base curriculum upon a discipline centered approach and conflicts with the traditional model in important respects. The following points represent the principal departures:

1. Change the school from a socializing environment to a situation for individual achievement.
2. Substitute a behaviorial approach for child study methods as the primary basis of teaching.
3. Move from a problem and unit centered structure to a concept or discipline centered structure.
4. Replace the teacher and school level determination of content selection and method with a "packaged" program.
5. Separate integrated content into its discrete fields of study.

Massive projects have been undertaken to develop instructional packages that are "teacher free" in the sense that the package is a self-contained course to be introduced wholesale rather than be developed in the school. Institutes supplant the usual in-service training in which the "package" is taught in much the same manner as the teacher is expected to teach it. The actual functioning of this model of large-scale curriculum making is well described in the literature through case studies of specific projects.[1] Its primary contribution has been to inject new knowledge into the curriculums of schools rapidly and to introduce, in an organized way, a conceptual approach to teaching.

Assessment of the Models: A Point of View

The three models outlined above are offered as descriptive rather than analytical accounts of approaches to program development now being employed. Admittedly, they are generalized descriptions that may not square point by point with what has transpired in a specific program design. The authors would argue, however, that they do reveal the essential features of three distinct operational models and that the de-

1. See: Robert Heath (ed.), *New Curricula* (New York: Harper & Row, 1964); Matthew B. Miles, *Innovation in Education* (New York: Bureau of Publications, Teacher's College, Columbia University, 1964).

scriptions are sufficiently valid to permit an assessment of issues and needs.

Following the analysis of the development of modular practice presented in Chapter 3, no new model for practice is likely to appear unless the current one fails to permit the solution of problems. Disenchantment with the old ways of proceeding set in, and alternative models to guide practice are put forward. One or more such models may prove to solve some of the relevant problems better and supplant the old. This appears to be a valid description of what has happened in the case of program design. Bear in mind, however, that no model permits the solution of all the relevant problems of a field; this is also the case with the two new models described above. What is needed is the assessment of the needs of program design and implementation that must be taken into account at the school level and an examination of how these needs can be met.

Essential School Level Elements. The one fact that seems to be unassailable in every attempt to influence educational program is that it involves *adopting or adapting at the local level.* Curriculum design and development draws its vitality from the understandings, beliefs, attitudes, perceptions, and skills of the teacher and those who work immediately with the teacher at the point that instruction takes place. Three elements are critical: (1) the personal-professional makeup of the teacher, (2) the social-organizational system of the school, and (3) the structure of the teaching situation—the curriculum plan and the resources available to carry out instruction.

Each of the three models reviewed in this chapter have made sustained, long-term impact upon educational programs when the target schools have been able (1) to effect professional growth and social system change at the school level, and (2) to integrate curriculum design and materials change in a coordinated, continuous fashion. Specific examples of individual schools that have been linked directly to large-scale project work stemming from one of the three models seem to have taken these elements into account as part of their commitment to the project. When the project work, as in the national curriculum projects, is disseminated widely, results generally have been disappointing. Curriculum construction and improvement are not a set of autonomous activities carried on apart from the ongoing school program.

Link-up Between School-Teacher Levels and District-External Levels. The three models for program development have had little success whenever they have operated upon the assumption that schools and the teachers in them either (1) constantly seek out new ways of teaching and eagerly accept and implement ideas offered, or (2) are a "target" for change and need only to be approached in the proper fashion. A school, like any other organization, is relatively stable and resistant to restructuring by external influences. At the same time, and for fundamentally the same reasons, few significant program innovations are invented or consciously developed in schools. Herein lies the dilemma of rapidly and systematically updating the total educational system—particularly, when many, including these authors, believe that education must not simply keep up with a fast-moving world, but must lead and determine its direction.

Apparently invention, trial, and development of significant materials and procedures require that they be generated in the "external" setting. The resources, variety of specialists, and production—field testing—evaluation requirements of major curriculum and instructional development work require large-scale projects. School districts, schools, and teachers need to be involved, but until the dissemination stage is reached, this kind of involvement is limited and determined largely by the needs of the project. The concern of the treatment here is at the point that large-scale project work is available for "public consumption."

Critical decisions in program planning and development for the principal occur in the link-up between the teacher-school levels of influence and the district-external levels. The nature of these decisions, the alternatives usually available, and the extent to which the principal can influence them are treated in the remainder of this chapter.

ADMINISTRATION OF PROGRAM DESIGN AND DEVELOPMENT

The principal operates within a structure of relationships within the school, the district, and the variety of external forces. He must mediate between influences generated within these relationships and do so in a way that will maximize the effects of the school in its educative role. He has the task of leading in long-range planning and relating that planning to day-by-day instruction; he is involved in both the psychological and practical aspects of these relationships; and he must help create stable patterns of work—both in the school's relationship to the district and in the internal operation of the school—while maintaining adequate flexibility for the school and the teachers.

Balance Between District-wide and School Approaches

Early efforts in "curriculum making" were district-wide in scope. One of the first efforts to establish what has been termed the traditional model in this chapter was begun in Los Angeles in 1922; statewide projects following this model were initiated in Connecticut and Virginia before 1925. They assumed a comprehensive approach involving very large numbers of teachers in committee and task force teams and resulted in "courses of study" that tended to be viewed as prescriptions of content and method to be enforced administratively. Although the early model has remained, it has been modified considerably.

Organizational Patterns. Highly centralized organization and control have given way to a coordinating role. The trend is toward assigning chief responsibility to the building unit. In 1960, Harold McNally and Harry Passow surveyed a large number of curriculum programs and concluded that:

The growing trend toward assigning chief responsibility to the building unit reflects recognition of the belief that continuity, unity, and balance are best achieved when the staff focus their efforts on behalf of their own pupils. It is within a particular school that curriculum plans must be translated into instructional practice. It is at this level that planning seems most meaningful to teachers.[2]

In this study McNally and Passow identified three patterns of organization. These are: (1) a centralized approach in which responsibility for activities, committees, selection of procedures, and the like are directed by central office personnel; (2) a decentralized approach in which planning and development are the responsibility of individual schools—problems studied, procedures used, resources employed, and the like—with the central office staff maintaining a consulting and advisory role; and (3) a centrally coordinated approach in which the individual school is maintained as the basic unit and source of initiating improvement, but with the central staff initiating some district-wide projects and coordinating activities by proposing joint criteria for studies, etc.[3]

Strategies of Operation. Perhaps the greatest single operational modi-

2. Harold J. McNally and A. Harry Passow, *Improving the Quality of Public School Programs* (New York: Bureau of Publications, Teachers College, Columbia University, 1960), p. 43.
3. *Ibid.,* p. 44.

fication to the traditional mode has been the acceptance of what has come to be called the broken front approach. Lack of provision for it has frustrated dissemination of many of the large-scale projects. In the comprehensive programs and large-scale projects, it is assumed that change takes place simultaneously upon the adoption of a new course of study or the publication and distribution of an instructional package. The dynamics of change in such cases is ignored with serious effects.

Almost every new proposal arouses doubts, questions, alternative suggestions, misunderstandings and a host of reactions that are *not necessarily outright resistance.* Unless the plan, the materials, and the advocates are able to diagnose the difficulty, handle it in a supportive fashion without hostility (and permit something less than total adoption at the beginning) resistance is likely to be the result. It is largely for this reason that the role of the principal is such a critical one, for he is the one in authority who is closest to the situation at the point of program implementation. He is the one who can best diagnose the problem *with teachers* and decide whether a given step will move practice in the desired direction.

Nature and Exercise of Authority. The point made above concerning the role of the principal at the implementation stage raises the question of authority and its use in program design and development. Authority is a critical element in organization and especially so in planning and change situations. Unfortunately, the study of the nature and exercise of authority in the educational setting has been neglected. The literature has tended to picture the teacher as an independent professional rather than one member of a professional organization. Authority of the administrator permits him to initiate or prevent action because administrative authority is necessary to rearrange the structure of the organization, allocate resources and personnel, coordinate activity, and precipitate decisions.

The authority to initiate and execute certain tasks is essential to sound progress. Unless a clear understanding exists about the sharing of administrative authority between the district office and building level personnel, disorganization and ineffectiveness will result. Some of these tasks include:

1. Evaluate and identify instructional patterns.
2. Search, investigate, and disseminate external project materials and resources.
3. Initiate in-service curriculum activities.

4. Secure consultants and resource specialists.
5. Communicate and share plans and ideas with other schools and groups.
6. Consult with individual teachers.
7. Initiate decision-making procedures.
8. Implement decisions reached.

These tasks may be shared differently depending upon whether the pattern of organization is centralized, decentralized, or centrally coordinated as found by McNally and Passow (above). In any case, they represent the foci of concern of the principal and could well form a list of items to negotiate with the superintendent and central office personnel so that authority relationships are clearly understood and the principal knows the extent to which he can go in building level activity.

Some evidence is available concerning the role of the elementary principal in shaping the curriculum, selecting instructional materials, determining specific teaching methods, and supervision of teachers. A recent study conducted by the Department of Elementary School Principals substantiates the trends documented by a number of studies of narrower scope. The DESP study, a survey of a representative sample of 2,292 principals, indicates that more than half of the elementary school principals have, and exercise, the responsibility to "modify and adapt" the school system's curriculum program to the individual school. More than one-third of the remaining principals indicated that they followed closely the prescribed program but exerted some influence in developing the educational program.[4] No significant differences in the percentage of responses were made due to size of school enrollment or region of the country. Between 45 and 55 percent of the principals in the same study indicated that they participated in faculty-principal cooperative action to select instructional materials and determine specific teaching methods. Finally, more than 80 percent of the principals indicated that they had the primary responsibility for the supervision of teachers. There is good reason to believe that these findings reflect the situation that exists nationally. The elementary principal, typically, is actively involved in these four important features of the educational program—curriculum, instructional materials, instructional methods, and supervision.

4. Department of Elementary School Principals, *The Elementary School Principalship in 1968* (Washington, D.C.: National Education Association, 1968), pp. 79–80.

BALANCE BETWEEN TEACHER AND SCHOOL APPROACHES

Several operational approaches are available to the principal as he works with staff. Evidence is reasonably clear that teachers left to their own devices have limited influence in effecting significant improvements. They do alter classroom procedures, change instructional techniques, update materials, and, in cooperation with other teachers, adjust content in terms of sequence and introduce new segments of units and courses.

Significant aspects of program—objectives, modes of instruction, major substitutions of content and learning activities—rarely occur without systematic planning at the school and even school district levels. Two reasons account for this. First, the most fundamental developments —introduction of new content, such as modern mathematics; changes in qualitative aspects of learning, such as discovery learning—require rather elaborate help. They involve retraining of teachers, new materials, new scheduling, technology, and the like. Second, fundamental developments require systemic changes that go beyond those arrangements and procedures handled by a single teacher or a small group of teachers. In short, they require a level of professional growth and a system change that should not be expected of the teacher alone.

Teacher Involvement: Professional Growth. Perhaps the principle upon which most agreement exists throughout the profession is that teachers be involved at all levels of planning and in all stages of activity. This is true in the large-scale curriculum projects, and it is true in any program development within the school or school district. The reasons are so varied that an examination of them here seems unnecessary. The rationale set forth at the beginning of this chapter established the assumption of the teacher as the first level of influence and that all planning and development work relating to the educational program must center upon his behavior, beliefs, attitudes, knowledge, and skills. Unless the teacher is involved and changed, there is little reason to believe that anything else that might be done could significantly improve instruction.

There are several types of involvement and activity that can foster professional growth. The principal should keep these in mind in planning any program development work, for most major program projects require staff involvement of each type:

1. Idea and general education type. Staff should be constantly oriented to new developments external to the school. Additional study,

travel and visitation, study groups, and the like provide opportunities to investigate, to broaden understandings and insights, and to give attention to ideas not typically a part of the teacher's experience.

2. Policy type. Within the school, the district, and the profession there is a need to clarify policy positions and formulate guides to action. Teachers should be the best source of determining the effect of current policies and needed policy changes.

3. Evaluation, problem-solving and research type. Sound evaluation is the first stage of change and often necessary to problem-solving and research-oriented activity. Usually this type of activity implies relatively unstructured group activity—the group defining the dimensions of its task and seeking solutions and recommendations or new knowledge about a given situation.

4. Production or task-centered type. Usually this type of in-service activity stems from an assigned, clearly defined task. Preparing a resource unit, writing a curriculum guide, developing evaluation instruments, and the like.

5. Skill acquisition type. Often acquiring or sharpening needed skills is important to improving—learning to write a programed text, learning a technique for teaching a particular aspect of science, and the like.

Each type requires different planning and resources and leads to different kinds of follow-up. The principal should plan specifically for staff improvement as an integral part of any program development activity. It should come about naturally in terms of the school plan and lead to some specific contribution to the school's program.

System Changes. The principal will be involved with staff personnel on two different but related activities in terms of changing the social system of the school itself. First, he will find that the members of the staff develop commonly shared attitudes, opinions, and beliefs which form the normative structure of their working relationships. He will need to be aware of the effect of group norms, of the patterns of interpersonal influence, of expectations held for his behavior and the exercise of administrative authority, and of factors which affect group effort. Chapters 5 and 6 should be of help in an understanding of the dynamics of the social system of the school and the leadership potential of the principal.

A second and related activity necessary to changing the social system of the school involves establishing the institutional arrangements and resources of the school to specifically foster change and the staff activity that contributes to program improvement even to a restructuring of the school itself. Few schools sustain development that do not have as a highly prized and widely shared staff attitude that the school is a place where improvement and change are taking place and are supported. Time, facilities, professional materials, secretarial help, and funds for travel and study are expressions of sound institutional support. Administrative encouragement and recognition and, more important, a school-developed plan are essential.

REFERENCES

Bennis, Warren G., Kenneth Benne, and Robert Chin, *The Planning of Change* (New York: Holt, Rinehart and Winston, 1966).

Eichhorn, Donald H., *The Middle School* (New York: Center for Applied Research in Education, 1966).

Foskett, John M., *The Normative World of the Elementary School Principal* (Eugene, Ore.: Center for Advanced Study of Educational Administration, 1967).

Frazier, Alexander (ed.), *The New Elementary School* (Washington, D.C.: Association for Supervision and Curriculum Development and Department of Elementary School Principals, 1968).

Hechinger, Fred M. (ed.), *Pre-School Education Today* (New York: Doubleday, 1966).

Jarvis, Oscar T., and Lutian R. Wootton, *The Transitional Elementary School and Its Curriculum* (Dubuque, Iowa: Wm. C. Brown, 1966).

Koopman, Robert C., *Curriculum Development* (New York: Center for Applied Research in Education, 1966).

Steiner, Gary A. (ed.), *The Creative Organization* (Chicago: University of Chicago Press, 1965).

Unruh, Glenys G., and Robert Leeper, *Influences in Curriculum Change* (Washington, D.C.: Association for Supervision and Curriculum Development, 1966).

Warner, Ruby H., *Elementary School Teaching Practices* (New York: Center for Applied Research in Education, 1962).

Watson, Goodwin, *Concept of Social Change* (Washington, D.C.: National Training Laboratories of the National Education Association, 1967).

Witt, Paul (ed.), *Technology and the Curriculum* (New York: Teachers College, Columbia University, 1968).

Chapter 8

PROGRAM SUPERVISION
AND EVALUATION

THE essential and basic components of one elementary school are very much like those of any other elementary school. Some of these components or characteristics are relatively easily observed, such as pupils, teachers, classrooms, textbooks, materials and supplies, media equipment, curriculum guides, programs of study, and general purposes. However, these common characteristics are also variant characteristics. Hence, elementary schools exhibit individual differences.

But individual differences also exist among some not so easily observed characteristics, such as the motivations of the principal and teachers, their commitments to service, their teaching behaviors, and the extent of their concern about goals. These characteristics are internal variables. The differences among elementary schools also reflect external factors in their environments, such as central office influence and society in general.

SYSTEMS MODELS FOR PROGRAM SUPERVISION
AND EVALUATION

Program supervision and evaluation cannot be undertaken in any meaningful way without due consideration of these characteristics and factors. The work of Etzioni, a sociologist, provides a convenient model or framework from which to view and to analyze program components of the elementary school. He designed a system model for organizations and identified two subtypes of models.[1] His system model consists of a

1. Amitai Etzioni, *Modern Organizations* (Englewood Cliffs, N.J.: Prentice-Hall, 1964), p. 19.

statement about relationships which, if actually existing, would allow an organization to maintain itself and to operate.

One of the subtypes of system models is a *survival model* which means that a given set of requirements, if fulfilled, allows the system to exist. Removal of any one of the requirements causes the system to cease operating, or at least some kind of curtailment. An obvious and extreme example is provided in the case of a teachers' strike or walkout. Operations do cease even if efforts are expended in keeping the children in school under the supervision of mothers and other noncertificated adults.

The second subtype of system model is an *effectiveness model* which defines a pattern of interrelationships among the elements of the system which would make it most effective in the service of a given goal, as compared with other combinations of the same or similar elements. An effectiveness model for elementary schools may be conceived as a hypothetical ideal toward which we direct our efforts, realizing full well that our attainments are approximations at best. To believe that full attainment is possible is to exhibit a curious utopian naïveté.

A Survival-Effectiveness Continuum

In order to generate the greatest utility of the system model for viewing and analyzing program supervision and evaluation, the submodels are exhibited as the two extremes of a continuum (see Figure 8–1).

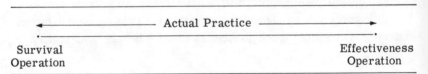

Figure 8-1. A Survival-Effectiveness Continuum

Thus, the actual practice of a given school can be conceived as fitting somewhere on the continuum between minimal operation at the survival level and optimal operation at an effectiveness level. The purposes of program supervision and evaluation become the means for propelling the actual practice in an elementary school toward a more effective level of operation. The conceptualization of the survival-effectiveness continuum has utility for viewing the total operational effectiveness as well as for evaluating certain components selected for microscopic analysis.

An effective elementary school, as contrasted with one operating at a survival level, is one in which the essential and necessary components or characteristics are given high development priority and consideration. An effectiveness operation does not "just happen." To attain the objectives or goals of an organization, functions must be delineated; these functions must be made operational by allocating them in the form of subtasks or roles with established behavior norms which will lead to the satisfactory performance of these subtasks and functions. Program supervision and evaluation are means which contribute toward the attainment of an effectiveness level of operation.

A Model for Viewing Organization Interaction Variables

Effectiveness derives from a carefully formulated pattern of interrelationships among the components of the system. Leavitt's model of interacting variables in an organization provides one way of ordering these components and of viewing their interaction. He conceptualized these components as fitting into four dimensions which are task (function), people (actors), technology (tools), and structure.[2] His observation that a change in any one of the dimensions will most probably result in compensatory or retaliatory change in the others has particular pertinence for effective program supervision and evaluation in the elementary school. The four dimensions of organization interaction are shown in Figure 8–2.

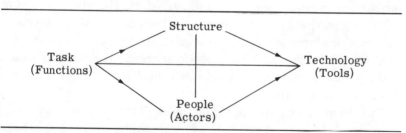

Figure 8-2. Four Dimensions of Organization Interaction

A classification scheme is inadequate for viewing and analyzing effectiveness in program supervision and evaluation. Such an approach has produced only lists of principles of supervision which possess very little meaning or prescription. The more demanding taxonomy tends to possess more purposeful utility; however, there does not appear to be a taxonomy

2. H. J. Leavitt, "Applied Organization Change in Industry: Structural, Technical, and Human Approaches," in W. W. Cooper, H. J. Leavitt, and M. W. Shelly II (eds.), *New Perspectives in Organization Research* (New York: John Wiley & Sons, 1964), p. 56.

appropriate to effective program supervision and evaluation. Not infrequently, the so-called taxonomies in education have been little more than lists of principles also.

Systems theory is a modeling approach or simulation process which provides a way of viewing an organization as a whole. From systems theory we derive the rationale for system analysis and function analysis which utilize relevant strategies to secure an end or an objective—solve a problem. The systems theory function has been enhanced with the development and use of computers and other servomechanisms, but analyses are not restricted to their deployment, as demonstrated in this chapter. Simply stated, the systems approach is a method of scientific inquiry in which we attempt to identify all possible alternatives and their probable consequences. Selection of the "best-appearing" strategies becomes possible before final decisions are made and actions taken. System analysis encourages the consideration of organization components and variables that would likely be overlooked in other modes of attack on the problem at hand.

The theory makes extensive use of models, both simple and complex, which serve, among other things, as mnemonic devices. The adaptation of Etzioni's survival-effectiveness models and of Leavitt's four dimensions of organization interaction provides a systems approach for analyzing effective program supervision and evaluation. The whole process of program supervision and evaluation—the interaction of the components and their development—becomes meaningful when it is examined and analyzed on the survival-effectiveness continuum. The complex nature of the process is ordered, if not somewhat simplified, by these mnemonic devices or bases of reference.

Task. In order to maximize the utilization of the survival-effectiveness continuum, the four dimensions of organization interaction require definitions and delineation. *Task* or function reduces to reasons for being. Just what are the reasons society has for maintaining and supporting the elementary schools? There are essentially two categories of reasons for being: (1) tasks which resemble generalizations, such as achieving good citizenship and love of the American way of life; and (2) tasks designed for the preparation (or a part of it) of the boys and girls for appropriate adult pursuits. Admittedly, these categorizations tend toward an oversimplification, and they tend to include more and more component subtasks. The first category is difficult to observe, quantify, and measure for the purpose of implementing redefined subtasks for greater effectiveness. The second category contains many subtasks which are operationally meaningful. The basic skills and their development and refinement as well as pupil personnel services are typical of the subtasks assigned to the elementary schools. This category tends to contain subtasks which can be more or less observed, quantified, and measured, but not exclusively.

Technology. The second variable of interaction is *technology.* Technology or the technical tools available in the elementary school differ vastly from those in industry in which this model was first developed. However, in either case, the desired results or outcomes are the same. Development of technology or tools is essentially related to attempts to be rational and to effect greater efficiency. Problem-solving inventions characterize technology as it is utilized in the model. Problem-solving inventions are becoming more and more available for utilization in the elementary schools. Many of these tools are admittedly still in the tryout stage, but this portends mainly a particularly important aspect for effective program supervision and evaluation.

The development of technology for the elementary schools has been a slow and uneven development. A chalkboard, a textbook, and a stereotyped teaching method were long the basic technical tools for the teacher. Development of technology is illustrated in the "better" textbooks and library materials; the vast array of media—equipment and support materials; and the various program teaching devices, including the sophisticated hardware for computer-assisted-instruction. Great strides have been made from the stereotyped single teaching method to the development of many methods.

Structure. The third of the interacting variables is *structure.* Concerned with systems for communication, and with systems of roles or positions, and with systems for work flow or accomplishment, structure is essentially a consideration of how the elementary school is "put together." And how these systems are "put together" or structured, implemented, and maintained will determine whether the organization is a survival model or an effectiveness model operation. Terms such as centralized, decentralized, formal, and informal, may be used to describe structure.

Further, these systems are used in at least four contexts of interaction: (1) within the school itself, (2) the school in its relationships with the school district of which it is a part, (3) the school in its relationships with other organizations and agencies, and (4) the school in its relationships with society in general. As an interacting variable for effective program supervision and evaluation, structure is principally used in the context of interaction within the school itself, but certainly not exclusively.

People. Concern with the member or *people* variable has, more frequently than not, ignored the intense interaction of these organization variables. Program supervision and evaluation have been defined and defended, at one time or another, as bringing about change in people— the organization members. There has not been any long term consensus on procedure; sometimes people have been the direct target of change and sometimes they were changed by indirection. Essentially, the people approach to pattern change or to pattern maintenance has experienced progress through two general periods of development. The first period of development is characterized by the work of Carnegie,[3] Lewin,[4] and the Western Electric researchers.[5]

Although methods and means varied, the common variable appears to have been some kind of manipulation. Change through manipulation was accomplished by emphasizing an interrelationship of one sort or another. Carnegie emphasized the personal relationship *between* two people—the change agent and the person to be changed. Lewin emphasized the interrelationships *among* the persons to be changed. The Western Electric approach may be described as a combination of the other two approaches.

The second period of development in the people variable is characterized as giving attention to power equalization, as developed by Bennis, *et al.*[6] Power equalization, rather than power differentiation, is an important variable in planning and implementing change. Bennis, *et al.*, defined change as a power distribution in which the change agent and those who are to be changed have equal, or almost equal, opportunities to influence.[7] This period of development, characterized by power redistribution, is appropriate for efforts to attain an effectiveness level of

3. Dale Carnegie, *How to Win Friends and Influence People* (New York: Simon and Schuster, 1936).

4. Kurt Lewin, "Group Decision and Social Change," in G. E. Swanson, T. M. Newcomb, and E. L. Hartley (eds.), *Readings in Social Psychology* (New York: Holt, 1952).

5. F. J. Roethlisberger and W. J. Dickson, *Management and the Worker* (Cambridge, Mass.: Harvard University Press, 1941).

6. Warren G. Bennis, K. D. Benne, and Robert Chin (eds.), *The Planning of Change* (New York: Holt, Rinehart and Winston, 1962).

7. *Ibid.,* p. 5.

operation. This approach provides communication networks for collaboration and deliberation. Also the expertise of specialization for teaching and the expertise of specialization for administration and supervision are allowed and encouraged to function independently of the principles of a single hierarchy.

THE PRINCIPALSHIP AND PROGRAM SUPERVISION AND EVALUATION

The principalship has not existed as long as have supervision and evaluation. Historically, supervision and evaluation have been considered to be essential and necessary activities. Whether the focus was on subtask accomplishment or on the technological method used to achieve it, supervision and evaluation activities almost invariably reduced to an evaluation of the teacher. The observed teacher's performance was judged satisfactory or deviant by the observer who was most frequently a district supervisor. The observation was usually a brief, formal affair with the resulting reward of being retained or the sanctions of being transferred for a second chance or of being dismissed based on perhaps but one such observation. One of the shortcomings of supervision and evaluation conceptualizations has been the tendency to practice as though they were ends and never means.

Just when the principalship was delegated the responsibilities of supervision and evaluation is not clear, but the conceptualization of *program* supervision and evaluation with the principal assigned major responsibility is still more recent. In fact, it is not a practice common to all elementary schools even today. Far too many of the elementary schools are operating too near a survival level. If there were to be designated a single contributory reason for survival operation, it would have to be the behavior of the elementary school principal in those schools.

This observation is given support by Gross and Herriott: "Programs designed to prepare school administrators should perhaps constantly stress the fact that the principal is there to accomplish organizational goals and, therefore, on this criterion his performance should be assessed." [8]

The assignment of goal accomplishment to the elementary school principal is not a great deal different from the assignment of first grade

8. Neal Gross and Robert E. Herriott, *Staff Leadership in Public Schools: A Sociological Inquiry* (New York: John Wiley & Sons, 1965), p. 159.

goal accomplishment to the first grade teacher. In neither case is a solo performance implied. And as the first grade teacher supervises and directs her pupils in their first grade activities, so must the elementary school principal assume a similar stance for his organization and its members. Because changing for improvement in most instances involves the organization dimensions or demands (structures, technologies, and tasks) or the individual (idiographic) dimensions as they affect the nomothetic dimensions, there is the necessity of assignment of the job to the one member who has the responsibility for the whole organization.

Shepherd suggested that:

The attitude of everyday life may be said to be characterized by at least three major propositions. First, that a person views the world about him from his *personal perspective,* not from a general perspective. Second, that a person is constrained to *routinize* the world about him. Third, that a person is engaged in a process of *typification,* a process of forming generalized judgments about the world about him.[9]

The personal perspective, routinized task performance, and typification of organization life are reflected in the division of labor or structures of the elementary school. Only the role or job description of the principal applies to viewing the total program. Striving to exceed a survival level operation is a behavior expected of the elementary school principal. Conscious efforts to attain effectiveness require optimum decision making as he seeks the best alternatives of choice from the mix of tasks, technologies, and structures. Because these interacting variables influence and are influenced by the fourth variable—people, most efforts to effect change soon involve two or more of the interacting variables with the people variable almost certain to be present.

Organization effectiveness and member efficiency have been subjected to considerable search activity. Arriving at the appropriate mix of effectiveness and efficiency is determined by the environment of the elementary school in which the effort is being made. Organization effectiveness derives from the mix of the components of tasks, technologies, and structures, and represents one way of meeting the organization's purpose. To the extent that organization demands are internalized by the individuals will efficiency obtain. The individual demands must be subordinate to, and supportive of, the organization's demands if the elementary school is to operate optimally—which is epitomized by a commitment

9. Clovis R. Shepherd, *Small Groups: Some Sociological Perspectives* (San Francisco, Calif: Chandler Publishing Co., 1964), pp. 9–10.

to improvement. The commitment to improvement reduces to consideration, and acceptance by the individual members, of how to redefine tasks, technologies, and structures to effect improvement. Individual demands can be an important dimension of redefinition, but the principal's task is to preclude goal distortion and displacement. Etzioni observed:

The distortion of goals that arises from over-measurement of some aspects of the organization's output to the detriment of others is one of a larger category of distortions that arise in the relations of organizations to their goals. . . . Distortions due to over-measurement are comparatively mild, since the main goals of the organization remain intact, though certain aspects of these goals become over-emphasized at the expense of other sometimes more important ones. Goal displacement is much more detrimental.[10]

Goal displacement obtains when an organization displaces its legitimate goal with some other goal. According to Etzioni: "The mildest and most common form of displacement is the process by which an organization reverses the priority between its goals and means in a way that makes the means a goal and the goal a means." [11]

Some telecourses via ETV demonstrate the reversing of a goal and a means in the elementary school setting. It was reasoned that certain aspects of teaching history could be enhanced through ETV because remnants, realia, artifacts, and other visuals could be more effectively utilized. Each student would obtain a better view than if some of these things were merely held up in the front of the classroom. This is a legitimate goal, and telecasting appeared to be a promising means. However, the telecast reveals that the lecturer or narrator is on camera most of the time. When this condition exists, goal and means have been reversed. Utilizing ETV for the sake of ETV is the goal rather than the means.

Commitment by the organization's members to changing for improvement of the education program in the elementary school is one thing when it is discussed in generalities of purpose, and then it tends to become something quite different when it is taken under consideration at the subgoal and task levels. Change *per se* is actually neither desirable nor undesirable; however, it tends to possess connotations implying destruction, elimination, and obsolescence for many persons in their

10. Etzioni, *op. cit.*, p. 10.
11. *Ibid.*, p. 10.

thinking. The short-lived teacher panic following the Skinnerian programed instruction innovation epitomizes this kind of fear. If planning for change for improvement of the education program can be done with a connotation of modification or alteration, meaning to change something in one particular without changing the whole thing, a delicate operation may be made less delicate.

Even the least suspected change proposal may generate emotional reactions by affecting some organization member's deep-rooted values. The elementary school principal as the leader in planning and effecting change for improvement may discern that the organization's preparedness and readiness programing has failed insofar as certain individuals are concerned. When this situation obtains, the ready members may well have to decide to proceed without the reluctant ones and hope to discover ways to gain support from the reluctant ones. However, before the decision is made, the principal must weigh the likely consequences of proceeding against the likely consequences of not proceeding. No matter how the issue is decided, one group will be satisfied; and another group will be dissatisfied. Another consideration for the principal, and perhaps basic to the others, is what are the anticipated effects on the total program if all, some, or none of the change is implemented?

Cunningham stated that changes for improvement result from manipulation of the environments of the profession and of the organization. He acknowledged the usual negative connotation of manipulation, but he asserted that manipulation was exactly what had to take place. Manipulation has to do with:

The assessment of circumstances, the planned arrangement of people, of conditions, of resources, and of events which will lead to the attainment of socially acceptable objectives for a school system. Manipulation, after all, may involve strategy, not cunning; intelligence, not deception; statesmanship, not demagoguery; discretion, not duplicity; premeditation, not impulsiveness.[12]

Cunningham further suggested that *diagnosis* becomes the administrator's responsibility and that *intervention* or mediation to effect the conjunction between expectations and needs is necessary.[13] Intervention is an act of interfering, and the principal is the interferer in this case. He must assume this role if he is to effect modifications in the status quo,

12. Luvern L. Cunningham, "Viewing Change in School Organizations," *Administrator's Notebook,* Vol. XI, No. 1, September, 1962, p. 2.
13. *Ibid.,* p. 2.

that is, if there is to be effective changing for improvement of the education program.

THE EDUCATION PROGRAM COMPONENTS

If the elementary school principal is to assume his role as leader and change agent in efforts to propel his school toward an effectiveness level of operation, then he must become informed about the variables that he can set in interaction toward this end. Effective program supervision and evaluation are vitally dependent upon his role interpretation and his level of understanding in leadership tasks. Task, technology, structure, and people have been presented as four interacting variables about which he must become informed. Over the years, educators have exhibited a typical behavior of becoming concerned with but one of these variables at a time. Even though it has been demonstrated that they are interacting and that an alteration in any one is likely to set in motion a compensatory or retaliatory reaction in others, far too many of the present day admonitions center around the people variables without concern for the others. In fact, a search of the literature reveals very little effort has been directed toward integrating the components of the education program. In the ensuing sections, these components and their interrelationships are subjected to a more intensive discussion and development.

Task Components

Organizations are generally created to serve a specific function. In this sense, organizations represent a division of labor. The elementary schools are special organizations created, maintained, and supported by society. They are also characterized by a division of labor; that is, the five-to-eleven-year-old children are the general responsibility of the elementary school. Some elementary schools are also responsible for the twelve-and-thirteen-year-old children, and, in recent years, some elementary schools have been providing programs for children under five years of age.

What the elementary schools do to and for these children and indirectly for society is represented by *task* or function. These tasks are frequently stated in the form of purposes, objectives, or goals. Tasks are the reasons for which the elementary schools exist, although not every elementary school has the same tasks.

It is one thing to discuss tasks as reasons for creating schools and quite another thing to make these tasks operational as subtasks to be performed. There is a category of tasks which are very generalized and which do not lend themselves to elementary school or secondary school assignment exclusively. These are shared tasks and are represented by goals of the nature of achieving good citizenship, good mental health, and respect and love for the American heritage. In fact, these goals are achieved as a result of experiences outside the school as well as in it.

A second category of tasks is made operationally meaningful through subtask development. Presumably a subtask is assigned to a role or position occupied by a teacher. When the teacher has performed the subtask, a goal has been accomplished. Teaching first-grade pupils how to read is an example, and the goal accomplishment can be observed and assessed for extent of quantifiable success. Another characteristic of this category is that there is an ordering of them. They prepare the pupils for the next set of subtasks and so on through the entire educative process.

Another concern of the task component is the fact that new subtasks are being assigned to the elementary schools by society. The public school leaders have rather generally accepted these new subtasks and have attempted to integrate them as part of the education program. The provision of preschool programs, especially for the disadvantaged children, is one type of expanding task. Another and more prevalent type is characterized by the development of health services, guidance and psychological services, and specialized services for the variously handicapped children. From time to time another subject area is added to the curriculum which is essentially another task assignment requiring subtask development. Immediately following the Sputnik episode, many elementary schools began to teach science for the first time.

It may be that tasks or the reasons that elementary schools exist do not lend themselves to change in the sense that the principal and the faculty can decide that a given task is no longer serviceable and that it should be excluded. There is literature which appears to support the discarding of tasks through change and leadership. However, it is obvious that the operational subtasks, even those which propose to accomplish a generalized goal such as good citizenship, demand persistent supervision and evaluation to make them the most effective means in the service of these goals.

Sometimes a redefinition of task or subtask is required merely to maintain the organization pattern or to maintain the task in relation to present society. This type of redefinition implies operation at the survival level. On other occasions dramatic changes or redefinitions may be implemented if effectiveness is sought. Either way, it is obvious that tasks and subtask variables involve the other components and particularly that of people. The example of elementary school science is relevant. Upon its acceptance as a task, the subtasks were developed and assigned to the teachers. Their roles were redefined to include the teaching of some segment of elementary school science.

Effective program supervision and evaluation takes place within this component of task, particularly at the subtasks level. Part of the difficulty encountered has been attributed to the nature of certain subtasks— their tendency to defy both observation and quantifiable assessment. Another part of the difficulty is that of not being able to distinguish among people, technology, and structure components as they affect task. But this inability to distinguish may also be a case of applying the assessment to the wrong variable. Good citizenship is likely derived in part from the social studies curriculum (task and subtasks), but there are many other operative variables, including teacher behaviors, pupil control and government, and lots of out-of-school variables.

One of the tasks of the elementary school is to socialize the pupils into roles. A first-grade pupil has not learned his role until he has learned to perform as a first grader; that is, giving his attention when it is needed, keeping quiet when quietness is indicated, working as indicated individually or as a group member, imitating when he is so directed. Much of this role learning through the elementary school years would operate toward the accomplishment of the subtasks of good citizenship. However, much of the socialization into role is viewed by the teachers from the more immediate necessity of socialization in order that teaching in the academic subjects can be undertaken.

Technology Components

Technology has been defined to include methods of teaching, tools, mechanical and electronic devices and instruments, media equipment; and summarized as problem-solving inventions. Technology is a means component; however, observation of practice and other evidence lead to the conclusion that very frequently the advocates tend to view them as ends. This kind of advocacy is not particularly unique to technology or to education; most problem-solving inventions or other developments are at first advocated as *panaceas*.

One of the problems facing the principal and his faculty members is the recent proliferation of problem-solving inventions being advocated for the elementary schools. A further confounding variable is that the advocates of the new technology are also spokesmen and decision makers for education program policy making in superordinate positions and high status organizations. Yet, the principal and his teachers are being forced to make judgments with very little more evidence than advocacy. If there is a wait and see attitude, then they are suspected of being *satisficers* and status quo maintainers. If there is an immediate acceptance of the problem-solving inventions, then the charge is that of jumping on the education bandwagon or of converting means to ends.

Yet, neither attitude is appropriate if an effectiveness operation is sought. Each promising technological invention must be evaluated as a means to be integrated in the mix of all the education program components. Until the identity of the problem-solving inventions that are most effective in the service of the goals of a given elementary school is known, the only justifiable utilization of new technologies is experimentation and tryout. Whether the technology is a new series of textbooks, a modified role system, or a new piece of media equipment—experimentation, tryout, and evaluation are the important activities of effective program supervision and evaluation.

The likely success of a given technical tool or methodology is dependent upon the attitude, understanding, and acceptance by the persons who will be affected either directly or indirectly. If the technology requires the teacher as an operator, then the teacher must become a capable operator. It may be that subtasks will be modified or changed, and this aspect must be considered carefully.

A most common example is found in the new mathematics or new arithmetic in the elementary school curriculum. For some teachers, the change to the method was not much more than a substitution of practice; for others acceptance was more difficult, and they may be only going through the motions because they lack understanding. There is still another group for whom the new method is a complete value disorientation. These people will likely never accede to the new technology. Even if they are forced to use the textbook, they will still be teaching arithmetic with their old method.

Structure Components

Structure is essentially a consideration of how the elementary school is put together. It is possible to identify at least three systems for examining structure: (1) a system of roles or positions, (2) systems for communication, and (3) a system for work flow. Although there is overlap or interaction among them, they are discussed as discrete systems.

1. *A System of Roles or Positions.* Organizations are characterized by positions or roles which differentiate positions, but organizations are also characterized by sets of norms which serve to integrate the organization. An examination of positions in the public school enterprise reveals that each position has attributes of power, authority, force, and responsibility. Some positions have more or less of each of these characteristics than do others—a condition which serves to produce a hierarchy of positions, graded levels of authority, division of labor, and departmentation or specialization. It is from these characteristics and variables that the conceptualization of superordinate-subordinate roles with higher and lower prestige and status has been derived.

In the elementary school, as in most organizations, there is a need for a system of superordinate-subordinate roles. However, there are at least three characteristics of the elementary school which modify the bureaucracy principles from which the position characteristics and variables are developed: (1) the unique line concept of position and roles, (2) specialization differences, that is, specialization for administration and supervision and specialization for teaching, and (3) the presence of the organization's clients (the pupils). Although the elementary school is a modified bureaucracy, the need for a system of superordinate-subordinate roles derives from the assignment or designation of decision making and policy implementing to appropriate positions in the organization.

The structure theorists were cognizant of deviant or unanticipated responses in role interpretation. Further, they all set about to establish controls designed to preclude or to minimize the human elements of unpredictability. The bureaucracy principles, the detailed task analysis, and the job description were all supposed to narrow and to circumscribe the incumbent's range of role interpretation. The early conceptualizations of supervision in education were based on the same utopian notions—notions that people preferred that planning be done for them and not with them. But it was not until role and role expectations were developed in conjunction with the people variable that any real progress was noted.

The elementary school principal must become expert in mediating role expectations and the members' needs as he seeks effectiveness in the program. March and Simon report on three consequences and the techniques used to install this emphasis on reliability of behavior or control of behavior: "(1) There is a reduction in the amount of personalized relationships . . . , (2) Internalization of the rules of the organization by the participants is increased . . . , (3) There is increased use of categorization as a decision-making technique. . . ." They assert that the combination of these variables result in a rigidity of behavior which makes behavior highly predictable.[14]

If these consequences and techniques are the dominant characteristics of an elementary school, there is little likelihood that it will ever surpass a survival level of operation. On the other hand, in a school without a measure of these, it can be anticipated that the survival model will also apply. Effective program supervision and evaluation depend upon the involvement of the members. Vroom recognized the dilemma of seeking the appropriate mix by stating: ". . . the necessity of taking individuals with diverse goals, habits, and skills and establishing the patterns of behavior that are consistent with the rational plan of the organization present an exceedingly difficult and complex problem."[15]

Perhaps the view of the dilemma taken by Katz and Kahn is more hopeful. System norms and values are a group product and may not be necessarily identical with the privately held values of a representative sample of the individuals in the system. Specifically, they wrote:

. . . three criteria define system norms: (1) there must be beliefs about appropriate and required behavior for group members as group members, (2) there must be objective or statistical commonality of such beliefs; not every member of the group must hold the same idea, but a majority of active members should be in agreement, (3) there must be an awareness by individuals that there is group support for a given belief.[16]

An elementary school is indeed characterized by a system of roles or positions. Further, this system is essentially an extension of a system

14. James G. March and Herbert A. Simon, *Organizations* (New York: John Wiley & Sons, 1958), pp. 38–39.

15. Victor H. Vroom, "Some Psychological Aspects of Organizational Control," in W. W. Cooper, H. J. Leavitt, and M. W. Shelly II (eds.), *New Perspectives in Organization Research* (New York: John Wiley & Sons, 1964), p. 73.

16. Daniel Katz and Robert L. Kahn, *The Social Psychology of Organizations* (New York: John Wiley & Sons, 1966), p. 54.

of roles that stem from the board of education and the superintendency in the central office.

If the school district tends toward a decentralized structure, considerably more autonomy may be anticipated in the elementary school's system of roles than if centralization is more characteristic. However, even decentralization retains connections and controls. In one sense, the elementary schools are becoming more autonomous, but on the other hand, there are observable factors of centralization. The present-day activity appears to be one of seeking the advantages offered by centralization without centralizing. Data-processing systems, or computer-based operations, portend of centralizing considerations because such systems are not justifiable without large-scale utilization. Decentralization is observable in such areas as program development, including supervision and evaluation.

Within the elementary schools, new systems of roles and positions are being developed. Rather traditionally, the hierarchy of superordinate-subordinate roles consisted of the principal, the teachers, and the pupils. Structure, as a system of roles and positions, is much like technology. There is a plethora of structure innovation advocates for nongrading, dual progress, continuous progress, and teaming, and so on. New roles and statuses are being generated: master teachers, coordinating teachers, and paraprofessionals. And technology is bringing about new and modified roles.

As though these developments were not enough to plague the elementary school principal and his organization members as they seek to develop effective program supervision and evaluation, the same developments are taking place in the role system of the central office. Many of these positions directly influence the elementary school and are essentially a part of the elementary school's system of roles and positions.

Much of the more appropriate literature relating to structure as a system of roles and positions is concerned with the people variable—primarily with role a secondary consideration. Thus, the problem of the principal in mediating the congruence between these components—structure and people—is viewed in the section on people.

2. *Systems for Communication.* Obviously, organizations could not exist without communication systems or networks. There is a positive correlation between an organization's effectiveness level and its systems for communication. Systems for communication are also particularly sensitive to the roles system. Most organizations are characterized as

possessing at least two systems for communication: formal and informal. Some theorists, such as Barnard, assert that both kinds of systems are necessary; neither one can be viable without the other one. The formal system is reflected in the interpretation and practice in the system of roles and positions. The informal system tends to lack any definite form or structure.

If the bureaucratic principle of impersonality and the rigid use of rules characterize the system of roles and positions, it is to be expected that the formal system of communication will consist of explicit channels of communication and carefully enforced protocols. A subordinate must report or communicate with an officially designated superordinate. Bypassing or communicating with an incumbent superordinate to the designated position incumbent is the epitome of deviant organization behavior. However, in an organization characterized by this kind of rigidity and formality, it is not unusual to observe that this protocol of communication is applied from subordinate to superordinate while the superordinate to subordinate channel is freely and unquestionably bypassed.

On the other hand, if the role system lacks structure or hierarchy, communication of a formal nature will be difficult because decision-making positions are not clearly identified. It should be noted, however, that this apparent nonexistence of authority designation is a dysfunction of role-incumbent interpretation to a greater extent than it is of role definition. All elementary schools have similar systems of roles, and the formality of communication depends, in a large measure, upon the interpretation and practice of the members.

An essential component of effectiveness attainment is a formal system of communication. The degree of formality of protocol is an important consideration; too much or too little is not conducive to effectiveness. The elementary school principal must seek the degree of formality that is comfortable for him and his organization members and at the same time enable them to function most efficiently in the activities of program supervision and evaluation.

Many elementary schools are experiencing structure changes which are products of communications systems and/or systems of roles and positions. Increasingly, specialization creates differences in understanding among members. Though it is more a phenomenon of recent awareness rather than of recent development, specialization for administration and supervision and specialization for teaching are examples of communications difficulties and their impact on the communication network and role system. The hierarchy of subordinate-superordinate roles is generally conceptualized in the school system as a single one of line extending from the classroom upward through the principalship to the central office and the superintendency. The lack of discernment of the differences imposed by the two kinds of specialization provides an unexplained discontinuity in the single hierarchy and hinders exchange of meaningful communication in the organization.

More recently, in some of the elementary schools, there have been implemented new communications systems or subhierarchies of roles. In the schools with teaming, there has evolved a new position with the master teacher being designated frequently as a superordinate of the other team members but subordinate to the principal. Of immediate concern is the pattern of channeling for communication. If communication flows up and down through the master teacher position, the incumbent becomes another communications filter. The implication of formal channeling portrays a mathematical model for communication; that is, A sends a message to B. Because exposure does not guarantee communication, the mathematical models have only limited utility for effective program supervision and evaluation.

Communication models, derived from sociology, embrace feedback and reciprocity and appear to be more appropriate because they enable power equalization. There is no implication that the informal system of communication can serve this function. If the elementary school principal is seeking effectiveness in program supervision and evaluation, he must learn about problems and teacher priorities by listening far more intently than he ever has. He can accomplish this by developing a communication system which encourages collaboration and deliberation, permitting an exchange of expertise of the kind held by teachers and of the kind possessed by the principal. The specialization for teaching component is the one in which program effectiveness is sought. In this sense, the specialization for administration and supervision serves as a means to the end through effective program supervision and evaluation.

3. *A System for Work Flow.* Intimately interwoven with role systems and communications networks, systems for work flow may be conceived as the aspects of structure that get the job done. The job to be done by the elementary school is sometimes described as getting the boys and girls ready for the secondary school experiences. For some boys and girls, the elementary school program is terminal; thus this adds another

dimension to the job of the elementary school. The view is broadened when the individual's interests and personal needs are developed in the elementary school experiences. The job to be done in the elementary school, as developed in the *Task* section of this chapter, reduces to the subtasks and their assignment to the various roles. Presumably the performance of these subtasks is getting the job done. If these subtasks have in reality mapped the tasks or the reasons for being a special organization, and if the performance is efficient, then the elementary school is characterized by a degree of effectiveness. Program supervision and evaluation become means, in this sense, toward facilitating work flow or articulation of the subtasks for goal accomplishment.

Communication systems and role systems are immediately obvious as prime considerations for facilitating work flow or the articulation of subtasks toward the goals. Program supervision and evaluation serve to assess performance, measure accomplishment, and aid in redefining the subtasks toward a more effective program.

Program supervision and evaluation are dedicated to the improvement of individual, group, and organization performances. People are reoriented toward subtasks and task goals; technology is updated; and people are retrained to perform with the new technology. Structure, in the aspects of role and position systems, is modified; communication networks are revamped toward greater efficiency and greater effectiveness—goal attainment. The components of structure, people, technology, and task are enhanced or hindered by the impact of any one of the components.

People Components

Two general periods of development in research of human behavior are identifiable. The first period is characterized as one in which the relationships toward influence were based on differentiated power. Much of the investigation was utopian in nature; that is, the people to be changed were assumed to be ready to accept change or to socialize their personalities to fit the role without difficulty or protest.

The second period is characterized, by and large, by the considerations given to power equalization in which socialization of the personality likely takes place; but, more important, the role is personalized. Both sides—the change agent and the changee—collaborate toward an effectiveness goal which will also generate individual and group efficiency.

The elementary school principal will discover that it is possible to effect change of a sort without obtaining the consensus of the members, but the effect of change is only a surface type and does not bring about the modification sought in the first place. Kelman proposed three processes of operative influence which have relevance as particularly appropriate bases of action for an elementary school principal.[17]

Compliance is one of the processes, and it is typified by an acceptance act for reasons other than the underlying reason for the change itself. A subordinate may express agreement to his superordinate or even to his coordinates, but inwardly and privately he disagrees and likely practices in his usual way unless he is closely supervised.

A second process of influence is *identification* in which an organization member adopts the change or activity because he identifies with the person or group advocating it. Essentially he takes over the other person's role and incorporates this role into his own self-image. A change in subtask performance will likely be observed, but the performance may be superficial because understanding is not a requirement of identification.

Internalization is the third process of influence delineated by Kelman. It occurs when an individual or group accepts the change because it is consistent with the individual or group's perspective and because the change represents a satisfactory solution to a problem.

Essentially, changing for improvement is feasible only when it comes through internalization, but it is somewhat difficult to ascertain that acceptance is indeed based on this process of influence. In the elementary school there is always the real and/or imagined presence of positions of graded authority or hierarchy. These implications may generate change acceptance through compliance and identification rather than through internalization. Likely, in the long view, these determinations will become apparent, but each short-term identification and compliance act can have a negative effect before it is realized.

The elementary school principal knows that the process of developing an effective organization through program supervision and evaluation is essentially that of mediating two sets of behavior-eliciting forces; that is, the organization's demands (expectations) and the individuals' demands (needs-dispositions). Research evidence asserts that morale and satisfaction are related to the compatibility between these two sets of behavior-eliciting dimensions. Effective program supervision and evalua-

17. Herbert C. Kelman, "Processes of Opinion Change," *Public Opinion Quarterly,* Vol. 25, 1961, pp. 57–58.

tion depend on this relatedness or compatibility. Guba observed that morale is a function of commitment, rationality, and belongingness. Morale is also related to the amount of energy output required by the individual to accomplish his assigned task.[18] When there is conflict in values or in interpretation, creating some kind of disharmony in the individual, he must generate more effort to produce a given outcome than if there is no essential conflict or disharmony, assuming that he does indeed produce a satisfactory outcome.

Morale and satisfaction are not ends per se, although there has been a tendency to view them as such in education. For effective program supervision and evaluation, morale and satisfaction are essential as environmental conditions. Supervision and evaluation contribute to them and are in turn made effective by them.

Satisfaction with the accomplishment of task performances is considered *effectiveness* from the vantage of the organization. Satisfaction with the accomplishment of task performance is *efficiency* from the vantage of the individual or group members. But one satisfaction is not the same as the other one. Effectiveness satisfaction derives from the conjunction of the participant's performance and the organization's dimensions of expectations, while efficiency satisfaction relates to the congruence of the participant's performance and his needs-dispositions. Chase distinguished between morale and satisfaction from the vantage of the individual.

... satisfaction grows out of a sense of achievement and of being valued in the organization; it is a result of past experiences and typically is uppermost in a state of rest between activities. Morale is compounded from a commitment to common purposes and a sense of unfulfillment or challenge and is powerfully influenced by the expectation (grounded in past experience) of satisfying future achievement.[19]

Effective program supervision and evaluation are dependent upon an appropriate mix of both kinds of satisfaction; however, the elementary school principal is always confronted with the task of determining how much organization satisfaction can be sacrificed for individual

18. Egon G. Guba, "Morale and Satisfaction: A Study in Past-Future Time Perspective," *Administrative Science Quarterly,* September, 1958, pp. 195 ff.
19. Francis S. Chase, "The Administrator as Implementor of the Goals of Education in Our Time," in Roald F. Campbell and James E. Lipham (eds.), *Adminstrative Theory as a Guide to Action* (Chicago: Midwest Administration Center, University of Chicago, 1960), p. 194.

satisfaction and vice versa. His decision in a given instance will be reflected in the morale of the members.

Morale has been defined in many different dimensions. Some of the definitions designate it as a condition of individuals; other definitions designate morale as a characteristic common to groups. Landis viewed morale in the latter sense.

Morale is a term to be applied to a state of mind shared by members of a group and moving [motivating] them to make the fullest use of their strength and skill to obtain their objective. It is not a state of mind existing in one man alone, but in many; it is close to *esprit de corps.*[20]

Although formal organization structure is represented by a system of graded roles or positions, the observed behaviors relate to the performances of the position incumbents. Satisfaction and morale are vital considerations as the elementary school principal seeks effectiveness through program supervision and evaluation.

Effective program supervision and effective program evaluation imply efforts and activities which very frequently involve or precipitate subsequent change action. These change variables may stem from task, technology, structure, or people; but invariably people are involved in one way or another. Katz and Kahn were concerned about this "psychological fallacy" which describes the attempts "to change organizations by working on individuals without redefining their roles in the system, without changing the sanctions of the system, and without changing the expectations of other role incumbents in the organization about appropriate role behavior." [21]

Accordingly, the fallacy obtains from a confusion between individual change and organization change. A change in an individual does not produce a reciprocal change in the organization; or, perhaps more importantly, an organization change does not necessarily produce a reciprocal change in the individual. Methods and approaches for eliciting change include:

... the direct use of information, skills training, individual counseling and therapy, the influence of the peer group, sensitivity training, group therapy, feedback on organizational functioning, and direct structural or systemic alteration. The primary target of change may be the individual as an individual personality, the interpersonal relationships between members of peer

20. Judson M. Landis, "Morale and Civilian Defense," *American Journal of Sociology,* Vol. 47, 1941, p. 331.
21. Katz and Kahn, *op. cit.,* p. 391.

groups, the norms of peer groups, the interpersonal relationships between members of an organizational family, the structure of a role, the role relationships of some segment of organizational space, or the structure of the organization as a whole. The difficulty with many attempts at organizational change is that the changers have not clearly distinguished their targets and have assumed that the individual or group-level target was the same as the social-structure target.[22]

The methods and approaches delineated for change eliciting are a heuristic listing, but they do represent a very "big bag of skills." There is no implication that an elementary school principal must possess this "bag of skills" if he seeks effectiveness in program supervision and evaluation. However, the implication is clear that he must be aware of them and of their potential. For many of the methods and approaches, he must seek the expertise of appropriate application from other sources. Some of them should be available in the central office; others will have to be brought in from other sources. His primary task may be that of diagnosis and recognizing what is needed and when it is appropriate. It is also obvious that a single elementary school's efforts toward an effectiveness level of operation is dependent, in a considerable measure, upon the commitment of the school district and community of which it is a part.

The elementary school principal should be cognizant of Wright's "administrative fallacy" as a serious retarding variable in program supervision and evaluation. The fallacy is ". . . that when affairs are working without apparent friction and through proper channels, they are working well. . . ." [23] In an organization as viable as the elementary school, lack of conflict and friction should be viewed with a degree of alarm. Such alarm would be more important today than ever before in view of the well-publicized wide-ranging efforts to improve both the quantity and the quality of the education program experiences. Harris observed that "Problems are generally caused by people, and solutions generally require changes in people." [24]

These observations provide relevance, then, to Cartwright's approaches to change in the organization components through people. He viewed the group from the administrator's vantage in three dimen-

22. *Ibid.*, p. 392.

23. David M. Wright, "The Administrative Fallacy," *Harvard Business Review,* Vol. 38, July-August, 1960, pp. 113–114.

24. Ben M. Harris, *Supervisory Behavior in Education* (Englewood Cliffs, N.J.: Prentice-Hall, 1963), p. 44.

sions: (1) as a *medium* of change, (2) as a *target* of change, and (3) as an *agent* of change.[25] The uses and implications of the three dimensions are important considerations for the effective elementary school principal in program supervision and evaluation.

Attempts to bring about change in group behavior, when the group is regarded as a *medium* of change, recognize the influence of pressures for acceptance or rejection within different combinations of individuals: how can individual A influence individual B? Cunningham's interventions concept is appropriate because the administrator must bring together human groupings wherein sustained contact brings about the desired change. Committees, department section groups, or even groups of two or three individuals are potential grouping patterns.

Individuals and groups as *targets* of change require a different approach to effect change. Such change plans may become a personal threat. Individual considerations are important variables, even though research evidence tends to indicate that morale and satisfaction are characteristics of group interactions. As Shepherd suggested, the personal perspective, routinized task performance, and typification of organization life are characteristics of the individual who is not ready for change for improvement.[26] For the reluctant organization member, special considerations must be made, if he is to be retained and ultimately contribute to the effective performance of the organization. Communications have not had the desired effect. The direct use of information, individual counseling and therapy, sensitivity training, feedback on organizational functioning may be utilized, as Katz and Kahn indicated,[27] or reutilized.

The third dimension or approach, *agents* of change, is the most common one, it is claimed. Using groups of individuals as agents of change may be regarded as a procedure of shifting the pressures for change from the administrator to another dimension—a group. Another view is that, as agents of change, the group members are exhibiting equalization of power. Bringing about desired change as a legislative function (involvement of the group) is likely to result in greater internalization of the changed situation, but it must be recognized that such legislative processes based on equalization of power are also subject to veto in an

25. Dorwin Cartwright, "Achieving Change in People: Some Applications of Group Dynamics Theory," *Human Relations*, Vol. IV, No. 1, 1951, p. 387.
26. Shepherd, *op. cit.*
27. Katz and Kahn, *op. cit.*

organization formulated on principles of hierarchy. This use of individuals and groups as agents of change is an appropriate approach when the members appear to be ready to deliberate and likely to concur in the desired direction in decision making. The reluctant member is not likely to be moved to change if this approach alone is utilized. In essence, a single change or modification may require all three approaches: members as mediums, targets, and agents.

TOWARD EFFECTIVENESS: THE ADVOCATES AND THE SOURCES

Isolated cases to the contrary, there is an environmental climate which encourages and demands increased and rational efforts at defining a pattern of interrelationships among the component variables of the elementary school which will make it the most effective in the service of its goals or purposes. Generalized and specific segments of society are responsible for the introduction of new tasks, new subtasks, and for the redefinition of others. Further, American society is involved in a technological renaissance. A lot of the encouragement and pressure from society in general to the school personnel derive from this state of affairs. Technology is being successfully utilized in solving many of the problems generated and perpetuated by society. Because people tend to focus on the apparent success aspects in general, it becomes "obviously logical" that the same application of technology in the elementary schools will bring about solutions for the problems encountered. Caution must be exercised by the school personnel because it is far too easy to identify technology as a genotypic class with the individual components which comprise the class.

Encouragement and advocacy for modifying the structure components of the elementary school tend to come from public school personnel to a greater extent than from external sources, but not exclusively. New patterns of departmentation by redivision of labor produce modified systems of roles and positions which influence communications networks, work-flow systems, and subtask assignments. Some of these modified role systems incorporate new technology as an essential component. At any rate, new patterns of grouping and regrouping of pupils and teachers are being advocated for more effective servicing of the purposes of the elementary schools. All of them are simply role systems being neither better nor worse than existing role systems. The successful or unsuccessful performance coming from any one of them is dependent upon other organization variables including, particularly, the individual teachers who are assigned to the roles or positions.

But the sources and advocacy are not exclusively external to the elementary schools. There are numerous factors within the elementary schools which encourage and demand renewed and persistent efforts which will generate greater efficiency and effectiveness in the education program.

Public school personnel, and particularly the elementary school personnel, are upgrading their initial preparation and are coming to regard career-long improvement activities as their way of life. Elementary school teachers actively pursue self-improvement through advanced degree programs, workshops, conferences, and other in-school in-service programs. They are becoming specialized for teaching. While a great part of their specialization for teaching consists of improving their knowledge about technology and its utilization, they are also pursuing, in various ways, specialization in subject matter content and in the psychology of behavior.

Research activity, recently intensified, may hold promises of new knowledge and more certainty about the knowledge we think we have. However, research projects possess a limiting characteristic which is relatively innate. By design most research projects are narrow in their scope which makes generalization of the findings to practice a relatively improper application. Yet the pressures and demands to improve and to implement innovations and effective change variables stimulate these generalizations into being. Recognizing these findings as observations derived under certain conditions, the elementary school principal and his faculty members must accept them as hypotheses for tryout and testing in their own program, evaluating and modifying them for use if they are serviceable in the realization of the goals to be accomplished.

Supervision and evaluation emerged as superordinate tasks designed to ensure acceptable performance. The conceptualizations of supervision and evaluation in education have paralleled or followed the general developments in other fields, particularly those in industry. Assuming a one-to-one correspondence between industry and education, the teacher and the production-line worker were subjected to the same kinds of supervision. When the variables to be observed were different, the supervisors apparently ignored the differences. There are vast differences between the production of learning or achievement in a social studies class (the teacher's performance of a subtask) and the production of a certain number of a component for a washing machine. There are survival-level elementary schools where this kind of supervisory practice is still utilized with only minor modifications.

Scientific management was the first major development to be extensively applied in industry. Thus, its central theme of seeking and enforcing the one best way to perform a task became the central theme for supervision and evaluation in education. In its application to education, it failed long before the failure was recognized or admitted. These early conceptualizations were formulated during an era of accepted power differentiation. Some of the ideas were right, some were inappropriate; but as a theoretical framework, scientific management was inadequate to explain all the relevant events. Admittedly, teachers and principals were not well prepared; they possessed virtually no specialization or expertise. They needed supervision for teaching, but the scientific management variety was inadequate. Acceptable performance was externally mediated by a superordinate incumbent who used a checklist of irrelevant characteristics to evaluate the observed performance.

The second major development to influence supervision and evaluation was the human relations approach. Variables omitted from the scientific management approach served as the base of the human relations approach, but it excluded the variables peculiar to scientific management. The human relations approach was doomed to failure also and for the same reason—inadequacy. Neither approach was adequate to account for all of the relevant variables.

One of the central themes of this book is that effectiveness in practice and performance in the elementary school principalship derives from adequate theoretical structures. Such is the view taken in this chapter. The functions and processes for program supervision and evaluation become effective and meaningful when there is an adequate theoretical structure for viewing and explaining all possible events and their interrelationships.

Systems analysis, in this case utilizing the survival-effectiveness models concept and Leavitt's dimensions of organization interaction, provides one theoretical structure for deriving a carefully formulated pattern of interrelationships among the elementary school components through effective program supervision and evaluation.

The boys and girls who attend the elementary school comprise the only group which has a clear and valid claim to vested interests. The content, sequence, and meaning of the subjects they study; the variety and depth of the activities they pursue; and the climate in which these teaching-learning experiences and situations are provided—all stem from the pattern of interrelationships of the task, technology, structure, and people variables effected in their school.

REFERENCES

Association for Supervision and Curriculum Development, *Supervision: Perspectives, and Propositions* (Washington, D.C.: the Association, 1967).

———, *Toward Professional Maturity of Supervisors and Curriculum Workers* (Washington, D.C.: the Association, 1967).

Bennis, Warren G., K. D. Benne, and Robert Chin (eds.), *The Planning of Change* (New York: Holt, Rinehart and Winston, 1962).

Carlson, Richard O., *Adoption of Educational Innovations* (Eugene, Ore.: University of Oregon, Center for the Advanced Study of Educational Administration, 1965).

———, *Change Processes in the Public Schools* (Eugene, Ore.: University of Oregon, Center for the Advanced Study of Educational Administration, 1965).

Cooper, W. W., H. J. Leavitt, and M. W. Shelly II (eds.), *New Perspectives in Organization Research* (New York: John Wiley & Sons, 1964).

Etzioni, Amitai, *Modern Organizations* (Englewood Cliffs, N.J.: Prentice-Hall, 1964).

Gross, Neal, and Robert Herriott, *Staff Leadership in Public Schools: A Sociological Inquiry* (New York: John Wiley & Sons, 1965).

Harris, Ben M., *Supervisory Behavior in Education* (Englewood Cliffs, N.J.: Prentice-Hall, 1963).

Hodgkinson, Harold L., *Education, Interaction, and Social Change* (Englewood Cliffs, N.J.: Prentice-Hall, 1967).

Katz, Daniel, and Robert L. Kahn, *The Social Psychology of Organizations* (New York: John Wiley & Sons, 1966).

Tyler, Fred (ed.), *Individualizing Instruction, 61st Yearbook, National Society for the Study of Education,* Part I (Chicago: the Society, University of Chicago Press, 1962).

Chapter 9

EXTENDING EDUCATIONAL
OPPORTUNITY

A FUNDAMENTAL ideal of American education is that every child has the right to education sufficient in amount and kind to realize the fullest development of his personal potential. Promoting this ideal has led educators to recognize unique needs of individual students which have been overlooked in systems of education not similarly committed, and the result has been an added dimension in curriculum: the extending of educational opportunity.

When the development of individual potential is valued, extending educational opportunity means making special provisions for individual student needs. From the viewpoint of administration, this involves initiating policy, structuring organization, staffing, and budgeting not only to provide for recognized needs but also to assess the effectiveness of current programs and the urgency of additional ones. Under the philosophy that each student should be developed to his maximum, the only limits upon implementing programs for extending his educational opportunity are lack of local leadership and lack of resources.

THE CHILD IN AMERICAN SOCIETY

Society is a mechanism employed by man to facilitate his survival as a living entity. With respect to the individual, using this mechanism has two aspects: the individual uses social institutions to serve his own ends, and the individual is used by society to build and maintain its institutions. Each of these aspects of social living provides a focus for justifying the extension of educational opportunity. On the one hand, a child should be equipped to use society's institutions. This means that needs generated by his social status should be considered and his adjustment to the social environment facilitated in such a way that he will capably employ social mechanisms. On the other hand, society should be able to use the child's social contribution for strengthening its institutions. This means that it should provide him with opportunity for developing his abilities and prompt him to use them for positive social contributions. In the United States, a country with democratic ideals, these imperatives must be understood to apply to every individual rather than any particular class of individuals; such is the burden of American education.

The Child's Needs in Society

It is widely recognized today that a child's social milieu is a prime determinant of his peculiar needs, and many people insist that the school should take an increasing role in satisfying them. Certainly the mass communications, urbanization, increased occupational mobility, and changing family patterns of today's society have an impact that changes the demands on a child for his successful social functioning. What, for example, are the effects upon a child of the following trends?

1. A changing status for family life leading to higher divorce (and remarriage) rates, fewer children per family, and increasing numbers of working mothers

2. The increasing massiveness of governmental, religious, economic, and other social institutions which minimize individual distinction

3. Compulsory education laws and indirect social pressures that trap "underachieving" or "unmotivated" children in environments of perpetual failure, increasing the emotional acuteness of their frustrations

Trends such as these characterize existing and emerging social climates which generate expectations and attitudes directed toward children. For example, today's child, as opposed to the child of America's traditional rural society, is neither expected nor permitted to make a significant contribution to his family's economic well-being. Does this role change forfeit certain positive values? Moreover, it is apparent that some parents use children as status symbols or for vicarious achievement of their own unattained childhood satisfactions. Little consideration is given to individual ability or inclination in pressing children to achieve such extrinsic ends. What kinds of emotional problems are created within children through such parental pressures? Also, it is striking to note the large portion of a child's activities that are "organized" today.

Children function in contrived environments managed by adults both in school and also on the playing field.

Factors such as the above define the social milieu known to children. An important question for educators is this: How can the schools assist children (as unique individuals) to adjust better to their environment? Moreover, how can the schools help children both to utilize their abilities and to circumvent their deficiencies, and also to function at optimum levels in society? Answers to such questions point the way to the special provisions needed in schools if citizens and educators are to structure effective plans for extending educational opportunities to all children.

Society's Need for the Child

That social climate affects the way a child responds to his educational environment cannot be denied. That special provisions should be made in the school to help the child overcome problems related to his unique condition in society has been justified by the democratic ideal that awards the right of fullest individual development. Recently, however, a more urgent justification has been recognized: the United States cannot afford to neglect maximum educational development of its youth as a national resource. This view was forcefully advocated by President J. F. Kennedy, who believed that the human mind is the fundamental resource and that to waste it through failure to provide the opportunity for maximum educational development is poor economics. He claimed that the United States was committed to investing in economic growth, and that research had indicated that ". . . one of the most beneficial of all such investments is education, accounting for some 40 percent of the Nation's growth and productivity in recent years." [1]

This view makes educational opportunity as much a matter of national survival as democratic idealism. Recognition of it has caused numerous federal programs for extending educational opportunity to come into being, many of which affect the elementary school child. Some of these are shown in Table 9–1, where annual appropriations for 1966 and 1967 are included to illustrate the magnitude of national investment they represent.

These programs are clearly aimed at reclaiming national wealth in terms of services apparently lost through failure to develop the country's human resources. The National Defense Education Act of 1958,

1. William T. O'Hara (ed.), *John F. Kennedy on Education* (New York: Teachers College Press, Columbia University, 1966), p. 155.

for example, makes federal assistance available for the purpose of acquiring equipment and training of teachers to improve instruction in critical subjects (science, mathematics, history, civics, geography, English, reading, economics, and modern foreign languages) that are related to broadening the student's technological and intercultural understandings. The above programs are coupled with provisions for maintaining guidance and testing programs to single out and encourage individuals to pursue studies related to their particular abilities. Students who otherwise might drop out of school can be encouraged to complete secondary programs and enter programs of higher education where their abilities can be developed to the fullest extent.

Children who suffer disadvantages either because they come from low-income families in areas of limited cultural opportunity or because they suffer physical or emotional handicaps are singled out for federal assistance. Title I of the Elementary and Secondary Education Act of 1965, recognizing a correlation between economic deprivation and low achievement in school, seeks to assist programs of all kinds directed at improving the educational opportunities of children from low-income families. Such programs may augment Project Head Start, provided for under Title II of the Economic Opportunity Act of 1964, which has facilitated the orientation of thousands of children coming from culturally and economically disadvantaged homes into the school environment.

Other federal programs, as indicated in Table 9–1, provide (a) for food and health services, to help prevent physical malfunctions from interfering with school activities, and (b) for construction of facilities and training of personnel to deal with handicapped children such as crippled, mentally retarded, deaf, and blind children. Funds for the various federal aid projects may be administered by the states according to a state master plan, or they may be granted directly to local agencies. Either way, they represent new resources for creating effective provisions to extend educational opportunity.

SPECIAL PROVISIONS TO MEET INDIVIDUAL STUDENT NEEDS

Earlier in the development of elementary education, the teacher, operating in a one-room school house, had the opportunity as an individual of providing for a number of special needs of students. He interacted with them in a context that allowed close acquaintance at all levels of elementary education. His capabilities were limited, however, by infe-

Table 9-1. Federal Investment in Educational Opportunity

Program	Purpose	Appropriation 1966	1967
Elementary and Second-ary Education Act of 1965		(in millions of dollars)	
Title I Programs for the Disadvantaged	Support educational programs in areas having high concentrations of low-income families.	959.0	1,053.4
Title II Library Resources	Support provisions of school library resources, textbooks, and other instructional materials.	100.0	105.0
Title VI Handicapped Children	Maintain and extend programs for handicapped children.	–	–
National Defense Education Act of 1958			
Title III Strengthening of Instruction Public Schools Loans to Private Schools	Strengthen instruction in critical subjects in elementary and secondary schools.	79.2 1.5	79.2 1.5
Title V-A Guidance, Counseling and Testing: State Programs	Provide for guidance, counseling, and testing in public elementary and secondary schools; testing in private schools.	24.5	24.5
Title XI Institutes for Advanced Study	Improve qualifications of elementary and secondary school teachers.	34.9	30.0
Economic Opportunity Act of 1964			
Title IIA. Community Action Program Head Start	Orient culturally disadvantaged preschool children to classroom environment.	–	352.0
Educational Television (P. L. 87-447)	Aid in acquisition and installation of transmitting and other type equipment necessary for broadcasting.	8.5	3.3
National School Lunch Program	Provide food for school children.	202.0	213.6
Food Distribution Programs	Improve diets of school children	140.2	169.0

Table 9-1. (Continued)

Program	Purpose	Appropriation 1966	1967
Special School Milk Program	Encourage increased milk consumption by children	103.0	104.0
Mental Retardation Facilities Act of 1963 (P. L. 88-164)			
Title IC. Construction of Facilities for the Mentally Retarded	Assist in the construction of facilities for the mentally retarded.	12.5	15.0
Title III Teacher Training	Prepare teachers and others who work with handicapped.	19.5	24.5
Research and demonstration	Promote research and demonstration on the education of the handicapped.	6.0	8.1
Mental Retardation—Project Grants for Training (P. L. 89-156)	Stimulate the development, expansion, or improvement of community services dealing with mental retardation.	4.5	5.5
Captioned Films for the Deaf	Provide cultural and educational services to the deaf through films.	3.0	5.0
American Printing House for the Blind	Distribute books and teaching materials to public institutions for the blind.	0.96	0.94
Training of Professional Personnel for the care of Crippled Children	Train professional personnel, such as doctors, nurses, psychologists and social workers for care of crippled children.	–	4.0
Services for Crippled Children	Extend and improve services for crippled children	45.0	50.0
Health Care of School and Preschool Children	Provide comprehensive health care and services for preschool and school-age children, especially in low-income families.	15.0	35.0
	Total annual investment	1,799.26	2,289.54

SOURCE: This table was adapted from "Federal Aid for Schools; 1967-1968 Chart" accompanying Howard S. Rowland and Richard L. Wing, Federal Aid for Schools; 1967-1968 Guide (New York: Macmillan, 1967).

rior technology and absence of professional training and sophistication.

In today's more complex setting, a number of specialized personnel are available to aid the teacher in extending educational opportunity. Thus, the teacher works in conjunction with administrators, guidance workers, student evaluation experts, and others who can help assess student potentials and deficiencies. The services of specialists aimed at providing programs to help students to develop their special potentials and to overcome their peculiar deficiencies are known as *pupil personnel services*. Their function in the school system is to create special programs and provisions to help individual students to succeed better in school.

Determining Need for Special Provisions

A system for collecting and collating data about students is fundamental to creating special provisions for extending their educational opportunities. Special needs cannot be met if no one knows what they are. For defining student needs, two pupil personnel services have come into being: pupil appraisal and pupil accounting.

Both of these services generate information which can be used to identify student needs. Perhaps the most important source of information is group testing, because it involves the majority of students and relates to the primary function of the elementary school—instruction. Determining levels of readiness and achievement is important to designing instructional programs, but group testing is also important because it can be used to screen students with special problems or potentials for further, more specialized testing or guidance.[2]

In elementary education, the fact that child development is a prime concern makes information derived from teachers' observations and classroom evaluations an important part of pupil appraisal. Such classroom devices as anecdotal records and sociograms can augment standardized testing in accumulating information for assessing students' needs. The observations of other pupil personnel specialists such as the school psychologist, sociologist, or health specialist constitute another important information source for selected students whom they contact.

The role played by the attendance worker brings pupil accounting into focus as an information source. Opportunities should be sought to use student attendance records (with their accompanying vital statistics)

2. See Warren G. Findley, "The Complete Testing Program," *Theory Into Practice,* Vol. 2, No. 4, October, 1963, pp. 192–198.

as aids in pinpointing individual problems. The attendance worker, in contacting students and their parents about attendance problems, often obtains information relative to physical or mental health problems that will aid other pupil personnel to help students adjust to school.[3]

In all, the sources of information that define student needs are diverse. The problem facing administrators is to organize a pupil appraisal service that coordinates and systematizes these sources so that a clear view of student needs emerges. If this is done, types of special provisions can be devised and programs implemented to satisfy them.

Types of Special Provisions

In elementary schools, three types of special provisions may be specified: individualization of instruction, remedial and corrective aid, and differentiated programs. For the majority of students, the classroom teacher has the responsibility of diagnosing individual needs and implementing one or more of these provisions. Even in extreme cases (those involving exceptional children) the classroom teacher carries the major burden of providing for special needs. Only a small minority of exceptional children are in special programs outside of the regular classroom.[4]

In those instances where the school district makes specialists available as part of the pupil personnel services, they most frequently serve the entire district rather than any particular attendance unit. The teacher must then learn to use them as consultants. He needs to augment his knowledge of the nature of child development with careful judgments about when it is necessary to refer cases to the specialist. Thus, a teacher should be able to decide whether a student can be motivated to work harder through the right kind of classroom support or whether he should be referred to the school psychologist for testing to determine if he is a retarded child. A teacher should recognize the signs of speech, hearing, or visual defects in children that require the attention of the school health specialist. The school administration should make it easy for the teacher to contact the specialists he needs. Pupil personnel services are the cooperative effort of many individuals.

One aspect of this cooperative effort that is particularly important

3. Some of these problems are outlined in I. N. Berlin, "Working With Children Who Won't Go to School," in Glenn A. Saltzman and Herman J. Peters (eds.), *Pupil Personnel Services; Selected Readings* (Itasca, Ill.: Peacock Publishers, 1967), pp. 134–140.

4. Walter F. Johnson, Buford Steffire, and Roy A. Edelfelt, *Pupil Personnel and Guidance Services* (New York: McGraw-Hill, 1961), p. 42.

to the elementary school is that parents are often closely involved with individual student problems. A pupil personnel specialist may work through a parent to help a child as readily as he would work through a teacher or directly with the child himself. The parent, child, teacher, and specialist may all work together or in any combination to provide the child with the type of special program he needs.

Individualization of Instruction

The elementary school is particularly well adaptable to the individualization of instruction. Special groupings, different sets of texts, individual and group student projects, and many similar approaches have tended to characterize elementary methodology in the American schools. Today, opportunities for individualizing instruction are being extended by the availability of new devices such as television, programed texts, and electronic computers. New concepts such as team teaching and flexible building spaces provide additional means to individualize a student's classroom experiences.

In such settings, the line between instruction and pupil personnel services becomes very thin. The teacher does as much to provide for individual student needs as he does to develop attitudes, skills, and knowledge. Indeed, for the majority of students in an elementary classroom, the teacher is the only one who deals intimately enough with students to assess properly what kind of instructional procedure best suits their needs. This he should be able to do for all but handicapped or gifted children.

Remedial and Corrective Aid

The problem of dealing with exceptional children (those who are retarded or gifted or who have physical or emotional handicaps) directs attention to providing the kind of aid that will help correct the condition that prevents their normal functioning in the school environment. For pupil personnel services, this focuses upon early detection, adequate diagnosis, and some means of referral. The teacher is closely involved in detection of exceptional children because peculiarities in classroom behavior are usually the first clues in discovering an exceptional child. On the basis of these clues, the teacher makes a tentative diagnosis and refers the child to a specialist who is qualified to make a more complete diagnosis and provide or recommend a procedure for helping him.

The school health service, which is responsible for health education, for providing a safe and healthful school environment, and for examining children for health defects, is in an excellent position to detect and diagnose physical handicaps. The school psychologist can determine whether a child is retarded or gifted and can diagnose mental or emotional disturbances, and, in connection with the school social worker, he can take measures to correct the disturbance.

Sometimes corrective measures involve these specialists in individual casework in which they either recommend to parents a therapist or actually perform therapy themselves. This has been true especially of the school social worker and the school psychologist, but the demand within the schools for their skills in behavioral sciences is calling them to a broader role. If the psychologist is charged with providing the student with a wholesome emotional environment (as the school nurse or physician is charged with providing a healthful physical environment), then his responsibilities will include working with teachers and administrators as well as students. He is qualified to advise teachers regarding such things as test interpretation and limitations, child development, group guidance activities, and the emotional needs of individual children. His skills in measurement can be used to devise and maintain pupil appraisal services and other types of evaluative procedures such as screening and selecting staff members. His value as a consultant to teachers and administrators may well exceed his value as a caseworker.[5]

When children have physical or mental handicaps that interfere with their classroom performance, the pupil personnel specialist can assist the teacher in providing individualized instruction. This is particularly important in light of the fact that most children in need of remedial or corrective aid must be served in the regular classroom. The help of specialists should be extended to in-service training where teachers can be helped to increase their professional repertory to include methodological devices and materials designed to help handicapped children.

Differentiated Programs

The design of individualized instruction to serve the special needs of students is at best a partial solution, because teachers are limited both in the time they can allot to individualized instruction and in special skills necessary to aid certain exceptional children. Recognition

5. For a discussion of broader roles for school psychologists, see Ralph H. Tindall, "Trends in Development of Psychological Services in the School," *Journal of School Psychology*, Vol. III, No. 1, Autumn, 1964, pp. 1-12.

of this fact has led many school systems to provide differentiated programs to aid students who are blind or partially blind, deaf or hard of hearing, physically handicapped, emotionally or socially disturbed, in need of remedial work (especially in reading), gifted, or retarded in mental development.

In some localities there are state-supported institutions for the deaf and blind, and for others with physical handicaps such as speech defects. These institutions are staffed by specialists who conduct programs not only to educate, but also to habilitate persons for effective functioning in society. Correction of defects is undertaken whenever this is feasible.

A growing number of programs in the public schools are staffed by personnel certified to teach special education classes. These people are trained to handle retarded and emotionally disturbed children in educational situations. They may also have specialized in speech correction, audiology, and remedial instruction. Additional programs are often instituted to allow gifted children to accelerate their progress or to undergo an enriched educational experience. In programs such as these, the line between instruction and pupil personnel services once again becomes indistinct because the child's special problem is intimately connected with his educational needs.

The process of instituting differentiated programs does not necessarily stop with the extreme needs of the exceptional child. It may be extended to more normal children who have varying degrees of academic ability. This brings into focus another pupil personnel service that is growing in the elementary school: guidance and counseling. The elementary school counselor has the responsibility of helping all children, normal as well as exceptional, to achieve individual understanding, social maturity and responsibility, and sound work habits.[6] Particular problems are encountered in helping the child make the transition from the home to the school and from the elementary to the secondary level. In assisting with such problems, the counselor will have to help the parent and teacher to understand the child, and the child to understand the school.

Two important functions of elementary counseling are (a) prevention and (b) placement. It is recognized that most of the emotional and social maladjustments encountered by secondary counselors have their roots in experiences at the elementary level. Prevention of these by identifying potential dangers early is an important job of the elemen-

6. Robert N. Schunk, "The Case for the Elementary Counselor," *Wisconsin Journal of Education,* Vol. 99, No. 3, November, 1966, p. 16.

tary counselor. Gathering data and conducting tests to identify potential
high school dropouts (or juvenile delinquents) may permit counselors
to place students in programs that will promote early adjustment, ward-
ing off future calamities. Whereas at the secondary level, placement
usually refers to vocational guidance, for the elementary counselor it
means identifying which of the programs available to the student would
best serve his needs. To help him take greatest advantage of his educational opportunities is to promote his best adjustment.

ORGANIZING PUPIL PERSONNEL SERVICES

The variety of highly trained personnel required to maintain a comprehensive pupil personnel program makes it unlikely that every school
district will be able to afford it. The Committee on Pupil Services estimates that only districts with a total enrollment of 10,000 or more
students will be able to support pupil personnel services of every kind.
Districts with fewer than 3,000 children will find it economically un-
sound to maintain an autonomous pupil personnel services unit.[7] Certainly, the typical elementary school could not expect to have available
all the services outlined in Table 9–2. This means that organizational
patterns will vary from district to district, with smaller districts seeking
to extend the scope of their services by sharing with other districts and
by taking advantage of public agencies in their communities.

The critical problem in administering pupil personnel services is
coordination, because several professional specialists trained in broadly
overlapping disciplines are involved. For small school districts, this task
may be performed by a guidance council consisting of competent professionals and community representatives who could advise the district
superintendent regarding pupil personnel services. Large districts which
can support a department within the structure of district organization
should have a Director of Pupil Personnel to coordinate services and
to make policy recommendations to the superintendent.

If the Director of Pupil Personnel carries out his responsibility to
maintain an organization that makes pupil personnel services readily
available to schools in his system, to minimize duplication by coordinating them, and to interpret the pupil personnel program to both school
and community, then success in his department will depend on leader-

7. The Committee on Pupil Services, "Organization of the Pupil Services Program," *Pupil Personnel Services; Selected Readings, op. cit.,* pp. 55–56.

Table 9-2. Pupil Personnel Services

Function	Staff Position	Typical Activity
Child accounting services	Attendance coordinator	Supervise data processing and maintain cumulative records to facilitate pupil guidance.
	Attendance officer	Check addresses of new students, check students not in attendance, etc.
Pupil appraisal services	Coordinator or director, psychometrician	Conduct testing program, do individual testing on referral, collate data and research, aid in curriculum development.
Health services	Physician, dentist	Make examinations, give emergency treatment, advise preventive medical practice, make referrals.
	Nurse, dental technician	Give emergency treatment, clear students returning to school from illness, maintain records, carry out prescribed medical practices.
	Food services	Typical activity: school lunch and breakfast supply, food distribution.
Guidance psychological services	Director of guidance	Coordinate all phases of pupil personnel, assign and supervise staff, plan budgets, etc.
	Teacher counselor, counselor	Conduct student orientation, give individual and group guidance counseling, consider general student welfare and assessment, handle parent conferences.
	Social worker, visiting teacher	Conduct casework, make referrals to psychologists and/or psychiatrists, represent student to outside agency such as court or welfare service, make home visits.
	Psychologist, psychiatrist	Do casework on referral, consult, participate in staff conferences, do individual testing, give therapy.
Special education	Special education teacher	Instruct physically, mentally, and emotionally handicapped children, participate in staff conferences.
	Speech and hearing	Provide therapy for children with speech and hearing handicaps, consult with teachers, participate in staff conferences.

ship by principals in individual schools. Especially is this true in the elementary school, where there is not likely to be a single full-time pupil personnel specialist employed. It will ordinarily become the task of the principal (1) to promote cooperation between staff members who do part-time guidance, remedial, or special education work and the other members of his staff; (2) to make facilities available to pupil personnel specialists from the district office for working with children in his school; (3) to keep his teachers informed regarding pupil personnel services available to them and open channels for their utilization; (4) to devise efficient procedures for providing information about students to pupil personnel specialists; and (5) to implement these procedures.

Since the nature of elementary instruction makes the classroom teacher a central person in providing personnel services to individual students, the principal should also exert his leadership to promote the competence of his staff in this area. If possible, he should exercise influence in selection of staff, and certainly he should promote in-service training aimed at making teachers better observers and keener diagnosticians of students' behavioral symptoms. Encouraging conferences and workshops with district pupil personnel specialists such as the school physician or psychologist will provide opportunities for teachers to improve their skills. These activities will also generate insights into better methods of providing pupil personnel services.

It is not likely that pupil personnel services will be effective without the active support of principals. No amount of formal organizational elegance can be a substitute for leadership in promoting the interaction, coordination, and cooperation among people that is the essence of effective pupil personnel work.

PROBLEMS AND ISSUES IN EXTENDING
EDUCATIONAL OPPORTUNITY

The role of pupil personnel services as an adjunct to instruction and administration in the schools is expanding rapidly. The term itself, used to describe all such services taken together, has come into general use only within the past decade. The elementary school counselor (as a person apart from the teacher or principal) and the special education teacher both represent roles that have primarily been a development of the present decade. Rapidly increasing enrollments and the encroachment of today's advanced technology are forcing changes in the manner of rendering services such as attendance accounting, pupil appraisal, and even counseling.[8] Services to pupil personnel are by no means stabilized in their scope or manner of administration; a number of problems and issues yet to be settled will bear significantly on their continuing development.

The Problem of Scope

One serious question in the light of expanding services offered by the school is what the proper scope of the school's activities is in relation to other social institutions that deal with the child. There is no question that schools today serve children in ways formerly considered the responsibility of the family or other community agencies. One view of this issue claims that the school has a responsibility to deal with problems in any department of a child's life that create or may create barriers to his success in school. Another claims that the school should shift its burden to proper community agencies.

One area of pupil personnel services that illustrates this issue is mental health. Allinsmith and Goethals outline potential mental health services for the schools which include detection, diagnosis, and prognosis, psychological first aid, referral, treatment, rehabilitation, followup, and prevention as desirable levels upon which the student should be served. The skills of psychiatrists are viewed as relevant to all of these levels.[9] At least one psychiatrist, however, claims that psychiatric services have no place in the schools and that mental health services should perform a diagnostic function, leaving therapy as an alternative for parents.[10]

Do parents have a fundamental right to decide when and by whom their children are to be treated, or is it the prerogative of public agencies such as schools to take the initiative when they feel that parents are remiss? Some authorities recommend that the school should take care of children's needs with respect to fatigue, disease, dental, visual, and hearing problems when parents fail to do so. They extend the obligation

8. A description of an experiment in counseling junior high school students by computer is given in System Development Corporation, *Final Report: Analysis of Instructional Systems* (Santa Monica, Calif.: System Development Corp., 1966).

9. Wesley Allinsmith and George W. Goethals, *The Role of Schools in Mental Health* (New York: Basic Books, 1962).

10. Thomas S. Szasz, "Psychiatry in the Public Schools," *Teachers College Record*, Vol. 66, No. 1, October, 1964, pp. 57–63.

even to providing food and clothing,[11] certainly a traditional function of the family. Whether this is an unwarranted encroachment on basic prerogatives has not yet been determined, but the question will have to be considered in determining what, in our society, is the proper scope for pupil personnel services.

The Problem of Methods

As pupil personnel services are extended, the need for effective methods of collecting and collating data about students becomes critical. The school's effort to help a student could end in total confusion if he were confronted with conflicting recommendations and contradictory prescriptions from counselors, attendance officers, school psychologists, and others. Fortunately, the progress being made today in the area of computer data processing offers broad opportunities for designing data processing systems that will both facilitate and help unify pupil personnel services.

Centralized data collection systems that minimize clerical time can be a boon to child accounting services [12] and can provide other pupil personnel specialists with more complete, up-to-date information than they have heretofore had at their disposal. If properly designed and organized, data processing systems can provide instantaneous retrieval of information supplied through pupil appraisal and accounting services from a centralized source. But Cooley points out that the use of computers to duplicate, however more efficiently, the information-gathering methods of pupil appraisal and accounting is to overlook the real power of computers in aiding pupil personnel specialists.[13] When the computer can be used to correlate several test scores along with other data (such as biographical data) and predict probabilities of success in various endeavors for students they characterize, using the computer merely for recording and displaying the test scores appears to represent gross underutilization. Thus, the challenge that automated data processing puts to pupil personnel workers is to devise new methods of describing

11. Benjamin S. Bloom, Allison Davis, and Robert Hess, *Compensatory Education for Cultural Deprivation* (New York: Holt, Rinehart and Winston, 1965), pp. 10–11.
12. See L. Donald Hahn, Richard A. Kaimann, and Peter P. McGraw, "Attendance Accounting: Yesterday—Today—Tomorrow," *Journal of Educational Data Processing*, Vol. 3, No. 3, Summer, 1966.
13. William W. Cooley, "A Computer-Measurement System for Guidance," *Harvard Educational Review*, Vol. 34, No. 4, Fall, 1964, pp. 559–572.

and studying (and even serving the student) which take advantage of such new tools. The question is not whether to utilize the computer but whether it will be used imaginatively to counsel, place, and appraise students or merely to reproduce existing methods of pupil accounting. Radical changes in future methods can be expected if educators plan now to use computers creatively.

The Problem of Focus

Traditional development of services rendered by people such as the school psychologist, social worker, or counselor has placed emphasis on dealing with the individual child. Needless to say, the performing of casework puts severe limitations upon the number of pupils one specialist can deal with effectively. Even if special problems requiring the services of school psychologists, social workers, or visiting teachers occur in but 2 percent of the population, recommended student-to-specialist ratios of 2,500 or 3,500 to 1 provide heavy case loads. Ratios of 1,200 to 1 have been recommended for elementary counselors, who should serve all the students. The fact that few schools are employing specialists in the recommended ratios to student population is evidence enough that pupil personnel services on a case basis are inadequate, and rising school enrollments (coupled with scarce resources to educate them) will likely prevent the situation from improving.

At the same time, pressure is on pupil personnel specialists to broaden their roles to serve greater numbers of students whose problems are not extreme but who, nevertheless, need some help. All this brings into question what the proper focus of pupil personnel services is. Is there an alternative to focusing directly on the individual student? Shaw and Tuel propose the alternative to school counselors of indirect (extrapersonal) focus. Counselors can serve students indirectly by improving their educational environment (extrapersonal influence) rather than directly dealing with the individual (intrapersonal influence).[14] This, of course, will require their dealing with people other than the child (such as teachers) who are responsible for the child's environment. It will result in transferring their services to a larger number of students.

The indirect focus may be used as well by specialists other than

14. Merville C. Shaw and John K. Tuel, "A Focus for Public School Guidance Programs: A Model and a Proposal," *Personnel and Guidance Journal,* Vol. 44, No. 8, April, 1966.

counselors, and it may lead to changing roles in pupil personnel services. It calls upon specialists to serve as consultants to teachers regarding special classroom problems; it calls upon them to be instructors in in-service training; it calls upon them to sit in council with school staff personnel. Indeed, pupil personnel specialists are being called upon more and more often to spend their time in activities such as these rather than in casework, and it may be that they can better serve school systems in this way.

The added demands placed upon the skills of the school psychologist are a case in point. Not only is he being required to examine and diagnose individual students, but he is also being asked to help teachers understand psychological measurement; to design research projects that will help evaluate school effectiveness or lead to innovation; to devise accurate and objective methods of selecting school personnel; to make his knowledge of child development and learning theory operative in the classroom; and to render other services indirectly touching the student. These are demands which require him to work with teachers and principals, not with pupils. They do not call for casework. Perhaps it is time for pupil personnel specialists to recognize a new focus for their services and accept the accompanying role changes.

The Problem of Organization

Problems dealt with by pupil personnel specialists are often interrelated. It is not uncommon for a physically handicapped child to have emotional disturbances brought on by his handicap or for a child to be hampered in school by a home environment that limits both cultural opportunity and adequate nutrition. In fact, many, if not most, of the special problems children have in school involve more than one pupil personnel specialist, and ought to be handled jointly by them. Furthermore, if the trend in pupil personnel is toward working with people in the child's school environment rather than the child himself, teachers and principals are drawn more closely into the picture. In other words, pupil personnel work should represent the cooperative effort of a number of people in the school system.

On the other hand, specialists in pupil personnel services are professionally trained people in different, though related, disciplines. They tend to look at their functions as central in importance and deserving of priorities in the allocation of resources. They expect autonomy in the rendering of their services and view their skills as being demanded by more situations than those of other professionals in the school.[15] This strongly profession-oriented outlook does not lend itself to cooperative effort in supplying services to pupil personnel.

Nevertheless, there is wide acceptance of the idea that pupil personnel services should be the result of teamwork. It is difficult to conceive how the many services described in this chapter can be effectively supplied under the constraint of scarce resources unless services are coordinated by specialists working as a team. Yet the question of who the coordinator should be is answered, "someone with a good foundation in psychology," by the psychologists; "someone with a background in sociology and social work," by the social workers; "someone with experience in guidance," by the counselors; and "someone with experience in teaching and training in administration," by the administrators.

Probably the most important qualification of an administrator of pupil personnel services is his ability to bring together people of widely divergent views and to achieve in them satisfaction with a role that fits into a team effort directed toward extending educational opportunity for children in a manner consistent with broad institutional goals. Making the "team approach" to pupil personnel services a working reality rather than lip service to a fictitious ideal is the imperative task facing administrators in this area. The character of future educational opportunity depends on their success.

15. Social workers and psychologists chose themselves as the ideal person to deal with various situations related to pupil services more often than they chose other school personnel in a study reported in John K. Fisher, "Role Perceptions and Characteristics of Attendance Coordinators, Psychologists, and Social Workers," *Pupil Personnel Services; Selected Readings, op. cit.,* p. 130.

REFERENCES

Allinsmith, Wesley, and George W. Goethals, *The Role of the Schools in Mental Health* (New York: Basic Books, 1962).

Arbuckle, Dugald S., *Pupil Personnel Services in American Schools* (Boston: Allyn and Bacon, 1962).

Association for Supervision and Curriculum Development, *Perceiving, Behaving, Becoming, 1962 Yearbook* (Washington, D.C.: the Association, 1962).

————, *Youth Education, 1968 Yearbook* (Washington, D.C.: the Association, 1968).

Bloom, Benjamin S., Allison Davis, and Robert Hess, *Compensatory Education for Cultural Deprivation* (New York: Holt, Rinehart and Winston, 1965).

Conner, Leo E., *Administration of Special Education Programs* (New York: Teachers College, Bureau of Publications, Columbia University, 1961).

Gowan, John Curtis, and George D. Demos (eds.), *The Guidance of Exceptional Children* (New York: David McKay Co., 1965).

Johnson, Walter F., Buford Steffire, and Roy A. Edelfelt, *Pupil Personnel and Guidance Services* (New York: McGraw-Hill, 1961).

Lord, F. E., and Robert M. Isenberg, *Cooperative Programs in Special Education* (Washington, D.C.: Council for Exceptional Children and Department of Rural Education, National Education Association, 1964).

Patterson, Cecil H. (ed.), *The Counselor in the School: Selected Readings* (New York: McGraw-Hill, 1967).

Peters, Herman J., Bruce Shertzer, and William Van Hoose, *Guidance in Elementary School* (Chicago: Rand McNally & Co., 1965).

Peters, Herman J., Anthony J. Riccio, and Joseph J. Quaranta (eds.), *Guidance in the Elementary School: A Book of Readings* (New York: Macmillan, 1963).

Peters, Herman J., and Bruce Shurtzer, *Guidance: Program Development and Management* (Columbus, Ohio: Charles E. Merrill Books, 1963).

Saltzman, Glenn A., and Herman J. Peters (eds.), *Pupil Personnel Services* (Itasca, Ill.: Peacock Publishers, 1967).

Chapter 10

T HE people who are grouped together for teaching and the supportive services in an elementary school determine in a large measure the extent of success or failure in meeting the purposes and goals of the school. The best organization structure, the newest curriculum guides and practices, the best equipment and materials are "best" only when we construct human groupings capable of making operative the tasks designed to realize the purposes, goals, and subgoals of the school. An elementary school is not so much a physical plant and supporting tangibles in the form of equipment and supplies as it is a set of roles or expectations of behavior from the incumbents who hold membership in the organization.

Slowly but surely two developments have become observable. In the first place, the importance of personnel functions is becoming appreciated. In the second instance, the importance of involving the elementary school principal in personnel functions is becoming recognized. Involvement of the elementary school principal in personnel functions has been, and is, a phenomenon of both external factors and internal factors relating to public school education in much the same sense as have personnel functions themselves emerged as important variables in public school education.

EXTERNAL FACTORS

Urbanism as a way of life, even in the less densely peopled areas, has a characteristic of forcing specialization upon people—in the usual sense of division of labor. And from this division of labor there emerges another and even more important kind of specialization. This specialization for teaching develops greater ability and awareness in the mix of subject matter, technology, and behavior psychology. Teacher training and preparation programs in elementary school education tend to preclude the training of generalists. Certification requirements and criteria in various states reflect this trend which may create some problems of personnel selection and retention in smaller schools because their structure requires generalists. Specialization in task assignment makes the larger elementary schools analogous to cities—they are collections of specialists with the number of specialties increasing as the size increases. The elementary school principal is likely the one who knows best which specialists are needed in his elementary school.

Public school education at all levels has become more complex with the ever increasing numbers of pupils with many and varied needs. New programs are being planned, implemented, and maintained which add to the complexity. As a result of these phenomena, many of the functions and tasks formerly performed by the superintendent and the central office staff members have been delegated to the elementary school principalship. One of these tasks relates to personnel functions.

Personnel functions were further complicated with the recruitment of a whole new group of personnel generally categorized as paraprofessionals. They serve as clerks, secretaries, and aides and are employed to free teachers from certain nonteaching tasks and to provide general support. The complexity related to paraprofessional personnel functions stems from the fact that the paraprofessionals do not possess specialty training and preparation and hold no certificate or license to perform in a classroom. The complexity of recruitment, selection, orientation, and development was more prohibitive at the central office level than in the elementary school because of the unique characteristics of the needs developed within an elementary school and of the paraprofessionals themselves.

Preparation programs for the elementary school principal have had an upgrading influence with some states requiring a minimum of two years of graduate level study. Thus, educational administration has evolved to a point at which the elementary school principal is more thoroughly trained and prepared to perform these kinds of tasks. He has also learned that if he is to be held responsible for the output or goal achievement of his elementary school he must have an important voice and involvement in determining the human groupings for his school.

A final dimension relating to external forces is the developing identity of the teaching corps as a consolidated force that has assumed responsibility for teacher welfare, working conditions, and other professional matters quite apart from the traditional administrative arrangements and channels for making decisions relating to these matters. Whether through the American Federation of Teachers' locals, the National Education Association's chapters, or independent locally organized union-type or professional units, teachers have created strong—sometimes militant—organizations that seek to effect personnel decisions.

INTERNAL FACTORS

The continuing expansion and the resulting complexity in the public school enterprise have served to force some modifications in the hierarchy of subordinate/superordinate responsibilities and tasks. On the one hand, the superintendent has added staff personnel, creating a large central office. This horizontal modification or expansion failed to meet all the requirements brought about by expansion and complexity in the public school enterprise.

Increasingly, functions, tasks, and responsibilities were delegated to the level closest to the implementation of these decisions and to a position commensurate with the demands generated by these responsibilities. Hence, there has been a resultant downward (vertical) assignment of functions, tasks, and responsibilities to the principalship which coincides with the upgraded preparation of the elementary school principals.

Within the elementary school, which tends to become larger and larger and more complex, there are numerous structural changes which require faculty members with varying specialties somewhat unlike the requirements for teachers in self-contained classrooms. Developing, implementing, and maintaining these peculiar human groupings are personnel function tasks most competently performed by the elementary school principal.

In general, the provision of adequate teaching-learning situations and experiences has benefited from a more objective view and evaluation of the total public school enterprise. A result of these activities can be observed in the emphasis on the critical nature of personnel functions.

The role of the elementary school principal has not been static. His responsibilities have evolved from the clerk-manager-record keeper to include also responsibilities for program development, implementation, and evaluation; facilitation and improvement of teaching-learning situations and experiences for all the boys and girls who enroll in the school; and the allocation of material and human resources to satisfy the needs of the organization and its clients.

This greater involvement has come from several sources. In part, it is the principal's own doing, and, in part, the involvement resulted from the downward assignment of functions and tasks. It must be granted that this greater involvement in personnel functions is essentially a superordinate control, but the elementary school principal who is still not involved sufficiently can effect and affect a change by demonstrating his abilities and showing relevant cause.

ORGANIZATION MODELS APPLIED TO PERSONNEL FUNCTIONS

Personnel functions in the elementary school have only recently been awarded a high priority concern. Obviously unanimity in practice has not been attained, but progress toward this state of affairs appears to be generating momentum. Concurrent and related to this concern with personnel functions has been the intense interest in organization theory relating to the system of public education. The intensity of concern with personnel functions in a given school or school district corresponds closely to the system model developed by Etzioni.[1] He defined a system model for organizations and identified two subtypes of models. One of the subtype models is a *survival model* which means that a given set of requirements, if fulfilled, allows the system to exist. The second subtype is an *effectiveness model* which defines a pattern of interrelationships among the elements of the system which make it the most effective in the service of a given goal, as compared with other combinations of the same or similar elements.

Concerned with minimal conditions and requirements for keeping the elementary school in existence and operating, the survival model level would require only that a teacher be assigned to each classroom or group of pupils. At the survival level, the involvement of the elementary school principal in personnel functions is not particularly important or crucial. Some districts still exhibit this kind of survival behavior. Teachers are given contracts for elementary school teaching in the district. Sometime before the school term commences, they are assigned

1. Amitai Etzioni, *Modern Organizations* (Englewood Cliffs, N.J.: Prentice-Hall, 1964), p. 19.

to a specific school and grade or classroom. Attempts to attain or to approximate an effectiveness model level require that the teachers in the school effect a pattern of interrelationships which will make it the most effective in the service of a given goal. It becomes immediately obvious that all personnel functions are tasks for which the effective elementary school principal must assume a major responsibility.

Personnel functions, and particularly the selection process, reduce to matching the right person and the right job or position. However, the survival model does not include a particularly demanding requirement. The organization will continue in existence, or survive, as long as persons can be employed to fill positions and as long as these persons can be induced to perform at least minimally. If an elementary school fits only the survival model, there is not much likelihood of observing education program development, implementation, and evaluation toward improved teaching-learning situations and experiences.

There are numerous factors which may operate to hold a school to survival levels. The school building inadequacies may contribute, but certainly most obvious is the assignment of teachers to a given elementary school by central office personnel officials without involving the elementary school principal. Teacher scarcity or specialization scarcity, inadequate funds for competitive hiring practices and for essential equipment and materials may contribute to operation at a near minimal level. Individual teachers or a group of them long entrenched in traditional self-contained classroom situations may contribute to survival level operation, especially if they have taught only in survival level schools. Self-contained classrooms do not necessarily imply the survival level, but most survival model operations would tend toward this structure.

Striving to exceed the survival level of operation is a behavior expected of the elementary school principal. The effectiveness model does not "just happen"; it requires the efforts of every member of the organization, as demonstrated in Chapter 8. The elementary school principal is the fulminator and prime planner in the undertaking whether consideration of the implications and ramifications of the effectiveness model is for program supervision and evaluation (Chapter 8) or for the present focus—the importance of personnel functions. Here the right person for the right job or position—professional and paraprofessional—is essential. The organization members, or human grouping, must come to agreement on purposes (both education program ends and member benefits); on subgoals and tasks; on the allocation of resources of every kind; and on priorities. New members must be selected and oriented to ensure their efforts toward the development of an organization that approaches an effectiveness model. This observation does not exclude the fact that new members do in some way or another alter or modify the ongoing program, but their efforts and contributions are essentially another part of the pattern of interrelationships which will lead to optimum effectiveness in the organization.

To paraphrase the intent of Simon, the elementary school principal whose orientation level is no higher than the survival model will *satisfice* rather than optimize.[2] Conscious efforts to attain an effectiveness level require decision making above the *satisficing* level which does not seek the one best alternative of choice but rather seeks an alternative which will continue existence. Involvement in and great concern for personnel functions are requisite for the elementary school principal who seeks to attain optimum effectiveness in his organization. There is no defensible alternative.

IMPROVEMENT: ORGANIZATION AND INDIVIDUAL DEMANDS

Identification of organization models for elementary schools provides a structure within which the principal, the teachers, and other members can determine where they and the organization are and under which conditions and activities they can move to an agreed-upon state of development at some future time. Knowing what the job is helps to assure its accomplishment. Utilization of the models serves in teacher selection and assignment, in goal defining and program improvement through the specific personnel functions of orientation, in-service programing, and evaluation.

Improvement is the key concept. If the organization and its members are not committed to improvement, then the acceptance of the survival model is sufficient. Personnel functions are then not really critical areas of concern for the principal and the teachers. However, there are both internal factors and external factors of environment operating to preclude the continuation of survival operations in the elementary school. But it is not always clear as to which variables are implied when reference is made to a commitment for improvement.

In recent years, organization and member effectiveness and efficiency

2. Herbert A. Simon, *Administrative Behavior* (New York: Macmillan, 1966), pp. xxv-xxvi.

have been subjected to considerable research activity. Whereas it is known that efficiency and effectiveness characteristics tend to correlate, it is also known that one characteristic does not automatically assure the existence or presence of the other. Elementary schools, and other organizations, are under pressure to be rational which is presumably a condition determined by the effectiveness and efficiency of the organization and its members.

The effective elementary school principal knows that his organization has expectations represented by sets of normative behavior. He realizes that if these expectations are internalized by the individual members and carried out, they contribute to the effectiveness of the organization. He is also acutely aware of the dimension represented by the individual and that each individual comes into the organization with special needs and dispositions which may either hinder or enhance goal realization.

The task of the elementary school principal is how best to effect member agreement on purposes and tasks, on the allocation of resources, and on priorities. To the extent that he is capable of deploying the personnel functions to these ends will efficiency and effectiveness obtain. Attainment of organization effectiveness requires attention to the improvement of organization purposes and goals. This attainment and its activities can be accomplished only through the individual members who are also seeking the satisfaction of their needs. If this dimension is satisfied, then the organization exhibits efficient behavior as well as effective behavior. Arriving at the appropriate mix of effectiveness and efficiency is determined by the conditions and situations or the environment in which the effort is being made. It should be noted that this environment will be influenced strongly by the manner in which personnel functions are developed and practiced.

The Getzels social process model (introduced in Chapter 5) is as useful for analyzing effectiveness and efficiency as they relate to personnel functions as it is for analyzing the program through supervision and evaluation. (See Figure 10–1.) The model consists of three dimensions. The nomothetic or organization dimension sets forth the role and role expectations or the sets of normative behavior. Personnel selection is essentially matching the candidate's likely performance with these norms because goal accomplishment is related to the extent these are realized. The idiographic dimension delineates the individual member's needs and desires. The third dimension or transactional dimension essen-

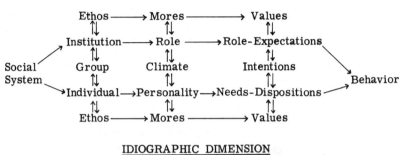

Figure 10-1. Getzels' Social Process Model

tially represents the situation. It is within the "wide" spectrum of the transactional dimension that the effective elementary school will be operating, being neither nomothetic nor idiographic and yet being both.

Effectiveness: The Organization Demands

Effectiveness is a characteristic of the organization or nomothetic dimension. Effectiveness is a relationship between an individual's behavior and the behavior expected of him by the "organization," and the correlation has to do with the presence or absence of disparity between the goals of the individual and of the organization. It should be acknowledged that the elementary school exists by virtue of a generalized purpose recognized by society at large. The functions, subgoals, and tasks are also generally developed. But the more microscopic official job description is the instrument of immediate interest to the teacher because it sets forth the functions and tasks upon which his performance will be evaluated. Operation at a survival level precludes the likelihood of well-defined tasks or job descriptions and such operation by the principal and teachers is in essence the acceptance of these generalized tasks and goals without question. They represent one way of meeting the organization's purpose.

Commitment to improvement in order to attain an effectiveness level reduces to considerations of how best to utilize personnel functions in redefining purposes, functions, subgoals, and tasks. In order to preclude goal distortion and goal displacement, the organization members must agree essentially that organization dimensions are the primary concern. Idiographic or individual dimensions must be defined relative to the organization demands. However, the conceptualization of personnel functions relates to the selection and development of members who enhance the chances of success in the improvement activities of the organization.

The more closely the behavior of the members approaches the behavior norms or expectations of the organization (the performance of assigned tasks which realize the subgoals and purposes of the organization), the greater the effectiveness of the organization. Effectiveness is the conjunction of expected behavior (the organization's demands) and the actual behavior (the individual's contribution and performance). The essential functions of organization expectations are to direct, to delineate, and to circumscribe personnel behavior in patterns that optimize organization goal achievement. Because the essential and undergirding parameters of these expectations are to set standards of desired behavior and to reduce behaviors which detract from effectiveness, the importance of personnel functions takes on ever increasing dimensions as the principal seeks to propel the elementary school toward an effective level of operation. Developing successively closer approximations between organization expectations and individual performances is a goal of personnel functions. If the selection function is well performed, it should be anticipated that expectations and performance will be in closer proximity than if selection is a haphazard procedure.

Efficiency: The Individual Demands

Internalization of the organization's expectations (demands) is necessary for the attainment of efficiency. If every member identified completely with the organization's expectations, exhibited absolute compatibility between his needs and his assigned role, and performed optimally his tasks, not only would the members attain efficiency but the organization would be an effective one. However, such utopian models do not correspond with reality. These models are based on the assumption that people prefer planning that has been done for them rather than with them. The matter of individual goals considers the fact that individuals evaluate their own positions in relation to the values of others and come to accept others' goals as their own. An individual enters an organization with a prior structure of preferences, or with a personality, which is the basis for the decisions he makes while he is a member. Thus, as

March and Simon observed, individual goals are not "given" for the organization, but can be varied both through recruitment procedures and through organizational practices.[3]

March and Simon presented four principal targets for identification which are available to an individual in an organization:

1. organizations external to the focal organization;
2. the focal organization itself (organization identification);
3. the work activities within the focal organization (task identification);
4. subgroups within the focal organization (subgroup identification).[4]

The first target suggested for identification is the least preferred one because extraorganizational identification introduces variables not related to organization. Development through personnel functions toward an effectiveness level is very difficult if this is the identification of very many of the members. Presthus' identification of the indifferent organization member illustrates the reasons that extraorganizational identification is not preferred or even desired.[5] The indifferent does his work, seeks nothing much, and leaves at the usual time each day. He is not interested in disturbing the status quo.

The other targets for identification are desirable ones and likely listed in order of preference from the organization viewpoint: organization identification, task identification, and subgroup identification. If the member identifies with the organization, he is perhaps a more valued member than if his principal identity is with a subgroup, depending essentially on the subgroup's goal-orientation. In the deployment of personnel functions toward an effectiveness level, members with organization identification would more likely assume ad hoc identity with tasks and subgroups than would subgroup members identify with task or organization levels.

Guba and Bidwell observed:

... There will always be a gap between expectations and needs in any real situation, for even the attempt to structure expectations congruent with needs of one role incumbent will produce results at least partially unsuitable for another incumbent. As a result, the administrator is always faced with the task of maintaining a balance between effectiveness and efficiency. The problem is to determine the extent to which effectiveness will be maximized

3. James C. March and H. A. Simon, *Organizations* (New York: John Wiley & Sons, 1958), p. 65.
4. *Ibid.*, p. 65.
5. Robert Presthus, *The Organizational Society* (New York: Alfred A. Knopf, 1962), Chapter 7, pp. 205–256.

at the expense of efficiency or vice versa. Clearly, it is through this effectiveness-efficiency relationship that the problem of staff motivation (expectation-needs congruence) can be approached.[6]

The interrelationships of effectiveness, efficiency, and satisfaction in organizations are shown in Figure 10–2. These interrelationships were summarized by Guba and Bidwell:

1. Effectiveness refers to congruence between expectations for behavior (role) and actual behavior.
2. Efficiency refers to congruence between an individual's needs and his behavior.
3. Satisfaction refers to congruence between expectations and needs.
4. A person in a given role may be effective yet inefficient; efficient yet ineffective; and satisfied while both ineffective and inefficient.[7]

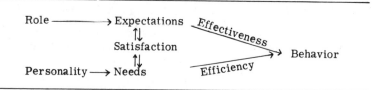

Figure 10-2. Interrelationships Among Effectiveness, Efficiency, and Satisfaction

Many of the incentives for deriving effective performance or behavior are tangibles, such as salary increments and promotions, which are essentially power controls of superordinates. These external incentives have long been considered as the "carrot and stick" toward job satisfaction. Vroom suggests that successful task performance may represent a source of satisfaction and unsuccessful task performance a source of dissatisfaction, independent of external mediated consequences of performance.[8] Thus, persons vary in the strength of their need for achievement which is defined as a "predisposition to gain satisfaction from success in competition with some standard of excellence."[9]

6. Egon G. Guba and Charles E. Bidwell, *Administrative Relationships* (Chicago: Midwest Administration Center, University of Chicago, 1957), p. 9.
7. *Ibid.*, p. 8.
8. Victor A. Vroom, "Some Psychological Aspects of Organizational Control," in W. W. Cooper, H. J. Leavitt, and M. W. Shelly II (eds.), *New Perspectives in Organization Research* (New York: John Wiley & Sons, 1964), p. 80.
9. *Ibid.*, p. 80.

Vroom's conceptualization of satisfaction sources appears particularly relevant for the effective elementary school principal who is seeking satisfied members who are both effective and efficient. At no time should the concepts of satisfaction, effectiveness, and efficiency be conceived as discrete variables as an are/are not dichotomy. In reality, all three concepts are at best approximations. It is by careful and diligent deployment of the tasks of personnel functions that the elementary school principal attempts to select and to develop satisfied, effective, and efficient organization members.

PERSONNEL FUNCTIONS

There are at least eight major tasks identifiable in the vast area of personnel functions. In sequence, they are recruitment, selection, nomination, orientation, in-service development, coordination, evaluation, and retention. These eight tasks of personnel functions may be assigned to the elementary school principalship or shared in certain aspects with central office superordinates. However, the general trend of development is greater involvement in these tasks for the elementary school principal. This development is mandatory for schools and administrators seeking effectiveness levels of operation. But, this development is also somewhat of a dilemma-producer because the elementary school principal can anticipate a more exacting evaluation of his own performance when he exerts an active role in personnel functions.

Recruitment as a Personnel Function

Recruitment of personnel is probably the most likely one of the eight tasks which will be initially and mainly retained at the central office level. This observation is particularly true for large school districts and even more so in school districts which recognize that teacher behavior is an economic behavior. A skillful teacher may have tendencies of mobility. He has but one commodity that possesses economic value, and that is his service to a school which needs his specialty. Therefore, a central office personnel recruitment officer frequently is assigned the task of traveling to various teacher-training universities to recruit the most promising candidates.

After the most promising candidates have been identified or cleared by the central office recruiting official, the elementary school principal is frequently given access to these candidates and in essence recruits for his own school from the list. This arrangement is an economic necessity because sending all principals on a recruiting tour would not only be prohibitive financially but also a duplication of effort.

Recruitment by a central office official can be conducted as a survival operation or as an effectiveness operation. The central office recruiter must know what teachers and specializations are needed, and this information has to come from the principals. Under the conditions of an effectiveness level of operation, recruitment by a single representative will have already done much of the usual and necessary screening. Thus the elementary school principal has essentially a select list from which to recruit his teachers. It is not difficult to conceptualize conditions at the survival level of operation.

Recruitment is an important personnel function. Most contacts are made with a university or college placement officer. The placement officer is essentially an agent for all the teachers who have active credentials on file—inexperienced as well as experienced teachers. Until the placement officer is satisfied that the school district recruiter is from a "good" school district with bona fide offers and competitive ones, there is very little recruitment possible. Development of needs and likely selection criteria is a required task shared by the central office recruitment official and the principals. To illustrate the importance of personnel functions in general and of recruitment in particular, note that a considerable amount of recruiting is done in November for the next school year. Long-range anticipation of actual needs for personnel requires that the elementary school principal know his organization and its member incumbents far better than has been true for any past period.

Recruitment of paraprofessional personnel is not a lot different from that of professional personnel, except it tends to be more local in nature. It may be anticipated that recruitment of paraprofessional personnel will reside largely with the elementary school principal. As an elementary school develops its program and surpasses the survival model of operation, it would be anticipated that there will be unique requirements for paraprofessional personnel more competently determined by the elementary school principal than by the more removed central office personnel.

Many of the larger school districts maintain a file of applications and frequently notify an applicant that an opening for his specialty may be a year away. Listing vacancies with placement offices in selected colleges and universities frequently alerts candidates who take the initiative of contact.

Selection and Nomination as Personnel Functions

If ever there were a problem without likely "correct" answers, selection of personnel would certainly qualify. Transcripts and personal recommendations typical of a teacher's credentials do not provide much evidence of how or how well that teacher will behave or perform in a given school and its environment. It has been known that a "successful" teacher in one school has performed "unsuccessfully" in another school, and conversely; but it is not *a priori* knowledge.

Some school districts still tend to exhibit a passive approach to personnel recruitment and selection. The officials notify placement offices of vacancies and then wait for applicants. This method does not ensure the most desirable candidates from which to select. With increasing stress on specialization and on operation at an effectiveness level, recruitment and selection must become active and demanding. We used to seek a fifth-grade teacher more or less on the untested premise that all of them were the same; that is, they were fifth-grade teachers. We know better now and have gone farther in seeking specialization of one kind or another and special characteristics within the general nomenclature of fifth-grade teacher. If teaming is practiced, specialization of one sort or another is immediately anticipated; however, even in less extreme structures, specialization is sought if only that the new member possess some extra interest or sophistication in a given area, for example, social studies, science, or language arts.

An important aspect of selection is the development of an accurate definition or description of the position. It is now apparent that every organization has a set or sets of norms for behavior control of individuals and groups. The job description should attempt to clarify the organization's goals and to delineate the task expectations for the position. A job description consists of two dimensions, and both of them are of considerable interest to the candidate or potential organization member.

One dimension is the job or position—the tasks to be performed by the member. Essentially these tasks represent sets of normative behavior and are called expectations. If they are internalized by the individual members and carried out, they contribute to the "successful" accomplishment of the organization's effectiveness model goals.

The second dimension of the job description includes the member benefits or the inducements. Member benefits are as much a part of a job description as is the other dimension which represents the education program means and ends. A job description is a list of inducements offered by the organization. The candidate or potential member weighs the expectations against the benefits and "selects" the organization for membership when the two dimensions of inducement are satisfactory to him. Likely the numerous cases of member dissatisfactions and failure to attain the organization's expectations at evaluation and retention time stem from inaccurate or incomplete job descriptions at the outset, or are due to a lack of real correspondence between the organization's expectations and the individual's needs-dispositions.

These job descriptions should encompass the presently conceived role and position and also the likely future aspects. If a vacancy in the fifth-grade level is being filled, the present organization structure may require or seek a teacher who is experienced in departmentalized teaching only. However, if a more sophisticated team approach or a nongraded organization structure is anticipated in a short time, this information ought to be included as part of the job description.

If the school district's personnel policies and practices require specific professional growth in graduate work, travel, or in other ways, this information ought to be considered as part of the job description. The more completely the expectations and inducements are delineated, the less the chance of having a disillusioned and dissatisfied teacher later when these facts are disclosed. The development of the job description will likely be a shared responsibility of the central office personnel staff and of the elementary school principal who will add the peculiarities of given requirements in a particular instance.

Certain items of information are sought from the candidate or potential member, in addition to the usual placement credentials. These items of personal information frequently include age; general health; experience; appearance; general knowledge; communication skills; motivations; interests; mental health; general rapport with pupils, faculty members, and community members. Granting that this information can be obtained in one way or another, some of it is difficult to assess. The school district personnel in charge of personnel functions, including the elementary school principal, must establish some acceptable criteria. Is a statement by the candidate asserting good mental health sufficient evidence?

Larger school districts may resort to some of the more sophisticated information-yielding processes and procedures, although they are not necessarily limited to the larger districts. Structured interviews, both individual and group; performance tests; written examinations; and rating scales are available or may be developed. But even with these processes and procedures, the elementary school principal who is involved in this aspect of personnel functions is still hard-pressed to make a final judgment without a margin of error.

Selection can and should be viewed from the candidate's side of the process also. A carefully delineated and delimited job description which sets forth the description of the position and role expectations can be handed to the candidate. The question asked the candidate is essentially: "Here is what we expect and demand of the person in this position, are you willing to place your professional career in this position?" If the candidate knows that evaluation and retention are based on these expectations, there is every likelihood to assume that the competent candidate will be the most persistent in being the selected one.

Personnel functions and specifically the matter of selection are nothing more or less than matching the right person and the right job. While a perfect record of selecting teachers should not be anticipated even with the best procedures, there is every reason to believe that the record can be much improved. Even the involvement of the elementary school principal as the person who makes the decision of selection has an upgrading effect on the process.

As illustrated by Table 10–1, the degree of involvement in the selec-

Table 10-1. Role of the Principal in selecting Faculty

| | | School System Enrollment | | |
Action	% of Total Sample	Over 25,000	3,000 to 24,999	300 to 2,999
Nothing to say	38.5%	46.8%	29.7%	28.2%
Accept-reject among candidates	32.7	34.4	33.8	24.7
Examine and recommend	25.2	14.4	27.8	40.3
Employ without central office	3.6	1.5	3.7	6.8

SOURCE: The Elementary School Principalship, Department of Elementary School Principals, National Education Association, 1968, p. 57.

tion decision varies greatly with a large percentage of principals having nothing to say about the selection of staff members. The table represents the findings of a survey conducted by the Department of Elementary School Principals that included responses from 1,841 principals. In the large systems relatively more elementary principals have nothing to say about the selection of teachers. In the smaller systems, a larger proportion of principals have the opportunity to state qualifications, examine applicants, and recommend those to be employed. This mode of operation is the one supported by administrative theory.

Selection should be tantamount to nomination and appointment, even though official appointment legally rests with the board of education. Generally, the practice is for the board of education to appoint the nominated candidate upon the recommendation of the superintendent who has been informed of the selection decision by the elementary school principal.

The selection function should include also the notification of candidates who are not selected. Sometimes their applications are desired for the district's personnel file. It is a good practice to inform the non-selected candidates of this procedure and to obtain their permission because they may or may not be interested in being considered at another time. This is a particularly good method for developing a "stockpile" of desirable candidates. If the school district is operating at an effectiveness level, the most desirable candidates will likely hope to be considered at a future time.

Orientation as a Personnel Function

The act of appointment of the selected candidate represents both a culminating activity and a beginning activity, if personnel functions are given serious consideration in the public school enterprise. With the act of appointment and the ensuing acceptance by the candidate, survival of the organization is essentially assured; a person has been placed in a position. School will keep, as the old adage states. Hopefully, this observation is a generalized oversimplification, especially if the selection process has been carefully planned and executed.

Even the best qualified teacher deserves a careful and meaningful orientation to the organization and its expectations. Orientation of new members is not a one-session-half-day affair. First of all, even for experienced teachers, the new school represents a new environment, new colleagues, new organization demands and expectations. No matter how explicitly these matters are stated in the job description and the interviews, they all take on added dimensions when the new teacher reports for work.

School policies, practices, goals, leadership patterns, organization communication structure, resource allocation, even community taboos or mores are important first-order concerns for a newly arrived oganization member. Orientation sessions are comprised of what has been, is, and what will likely be insofar as the role of the elementary school is concerned. In short, orientation is a presentation designed to provide the new member with an "immediate adjustment" to his new environment.

The beginning of the school term brings together the members of the faculty. Is it a group with relatively common purposes, and are these purposes common to the organization's administrators? Does the faculty appear to possess cohesiveness? Is the organization held together by consensus or coercion? Autonomy is a concern of the new teacher; every organization member tends to "see" the organization with himself as the focal point or center of the organization. Further, does the school itself tend to possess any autonomy—to develop and to pursue subgoals and tasks which will enhance its effectiveness? Performance will be evaluated, but by whom and on what bases? Where do the members of the organization plan to implement improvements, and what part does an individual have in the process? Questions of these kinds are of vital concern to the new member. And even though they may have been discussed in the selection interviews, they now possess a different imperativeness.

Orientation sessions will involve the new members principally; however, inclusion of the other members appears to enhance the adjustment to organization expectations for the newcomers. Orientation sessions are not to be designed for the principal to be the sole actor. Much of the total orientation adjustment-integration is enhanced when the elementary school principal and the teachers share in it. The principal has the major responsibility, but it cannot be successful if he fails to delegate relevant aspects of it.

Just where orientation ends, if ever, and in-service development begins is a moot concern. Essentially both personnel functions are continuous rather than discrete entities. The adjustment-integration concepts generated from Getzels' social process model suggest one way of categorizing these two functions. Adjustment is a phenomenon of the nomothetic or organization dimension wherein an individual exhibits adjustment to the extent that his behavior is compatible with the role expectations. Orientation is an adjustment effort to "catch up" the new members with the other members to provide a common starting point. At first consideration, it may appear that these activities are associated with the preschool activities, but reflection reveals that this is only an important part of orientation. Orientation may be viewed as the presentation of a good outline or overview with critical areas developed early. Orientation is member-directed in the sense that the efforts are designed to socialize the new member's personality, or to preclude unanticipated responses to role.

In-service development is explained as integration which is associated with the idiographic dimension. The integrated individual is one whose behavior is compatible with his needs-disposition. In-service development may be member-directed, but more likely it will utilize the members indirectly with curriculum matters the focus—all those tasks which contribute to organization effectiveness.

In-service Development as a Personnel Function

The importance of in-service programs as a personnel function was lucidly demonstrated in the decade of Sputnik-inspired changes. Far too many schools began to implement changes and innovations without due regard to the organization members. For example, some elementary schools began to teach the "new math," but the teachers had not been instructed, retrained, or even retooled to do the job.

In-service development of both teachers and programs is a personnel function which may have school-district-wide activities as well as activities within a given school or attendance center. Priorities have to be established, schedules developed, participation made meaningful and desirable—all of which lead to a common goal. If there is a district-wide in-service project, it is possible that a given elementary school faculty may engage in it also locally in greater depth. One important principle is to keep away from too much diversity. Closed circuit television has made possible some large scale in-service programing which was prohibitive prior to closed circuit television. One large district conducted a year-long in-service program for its elementary school teachers preparing them for the "new math" program which was implemented the following year.

Such large scale in-service activities are being undertaken via television by a number of school districts cooperating. There are a number of advantages to consider when a common interest, such as preparation for the "new math," is prevalent among school districts. Costs are reduced. Experts can be obtained. Exchange discussions can be arranged in one way or another. The author participated in a six-district in-service program in which all the teachers of a given grade level or subject area met for discussion and exchange of information with expert consultants.

But there are many single organization in-service aspects which must not be overlooked if organization effectiveness is to be realized. Each elementary school tends to have unique or peculiar problems which can be satisfactorily resolved only at the single organization level. The needs and abilities of the pupils and of the organization members document this "local" need. There are single organization activities and projects which may involve all the members simultaneously, but much of the in-service development involves the members in groups, committees, and even a single individual working on some problem. Consultants and resources are made available as the need arises. Program supervision and evaluation, developed in Chapter 8, are particularly relevant to in-service programs within the elementary school.

Whether district-wide or "local" and whether teacher-directed or subject-matter directed, the success of in-service development will depend in part upon certain general considerations. The elementary school principal has the responsibility of ascertaining the appropriateness for his organization members, as their chief spokesman. Specifically the features or characteristics of in-service programing should embrace certain minimal considerations.

1. Any in-service program should be designed to improve teacher competence whether the mode is direct or indirect. The organization purpose and subgoal improvement and realization represent the end sought, but the members are the instruments through which this end becomes a reality. If this consideration is not clear to the teachers and others, active participation is not likely.

2. An atmosphere conducive to inquiry and search is important. Both self-evaluation and program evaluation become meaningful and useful by testing objectively the validity of ongoing programs and procedures. On the basis of research data, new directions, changes, and methodologies take on full meaning. Continuation of ongoing programs should be justified by these processes also.

3. Group and individual projects should be encouraged and planned.

Organization members from one school or several should be encouraged to develop research-oriented studies designed to provide more knowledge relating to the ongoing programs. There are many activities and programs, emanating from the federally subsidized interests and the rash of innovations, which lend themselves to this kind of scrutiny.

4. Avoid trivia. Nothing will succeed in scuttling an in-service program so well as the introduction of trivia. The definition of what is or is not trivia must be viewed from the reference point of the participants —the teachers.

5. Schedule in-service programs at times when they will do the most good. Scheduling is a major deterrent to in-service program development. Every Monday 15 minutes after the pupils are dismissed is not generally the most productive time. Just what schedule is best is a local determination, but immediately after pupil dismissal brings together a group of tired, unreceptive teachers. The utilization of paraprofessionals and special teachers in music, art, and physical education may make possible some in-service periods.

One important basic principle is a commitment to in-service programing by the board of education. Far too many school districts have attempted to develop an in-service program by "adding it on," without providing a calendar and a contract extending the period of compensated service to the district. In-service programs can begin prior to the opening of school; extra days can be set aside during the year, and even carry over into the days immediately after the school term ends for the pupils. One group of six school districts in an intermediate school district undertook a five-year plan. In the first year, two days preceding the school term, one day in each quarter, one day between semesters, and a day after the term closed were scheduled for the planned in-service program, in addition to the preschool programs of the individual schools. One goal was to establish a longer school service calendar for the teachers with remuneration reflecting the extended school year. The effect was to discern similar calendars among the participating districts. They began and concluded the extended school year on the same dates. The days between semesters increased and were the same among the districts. But other periods within the school year began to reflect the local nature of in-service programing.

Effective in-service programs are judged effective from the point of view of what they accomplish through the individual teachers for a given school. If this premise is accepted generally, then the principal emphasis on in-service program development must focus on the individual school and its needs. A system of communication is essential because duplication of certain efforts can be identified. If several individual schools possess a common problem or interest, forces can conceivably be united. How district-wide communication can be implemented and maintained will vary from one district to another. An all-administrator/supervisor cabinet works well in some districts. Other districts have effected successful communication with teacher committees. Someone in the central office generally serves on these committees to ensure continuity and to disseminate the proceedings.

Coordination as a Personnel Function

Coordination is a category in Urwick's POSDCORB administration classification schema. (See Chapters 1, 5, and 11.) He defined coordination as the "all important duty of interrelating the various parts of the work." [10] Gulick suggested that if an organization requires continual resort to special coordinating devices in the discharge of its regular activities, then something is wrong with the organization.[11] A decade and a half later, Newman observed: "In administration, coordination deals with synchronizing and unifying the actions of a group of people. A coordinated operation is one in which the activities of the employees are harmonious, dovetailed and integrated toward a common goal." [12]

The elementary school is characterized by some form of division of labor. The simplest form is the self-contained classroom structure. With specialization making phenomenal inroads in public education, the complexities of division of labor are expanding at essentially exponential rates. Although the authors quoted were not addressing coordination to the public school enterprise, the definitions and discussions are appropriate. As a concept for administration, coordination possesses at least two applications at the elementary school level. The concept of coordination is relevant for the analysis of external functions whereby the development and maintenance of optimum relationships with its environment—other schools and the many groups in the community—are a consideration. The second application of the concept of coordination is to person-

10. Luther Gulick, "Notes on the Theory of Organization," in L. Gulick and L. Urwick (eds.), *Papers on the Science of Administration* (New York: Institute of Public Administration, 1937), p. 13.

11. *Ibid.,* p. 26.

12. William H. Newman, *Administrative Action* (Englewood Cliffs, N.J.: Prentice-Hall, 1951), p. 340.

nel functions and is internal. This application is task coordination or the assignment of task responsibilities to persons and has as its purpose the synchronization of activities and events to enhance work flow in the organization. Elementary school tasks can be classified into three general categories: (1) completed tasks, calling for some kind of culminating event; (2) ongoing tasks, which are the here-and-now activities; (3) future tasks, which develop from ongoing tasks and are characterized by still other coordinating events and activities. Reduced to its simplest form, coordination amounts to keeping the school in existence, but this observation implies operation at only the level of survival.

The elementary school principal who gets bogged down in the administrivia of survival operations is likely the hierarchical head of an organization which requires continual resort to special coordinating devices. This type of coordination seems never to get beyond the here-and-now operations with each succeeding day putting the organization in greater arrears.

There is, and apparently always will be, the here-and-now coordinating activities for the elementary school principal. Materials, supplies, ETV schedule synchronization, shared facilities and media scheduling, and making certain that necessary arrangements have been affirmed are a few examples. It would be inaccurate to assert that these activities are mere routine because they are important aspects of coordination at the effectiveness level. They do, however, need to be routinized, and many of them can be delegated to the principal's clerical personnel. The main concern is that they do not become the principal's major time-consumers.

When the elementary school is functioning at the effectiveness level, there are certain characteristics observable. Both delegation (the act or activity) and responsibility (the right to make decisions) are assigned to personnel at appropriate levels in a manner that neither hinders nor postpones operation. No one seems to get in another person's way; no activity comes into conflict with another for time, place, or priority. The tasks designed to satisfy subgoals at one grade level or equivalency in grouping arrangements prepare the pupils for the next step and so on. The work of the organization flows; structure and function assignment are comfortable and natural. The members of the organization have internalized the organization procedures and the agreed upon expectations. In essence there is communication, but some of it took place during the orientation sessions and continued into the in-service development programs.

Smith defined communication as "the reciprocal exchange of signals," and explained communication as a nonlinear type.

I emphasize reciprocity here in order to distinguish the human and social approach to communication from the engineering and physical approach to communication. The mathematical theory of communication conceives of messages originating with a sender and a receiver. That theory presents a linear model: the message goes from A to B. The social model we need is not a thing of straight lines. Instead it is something round and curvy. Human communication is more circular and helical because it involves interaction and feedback between sender and receiver. In a word, repicrocity.[13]

The mathematical theory of linearity was discussed as one of two models with relevance for coordination by Dahl and Lindblom.[14] They identified it as a leader model in which the work flow and the activity flow are coordinated from a central source—likely the principal. The underlying presumption is that perhaps some but not all the members of the organization are sensitivized to cues or signals or that they are not all capable of making the automatic and appropriate response to the cue. Thus, rather than to take chances of misinterpreted cues and inappropriate responses, coordination is vested in a central position.

They discussed the second model also as one of reciprocity in which work flow and activity flow are coordinated by cues and signals. It presumes that every organization member is sensitivized and "automatically" responds to the cues and that upon receiving the cue makes the appropriate response. This desirable state of awareness does not always obtain. Kaufman noted that the models possess limitations and strengths:

. . . channels of distribution often break down when regulated exclusively by reciprocal methods. Information is not always distributed, communications are often incomplete and ambiguous and contradictory. The timing of flow permits the accumulation of excess materials in some places, shortages of the same materials in others. Things and messages go to the wrong people, generate the wrong actions. People undo each other's work, impede each other. The basic processes are all jeopardized.

A leader, or a leadership group, devoting time specifically to the detection of such situations and to the issuance of messages that inhibit some actions, encourage others, slow some down, speed up others, change the directions and intensities of flow, open new channels, and so on, can often end block-

13. Alfred G. Smith, *Communication and Status* (Eugene, Ore.: University of Oregon, Center for the Advanced Study of Educational Administration, 1966), p. 3.

14. R. A. Dahl and C. E. Lindblom, *Politics, Economics, and Welfare* (New York: Harper & Row, 1953), pp. 357 ff.

ages, prevent jams, and thus facilitate the vigorous performance of the basic processes. . . .[15]

The size of the organization, that is, the number of members and divisions of labor, is an important variable but not the only one in the consideration of a communication model for coordinating the activities of the elementary school. The leader model is a tendency of an organization with positions of graded authority, such as the elementary school. The elementary school principal will have to seek a mix of the two models appropriate to his school. Neither model alone is sufficient for ensuring effective communication and effective coordination. The members of the organization represent another variable for consideration. If the two models represent the two extremes of a continuum, then the elementary school principal will discover the point of effective communication and coordination lying somewhere between the two points. As the organization approaches the effectiveness level, it can be anticipated that the point of effective coordination will move toward the reciprocity model.

Haskins, writing of organizations other than those in the system of public education, discussed a relevant conceptualization for coordination as a personnel function. ". . . It is far too easy to identify the organized group with the members who compose it. It is far too easy to forget that the very essence of creativeness must be with the individual as contrasted with the group." [16]

Obviously there are uses for communication based on both models in the elementary school, and the effective principal will capitalize on both of them. With Haskins' conceptualization, the elementary school principal will be cognizant of the fact that leadership is not ideally aimed at the development of monolithic organizations. Rather, leadership is utilized to develop the individual members toward patterns of effective behavior and for effective coordination.

Evaluation and Retention as Personnel Functions

Evaluation as a personnel function has a high-frequency utilization in discussions and literature relating to public education. Just what it is and how it is made operative and for what real purposes are not very

15. Herbert Kaufman, "Why Organizations Behave as They Do: An Outline of a Theory," in *Administrative Theory* (Austin, Tex.: University of Texas, 1961), p. 46.
16. Caryl P. Haskins, "Society and Scientific Research," *Bulletin of the Atomic Scientists,* Vol. 16 (May, 1960), p. 150.

clearly delineated. According to superintendents queried in a National Education Association survey, the chief purpose of evaluation is the improvement of instruction.[17] Whether teacher evaluation is conducted as a means toward program effectiveness or as the end of evaluating the teacher per se is not always clearly delineated. Evaluation of programs and their accomplishments and evaluation of the organization members do appear as high priority tasks of the elementary school principal, but some of these tasks are also assigned as functions of central office supervisory personnel in many articles—and in practice. Until recently much of this evaluation of teaching personnel was done by a district supervisor, and more frequently than not the principal occupied a subordinate role in the task. The practice has not been eliminated entirely, and very likely there may remain a need for some shared responsibility, especially for evaluation of programs and their outcomes. The principal is more and more frequently assuming the primary responsibility for evaluation because it is recognized now as an important part of the personnel functions and of the whole program.

The infrequency of contacts with a teacher by a district supervisor made evaluation of teachers a shallow and, far too frequently, an inequitable event. Decisions were based on hasty generalizations. It was both possible and probable for effective teachers to be dismissed and for ineffective teachers to be retained.

If the elementary school is to attain an effectiveness level, then evaluation must be a meaningful, valid, and defensible process. Evaluation is not a discrete function to be done once or twice a year, but rather it is an integral process in the mix of activities and procedures in personnel functions which are vital aspects of the elementary school program. Its assignment to the elementary school principal to be utilized by him and his faculty members toward the attainment of organization effectiveness is a requisite of personnel functions.

The conceptualization of evaluation is preferred over the older concepts of "supervision." Supervision was used to describe the observation of the teacher to determine if the teacher was exhibiting behaviors which met the expected norms of the organization. Supervision in this sense was personnel management, and the norms of expected behavior tended to be those of the supervisor. To presume that this kind of evalua-

---

17. National Education Association, Research Division, *Evaluation of Classroom Teachers, Research Report 1964 R14* (Washington, D.C.: the Association, October, 1964).

tive observation could be done by a district supervisor was indeed a narrow and unrealistic conceptualization.

Determination of satisfactory accomplishment of the organization's purposes certainly includes the performance or behavior of the teachers, but this performance must be related to other variables, as delineated in Chapter 8. Considerations of the clients, the nature of the program and its stage of development, evaluation of task accomplishment toward previously designated subgoals and purposes are obviously personnel functions calling for activities and involvement far beyond the narrow concept of observing the teacher teaching. Evaluation is a continuous process, in interaction with other variables and activities, and to be effective it must include all members of the organization who have a role in the functions of the organization. Methods of evaluation are many, but they should all contribute to reliable, valid, and objective determinations of accomplishment, behavior, and change. Evaluation of individuals and groups of teachers requires consideration of subtasks, role expectations, and the technological tools available and used. Provisions for group and individual self-evaluation, using rating-scale instruments and followup techniques, are important parts of evaluation.

One of the realities of membership in the elementary school is the requirement of an official personnel individual performance report for the purposes of retention and reward. The effective elementary school principal formulates his evaluation of individual members out of the continuing activities of organization and program evaluation. Thus, a realistic evaluation of individuals based on continuing observations results and contrasts with the single observation typified by the older external supervisory observation-evaluation of the survival-type model.

An important product of evaluation as a personnel function at an effectiveness level is the opportunity to confer with individual members on matters of observed behavior as it relates to expectations. This process, as individual in-service projects, effects modifications toward effectiveness and eliminates cases of ineffective performance before they have an opportunity to become incurable serious dysfunctions.

PERSONNEL FUNCTIONS AND CHANGING FOR AN IMPROVED EDUCATION PROGRAM

The personnel functions which have been described as internal processes of an effective elementary school and which, both ideally and realistically, involve the principal and the other organization members are not discrete activities and events. They are rather a coordinated operation "in which the activities of the employees are harmonious, dovetailed, and integrated toward a common goal." [18]

Two models, a survival type and an effectiveness type, were developed to demonstrate the essential importance of personnel functions in the elementary school. The extent of success or failure in realizing the goals and subgoals through satisfactory task delineation and accomplishment is determined in a large measure by the personnel within the school. Striving to exceed a survival model operation is a behavior expected of the elementary school principal; but the effectiveness model does not "just happen," nor is it the result of the efforts of the principal alone. The organization members must come to essential agreement on purposes (education program ends and member benefits), subgoals and tasks; on the allocation of resources, and on priorities. Conscious efforts to attain effectiveness require decision making above the *satisficing* level which does not seek the one best alternative of choice but merely seeks an alternative which will continue existence.

Concern for the people variable has, more frequently than not, ignored the intense interaction of other organization variables. In recent years, the literature relating to changing for improvement in organization effectiveness has almost exclusively aimed at individuals and groups in organizations. However, there is an increasing awareness of these interaction variables as well as an awareness of a redistribution of power among the members. Coffey and Golden [19]; Ginzberg and Reilly [20]; Lawrence [21]; Lippitt, Watson, and Westley [22]; Bennis, Benne, and Chin [23]; Guest [24];

18. Newman, *op. cit.*
19. Hubert S. Coffey and William P. Golden, Jr., "Psychology of Change Within an Institution," in *In-service Education of Teachers, Supervisors, and Administrators, Fifty-sixth Yearbook of the National Society for the Study of Education, Part I* (Chicago: University of Chicago Press, 1957).
20. Eli Ginzberg and Ewing W. Reilly, *Effective Change in Large Organizations* (New York: Columbia University Press, 1957).
21. P. R. Lawrence, *The Changing of Organizational Behavior Patterns* (Boston: Harvard University, Graduate School of Business Administration, Division of Research, 1958).
22. Ronald Lippitt, Jeanne Watson, and Bruce Westley, *The Dynamics of Planned Change* (New York: Harcourt, Brace, and Co., 1958).
23. Warren G. Bennis, Kenneth Benne, and Robert Chin, *The Planning of Change* (New York: Holt, Rinehart and Winston, 1962).
24. R. H. Guest, *Organizational Change: The Effect of Successful Leadership* (Homewood, Ill.: the Dorsey Press, 1962).

Blau and Scott [25]; and Katz and Kahn [26] reveal the tendency to focus the process of change on the organization members.

In this chapter, the eight major tasks identified as personnel functions, from recruitment through retention, have been viewed as integrated functions essential to education program effectiveness. Implicit in all of them is the recognition of the specialization for teaching in the sense of having greater ability and awareness in the mix of technology, subject matter, and behavior psychology. This meaning of specialization is far more appropriate than the one so frequently projected in which the teacher is characterized as having a deep and intense knowledge of a particular narrow area.

Recognizing the differences between specialization for teaching and specialization for administration permits deliberation and collaboration in the elementary school which have not been characteristics of personnel functions when the organization structure was explained on the principles of a single line hierarchy.

Out of this new awareness of specializations emerge two vital variables for the elementary school principal as he seeks organization effectiveness which is essentially based on a generalized commitment to changing for improvement. One variable is the scarcely explored potential of personnel functions within the parameters of specialization. The second relates to the ever increasing body of knowledge about individual and group psychology. The principal's leadership and success hinge upon his ability to effect with these variables the unique mix appropriate to his organization and its individual members.

Concluding Comment

Berenda's observations and comments serve well as a concluding statement for those administrators who have responsibility to the teachers and pupils in the elementary school.

Educational administration places a special burden upon the administrator. ... To be an educational administrator without being a traitor to education is a difficult art indeed. It demands the highest courage, sensitivity, and insight. One must have the courage to encourage creativity in the teacher, who is the final source of new ideas for all good teaching, and to run the risks that inevitably go with that sort of teaching, and to take the respon-

25. Peter M. Blau and W. Richard Scott, *Formal Organizations* (San Francisco, Calif.: Chandler Publishing Co., 1962).

26. Daniel Katz and Robert L. Kahn, *The Social Psychology of Organizations* (New York: John Wiley & Sons, 1966).

sibilities of supporting such teachers against the consequent outcries that sometimes come from society, parents, and legislatures. . . .

. . . it is well to emphasize that what we administer is some program *through people.* And the programs depend for their origination and implementation upon people. Advice and decision are made by people. Plans and purposes are generated by people. . . . Efficiency is good only so far as it does not override the human values of personhood. And ultimately the highest efficiency is obtained when the administrator is deeply sensitive to the persons under his administration. We operate within social organizations whose basic unit is men. The administrator must help to establish and maintain whatever creativity can be encouraged within his organization. New ideas that can help the efficiency of the organization can come from the individuals that compose the organization and not merely from outside "efficiency experts." New ideas are best generated in an atmosphere of cooperation, and cooperation itself emerges most often under an administrator who respects and encourages the personhood of the people working under his direction. . . . And, finally, there is the basic philosophical question we must all keep in mind: of what ultimate use is efficiency in any organization, if dehumanization and mechanization of man are its outcomes? [27]

Professional-like career teachers, aided by paraprofessionals, are the key to development of an effective elementary school; this is the idiographic or member dimension. But an effective elementary school is one which has also delineated and defined the nomothetic or organization's demands. The need for total involvement of the elementary school principal in all of the personnel functions is obvious because the organization moves toward effectiveness when the members' demands are essentially an internalization of the organization's expectations.

27. Carleton W. Berenda, "What is Man?" in R. E. Ohm and W. G. Monahan (eds.), *Educational Administration—Philosophy in Action* (Norman, Okla.: the College of Education, the University of Oklahoma and the University Council for Educational Administration, 1965), pp. 17–18.

REFERENCES

Boguslaw, Robert, *The New Utopians* (Englewood Cliffs, N.J.: Prentice-Hall, 1965).

Cooper, W. W., H. J. Leavitt, and M. W. Shelly II (eds.), *New Perspectives in Organization Research* (New York: John Wiley & Sons, 1964).

Culbertson, Jack A., and Stephen P. Hencley (eds.), *Educational Research: New Perspectives* (Danville, Ill.: the Interstate Printers and Publishers, 1963).

Davis, Donald E., and Neal C. Nickerson, *Critical Issues in School Personnel Administration* (Chicago: Rand McNally, 1968).

Griffiths, Daniel, *et al., Organizing Schools for Effective Education* (Danville, Ill.: the Interstate Printers and Publishers, 1962).

Hodgkinson, Harold L., *Education, Interaction, and Social Change* (Englewood Cliffs, N.J.: Prentice-Hall, 1967).

Katz, Daniel, and Robert L. Kahn, *The Social Psychology of Organizations* (New York: John Wiley & Sons, 1966).

Lichtenberger, Allen R., and Richard J. Penrod, *Staff Accounting for Local and State School Systems* (Washington, D.C.: U.S. Government Printing Office, 1965).

Presthus, Robert V., *The Organizational Society: An Analysis and a Theory* (New York: Alfred A. Knopf, 1962).

Simon, Herbert A., *Administrative Behavior* (New York: Macmillan, 1959).

Part IV

Management and Operations

Chapter 11

ELEMENTARY SCHOOL
MANAGEMENT FUNCTIONS

M AKING certain that school keeps and meets the day-to-day demands on it is one way of describing the elementary school office and its functions. Such a description is appropriate for describing an elementary school which is functioning at a survival level. The personnel in the school office operate on a day-to-day or crisis-to-crisis basis. Survival operation precludes the opportunity of looking beyond the here-and-now operations.

Any attempt to attain an effectiveness level of operation reveals this conceptualization as grossly inadequate. The effective elementary school office is the school's nerve center and has but one *raison d'être,* which is service or meeting demands. The demands are numerous and varied, emanating from the organization, the members, the clients, and the environments of the elementary school. The characteristic which distinguishes between the survival level and the effectiveness level is that the demands and services are anticipated ones at the effectiveness level.

To demonstrate the essential functions of the elementary school office and their role in the total organization as effectiveness is sought is the purpose of this chapter. Organization effectiveness is impossible until the school office is effective. The functions of the school office and the performance tasks serve to communicate, to expedite, and to coordinate in ways to maximize the work flow and activity flow of the organization.

Historically, the elementary school office has exhibited characteristics common to the survival model. Efficiency, as advocated by Taylor's disciples, was the apparent goal. "Saving money" seemed to be the operating principle, rather than seeking the optimum return or benefits from an investment of that which could be made available. Callahan described succinctly the efficiency era and demonstrated the lingering and persistent aspects of misapplication of the principles of efficiency.[1]

But even today the elementary schools reveal a wide range of development of services. While size of the school is one determinant in the provision and development of services; it is not, in any sense, the most important one. The attitude and role interpretation of the principal have a great deal of bearing upon the scope of services and their organization structure. There are certain functions and tasks which are basic and which represent the minimum requirements of the survival model of operation as developed by Etzioni.[2] (See Chapters 8 and 10.) Failure to provide or to perform them in the school office would cause the organization to cease operating, or at least certainly curtail its normal operation. Some of the tasks to be performed are not continuing activities, but once performed they tend to be self-sustaining. Room and teacher assignments, pupil assignment to sections or classrooms, schedules for special programs such as orchestra, ETV programs, recess and physical education schedules are examples.

Once a service is decided upon as appropriate, its maintenance is a required performance task. The cumulative information records including the pupils' academic and activity performance, test results, health records, and attendance records involve the decision to provide; but maintaining them is a continuing task, and to be of service to the organization, the members, and the clients, they must be kept current and readily available.

An understanding of the total of the management functions is dependent upon the extent to which each function and its tasks are identified and defined and upon the point of view held by the elementary school principal relative to his responsibility for these functions. The model of administration for elementary schools, Figure 1–1 in Chapter 1, depicts how management functions and their tasks relate to the job of maintaining the school in its day-to-day operations. Contemplation of their importance as the school is propelled toward an effectiveness level of operation suggests the increasing complexity and importance of them. Each function and its performance tasks must be kept under surveillance, because even at the survival level monitoring and change are realities.

1. Raymond E. Callahan, *Education and the Cult of Efficiency* (Chicago: University of Chicago Press, 1962).

2. Amitai Etzioni, *Modern Organizations* (Englewood Cliffs, N.J.: Prentice-Hall, 1964), p. 19.

The performance tasks that can be routinized must be identified; those which cannot be must be brought under appropriate control. In the long run, meeting each crisis or demand as it comes up is more costly and time-consuming than is the investment for planning and maintaining these management functions at the effectiveness level. Providing and maintaining these management functions and tasks at any level of operation become the issue discussed by Etzioni who observed that:

Organizations are social units which pursue specific goals; their very *raison d'être* is the service of these goals. But once formed, organizations acquire their own needs, these sometimes becoming the masters of the organization . . . organizations reduce the service of their initial goals in order to satisfy their acquired needs, rather than adjust the service of their acquired needs to that of their goals.[3]

The elementary school in which the amounts of data, information, and other reported items going to the school office are greater than the amounts coming from the school office may well be an example of the school office becoming the master rather than the provider of service.

Changing for improvement of the education program is an ever increasing admonishment from both the internal environment and the external environment of the elementary school. It has been suggested that change occurs even in the schools operating at the survival level. However, improvements in the education program cannot be anticipated as lasting improvements without prior and concurrent concern for the management functions and their performance tasks. How to bring the management functions into an appropriate perspective is a gigantic undertaking which will involve all the organization members and other persons from outside the organization.

There is a tool or technique which facilitates the process and which is being utilized more and more commonly as the elementary school becomes more complex and as its scope of services increases. The technique is systems analysis which involves looking at purposes, at alternatives of choice and their possible and probable consequences, at inputs, throughputs, and outputs. Costs, sequence and schedules, personnel, and benefits are also involved. Systems analysis is essentially a simulation process in which the "best" system is delineated and designed prior to the making of commitments to a system. (See Chapter 8 for additional information.)

The systems approach (in which data must be gathered, organized,

3. *Ibid.,* p. 5.

analyzed, and evaluated during the selection of a subsystem from among several alternatives) is depicted in Figure 11–1. An initial study—to define alternatives and subsystems, to build models, and to analyze data (often through cost-benefit studies)—may culminate in the selection of an alternative as indicated in the figure. Frequently, however, the evaluation leads to further studies which often culminate in still more sophisticated selections of options or alternatives.

The management functions and their performance tasks are uniquely appropriate for this kind of *a priori* scrutiny. If the elementary school is "programed for change" as it often is by unrelated efforts of individuals

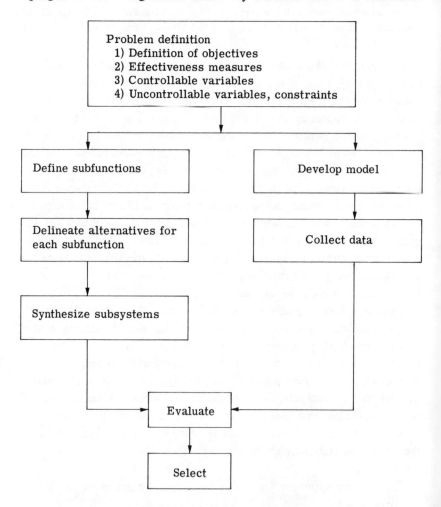

Figure 11-1. Flow Chart Illustrating the Systems Approach.

and groups, there is a curriculum problem, there is a materials and equipment problem, there is a personnel problem, there is a media problem, there is a scheduling problem, there is a school office problem, there is a records problem. Granting that each of these problems is subjected to still more balkanization demonstrates the chances for goal distortion and goal displacement. Resources are allocated, reallocated, and misallocated without benefit of the knowledge of the effect on the total organization.

It was Leavitt who demonstrated that a change or alteration in an organization, while it may be focused on but one aspect, can be anticipated to produce compensatory or retaliatory change in others.[4] A study of the four major variables comprising an organization, shown in Figure 11-2, reveals the major importance of the school office functions as they relate to the rest of the elementary school enterprise. (For additional discussion of Leavitt's model, see Chapter 8.)

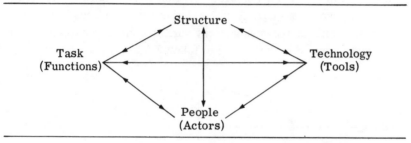

Figure 11-2. Model for Viewing Interrelationships of
Organization Variables

MANAGEMENT: THE KEY TO AN EFFECTIVE ORGANIZATION

The renaissance of interest in and commitment to an appropriate education program for all persons who present themselves for the opportunity contributed to an already existing frustration. The efforts of elementary school personnel had been directed largely toward the problems of increasing enrollments and the longer time the students remained in school. The mobility of people had a confounding effect. As more and more students remained for longer periods of time, the elementary school

4. Harold J. Leavitt, "Applied Organization Change in Industry: Structural, Technical, and Human Approaches," in W. W. Cooper, H. J. Leavitt, and M. W. Shelly, II (eds.), *New Perspectives in Organization Research* (New York: John Wiley & Sons, 1964), p. 56.

principal was confronted with the provision of more pupil-spaces, more equipment and materials, more record keeping, and greater differences among the school clients. These problems related generally to quantity logistics. Then the sudden renaissance of interest in and commitment to improved education programs introduced problems relating to quality, but in essence the problem was that of providing quality education programs to still greater quantities of clients.

The resultant greater social and school achievement and aptitude differentiation among the elementary school clients required the addition of still other management functions or services. Health services and guidance and testing programs became essential service functions of the elementary school office. The management aspects of elementary school administration were too complex to be operated as in the past. In order to meet the demands being made upon the organization, an ordering for understanding the whole school management operation is necessary. Utilizing the classification schema of functions, tasks, procedures, and records is one way this ordering can be accomplished. The interrelationships of the management variables are depicted in Figure 11–3, and discussed in the section to follow.

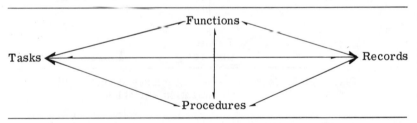

Figure 11-3. Model for Viewing Interrelationships of Management Variables

FUNCTIONS, TASKS, PROCEDURES

Functions represent the major service areas of management concerns. The major management functions of the elementary school are organization structure, pupil personnel services, personnel services, curriculum services, activities, and business services. A seventh function which is superimposed over the other six is that of attaining organization effectiveness. The seven major management functions are shown in Table 11–1 with a listing of selected performance tasks. This list of tasks is not presumed to be exhaustive; rather it is a heuristic listing. A review

Table 11-1. Management Functions and Tasks

Function	Task Category	Performance/Record

Organization Structure Coordination	Schedules	Master
		Bell
		Special TV Programs
		Music
		Art
		Physical Education
		Recess/Lunch
		Shared Facilities
		   Playground
		   All-Purpose Room
		   Library
		Parent/Teacher Conference
		Daily Pupil Sections
		Activities
		In-service Events
		Summer School

	Assignments	Room Teacher Pupils Nongraded Group Sections
	Other	Activity and Events Calendar Faculty Handbook Administrative Report Calendar Substitute Teacher List
Pupil Personnel Services	Information Records	Academic Activity Test Data Health Data Attendance Anecdotal Counseling Discipline Psychological Progress Evaluation Census Social Services Child Welfare
	Attendance	Daily Monthly Quarterly Annual
	Reports to Parents	Quarter Grade Report Behavior/Conduct Report Parent/Teacher Conference
	Discipline	Principal/Teacher/Pupil/Report Formal Investigation Report
Personnel Services	Professional	Personal Data Inventory Professional Growth Record

Table 11-1. (Continued)

Function	Task Category	Performance/Record
Personnel Services (cont.)	Professional (cont.)	Salary and Tenure Record
		Assignment Record
		Health Certificate
		Teaching Certificate Record
		Cumulative Evaluation Record
		Job Descriptions
	Paraprofessional	Personal Data Inventory
		In-service Development Records
		Experience and Salary Record
		Health Certificate
		Assignment Record
		Cumulative Evaluation Record
		Job Descriptions
	Noncertificated Service	Personal Data Inventory
		In-service Development Record
		Experience and Salary Record
		Health Certificate
		Assignment Record
		Cumulative Evaluation Record
		Job Descriptions
Curriculum Services		Statement of School Philosophy
		Statement of Purpose, Subgoals
		Curriculum Guides
		Courses of Study
		Resource Units
		Library Listings
		Media Listings
		Inventory of Equipment
		Inventory of Supplemental Material
		Inventory of Texts, etc.
		Inventory of District Requirements
		Inventory of State Requirements
		Inventory of Professional Texts
		Test Schedules
		Schedule of In-service Events
		List of Consultants
		List of Resource Persons
		Criteria for Evaluating Textbooks
Activities		Student Government
		Assembly Policies
		School Events Calendar
		Special Events Outside School
		Teacher Activity Assignment
		Safety Patrol Guards
		School Newspaper
Business		Budget Construction
		Budget Administration
		Payroll Accounts

Table 11-1. (Continued)

Function	Task Category	Performance/Record
Business (Cont.)		Internal Accounts
		Insurance Administration
		Specifications: Equipment
		Specifications: Materials
		Specifications: Supplies
		Purchasing Procedures
		Inventory of Equipment
		Inventory of Materials
		Inventory of Supplies
		Accounting Auxiliary Services
		Reporting State and Federal Funds
		Sick Leave Accounting
		Building Maintenance Records
Effectiveness Attainment		Procedures for Bulletins and Announcements
		Procedures for Fire, Safety, Storm, Emergencies, Defense, Accidents
		Inventory and Procedures for Substitute Teachers
		State and District Record Statistics
		Bell Schedules and Special Events Programing
		In-service Program Calendar, Goals, and Priorities
		Curriculum Priorities
		Summer School Schedules and Classes
		Special Projects Underway
		Regulations and Rules for Teacher-Student Relations

of the related performance tasks indicates the all-pervading nature and influence of these management functions. Under the classification of organization structure, the many tasks reveal that coordination of the division of labor or responsibilities is a principal concern. The complexity of this management function can be appreciated by contemplation of the intricacies of coordination as the organization moves from self-contained classroom structure to a nongraded form or structure. The master schedule, room assignments, teacher assignments, and pupil assignments immediately become different. Achievement data and psychological information are necessary for sectioning the students. Because students progress differently, this kind of information must be continuously available on demand for reassignment of students to appropriate sections.

If a given management function represents categories of performance tasks, then the performance of these tasks indicates that the function is "completed" or satisfied at that point in time. It is at this point that mere survival or the extent of effectiveness can be observed. Administration entails a sequence of steps which facilitate the performance of these tasks or the completion of the function. Evaluation or assessment procedures essentially reverse the sequence of steps.

Procedures are prescriptions for task performances. Coordination of task performances, rather than performing each task separately, is a characteristic of the procedures. POSDCORB, Urwick's famous management taxonomy (see Chapters 1, 5, and 10), has basic applicability because it is through planning, organizing, staffing, directing, coordinating, reporting, and budgeting that management functions and their tasks can be designed to facilitate the work flow and the activities flow of the school. Sometimes order and timing are essential; sometimes assignment of responsibility is essential, sometimes priorities establishment is essential; but the procedures must be designed on the basis of what is needed at the completion of the task. Procedures are means to ends and the ends have to be identified and known. An important variable is the recognition that these management functions, tasks, and procedures are supportive services and performances to facilitate the needs of the teachers who are responsible for the work flow and activities flow of their assigned parts of the elementary school program.

These elementary school office procedures reduce to procurement and supportive allocation of resources, to procedures facilitating classroom "autonomy," norm establishment, and morale and satisfactions among the members and clients. To design, implement, and maintain through effective procedures these school office management functions, it is imperative that the personnel involved recognize the importance of leadership. The requisite leadership pattern was identified by Barnard as leadership in the sense of the guidance of people in organization.[5]

5. Chester Barnard, *Organization and Management* (Cambridge, Mass.: Harvard University Press, 1962), p. 81.

RECORDS AND RECORDS SYSTEMS

Records and a records system are common to all elementary schools as an essential characteristic of an organization. What kinds of records and what kind of records system will be discerned depends upon a number of variables. Most records systems, like Topsy, just grew. A records system and records are products of completing the management functions and the performance tasks. The purpose of the records is to facilitate the work flow and activity flow of the organization. Thus, meeting the service demands of the organization members, clients, and others is dependent upon the availability and viability of records.

Red tape is being replaced with magnetic tape, but the same dysfunctional complaints are heard. A considerable quantity of the data, statistics, and information derives initially from the organization members and clients. Duplication of records by different departments within the elementary school office is not unusual. Guidance personnel collect information which may also be collected by other departments. Duplication cannot be defended, but it is confounded by the fact that much of what is collected serves no real purpose. Files are full of information that serves or has served no purpose other than filling space.

Planning a records system and designing the record gathering, storing, and dispensing forms and the procedures must be approached with a pragmatic point of view. What difference does it make if the information is collected? How can it be recorded for the greatest utility? A definition of the utility and of the need for a certain kind of information lies in the difference it makes. The entire procedure from source to ultimate ends must be considered. Coordination, consolidation, and reconfiguration are the key processes. It is possible that the organization itself, the district central office, and the state department of education, and/or a federal agency may have similar needs or demands for a particular kind of information. If the procedure is planned and executed carefully, it may be that the organization itself requires the most complete set of information and that the demands of the district office and of the state and federal agencies can be taken from the records of the elementary school office. One initial compilation with subsequent résumés may then satisfy all the organizations' demands. Incidents where three different demands result in three separate collections are not unknown.

A list of the pupils assigned to Teacher A is not an unusual piece of information, provided as a service of the elementary school office. When the school term begins she has a list of pupils for checking the first day's attendance. But in the files of the records system there are many other bits of information pertaining to each of the pupils on the list. There are achievement measures in various subject areas from each year the student has attended school; there are intelligence scores, attitude notations, attendance habits, teacher-given marks or grades, and health data. This information in a usable print-out would benefit Teacher A and her students considerably more than the mere knowledge of their names.

There are some boards of education, superintendents, and elementary school principals who look upon clerical support as a wasteful expenditure. But many of the tasks and procedural details in maintaining the records system—input, throughput, and output, are appropriate assignments for clerks rather than for professionally certificated personnel. The effective elementary school principal must be able to demonstrate the benefits of an effectiveness model records system. One way to accomplish this is to use a form of system analysis. Program evaluation and review technique (PERT) has become a common control process in management functions and tasks. The development of an effectiveness model records system is an appropriate utilization of PERT. After goals or ends are identified, PERT, as a process, can help identify possible breakdowns or serious weaknesses as the "best" procedure is developed. The quality of a PERT production is determined by the kind and level of decision making that go into it.

Improved records systems are essential for at least five good reasons:

1. The expanding and varied needs for instant information
2. The increasing magnitude of records required for expanded education programs
3. The greater complexity of the organization structure; for example, the nongraded elementary school
4. The increasing costs of installation, maintenance, and operating personnel
5. The pressure to free teachers from as much administrative detail and reporting as possible

Undoubtedly the list can be expanded, but these five reasons leave no doubt that improved records systems are essential and that keeping them appropriate will require continuous evaluation and improvement.

COMPUTERS AND DATA-PROCESSING SYSTEMS

Data-processing systems, or computer-based operations, have a great potential for facilitating and improving the elementary school office management functions and records systems. Although there is extensive utility for computer-based operation in effective elementary schools, these operations are usually a part of a school district installation. While the likely extent of involvement of an elementary school will depend upon the district's commitment, the actual utility of the available system for a given elementary school will relate in a large measure to the principal and other personnel in decision-making positions.

Not every elementary school office management function can be computerized, and some of them are more amenable than are others; but a systems analysis will reveal those which can be made more effective by computer-based operations. The management aspects of the role of the principal are associated with the tasks of facilitating and improving

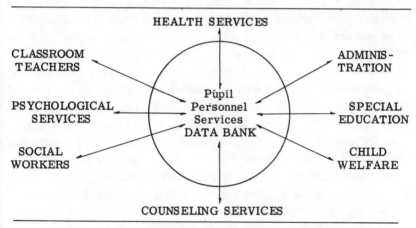

Figure 11-4. Data Bank for Pupil Personnel Services

the work flow and activity flow of the elementary school. To these ends, Loughary proposed the conceptualization of an integrated information system which he called a data bank, as shown in a modified form in Figure 11–4. It illustrates how a data bank operates with each of the pupil personnel service functions as an input to the data bank and with each of them having access to data in the bank.[6] It is easy to see how

6. John W. Loughary, *Man-Machine Systems in Education* (New York: Harper & Row, 1966), p. 199.

a computer-based operation can enhance service functions performance and also to conceptualize a further extension of the data bank.

Data-processing systems have come into rather general use and acceptance in public education, perhaps earlier in the secondary schools than in the elementary schools. A number of reasons encouraged the adoption of data-processing systems: (1) an increasing demand for information, (2) larger numbers of pupils to be served, (3) a demand for "instant" and current information, and (4) a need to effect greater efficiency and effectiveness by freeing professional personnel from as many clerical tasks as possible. A particular advantage obtains from the flexibility of the system, providing easy input and access to information at tremendous speed, accuracy, and increasingly lower costs.

A schematic flow chart of selected applications of data-processing to management functions is presented in Figure 11–5. The flow chart depicts the range of outputs from several common sources: (1) the census cards, (2) the master pupil file, (3) the master teacher file, and (4) the list and specifications of the classrooms. Two other sources are depicted: the individual subject grades and the attendance cards. With these sources of information, there are shown four management functions that can be accomplished by the computer operations. The tasks performed include: (1) the external demands for information reports, (2) the various necessary schedules which facilitate the work flow and the activity flow of the school, (3) individual and group achievement and progress record keeping and reporting, and (4) the various attendance reports. Essentially, the illustration is heuristic and demonstrates the kinds of effective outputs that can be generated by variously combined inputs. One unique output of the data-processing system is the statistical reports for analysis and evaluation. The data have generally existed but noncomputer operations are too cumbersome and expensive to generate detailed statistical reports for these purposes.

The increasing complexity of the elementary school with major restructuring to accommodate the variously practiced forms of nongrading and team teaching, which require much more information for pupil sectioning and resectioning, can be conceptualized as an effective operation when computer-based operations are available.

THE PRINCIPAL'S ROLE INTERPRETATION AND
MANAGEMENT FUNCTIONS

The elementary school office is the nerve center which facilitates the work flow and the activities flow of the school. Several factors have operated to retard the optimal development of the management functions which are an essential prerequisite to effective operation. One retarding factor has been the apparent lack of understanding of the essential nature of the management functions and of their interrelationships with other aspects of the organization. Conceptualization of the elementary school office and of the principalship as peripheral aspects of providing adequate teaching-learning experiences for the pupils has been too long perpetuated by too many of the decision makers: boards of education, superintendents, principals, and teachers.

A second retarding factor is the tendency among principals to misinterpret their role. Every principal assumes a headship role or the hierarchical position. What ensues from this common beginning is varied. Headship roles have been associated with management or administrative functions. But many principals have interpreted the management role status only as involvement in routine survival task performances. The performance of these tasks becomes a ritual. The tasks become ends rather than means. These principals devote their time to detail work and it soon becomes all-consuming. Each day seems to put the principal and his office in greater arrears. Changing for improvement of the education program cannot be anticipated until the position incumbent changes or is changed. Management functions exist for their own sake, and there is no apparent realization that they do indeed relate to the effectiveness of the work flow and activities flow of the school—other than to keep it in day-to-day operation.

Another type of principal is discernible. These principals view management functions as irrelevant and distasteful symbols of the red tape of bureaucracy. Their goal is to ignore these management functions to the fullest possible extent. They may have assumed another or a substitute concept of the principalship role which is essentially a misinterpreted concept of leadership. They attempt leadership activities because they are convinced that management is not an appropriate role of the elementary school principal. They spend much of their professional day visiting classrooms, making contacts and plans for new projects, explaining their school and all of education to service groups and to whoever

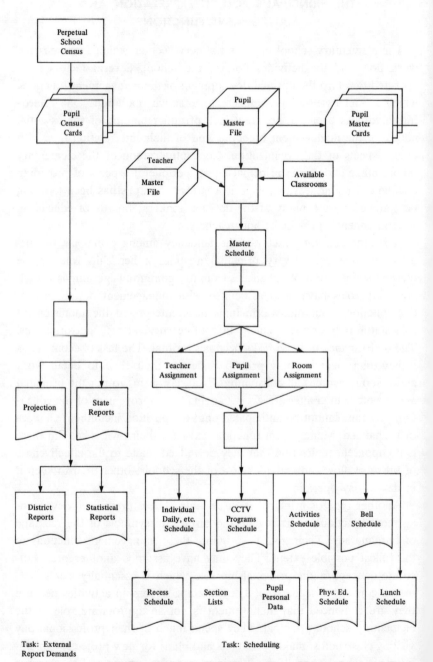

Task: External
Report Demands

Task: Scheduling

Figure 11-5. Schematic Flow Chart: Selected Task

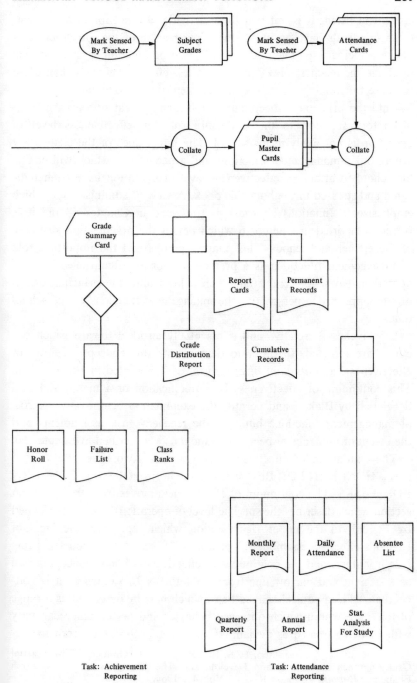

Task: Achievement
Reporting

Task: Attendance
Reporting

Performances in the Elementary School

else might listen. It is not that these activities are not important; rather these principals have an out-of-focus perspective of the job description of the principalship. Their schools will also be functioning at a survival level and the teachers may exhibit even less efficient behavior than those who are functioning under the management-detail principal.

Until the principal conceptualizes the management role as a prerequisite for ascension to the leadership role, an effectiveness level of operation is not likely in his school. The importance of the elementary school office management functions and a perspective which will enable the school to attain an effectiveness level of operation have been indicated and stressed throughout this book. A view of administration which emphasizes a functions approach is presented in Chapter 4, and it is further supported in Chapter 6 which details the organization structure of the elementary school. This chapter emphasizes the important role of management functions as a prerequisite for an effectiveness level of operation. No school can attain such a level until the principal brings into an appropriate perspective the management functions of the school office.

Effectiveness is relative and is essentially an ideal toward which our efforts are directed. In order to demonstrate this conceptualization of effectiveness, a *continuum of effectiveness* is presented in Figure 11–6. This continuum of effectiveness is a modification of a managerial grid developed by Blake [7] and permits the examination of not only the role of management functions but also the teachers' task assignments and the extent of influence of personnel functions as described in Chapter 10.

The continuum of effectiveness derives from two axes: the vertical axis is CONCERN FOR PEOPLE and the horizontal axis is CONCERN FOR TASKS. The continuum of effectiveness moves from the lower left section which describes the survival level of operation (1 x 1), as defined by Etzioni, to the upper right section which represents the ideal of Etzioni's effectiveness model of operation (9 x 9).[8] The model is heuristic in nature, and the continuum of effectiveness is not conceptualized as a straight and narrow line from 1 x 1 to 9 x 9 so much as it is conceptualized as a conical-shaped band which may be described as a range of tolerance within which observed behavior and performance can vary without being treated as deviant. By giving appropriate concern to per-

---

7. R. R. Blake, J. S. Mouton, L. B. Barnes, and L. E. Greiner, "A Managerial Grid Approach to Organization Development: The Theory and Some Research Findings," *Harvard Business Review,* Vol. 42, 1964.
8. Etzioni, *op. cit.,* p. 19.

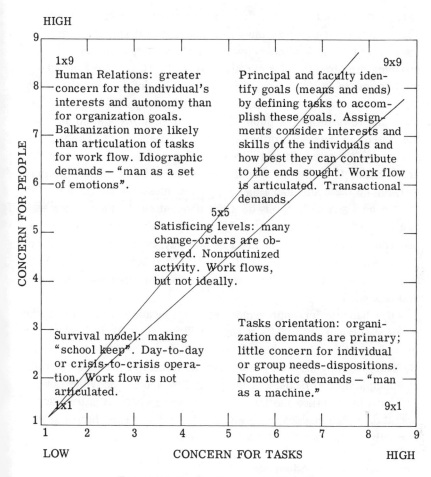

HIGH

1x9   9x9
Human Relations: greater   Principal and faculty iden-
concern for the individual's   tify goals (means and ends)
interests and autonomy than   by defining tasks to accom-
for organization goals.   plish these goals. Assign-
Balkanization more likely   ments consider interests and
than articulation of tasks   skills of the individuals and
for work flow. Idiographic   how best they can contribute
demands — "man as a set   to the ends sought. Work flow
of emotions".   is articulated. Transactional
                                demands.

                        5x5
                Satisficing levels: many
                change-orders are ob-
                served. Nonroutinized
                activity. Work flows,
                but not ideally.

                                Tasks orientation: organi-
Survival model: making   zation demands are primary;
"school keep". Day-to-day   little concern for individual
or crisis-to-crisis opera-   or group needs-dispositions.
tion. Work flow is not   Nomothetic demands — "man
articulated.   as a machine."
1x1   9x1

LOW   CONCERN FOR TASKS   HIGH

CONCERN FOR PEOPLE

Figure 11-6. Continuum of Effectiveness

sonnel needs and to management functions and task requirements and assignments, including the teachers' job descriptions, an effectiveness level of operation is approximated. It will be noted that Simon's equilibrium and search theory [9] is applicable in the development and design of effectiveness, which is to state that as alternatives of choice in decision making increase in quantity and quality, and, as aspirations mount, the observed effectiveness of a given elementary school moves toward the 9 x 9 ideal.

The teachers cannot accomplish their task assignments unless they

9. Herbert A. Simon, *Administrative Behavior* (New York: Macmillan, 1966).

have a stable and well-articulated organization in which to perform. The organization structure must facilitate the goal specifications which are manifested in the teachers' job descriptions. Pupil-teacher ratios and grouping are important for effectiveness in the classroom. Schedules or mechanisms to facilitate work flow and activity flow are necessary. The teachers need procedures, regulations and rules, and channels for punishment and reward of their pupils. They need authority and autonomy in the classroom with superordinate and colleague support. The principal knows that procurement and allocation of materials and other resources are essential. Ordering the school office functions, tasks, and procedures to facilitate these stabilizing and supportive measures and materials for the teachers and their pupils does not demand all the time of the effective elementary school principal. He routinizes those function tasks and procedures which can be handled in this way, delegates to clerical personnel whenever delegation is appropriate, and brings into control the function tasks and procedures which can not be essentially routinized and delegated.

Any changing for improvement of the education program, whether it is for survival or for effectiveness, will be more likely implemented in an elementary school where the principal has an effective school office. By demonstrating his ability, skill, and awareness of the total enterprise in anticipating and facilitating the work flow and the activities flow, he will have have earned the teachers' trust and respect. It is this kind of operation which enables the principal to move from the headship position only to one including leadership potential.

Two Tools of the Administrator

Observation of principals in action reveals practices on a continuum from minimal survival operation almost to the hypothetical ideal of effectiveness operation. The wide range of practice obtains from the two "tools" of administration of the elementary school principal which are (1) role interpretation as he practices it, and (2) the school management functions. These two tools are complexly interrelated, but role interpretation—what the principal does with the other tool—determines in a large measure the level of effectiveness.

The effective elementary school principal recognizes that his role involves both management and leadership and that his overall success emanates from an appropriate mix which produces at least three interdependent activity categorizations: (1) control, (2) evaluation and decision making, and (3) facilitation of work flow and activities flow for implementing and maintaining effectiveness.

Control is an essential characteristic of organizations. The methods of obtaining and maintaining control and the uses to which control is put are the important considerations. If the school is to attain its goals, then a stable organization is imperative and stability derives from control. According to Etzioni, there are three types of control: (1) coercive, (2) remunerative, and (3) normative.[10] Using the tools of administration—role interpretation and management functions—as means of control, the principal could apply each of the types of control to both of the tools of administration, as depicted in Figure 11-7, which illustrates that not all of the six possible combinations or applications are desirable if effective operation is sought. Further, the principal must exercise caution to prevent controls from becoming ends in themselves rather than means to ends or goal attainment.

Kind of Control	Applied to: Role Interpretation	Management Functions
coercive	1	2
remunerative	3	4
normative	5	6

Figure 11-7. A Typology of Control Relations

Using the tools of administration—role interpretation and management functions as means of evaluation and decision making—presumes possible change strategies. Changing for the improvement of the education program may be a simple substitution or a complex disruption of value orientation. Chin offered three general change strategies which are available to an elementary school principal.[11] *Empirical-rational strategy* is a logically derived decision-making process to effect change. Evaluation and analysis for decision making are obvious prerequisites of the empirical-rational strategy of effecting a change. The teachers can conceptualize the benefits and gains to be derived for organization effectiveness and individual efficiency when they are presented evidence to support a change recommendation.

10. Amitai Etzioni, *A Comparative Analysis of Complex Organizations* (New York: Free Press, 1961), pp. 4–5.

11. Robert Chin, "Basic Strategies and Procedures in Effecting Change," in Edgar L. Morphet and Charles O. Ryan (eds.), *Planning and Effecting Needed Changes in Education* (Denver, Colo.: Publishers Press, 1967), pp. 39–57.

A second change strategy is *normative-reeducative* and is a very important change strategy for the elementary school principal. Any change variable can be measured on an intensity continuum from a substitution for a stabilizing change to a value disorientation or disrupting change. Even a moderate version of the "new math" ranged from a substitution of practice to a value disorientation when it was introduced into the elementary schools. The elementary school principal who utilized the normative-reeducative strategy in the in-service program to ready his teachers for the introduction of the "new math" program would more likely observe a stabilizing change than would the principal who had failed to provide a readiness program or a retooling program prior to its introduction.

Power is the third change strategy; however, like coercive control, power tends to be disruptive and would preclude stability and internalization by the members. There is no doubt that power and coercion can produce change, but the change that is effected is frequently in the opposite direction. If effectiveness and improving the education program are the ultimate targets, these procedures do not possess much utility.

Facilitation of work flow and activities flow for implementing and maintaining the organization effectiveness is a third role activity of the elementary school principal. There are a number of factors which condition the role of the principal in the administration of the school office. Some of them are more easily controlled than are others. Getzels' social process model, depicted in Figure 10–1 in Chapter 10, indicates that there are both external factors and internal factors. The role of the principal is interpreted from its relationship with a reference group or individual. The board of education, the superintendent, and various groups and individuals in the community have differing expectations and role definitions. These definitions are external factors and may have certain conditioning effects upon the principalship and the principal. The teachers, pupils, and other personnel have differing expectations and role definitions also, and these represent the internal factors. Although the external factors may be more difficult to change or to modify than are the internal factors, they tend to have less relevancy to the facilitation of work flow and activity flow than do the internal factors. Thus, the principal possesses a considerable freedom to structure and operate his school and still remain within any limitations imposed by external factors. If the school office functions are redesigned by task and performance to help the teachers, pupils, and other person-nel, the principal has no real internal curtailing dysfunctions.

As the elementary school principal considers his role in school man-agement functions as they may facilitate the work flow and the activities flow for implementing and maintaining organization effectiveness and individual efficiency, there are several principles which possess relevancy:

1. Utilize systems analysis to determine the extent to which administra-tive action, reports, and records are required by external agencies of constituted authority and by the needs and demands of the organiza-tion members and clients.
   a. Develop a system for anticipating these demands and maintain a time schedule and calendar.
   b. Evaluate the integrated records system and data bank, and elimi-nate duplication and obsolete data-yield by revising the record forms.
2. Analyze each of the major management functions, the tasks, and performance procedures involved in fulfilling them as they relate to and contribute to an effective school.
3. Prepare a handbook or guidebook of administrative functions pro-cedures. Trace the process from beginning to completion of each major task. Assign position responsibility for each phase of each task. Indicate the record-storing procedures and the reporting for which these tasks are undertaken.
4. Gain experience with the procedures, records, and the record system. Avoid becoming engrossed with detailed clerical tasks, but use the skills to monitor and to redesign procedures as necessary. Involve other personnel—both clerical and professional—in the monitoring and evaluating processes, in order that they can also make effective change recommendations.
5. Make certain that the records system and the records are a service to the organization, its members, and clients rather than serving primarily as a means of regulating and controlling the organization or of serving the external demands.

The tools of one elementary school principal are very similar to those of other elementary school principals. It has been demonstrated in this chapter that the greatest differences abound in the ways the tools are utilized and the variables to which they are applied. Granting that both external factors and internal factors tend to condition the administra-tion of the elementary school, the principal's role interpretation of the principalship emerges as the single most important and crucial tool of administration. Further, it has a pronounced effect on the other tools commonly available to the elementary school principal.

The principal operates in three distinct, but interrelated, spheres of influence: management, organization leadership, and policy-making participation, as depicted in the model developed in Chapter 1. The extent to which the principal has attained an effectiveness in the management functions has a direct bearing on his influence in organization leadership and policy-making participation.

REFERENCES

Callahan, Raymond E., *Education and the Cult of Efficiency* (Chicago: University of Chicago Press, 1962).

Clark, Harold F., *Cost and Quality in Public Education* (Syracuse, N.Y.: Syracuse University Press, 1963).

Etzioni, Amitai, *Modern Organizations* (Englewood Cliffs, N.J.: Prentice-Hall, 1964).

Holz, Robert E., *School Scheduling Using Computers* (Cambridge, Mass.: Massachusetts Institute of Technology, 1964).

Kershaw, J. A., and R. N. McKean, *Systems Analysis and Education* (Santa Monica, Calif.: Rand Corp., 1959).

Knezevich, Stephen J., and John Guy Fowlkes, *Business Management of Local School Systems* (New York: Harper & Bros., 1960).

Loughary, John W., *Man-Machine Systems in Education* (New York: Harper & Row, 1966).

Yeager, William A., *Administration of Noninstructional Personnel and Services* (New York: Harper & Bros., 1959).

Chapter 12

BUSINESS MANAGEMENT
FUNCTIONS

A CENTRAL role of the elementary school principal is that of maintaining, facilitating, and implementing more effective education program components relating to the teaching-learning situations and experiences for the boys and girls. This central role is to be encouraged, and one very important way is to make certain that the various school management functions are optimally focused into an integrated system. A principal thesis of this book has been the vital importance of the school management functions as they contribute to an effective elementary school. A detailed perspective was developed in Chapter 11 and supported in Chapter 4 which deals with a functional view of administration and in Chapter 6 which is concerned with elementary school organization and structure.

Business management functions relate to the administration of school funds and the things these funds purchase, including other considerations such as obtaining these funds and establishing priorities for allocation. As the size of the elementary school increases in numbers of pupils and in program breadth, competition for funds increases not only within a given elementary school but also among elementary schools and other levels within the school district. With increasing availability of funds from special state and federal programs, the competition for these funds increases also. These developments in fiscal matters carry important implications for the elementary school principal as he seeks to propel his organization toward an effectiveness level. He can no longer concern himself with only the fiscal matters pertaining to his particular school. Competition for the funds available to public education precludes such a narrow interest and concern.

Every education program—whether minimal or optimal—is based on business management functions. Knezevich defined business management as: "... that phase of educational administration that is primarily concerned with procuring, expending, accounting for, protecting, organizing, and maintaining fiscal and material resources in an efficient manner so that human resources and efforts are aided in achieving educational goals." [1]

Business management functions permeate every facet of the elementary school operation. An increased effort, usually measured by an increased amount of money, in one of these facets will likely exert an influence on one or more of the other facets. When a long-range education program is kept responsive to needs and viable priorities, these fluctuations and added or reduced allocations will tend to be better understood by the organization members. As Etzioni observed: "The establishment of a set of priorities which clearly defines the relative importance of the various goals reduces the disruptive consequences of such conflicts, though it does not eliminate the problem." [2]

Development of an effective education program, attained by appropriately involving all organization members, is not likely unless the all-important areas of business management functions are also related to the process. The interrelationships of program development and of the business management functions are demonstrated in Figure 12–1 which depicts the influence of resources (income) and planned expenditures on the education program. Any attempt to evaluate the scope and quality of the education program requires probing the other two variables for information-yield.

Because money is the basic underlying variable utilized in obtaining the components which comprise an effective elementary school, its importance cannot be overstressed. However, there are numerous instances in which its impact on the organization in terms of allocation, reallocation, and even misallocation has resulted from lack of understanding of the interrelationships depicted in Figure 12–1. A very common fallacy in public education stems from the notion that more money is a certain cure for the various shortcomings of the elementary school. Careful analysis reveals this to be erroneous in many instances; definite goals, carefully delineated priorities, and reallocation of funds accordingly are

1. Stephen J. Knezevich and John Guy Fowlkes, *Business Management of Local School Systems* (New York: Harper & Bros., 1960), p. 2.
2. Amitai Etzioni, *Modern Organizations* (Englewood Cliffs, N.J.: Prentice-Hall, 1964), p. 15.

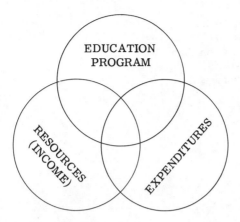

Figure 12-1: The Interrelationships of the Education Program and the
Business Management Functions

often more likely to improve the situation than will merely providing
more money for the same old problem. This contention does not presume
to exclude the necessity for seeking additional support to continue and
to improve the efforts toward an effectiveness model of operation.

THE BUDGET DOCUMENT

The budget document consists of three essential parts: (1) the education program to be provided for the budget year, (2) the cost or spending plan, and (3) the estimate of revenues and their anticipated sources.
These three parts coincide with the three circles depicted in Figure 12–1.
The terminology is changed to some extent to accommodate the peculiar
nature of the budget document. The budget document for a given school
year is essentially a segment of the long-range plan that has been formulated by the principal, teachers, and others who have responsibility for
the elementary school, as illustrated in Figure 12–2.

The Education Plan

It is the education program or plan that is frequently omitted from
the budget document, yet there is every reason to assume that it is the
most important part. This is not to state that an education program or
plan does not exist, if there is this omission from the budget document.
The assertion is far more realistically oriented. Operation at a survival

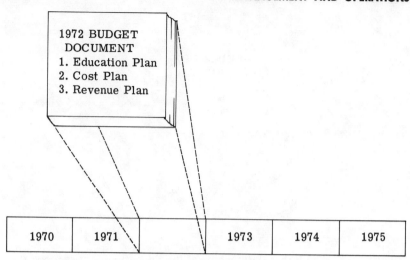

Figure 12-2. The Budget Document as a Segment of
Long-Range Program Implementation

level should be anticipated. There are many shifts—emphases and de-emphases—based on the unplanned day-to-day operations. A low grade of *satisficing* characterizes the organization behavior. Work flow and activity flow are not articulated as described by Parsons' integrative function of organization behavior. "... it is of fundamental importance that in any given case the basic institutional patterns constitute a relatively integrated system and not a mere agglomeration of distinct elements or 'traits.'" [3] The development of the education program or plan for inclusion in the budget document serves this integrative function of viewing the various components of the education program as they interrelate and the various emphases allotted to them as revealed from the amounts of allocated support in the budget process.

How an elementary school principal can defend professionally or otherwise a budget document without the education program is a bit difficult to conceptualize, yet such has been the case in thousands of school budgets. The education program plan is a detailed presentation of the teaching-learning situations and experiences to be provided in the school year which is covered by the proposed budget. It is in this presentation that new programs and expanded ones are justified. Allocation and reallocation of resources and emphases are demonstrated as essential components of the education program. A budget document

3. Talcott Parsons, *Essays in Sociological Theory Pure and Applied* (Glencoe, Ill.: Free Press, 1949), p. 276.

lacking this information and explanation is somewhat akin to requesting a blank check to be filled in and spent for whatever happens to be momentarily attractive.

Sweeping generalizations and broad categories are not sufficient for presenting the education program or plan. Specific goals to be realized; number of teachers and their assignments; the supporting equipment, materials, and supplies; and special projects which require special allocations should all be specified in the education program presentation. Any new projects or expanded services should be detailed. An education program plan of this nature serves another function in case the available funds for the budget year require any sort of curtailment. Rather than having to "lop off" a percentage of the total request, the priority system permits a reasoned reduction.

The following outline suggests the comprehensiveness and the amount of planning involved in preparing the education program plan.

A. Statements of the school's philosophy of education
B. Statements relating to the general objectives of the district and of the given school
C. District and school policies, rules, and regulations
   1. Type of organization
   2. Calendar for school term
   3. Special and regular "grade-level" structure
   4. Pupil data: preschool census, enrollment, attendance, age-grade tables, achievement summaries, progress reports
   5. Personnel practices and policies: salary schedule, leave policies (and utilization), tenure, pension and health insurance programs
   6. Education program specifics: content by levels, requirements, activities, and field trips
   7. Textbooks, equipment, and supplies: needed for the ensuing year, used during the past period, disposal of items being replaced
   8. Services relating to transportation, health, safety, food services, and others
   9. Plant description: space utilization, needs for improvement, and adaptability of the building to program needs.[4]

The Cost or Spending Plan

The spending plan is the translation of the proposed education program into relatively accurate cost or expenditure estimates. It is no easy task to make this translation, but an effective school office in

4. Adapted from *Uniform Financial Accounting for Iowa Schools* (Des Moines, Iowa: State Department of Public Instruction, 1963), pp. 4–5.

which computer-based accounting procedures are utilized will be able to make more accurate estimations than will be the case in survival-type operations.

There are two principal categories in the expenditure or spending plan: (1) salaries, usually for contracted services, and (2) anticipated purchases. The contracted services are listed by *function:* that is, administration, instruction, maintenance, and operation; and are also listed by *object:* administrator's or teachers' salaries, paraprofessional and nonprofessional salaries, and fixed charges. These contracted services for the elementary school include mainly the instructional and supportive salaries and account for 70 to 80 percent of the spending plan request. There is not a lot of flexibility or discretion in budgeting for this category. Established salary schedules, returning teachers and other employees, and fixed schedules for retirement and other appropriate fixed charges tend to preclude manipulation. There are some practices which have an indirect influence, for example, the policy of requiring or not requiring prior teaching experience for employment.

The remaining 20 to 30 percent of the spending plan request is devoted to the second category—anticipated purchases. How specifically and clearly the education program and the school's needs are detailed determines in a large measure the effectiveness extracted from the available funds for these supportive purchases. Textbooks, paper, utilities, fuel, media equipment and supplies, library books, janitorial supplies and equipment serve to demonstrate the wide range of supportive purchases. If adequate funds are not available to match the budget document requests, it is this category that sustains the cutback.

Since early in the twentieth century, there has been an interest in and an obvious need for uniformity in terminology and practice in public education accounting, including the preparation and presentation of the budget document. The United States Office of Education has exerted its leadership in this interest, and in 1957 a manual was published which has received widespread acceptance.[5]

There are 14 major accounts set forth in the manual, but not all of them are applicable to every elementary school either in budget development or in accounting for expenditures. In the usual context, an elementary school is a part of a school district which maintains junior high

5. Paul L. Reason and Alpheus L. White, *Financial Accounting for Local and State School Systems, Standard Receipt and Expenditure Accounts, Bulletin 1957, No. 4,* U.S. Office of Education (Washington, D.C.: U.S. Government Printing Office, 1957).

schools and senior high schools also. There are elementary school districts which operate only through Grade six or Grade eight. In these districts, the principal has the role of a superintendent and is responsible for an entire operation which embraces potentially all 14 major accounts. Because of these variances of practice, each of the major accounts is listed and commented upon with a notation of its general applicability. It should be noted that each applicable account must be considered in budget construction as well as in financial accounting (keeping a record of expenditures). Certain accounts, budgeted and expended by the district central office, should be maintained by the elementary school principal because they represent a portion of the cost of his program. Fixed charges account is a case in point. Retirement and health insurance contributions for faculty members represent costs to be charged against a given school. These costs, such as retirement, reflect the employment practices of the elementary school principal. If a majority of the faculty members are eligible for salaries at the top of the salary schedule, then the social security and additional retirement costs will be greater than if the faculty is eligible for salaries at the bottom of the schedule.

THE MAJOR ACCOUNTS SERIES

1. *Account Series 100—Administration.* These accounts include cost for the general control, direction, and planning of public education on a district-wide basis. This account is generally not applicable to an elementary school budget.

2. *Account Series 200—Instruction.* Salaries of teachers, principals, and other professional personnel as well as the costs of textbooks, materials, and supplies used in the instruction program are recorded in these accounts. The greatest portion of the budget request is spread in this account series.

3. *Account Series 300—Attendance Services for Public Schools.* The elementary school office functions relating to pupil attendance matters are recorded in this account under two principal classifications: (1) salaries and (2) other expenses for attendance services.

4. *Account Series 400—Health Services for Public Schools.* Medical, dental, psychiatric, and nurse care costs in the form of salaries and supportive expenses are recorded in this account. This account may be district-wide, an attendance center account, or it may be shared at both levels.

5. *Account Series 500—Pupil Transportation Services.* This service is generally district-wide in its provision; however, budget requests for field trips and excursions requiring pupil transportation may be a concern for the elementary school principal when he prepares the budget.

6. *Account Series 600—Operation of Plant.* Salaries, contracted services, utilities, and supplies which contribute to keeping the plant in day-to-day operation are included in this account. Some of this account series may be provided for at the district office level.

7. *Account Series 700—Maintenance of Plant.* In this account, the salaries, contracted services, replacements, and other expenditures required for maintaining the buildings, grounds, and equipment in "original" condition are recorded. This category of accounts may be anticipated generally as a district-wide provision.

8. *Account Series 800—Fixed Charges.* District-paid contributions to social security, retirement and various insurance programs, rents paid for land and buildings are indicative of expenditures placed in this account. Essentially, it is a "catchall" account for expenditures which are not easily allocated to the other accounts. Although the account is likely a responsibility of the district's central office, the elementary school principal must consider these costs as they pertain to his school.

9. *Account Series 900—Food Services.* The elementary school principal's involvement in food services as they relate to the budget process depends upon the district's practice. If the elementary school has an independent food service, then the principal must budget for salaries and other costs.

10. *Account Series 1000—Student Body Activities.* The costs of activities which are not a part of the regular instruction program are provided for in this account. There is not a lot of applicability for the elementary school because most of its activities are viewed as part of the regular instruction program.

11. *Account Series 1100—Community Services.* Community services are those activities and services provided beyond the regular public school and adult education programs. Usually they are district or area services and include recreation, civic activities, public libraries, and certain welfare activities.

12. *Account Series 1200—Capital Outlay.* This account includes funds for land, improvement of grounds, construction and remodeling of buildings, and both initial and additional equipment, which result in the acquisition of fixed assets. This account is usually a district concern;

however, an elementary school principal seeking equipment, remodeling, or grounds improvement would include this line in his budget request.

13. *Account Series 1300—Debt Service from Current Funds.* Debt service is the retirement of debt, including principal and interest payments. This account has district-wide applicability rather than individual school concern.

14. *Account Series 1400—Outgoing Transfer Funds.* This account consists of payments to other school districts for services such as tuition and transportation and is not generally a concern of the elementary school principal.

The Estimate of Revenues and Their Sources

Once the education program is translated to the dollar cost of the spending plan, the elementary school principal must next determine if there are reasonable expectations of acquiring the funds necessary to make operative the proposed program. When public school financing is generalized to the practices among the 50 states, about the only observable common variable is the source of funds. How they are obtained and even the relative proportions of participation vary from state to state. Income for public education is derived essentially from six sources.

1. *Local property tax levy.* Local property taxation yields a substantial proportion of the funds for public education. In some states, the actual amount available is determined by a fixed mill rate which limits the school to whatever the mill rate will produce. In other states there is no essential maximum limit.

2. *State nonproperty funds.* Many states have established some form of equalization or a minimum support program for public education. The formulas utilized in apportioning these state funds enable the school administrators to determine relatively accurately the amounts to be anticipated from state sources.

3. *Federal nonproperty funds.* Two patterns of distribution are discernible for obtaining federal funds. The older pattern is the state-administered-federal-subsidized support program. The state education agency designs the program and establishes the guidelines for local district participation. The participating local district then obtains federal funds in varying amounts, usually on a matching basis. Although the pattern of distribution is still being widely utilized, another pattern of distribution has developed since the mid-1960's. The federal agency is

dealt with directly by the local school, and the state agency is eliminated almost completely. Many federal subsidized programs are special purpose, but they do serve to permit reallocation of other funds within the local school district.

4. *Proceeds from land sales.* In certain states, the proceeds from land sales represent a sizable amount of revenue. This situation holds particularly for the states of the far west. The older states in the midregion received less land from the federal government and, in many instances, failed to protect a potentially valuable asset.

5. *Rentals and fees.* At the elementary school level, these sources of income have tended to decrease as free textbook policies have become more general. In the schools where rental systems persist, the rents are usually presumed to replace textbooks on some time schedule.

6. *Tuition.* As a source of income, tuition payments from other districts have tended to decrease because the number of nonoperating school districts has been decreasing through reconfiguration efforts. Where this source of income does exist, it is largely at the secondary level.

Changes in support programs and particularly the actions of the federal government in the support of education require that the elementary school principal keep himself currently informed about revenue sources as he seeks to develop the school's education program.

There are several ways to approach budget preparation for the elementary school, and they are not all equally appropriate or desirable. One of the more inappropriate ways is to provide the elementary school principal a flat sum, derived from some kind of formula based on the number of teachers, number of pupils, or a percentage of the district's anticipated revenues. When this mode of operation is used, a negative situation obtains. The allotment becomes the cost or spending plan and serves to define the education program. The elementary school principal, and his faculty, must then determine priorities of the essentials that must be retained and which activities and program components can be or have to be curtailed or eliminated in order to make the education program fit the allotment. Progression toward an effectiveness level of operation is not likely to be observed under these conditions. Some state support programs effect the same sort of limiting circumstances as do the states which deny fiscal independence to the school districts.

At the other end of the continuum is the more appropriate and ideal procedure of budget construction. The education program for the ensuing school year is detailed by the principal and his faculty. Then this program is converted to anticipated costs which is the spending plan. When this spending plan is correlated with the anticipated revenues, it may well be that certain parts of the education program may require curtailment, modification, or even postponement. The action, though undoubtedly disappointing, assumes a more positive atmosphere. The hindrances are essentially worked out according to the previously derived priority system with curtailment or postponement only until the next time rather than being essentially precluded as is the case in the allotment approach.

Construction of the budget document for an elementary school is obviously delimited by district policy and practice, but within these limitations there is a considerable freedom available to the principal and his faculty. The quality of the budget document likely influences the superordinate decision makers as they ponder the various documents which they must fit into the district's budget requests.

An account of methods in budget procedures in a suburban school district serves to demonstrate the importance of careful budget document preparation. With 65 schools and 60,000 boys and girls, school business administration functions have reached "big business" proportions. It is estimated that the Data Processing Department using an IBM 1440 computer will have reached the machine's capacity for work output within the next two or three years.

The district is the first in the state, to its knowledge, to employ a professional school business manager who has been trained in both school administration and school business management. His job is to supervise a $39,000,000 budget in such a way as to secure the best education for the boys and girls of the district. To do this, the money is divided into 457 budget classes, and is spent by 201 suborganizations. Monthly budget summaries totaling 1,200 pages are given the business manager by modern data-processing methods. Each of these 201 organizations also receives a monthly report as to their budget allotments and monthly expenditures. In February of this year, each organization submitted budget requests for the next year. After processing the requests and determining salaries, the board of education and administrative staff have to determine which programs it can afford and to what extent it can finance them in the coming year.

The business manager must bring together all the needs of the district and translate those needs into dollar amounts so that in the spring of each year the superintendent and staff will be able to make wise choices as they set out the educational direction for the district, the school, and the boys and girls.[6]

6. Granite School District *Newsletter,* Vol. 6, No. 2, May, 1967 (Granite School District, Salt Lake City, Utah).

FINANCIAL ACCOUNTING

With the increased utilization of computers in the public schools, there is a concomitant tendency for centralization of financial accounting. This set of circumstances does not, in any sense, preclude the necessity for the elementary school principal to engage in an effective accounting process. The sophistication of data-yield actually enhances the business management functions that must be executed by the elementary school principal.

It is through financial accounting that the principal procures, expends, protects, organizes, and maintains the resources that propel his school toward an effectiveness operation. Accounting keeps track of the expenditure of funds according to the allocation granted to the various accounts, but it also serves the function of budget document preparation. In other words, records that facilitate audit requirements also facilitate cost analyses for budget construction.

The actual receipt of funds and the ensuing disbursement of these funds for the elementary school are generally functions performed by the district's central business office. Procedures for requisitions, purchasing, and memorandum accounting are essential procedures in the elementary school office.

Memorandum Accounting. Memorandum accounts are essentially a system of accounting which permits the principal to maintain a current and accurate record of budget allotment, amount expended, and the balance remaining in each budget account. The central business office issues monthly statements of the status of the various budget categories in many districts with centralized financial accounting; however, memorandum accounting besides maintaining a check system enables the principal to analyze his expenditures as they relate to his school's education program independently.

The financial accounting system of the central office and the memorandum account system of the elementary school principal's office should utilize the same system which will likely be the one recommended by the United States Office of Education. The principal may develop greater detail or subdivisions within his system if it facilitates his evaluations and analyses.

Of particular interest to the elementary school principal are the categories of payroll and leave utilization because they both exert a peculiar influence upon the effectiveness of the education program. It is likely that the kind of reporting executed by the central office will not suffice for analysis and evaluation of these categories as they influence the effectiveness of the education program.

The plant operation program and the plant maintenance program represent areas of complex problems which may be other categories the elementary school principal will develop beyond the usual scope of memorandum accounting. The two categories bear a direct effect upon the education program and the health and safety of the pupils and teachers. Further, a poor program of operation and maintenance ultimately diverts valuable funds from the education program. Far too typical is the practice of waiting until a crisis develops rather than developing a continuous maintenance program. Finchum reported seven maintenance objectives:

(1) promote health and safety,
(2) provide operating economies,
(3) prevent time loss,
(4) preserve property values,
(5) retard deterioration,
(6) prevent obsolescence, and
(7) develop community pride.[7]

Cost Analyses. Cost analyses of school expenditures are essential prerequisities of effective operation. Because funds for public education are essentially limited and scarce, their allocation and utilization are a major concern of the principal. Cost analyses reveal patterns of distribution and utilization of funds which are necessary for program evaluation. From these analyses, it is possible to discern areas of overallocation or underallocation of resources. This information suggests ways of reallocation to areas of desired greater development and concentration as the faculty members and the principal seek to improve the education program, and especially when priorities must be developed.

Cost analysis yields information permitting comparisons with comparable schools, but extreme caution must be exercised to preclude the use of comparisons for the mere purpose of maintaining the status quo. If extreme deviations in practice are revealed, then it should be determined whether the condition is a case of unusual circumstances which justify the practice or whether there is in fact an inappropriate allocation. Cost analyses should be primarily applied to the school in which

7. R. N. Finchum, *School Plant Management, Organizing the Maintenance Program* (Washington, D.C.: U.S. Government Printing Office, 1960), p. 7.

they are made. Efficient operation or the ultimate disposition of available funds is relative to the school's education program, and one school's efforts at developing and maintaining an effective education program are not necessarily comparable with those of other elementary schools.

Activity Accounting. A comprehensive handbook of finance accounting for activities was prepared by the United States Office of Education.[8] The introductory remarks serve to illustrate its purpose:

The major purpose of this handbook is to establish standard accounts and terminology to be used in accounting for school activity money. It classifies and defines standard receipt and expenditure accounts, and includes a system of accounting for illustrative purposes. The handbook is adaptable for use by elementary schools, junior high schools, senior high schools, and community colleges, and may be used by school systems or by individual schools within a system.[9]

A school activity program is defined as those activities (either curricular or extracurricular) that are financed at least in part by the operation of the program. The accounting is the responsibility of the individual school, although periodic and annual reports are filed with the central business office. The elementary school tends to have fewer activities than do the other levels, but an activity accounting system is just as necessary for the fewer activities. Two accounts are recommended. *Regular Accounts* is for receiving and expending money for the actual operation of the activity program. An example for the elementary school is the paid admission assembly program. The admissions are received and then paid out to the provider of the program. "Profits" or excesses are used for various purposes depending upon the school's policy and practice. The second account category is *Clearing Accounts* and is used for receiving and disbursing funds such as March of Dimes collections in which case the money is paid to the March of Dimes organization. Rentals from school-owned musical instruments or books are also accounted for in clearing accounts and paid to the board of education. This account serves to preclude distortions in regular budget categories. An examination of Table 12–1, *Regular Accounts,* and Table 12–2, *Clearing Accounts,* clarifies the utility and purposes of the two accounts. Both receipts and expenditures are shown.

Activities in the elementary schools are financed in different ways.

8. Everett V. Samuelson *et al.* (compilers), *Financial Accounting for School Activities* (Washington, D.C.: U.S. Government Printing Office, 1959).
9. *Ibid.,* p. xi.

Table 12-1. Regular Accounts

Receipts	Expenditures
10. ACTIVITY INCOME	100. ACTIVITY EXPENSE
11. Admissions	110. Basic Operating Expendi-
12. Prorated Share of	tures
General Activity	111. Personal and Con-
Tickets	tracted Services
13. Dues and Fees	112. Supplies
14. Sales	113. Purchase of Merchan-
15. Student Rentals	dise
from Materials	114. Other Activity Ex-
16. Advertising	pense
17. Guarantees	120. Supplemental Operating
18. Other Activity	Expenditures
Income	121. Health Services
20. GRANTS FROM THE	122. Pupil Transportation
SCHOOL DISTRICT	123. Operation of Plant
30. GIFTS FROM OTHER	124. Maintenance of Plant
SOURCES	125. Fixed Charges
40. OTHER RECEIPTS	200. CAPITAL OUTLAY

SOURCE: Everett V. Samuelson et al. (compilers), Financial Accounting for
       School Activities (Washington, D. C.: U. S. Government Printing Office,
       1959), p. xiv.

Table 12-2. Clearing Accounts

Receipts	Expenditures
1010-a. Board of Education	1010-b. Board of Education
1020-a. Out of School Campaigns	1020-b. Out of School Campaigns
1030-a. Taxes and Deductions	1030-b. Taxes and Deductions
1040-a. Nonstudent Organizations	1040-b. Nonstudent Organizations
1050-a. Returnable Deposits	1050-b. Returnable Deposits
1060-a. General Activity Tickets	1060-b. General Activity Tickets
1070-a. Abatements	1070-b. Abatements
1080-a. Loans from the School	1080-b. Loans from the School
District	District
1090-a. Interfund Transfers	1090-b. Interfund Transfers
1100-a. Petty Cash	1100-b. Petty Cash
1110-a. Miscellaneous Clearing	1110-b. Miscellaneous Clearing
Accounts	Accounts

SOURCE: Everett V. Samuelson et al. (compilers), Financial Accounting for School
       Activities (Washington, D.C.: U.S. Government Printing Office, 1959),
       p. xiv.

In some cases and in some schools, the activities must be self-supporting or nearly so with deficits made up with district funds. In other schools, almost every activity is interpreted as a part of the instruction program and is financed by the district. No matter how the activity program is financed, the principal of the school is responsible for an accurate accounting of the transactions.

Some elementary school principals utilize the activity program and its accounting procedures as a learning activity, especially in the upper elementary school grades. The various grades or classes elect student treasurers who maintain "memorandum" accounts.

PROCUREMENT FUNCTIONS

In a sense, the approval of the budget document by the board of education and its official adoption is *a priori* evidence that the line items have been approved for ultimate purchase. The realities of practice reveal that the case is not quite so pure and simple. Practice varies in the latitude granted to the elementary school principal as he proceeds to expend the funds allotted to his school. The policies and operating procedures of the school district as well as its size and the extent of centralization set the pattern of operation for the elementary school principal.

There are several basic procedures accompanying the expenditure of the budget funds. The ultimate purpose or end of purchasing is procurement of resources. Each school district has established some system within which the elementary school principal operates. A request or requisition initiates the procedure. In most districts a form has been devised to serve this request for equipment or supplies.

Requisitions

When a requisition is initiated by a teacher or other organization member, the item requested may be in the elementary school's storeroom, in the central stores of the district, or it may have to be purchased from some vendor. The principal or his delegated representative will determine this and also whether the item is a legitimate request and whether the budget account's unencumbered balance is adequate to cover the request.

If the item is not in the elementary school's storeroom, the principal will requisition the item from the district's central stores. It will be charged against the budget account for that school. If a purchase is necessary, the school's purchase order will probably be completely executed by the district's business office in order to complete the procurement procedure.

Supply Items and Equipment

There are differences between an item of supply and an item of equipment, but the differences tend to be arbitrary among school districts. In many school districts, the procedures for procurement of a supply item differ from those for equipment items. The United States Office of Education attempted to develop some clarifying criteria in its 1957 accounting handbook.

A supply item is any article or material which meets any one or more of the following conditions:

1. It is consumed in use.
2. It loses its original shape or appearance with use.
3. It is expendable. That is, if the article is damaged or some of its parts are lost or worn out, it is usually more feasible to replace it with an entirely new unit rather than to repair it.
4. It is an inexpensive item having characteristics of equipment whose small unit cost makes it inadvisable to capitalize the item.
5. It loses its identity through incorporation into a different or more complex unit of substance.

An equipment item is an immovable or fixed unit of furniture or furnishings, an instrument, a machine, an apparatus or a set of articles which meets *all* of the following conditions:

1. It retains its original shape and appearance with use.
2. It is nonexpendable, that is, if the article is damaged or some of its parts are lost or worn out, it is usually more feasible to repair it rather than replace it with an entirely new unit.
3. It represents an investment of money which makes it feasible and advisable to capitalize the item.
4. It does not lose its identity through incorporation into a different or more complex unit or substance.[10]

Purchase Orders and Inventory

A requisition is a request; but a purchase order creates a liability; that is, it creates an encumbrance against the funds in the budget account

10. Paul L. Reason and George G. Tankard, Jr., *Property Accounting for State and Local School Systems* (Washington, D.C.: U.S. Government Printing Office, 1959), pp. 98–99.

to which the item is to be charged. Regardless of the amount of time between issuance of the purchase order and the actual payment for the item, the amount is encumbered from the time of the purchase order issuance. Larger school districts stock supply items and many of the more common equipment items based on the experience of previous utilization and current requests in the budget document. The various schools "purchase" by requisition and order from these stocks. Many of the items have been standardized by district policy and are purchased on bids.

With largeness and centralization, a first impression might well be that the elementary school principal has but minor responsibility in purchasing and procuring items of supply and equipment, but such is not the case. The basic importance of school office functions, including the business management functions, was detailed in Chapter 11. An effective level of operation was declared to be based in part on the kind of management support provided the teachers as they perform their task assignment. The matters of procuring items of supply and equipment are obvious. Timing is important because teacher effectiveness in the classroom relates to having the resources at hand when they are needed. Satisfactory timing in procurement comes from anticipation of needs, and both teachers and principals have responsibilities in this matter. However, the effective elementary school principal will have devised a system of inventory control based on past experience of utilization and on the approved items in the current budget document. A perpetual inventory is a general recommendation that is as applicable for the elementary school as it is for the school district. An actual count is made and recorded when items enter the storeroom and again as the items are withdrawn for use. This practice does not imply hoarding, only maintaining an adequate amount in order to anticipate the needs of the school. Such inventorying procedures serve well in preparation of budget documents.

Specifications

Although items of supply and equipment are initially procured by the district's business management officials, the specifications developed for these items should emanate from active participation by those who use them—the teachers and principals. Purchasing large quantities of paper on the single variable of lowest apparent bid is not necessarily efficiency in operation, especially if the quality or another characteristic renders it unsuitable for classroom use. The involvement of teachers and principals is an obvious necessity, if effective levels of operation are sought.

The development, implementation, and maintenance of specifications for supply and equipment items must fit into a policy which accommodates review and modification. There is a need to keep specifications current in order to take advantage of new products and improved products. In this era of astonishing technological development there must also be an opportunity to try out promising products and equipment. Development is so revolutionary that it is difficult to keep specifications current. If the purpose of specifications were only efficiency in procurement, there might be a question of investing time and talent in their development; however, the original underlying purpose, which was the prevention of fraud, coupled with efficiency would appear to justify the investment.

PROPERTY ACCOUNTING

A particularly important part of the business management functions, frequently underemphasized, is that of property accounting. The elementary school principal is involved in property accounting in several ways. On the one hand, he maintains "memorandum" property accounts because the district's central office assumes primary responsibility for the function. But the elementary school principal must also maintain certain property accounts which serve his school as effective operation is sought.

The United States Office of Education has published a handbook for classification of property accounts which has served to promote much-needed standardization within and among the public schools.[11]

A property account ... is a descriptive heading under which is recorded specific information about land, buildings, and equipment under the jurisdiction and control of school districts and any other units that operate schools.

Property accounts are items of information that would be kept on an appropriate accounting or record form. They provide the basis for making essential reports to agencies concerned and to the public.[12]

An abbreviated classification of the major classes of property accounts is shown in Table 12–3. An examination of the categories reveals the importance of property accounting for the effective elementary school

11. *Ibid.*
12. *Ibid.*, p. 3.

Table 12-3. Classification of Property Accounts

SITES (100 series)

110. Site Identification
120. Area of Site
130. Cost of Site

BUILDINGS (200 series)

210. Building Identification
220. Size of Building
230. Cost of Building
240. Instructional Areas in Building
250. Administration Areas in Building
260. Circulation Areas of Building
270. Service Areas in Building
280. Service Systems in Building

EQUIPMENT (300 series)

310. Equipment under Unit Control
320. Equipment under Group Control

SOURCE: Paul L. Reason and George G. Tankard, Jr.,
Property Accounting for State and Local
School Systems (Washington, D. C.: U. S.
Government Printing Office, 1959), p. 4.

principal, even though prime responsibility for a considerable part is assumed by the district's central office.

There are three distinct property accounting categories, and all of them have relevance for the elementary school business management functions.

1. *School Plant.* A school plant consists of the site, buildings, and equipment. In this category an elementary school is the *unit* for property accounting.

2. *Supporting Services Facilities.* A supporting services facility is a noninstructional facility such as an administration building or a bus maintenance garage and parking lot. This category is of least interest and importance to the elementary school principal.

3. *Equipment Unassigned to a Plant or Facility.* Accounting in this category is done for the individual item of equipment or equipment group. School buses, power mowers, and certain media equipment used in several plants would be units for accounting in this category.

The unit of accounting for property of greatest importance to the elementary school principal is the school plant with the equipment

(300 series) classification serving to yield information as well as the account for recording of school property, for improved budget preparation, and for greater utilization of available property.

In equipment (300 series), there are two subcategories: equipment under unit control and equipment under group control. The difference lies in whether the equipment is assigned to a specific school plant or whether the equipment is unassigned and is utilized by several different school plants. The elementary school principal will maintain the property account of equipment under unit control, keeping records of his school's furniture, desks, chairs, media equipment. Certain other equipment and particularly items, such as media equipment, which are shared by several school plants will be recorded in a group control account in order that these items of equipment can be used in the school as needed. A particularly important account entry is that for library books. The property accounting handbook includes the following explanation under *Library Books:* "Library books are purchased for general use and not primarily for use in certain classes, grades, or other particular student groups. They include reference sets and dictionaries, but not periodicals and textbooks." [13]

One of the important developments in the public elementary school is the increase in instructional media centers. Instead of the school library serving as an adjunct to the curriculum or as an appendix of the school, the library has become a part of the curriculum. Actually the library, its functions, and its tasks have been redefined as to its purpose. The result has been the structuring of instructional media centers. With the increased utilization of library and media materials and equipment, accounting for this property and procuring equipment to ensure work flow and activity flow assume new dimensions of involvement for the elementary school principal's office.

Business management functions present many tasks for the elementary school principal. As they become systematized and routinized, the principal obtains more viable information which can be utilized for improved effectiveness in the total operation. A well-developed budget document and an orderly financial accounting system are vital, but they represent only a portion of the school business management functions. Cost analyses, procurement functions, and property accounting, frequently ignored or underdeveloped, contribute immensely to the level of operation in an elementary school.

13. *Ibid.,* p. 81.

REFERENCES

Burke, Arvid J., *Financing Public Schools in the United States* (New York: Harper & Bros., 1957).

Finchum, R. N., *School Plant Management, Organizing the Maintenance Program* (Washington, D.C.: U.S. Government Printing Office, 1960).

Johns, Roe L., and E. L. Morphet, *Financing the Public Schools* (Englewood Cliffs, N.J.: Prentice-Hall, 1960).

Knezevich, Stephen J., and John Guy Fowlkes, *Business Management of Local School Systems* (New York: Harper & Bros., 1960).

Mort, P. R., W. C. Reusser, and J. S. Polley, *Public School Finance* (New York: McGraw-Hill, 1960).

Reason, Paul L., and George G. Tankard, *Property Accounting for State and Local School Systems* (Washington, D.C.: U.S. Government Printing Office, 1959).

Reason, Paul L., and Alpheus L. White, *Financial Accounting for Local and State School Systems, Standard Receipts and Expenditures Accounts* (Washington, D.C.: U.S. Government Printing Office, 1957).

Samuelson, Everett V., et al. (compilers), *Financial Accounting for School Activities* (Washington, D.C.: U.S. Government Printing Office, 1959).

Chapter 13

SPECIAL OR AUXILIARY
SERVICES AND
CUSTODIAL FUNCTIONS

M AINTAINING, facilitating, and implementing education program components for more effective teaching-learning situations and experiences is the central role of the elementary school principal. To be effective in this role, the principal seeks to ensure work flow
and activity flow by integrating the numerous management functions of
the elementary school. This chapter is concerned with certain special
or auxiliary services and custodial functions which contribute to the
teaching-learning experiences either directly or indirectly. These services
and functions are frequently taken for granted and thus remain at survival
levels. Yet no school can be described as effective until these services
and functions are operating optimally. The effective elementary school
principal recognizes the vital aspects of the direct and indirect benefits
emanating from an integrated materials-media center, from health, transportation, school lunch services and from custodial functions; and he
attempts to maximize the contributions of each.

SPECIAL OR AUXILIARY SERVICES

Recent developments have served to stimulate interest in certain special or auxiliary services. These developments derive from a number of
sources and interested groups. Federal program funds have furnished
prime motivation for much of the development. Specialization and professionalization have provided additional impetus with state, regional,
and national organizations to alert the members of the essential need for
continuing and upgrading their efforts.

New knowledge, new relationships, and new applications in the library, audiovisual, health, transportation, and lunch services have stimulated increased preparation and certification requirements for personnel. Improvements in the technological characteristics of many of these services have operated to make their utilization more acceptable to teachers; for example, almost anyone can make a transparency today, and projectors do not require standby operator-technicians.

Instructional Media Centers

The instructional media center is a complex formed by combining numerous facilities and services. Ahlers provided a definition of a library which is applicable to an instructional media center. "A school library today, both elementary and secondary, must be a centrally organized collection, readily accessible, of many kinds of materials that, used together, enrich and support the educational program of the school of which it is an integral part." [1]

Beggs was more specific in his description of an instructional media center which ". . . is a place where ideas, in their multimedia and diverse forms, are housed, used, and distributed to classrooms and laboratories throughout the school. The IMC contains books, magazines, pamphlets, films, filmstrips, maps, pictures, electronic tapes, recordings, slides, transparencies, mock-ups, and learning programs." [2]

An instructional media center serves almost to remove it from the category of an auxiliary service in the elementary school; however, it is very obviously a special service and one that an effective elementary school principal must develop. These centers are vastly different in their services even when compared with the various separate facilities provided in certain schools. Many schools and school districts still provide minimal libraries and even more minimal audiovisual or media facilities. But there are both internal and external factors which portend an end to survival levels of operation in these services.

Teacher preparation programs in the colleges tend to provide more and more training and experiences in instructional media centers. With this orientation, the more recently prepared teachers expect and demand these facilities, and they also influence other teachers in the schools. There are numerous teachers who specialize in media areas as they

1. Eleanor E. Ahlers, "Library Service: A Changing Concept," *Educational Leadership*, Vol. 23, March, 1966, pp. 452–453.
2. David W. Beggs, "Organization Follows Use . . . The Instructional Materials Center," *Audiovisual Instruction*, Vol. 9, November, 1964, p. 602.

pursue advanced study programs. Institutes in media areas are common-place during the summers, with librarians, audiovisual personnel, and teachers preparing themselves as building media specialists or as district-level media administrators. Other factors which stimulate interest in instructional media centers would include the saturation of the nation with educational television programing, state departments of public instruction giving added impetus, and the general national alert in the various journals commonly used by educators and teachers.

Much of the activity in the effective elementary school does in fact center upon the generalized concept of an instructional media center, although there is no firm agreement on just what constitutes an instructional media center. The development of instructional media centers may take a library (printed material) orientation or a media (non-printed material) orientation. Factors which tend to influence the direction include the orientation of the personnel involved, the general condition of the library and/or media facilities, and the general emphasis of the teachers in the school. The elementary school principal must assess his school in terms of what it possesses, what it needs, and what appears to be the desired form of the instructional media center for the school. The present flexibility in instructional media center orientation is a prime consideration of administration to be encouraged because of the continuing change effected by new knowledge and developments.

The direction and extent of development of an elementary school instructional media center will be determined at least in part by the pattern which emerges for the school district. Just as centralization poses advantages and disadvantages, so too does decentralization. Likely, there are parts of an instructional media center which should be district-wide and other aspects which can be most satisfactorily developed in the individual school.

Media specialists and materials production personnel are two relatively new position developments. The media specialist tends to be either a librarian or an audiovisual coordinator who has acquired additional training and preparation to qualify for administering the emerging instructional media center, either at the district level or school level. Materials production personnel prepare materials, advise in the production of materials, or counsel in the selection of acceptable commercial materials. Materials production personnel tend to have district-wide responsibilities, but not exclusively.

The elementary school principal has prime responsibilities in the development, implementation, and maintenance of the instructional media center for his school, and these responsibilities extend beyond the recruitment and selection of personnel and the procurement of financial support.

Health Services

Educators have long emphasized the importance of health and safety services and facilities with virtually every pronouncement of goals of education issued by national commissions and committees including a statement relating to health. Yet in practice the general level of development is varied—from virtually nonexistent in some schools to well-articulated and effective programs in others. The scope and quality of health services vary so much from one school district to another that no consistent pattern of development is apparent. Size of the school, rural isolation, lack of funds, state legal restrictions, other agencies delegated the responsibility, and other reasons are offered to explain the lack of health services in the schools; yet none of them is really tenable under close scrutiny. Likely, the primary reason underlying the presence or absence of such services relates to the interest in and commitment to their development by the school administrators.

Essentially, the scope of the elementary school's health services cannot develop much beyond the limits allowed by the district's policy and practice. But the health services that are available can become effective ones, if the principal and his faculty become concerned about the well-being of the children. Leadership in developing this interest is the responsibility of the elementary school principal. He is also responsible for demonstrating to his superordinates the need for expanded programs, especially in view of the fact that more and more children from all socioeconomic levels are spending longer periods of time in the elementary schools.

In recent years, we have witnessed an urgent appeal for the mental and emotional health aspects in addition to the more traditional concern for the physical aspects of health services. These aspects require the services of physicians, psychologists, and psychiatrists. Programs including these aspects are limited to schools where there are funds available to support the commitment and to schools where community clinics and services have been organized to provide these services.

School health services should minimally provide for correction of problems that hinder maximum effectiveness in learning and for an understanding and desire for good physical and mental health in all phases of life. Essentially, three major dimensions constitute the school health services program.

1. *Preventative and Ameliorative Dimension.* It is this dimension that includes activities and services which attempt to detect problems or possible problems so they may be treated and corrected before they become serious health problems. Physical examinations and dental examinations either by school-employed physicians and dentists or by encouragement of parents to obtain these examinations for their children are rather common practices. Usually the minimum program seeks an annual dental examination and a physical examination twice during the elementary school years, and once each in junior high school and in senior high school. Some schools insist on these periodic examinations before a child is admitted to a certain grade, but such insistence must be measured in terms of values and mores of the various groups in the community.

Immunization programs are frequently conducted in cooperation with public health groups and have been very successful. Vision and hearing screenings are more and more frequently conducted annually. Speech and hearing correctionists and therapists and school nurses can process large numbers of examinations in a relatively short time. Their aim is to detect possible problems for referral to remedial attention.

Although there is no established pattern for the provision of the preventative and ameliorative services, they should be considered essential minimal services within the realm of realization for every school. Utilization of the various health agencies of the county and/or city should be emphasized whenever it is feasible because they have been established to provide these services. If the elementary school principal initiates efforts to obtain the cooperation of these health agencies, the minimal health services of the school are certain to be improved. There are too many known instances of school districts developing duplicate services with the result that neither program is very effective.

2. *Guardianship Dimension.* The school day is an extended period of time with a number of activities scheduled which can produce accidents. Further, the chances of illness and emergencies of one sort or another increase as the number of individuals increase which seems to be a characteristic of the elementary school. Provision of rest and isolation facilities and emergency and first aid treatment would appear to be minimal aspects of this health service dimension. The typical ele-

mentary school tends to lack the facilities, and provision is difficult in older buildings because space is not available. However, the provision of first aid treatment and emergency care is easier. Lack of full-time school nurses would suggest that someone in the school should be trained in first aid and emergency treatment.

3. *Educational Dimension.* An effective health education program can be developed when the principal coordinates the efforts of the persons who have responsibilities for *teaching about* health and of those who are concerned about *caring for* health.

Health education classes should include instruction about the body and its hygiene, about safety, about mental health, contagious and communicable diseases, community health hazards and problems, including drugs, and nutrition. The school lunch program and the physical education program can be integrated with health education instruction. Many school districts have supervisors for school lunch programs and also for physical education, but all too few of these school districts exhibit any evidence of cooperative planning. The initial interest and effort appear to rest with the elementary school principal in bringing together these persons, his teachers, and other persons and agencies from the community to plan, implement, and maintain an effective health education program.

Pupil Transportation Services

From rather modest and meager beginnings, pupil transportation services have become a major activity in the public schools of the nation. Pupil transportation services have implications for virtually the entire education program.

Pupil transportation was a characteristic phenomenon of rural sparseness. To encourage attendance was the first purpose, but it soon became obvious that more effective education programs could be provided if larger numbers of pupils were brought together. Thus, with reconfiguration of school districts into larger units, pupil transportation emerged as the enabling service. It is not unusual to observe pupils from one small community being transported to a nearby community to attend school.

Pupil transportation in urban areas is a more recent phenomenon. A principal reason for pupil transportation in urban areas is safety from hazards. Pupils are transported to and from school simply because there are too many hazards emanating from traffic congestion.

In other instances, it is necessary to transport pupils from one neighborhood to an underpopulated attendance center in order to maximize the utilization of classrooms. Sometimes it is wiser policy to transport urban pupils than it is to construct new school buildings. New neighborhoods develop, but only the experience acquired over a period of time will determine whether the people will remain in the neighborhood until the children complete school. In some cases, a neighborhood continues to be a "young" one; that is, the people tend to remain until their children have completed their elementary school years, and then they move to other areas. Young parents follow into the neighborhood perpetuating the need for elementary school facilities with secondary schools not a major problem. Thus mobility and "age" of the neighborhood within an urban area create problems of providing building facilities and/or pupil transportation services.

A number of approaches to the provision of pupil transportation have developed. Contracting with private carriers was among the earliest methods. In some areas, an individual purchased a bus and a chassis and was assigned a given bus route by the contracting school district. In cities, the practice of contracting for pupil transportation with the city transit company is not unusual. Many school districts own their fleets of buses and employ drivers and maintenance personnel.

In some instances, and for a variety of reasons, there are school districts which contract with parents to transport their children by private automobile. Sometimes, it is less costly in terms of time and scheduling to contract with parents than it is to schedule a school bus for an isolated pupil pickup, especially if the road system is poorly developed. On other occasions, it is easier for private transportation than it is for bus transportation when a pupil has a physical handicap.

Although pupil transportation is an added cost, the benefits derived by bringing the pupils to larger schools represent very compelling arguments. Cost studies tend to reveal school-owned fleets as the least costly method, and the fact of complete control and its resulting independence permit a greater utilization of the buses in the total education program.

Although pupil transportation services tend to be centralized at the central office level as a district-wide service, there is major involvement for the elementary school principal. The fact of having pupils in school who are transported poses one kind of involvement. The method of transportation service also poses various kinds of problems and involvement. These aspects have to do with getting the pupils to and from school. School day schedules must mesh with transportation schedules. If the district uses a bus for elementary and secondary school pupils, the problems are different from those when a bus is used only for transporting elementary school pupils. Early arrivals, early departures, and late arrivals create problems.

There are management functions relating to boarding, riding, and unloading the bus—all more or less relating to safety, well-being, and acceptable pupil behavior. These functions are shared by the teachers in the classroom and tend to blend with another important aspect of pupil transportation services—namely, how they can be utilized in developing more effective education programs.

In addition to safety, acceptable behavior, and citizenship, punctuality and community interest are promoted. Utilization of transportation service for field trips and excursions to enrich the classroom experiences present scheduling tasks for the elementary school office.

There are school districts which transport pupils during the school day to other centers for varying special services. These services and activities include therapy for children with speech, hearing, and/or vision handicaps. Occasionally pupils are transported for music, physical education, and school lunch participation.

The involvement of the elementary school principals in policy evaluation and determination is particularly desirable practice. They are responsible for the administration of the district's policies, and their experiences should be valued for policy evaluation. Keeping both parents and pupils informed of schedules and regulations and of any changes or variations become tasks of the elementary school principal.

School Lunch Services

School lunch programs have grown at exponential rates since their early inception. Although Bryan cites the first school lunch program as that of the Children's Aid Society in New York City in 1853 and credits the Boston School Committee with the beginning of the school lunch movement in 1894,[3] the national school lunch program has gained from events since 1946. Federal participation in money and "surplus" commodities since World War II has been an enabling service. National interest in the elimination of poverty and culture lag more recently has had an effect of stimulation. Reconfiguration of school districts and

3. M. deG. Bryan, *The School Cafeteria* (New York: Appleton-Century-Crofts, 1936), p. 3.

the transportation of pupils to schools away from their residences have necessitated a concern about lunch programs and nutrition. Further, the school lunch program has been popularized by providing attractive and nourishing lunches.

School lunch services are generally shared by the district's central offices and the individual school personnel. Some elementary schools have complete self-contained facilities including the kitchen and dining areas. In other schools, the food is catered from a district central kitchen to serving and dining facilities. There are some very successful programs with the food prepared in a central kitchen and served in the individual classrooms. Enrollment, participation, and available facilities determine in a large measure the procedure.

Involvement of the elementary school principal ranges from almost complete responsibility to very little direct responsibility. But he is responsible for scheduling, controlling, serving, and utilizing the lunch program for learning experiences. The number of lunch periods is determined by the number of pupils and the seating capacity of the dining area. If a 30-minute lunch period is desired, not more than four and preferably only three periods can be scheduled. Some facilities force staggered class dismissals to prevent a pileup of pupils in the serving line. When inadequate facilities create these kinds of management problems, the elementary school principal is faced with the possibility of an auxiliary service becoming master of the school program.

Actually, many of the school lunch management functions can be routinized and performed by paraprofessional and noncertificated personnel. Developing operational efficiency with the facilities available remains the responsibility of the principal. Close cooperation with the school lunch personnel is important. In those districts where the school lunch program is decentralized, the management functions, including budget considerations, may represent a major responsibility and involvement of the principal.

Involvement of the elementary school principal, then, concerns the managerial tasks and also the maintenance of attractive and nourishing lunches which encourage pupil participation. Actually, it is easy to conceptualize the importance and desirability of the involvement of the pupils and teachers as well as of the school lunch personnel and the principal. Utilization of the school lunch program in the health education program is desirable in all elementary schools and especially so in schools with pupils from the low socioeconomic neighborhoods.

CUSTODIAL FUNCTIONS

Commitment to continuous and improved plant operation and maintenance programs is a characteristic behavior of an effective elementary school principal. Successful program implementation involves the cooperation of the faculty members and the students, but the key variable is the level of performance of the custodial personnel. Frequently the selection and assignment of custodians to the school plants are functions of the district's buildings and grounds department. An effective school district will have personnel policies which enable the principal and the custodians to develop appropriate job descriptions for the elementary school. Within this framework, it is possible to realize the following maintenance objectives, as reported by Finchum.[4]

1. *Promote health and safety.* Heating systems, ventilating systems, lighting, and other essential service systems must be maintained in optimal working condition. Cleanliness of the building tends to generate greater care among the pupils to keep it clean and attractive. Good housekeeping attitudes and habits are encouraged by most teachers, and a clean school will help reinforce this teaching.

Closely related to health and cleanliness is safety. Regular and routine safety checks should be developed by the custodian and the principal. Many lives are at stake: fire doors must be kept closed and operative; storage areas must be kept clear of flammable materials; exits must be kept unlocked; grounds and play equipment must be maintained in good repair.

2. *Provide operating economies.* Economy is closely associated with efficiency which is defined as the ratio of useful output to total input. But far too many schools are characterized by misapplications of efficiency and economy. The apparent concept is that of "saving money." There is no evidence of preventive maintenance nor little evidence of a planned, continuous maintenance program. As a result, roofs are repaired after water has soaked through the interior ceilings, plumbing and toilet fixtures must be replaced because of long neglect, and heating systems are cleaned and repaired after a period of cold weather has caused a breakdown. The custodial personnel and the principal must prevent these occurrences by developing job descriptions, with the prin-

4. R. N. Finchum, *School Plant Management, Organizing the Maintenance Program* (Washington, D.C.: U.S. Government Printing Office, 1960), p. 7.

cipal ascertaining that the work and periodic checking are done on schedule.

Another application of economy and efficiency relates to the determination of how best to accomplish the work to be done. This is a justifiable application of the principles set forth by Taylor.[5] Thus, schedules for cleaning and other tasks are developed, specifying those which must be accomplished daily, weekly, monthly, and for other periods. These schedules ensure that the primary programs of the school are not interrupted and that the purposes of the plant operation and maintenance programs are realized. Appropriate materials and equipment are specified and procured.

3. *Prevent time loss.* An effectively developed operation and maintenance program which includes functions and tasks of an anticipatory nature will serve to ensure that the school plant can operate each scheduled day. This is not to state that a rare or occasional breakdown will be precluded. With each year of use, and even "normal" use is hard usage when the number of pupils is considered, the sanitary system, the heating and ventilating systems move closer to obsolescence. There are incidents on record of a desire to "get" one more year of service from a worn-out boiler. Replacement during the summer shutdown would have ensured full-time operation the ensuing school year.

Effective accounting procedures, procurement, and inventorying systems will ensure the availability of equipment and materials for the operation and maintenance of the school plant. There is no justification for shortages of towels, soap, cleaning agents, and other items so essential to the school program.

4. *Preserve property values.* School plants are usually utilized much longer than the planners and builders generally anticipate. This is focused into reality when it is realized that some elementary school buildings in the eastern sections of the nation were in use before Abraham Lincoln moved into the White House.

Replacement is difficult and is becoming ever more difficult with the increasing school population requiring new and additional school plants. The trend of inflation in construction costs and the extra wear and tear created by overcrowding in many of the schools represent relevant factors in the urgency for maximum repair and maintenance programs.

5. *Retard deterioration.* School plant maintenance tasks relate gen-

5. Frederick W. Taylor, *Principles of Scientific Management* (New York: Harper & Bros., 1911).

erally to the making of major and minor repairs or replacements which serve to prolong the utility of the grounds and plant. School plant operation is concerned with tasks relating more to the day-to-day tasks such as sweeping, dusting, damp mopping, scrubbing and polishing, chalkboard cleaning, light bulb replacement, and equipment and supply storage. Cleanliness of classrooms, toilets, halls, and service areas should be noted. In practice, it is difficult to separate the two programs because they are both designed to accomplish the same general ends.

6. *Prevent obsolescence.* School plant operation and maintenance programs serve to prolong the useful life of the school building, its equipment, and its furniture. Undoubtedly there are many ancient buildings which should be demolished and replaced. There are agencies which in recent years have had an interest in the health and safety of the pupils. State fire marshals have issued minimum standards for safety and also have a record of enforcing them. These actions have served to prevent obsolescence on the one hand, and to close down hazardous structures on the other. Furthermore, new plants must meet the regulations and standards set forth in these codes.

7. *Develop community pride.* A school with an effective education program is not as easy to observe as is a school with clean and orderly interiors and attractive school grounds. Thus, the latter aspects—the physical appearance—often represent the basis or source of the community members' impressions of a school. Frequently, participation in public meetings held in the school building is the only contact many people have with the school. Cleanliness and attractiveness tend to generate community support.

But equally important are the pride and care that cleanliness and attractiveness generate in the pupils who use the buildings. In some neighborhoods of low socioeconomic means, the school building may be the only place where some children are exposed to cleanliness and attractiveness. There have been accounts relating how the teachers and the pupils have helped in cleaning the school grounds and even in repainting the classroom walls to create more attractive surroundings. Not infrequently, these children have effected the same sort of rejuvenation of the entire neighborhood. If these things are this important to these children, it is obvious that good teaching and learning can be best attained in a clean and attractive environment.

In order to realize these seven objectives, the custodial personnel, the principal, the teachers, and the pupils will be actively involved in one way or another. But the prime responsibility for effecting the desired outcomes rests with the custodial personnel. Often the level of effectiveness of the custodial program is directly proportional to the involvement of the elementary school principal in developing schedules, standards, and an insistence on performance.

Another important aspect of custodial functions which involves the cooperation of the custodial personnel and the principal concerns the use of the school building by community groups and agencies. Educators have long advocated the concept of the school as a community center, but such utilization incurs numerous problems. Even after policies have been developed to regulate which groups and agencies are to be permitted to use the building, the principal is faced with scheduling these activities around the regular school program.

The importance of the cooperation of the custodial personnel is obvious. Preparing for the outside group entails cleaning the area and setting up the furniture and equipment needed by the group. Rearranging the area after the meeting to ready it for regular use is another chore for the custodial personnel. If the meeting is scheduled for evening hours, the building must be opened, lighted, heated, and closed at the end. These tasks are frequently shared by the custodial personnel and the principal.

REFERENCES

Ahlers, Eleanor E., "Library Service: A Changing Concept," *Educational Leadership,* Vol. 23, March, 1966, pp. 452–453.

American Association for Health, Physical Education, and Recreation, *Teaching Safety in the Elementary School* (Washington, D.C.: National Education Association, 1962).

American Association of School Librarians, *The Elementary School Library* (Washington, D.C.: National Education Association, 1966).

American Library Association, *How To Start an Elementary School Library* (Chicago: American Library Association, 1962).

Association for Supervision and Curriculum Development, "Centers for Learning," *Educational Leadership,* Vol. 21, January, 1964.

Association of School Librarians, *Standards for School Library Programs* (Chicago: American Library Association, 1960).

Beggs, David W., "Organization Follows Use . . . The Instructional Material Center," *Audiovisual Instruction,* Vol. 9, November, 1964, p. 602.

Brown, James W., *et al., A-V Instruction: Materials and Methods* (New York: McGraw-Hill, 1964).

Featherstone, E. Glenn, and D. P. Culp, *Pupil Transportation* (New York: Harper & Bros., 1965).

Finchum, R. N., *School Plant Management: Administrating the Custodial Program* (Washington, D.C.: U.S. Government Printing Office, 1961).

——, *School Plant Management: Organizing the Maintenance Program* (Washington, D.C.: U.S. Government Printing Office, 1960).

Hodges, Elizabeth D., "Central Libraries and Classroom Libraries—Ten Arguments For Both," *School Activities and the Library* (Chicago: American Library Association, 1963).

Joint Committee on Health Problems in Education, *Health Aspects of the School Lunch Program* (Washington, D.C.: National Education Association, 1956).

Langton, Clair V., Ross L. Allen, and Philip Wexler, *School Health—Organization and Services* (New York: Ronald Press, 1961).

Mahar, Hubert H. (ed.), *The School Library as a Materials Center* (Washington, D.C.: U.S. Government Printing Office, 1964).

National Council on Schoolhouse Construction, *Elementary School Plant Planning* (Nashville, Tenn.: George Peabody College, 1958).

——, *Guide for Planning School Plants* (East Lansing, Mich.: University of Michigan, 1964).

Yeager, William A., *Administration of Noninstructional Personnel and Services* (New York: Harper & Bros., 1959).

Part V

The Principal and His Profession

Chapter 14

PROFESSIONAL
MISSION

A S we scan the demands that appear to be posed for administration in the next decade, it becomes clear that knowledge, competence, and commitment will continue to characterize the essence and emphasis of the elementary school principal's professional mission. Management and leadership necessary to the creation of outstanding elementary schools will require broad administrative competence and extensive knowledge of the purposes, processes, and technologies underlying elementary education. Significant avenues to the attainment of administrative excellence will include sustained scholarly effort, attention to worthy educational purposes, awareness of important professional movements, sensitivity to inadequacies in both knowledge and performance, and commitment to professional improvement.

EVOLVING MISSION OF ADMINISTRATORS

The historical antecedents of current administrative theory are at least a century old. According to one writer,[1] administration of the 1870's was the ability to teach pedagogy—since the chief function of the administrator was to train teachers. Around the turn of the century, administration was regarded as applied philosophy. A quarter-century later the prevailing concept was one of business management. In the period 1935–1950, administrative focus was on technical expertise. Matters such as budgeting, accounting, and purchasing were considered to be the essence of administration. Coupled with this new movement

1. H. Warren Button, "Doctrine of Administration: A Brief History," *Educational Administration Quarterly,* Vol. XI, No. 3, Autumn, 1966, pp. 216–222.

was confidence in the belief that schools should serve democracy and that schools themselves should become democratic institutions. During the past decade, educational administration has come to be regarded by many as an applied behavioral science, albeit with persisting overtones of business management, technical expertise, and democratic supervision.

Close and analytic examinations of past modes of thought about educational administration reveal not only a gradual evolution of concepts but also a series of new directions and emphases—often paralleling or accompanying extensive social change. The fact that skill in the conceptualization and development of educational purposes, goals, and policies appears to be of equal importance today with high level competence in the technical and process dimensions of administration may be intimately related to the rapid social change documented in earlier chapters. Particular attention was directed to the explosions of knowledge and population, to domestic and international crises and tensions, and to the impact of science and technology. These forces and changes appear to have had great impact on current thinking about the administrator's professional mission. The critical nature of this mission has been much emphasized in recent years.

It may be that the strong management flavor of administrative roles of the past may become less tenable as the purposes and missions of today's educational enterprise are subjected to closer scrutiny and reappraisal. Leadership in school administration appears to have emerged as a critically important factor. As yet, however, there is no prototype, complete in detail, for the professional school administrator. Perhaps the construction and delineation of these prototypes will become tasks of high priority for both students and practitioners of administration in the decade ahead.

COMPETENCE IN ELEMENTARY SCHOOL ADMINISTRATION

For many years, principal emphases in the study and teaching of school administration centered upon the technical-managerial tasks of administrators, upon administrative organization and structure, upon important administrative processes, upon human relations skills, and upon administration as a social process. Contemporary thinking has achieved a solid synthesis of such emphases.

Within the past 15 years, moreover, much has been accomplished in incorporating knowledge relevant to school administration from both the social sciences and humanities. New understandings of organizational behavior, authority and responsibility, conflict resolution, and similar phenomena have resulted from studies in social psychology and sociology. Human relations and leadership studies have contributed insight into efficiency and effectiveness of organizations. Decision making both within a system and in the larger community setting has been improved by the contribution of concepts from studies in public administration and from the application of political science theory to educational administration. Social science models and theories have provided a means of organizing and relating the complex social phenomena encountered in administration.

Most recently, major attention has been directed toward reappraisal of the administrator's responsibility for the analysis of social change and for active participation in shaping educational purposes and directions. Stress has been placed upon the need for educational leaders to be finely attuned to the interrelationship between education and culture and to the educational implications of broad social movements.[2] Competence in the generation of educational policies and participation in policy determination and legitimation processes have also been advocated for school administrators. This view sees the administrator as one who is conversant with the history of human purposes, who is active in educational policy development, and who operates within the mainstream of societal forces that initiate and guide social reform.[3]

Purpose Competencies

Competence in conceptualizing and developing educational goals, purposes, and policies is becoming as important to the total professional mission of the elementary school principal as skill in the technical and process areas of administration. Competence in this new and vital area of administration will be difficult to acquire in the absence of sustained professional commitment and continuous study and self-improvement. The practitioner who aspires to outstanding performance will seek improvement of a number of salient abilities. Chief among these are the following: (a) the ability to generate viable educational policies from

2. See, for example, Arthur W. Munk, "Education and the Challenge of the Future," *School and Society*, Vol. 95, No. 2290, March 18, 1967.

3. See, for example, James G. Harlow, "Purpose Defining: The Central Function of the School Administrator," in Jack A. Culbertson and Stephen P. Hencley (eds.), *Preparing Administrators: New Perspectives* (Columbus, Ohio: University Council for Educational Administration, 1962).

complex and interrelated social movements and changes, (*b*) the ability to provide leadership in the resolution of value dilemmas and social conflicts surrounding education, and (*c*) the ability to propose ways in which education can assist in the development and implementation of cultural purposes.

1. *Ability to perceive educational policy in relation to evolving cultural change.* An administrator with this kind of competence is skilled in the analysis of highly complex problems with complicated interrelationships. He has a deep appreciation of the role of the schools in society and is adept at decision making which involves the social, economic, psychological, and political components of educational problems. He is sensitive to powerful forces affecting education and is skilled in abstracting essential educational implications from the currents of social change. The professional mission of elementary school administrators calls for continuous development of these competencies. Competence in purpose-definition activities can significantly affect the quality of educational decision making and operation in local school districts.

2. *Ability to propose and to plan ways in which education can implement societal purposes.* The need for sound leadership in appraising educational directions is evident at every level of education. Educational leaders will need to accept increasing responsibility for developing constructive solutions to.major social problems through education. The functions suggested by Culbertson [4] for educational planning agencies suggest that educational administrators should seek involvement in each of the following activities:

a. determining through analysis and assessment those educational objectives which should receive high priority for given time periods;

b. developing long-range master plans to ensure attainment of objectives at various educational levels;

c. delineating program alternatives for achieving educational goals and dimensionalizing the alternatives in terms of cost-benefit analyses;

d. assessing state and local financial resources available to education and, if needed, developing legislative proposals and support to deal with inadequacies;

e. developing adequate school district structures for achieving accepted educational objectives; and

---

4. Jack A. Culbertson, "State Planning for Education," in Edgar L. Morphet and Charles O. Ryan (eds.), *Planning and Effecting Needed Changes in Education* (Denver, Colo.: Publishers Press, 1967).

f. interpreting to public decision-making bodies the flow of quantitative data about education which has implications for master planning.[5]

3. *Leadership in helping to resolve substantive value conflicts in society.* Our history catalogs an unending sequence of value dilemmas. Independence, separation of church and state, state rights, federal rights, slavery, labor rights, and freedom and control of private enterprise are illustrative of the many value conflicts which have occupied central positions in the public forum at various times.

Today's school administrators must face value-laden problems associated with integration, with equal educational opportunity, with excellence in education, with local versus federal control of education, with alienation of today's youth, with the source and amount of financial support for education, and with the relationship of public education to projects such as head-start, job corps, and community action programs.

A major demand on administrators is provision of leadership in untangling conflicting community values and weaving them into acceptable purposes for public elementary education. Effectiveness in this area requires a global and defensible concept of elementary education based on sound purposes in a broad social setting. At times, performance will involve mediation in relation to incompatible proposals, and the formulation of policy in a matrix of social and ideological conflict.

Process Competencies

In relation to process, the elementary school administrator is responsible for his own in-service education in two major directions. He must seek constantly to improve the process of elementary education in his own system. This will doubtless involve continuing change in both organization and educational processes. The second direction is self-improvement in the processes of administration which are basic to effective performance.

The process of elementary education. Elementary education is a conscious effort to provide students with the basic tools of learning. These include mastery in the use of language; the basic skills of reading, listening, and communication. Included also are the fundamental attitudes and modes of thought which characterize scientific inquiry and its major

5. For a description of emerging planning patterns in government and business see Max Ways, "The Road to 1977," *Fortune Magazine,* January, 1967, p. 95. See also U.S. Bureau of the Budget, *Bulletin 66–3, Planning-Programming-Budgeting,* October 12, 1965.

tool, mathematics. An introduction is given to some of the social sciences, and a foundation is laid for responsible citizenship. Beginnings are made in appreciation and skill in some of the fine arts. Moreover, it is in elementary schools that motivation for learning is developed. Learning skills are nurtured, and the zest for inquiry is encouraged and maintained among the young.

Achievement of the true mission of elementary education requires understanding of the purposes of elementary education, of the processes of learning as they relate to elementary children, of child growth and development, and of the nature and process of motivation. Fundamental to the administrator's own motivation is a realization, substantiated by both observation and recent research, that the elementary years are precious in the educational life of a child and that losses suffered at this stage may be irretrievable.

Administrative processes. Understanding must be bolstered by skill. Fundamental to successful operation as an administrator is sophistication in deciding, communicating, organizing, innovating, evaluating, maintaining an organization, and in human relations. These skills are essential (1) in formulating and achieving the purposes of elementary education, (2) in unifying work-flow patterns, (3) in developing operational policy, (4) in maintaining an appropriate school-society relationship. Sections of preceding chapters have dealt with the use of the above processes in settings within and outside the school organization.

The DCS (Determination of Criteria of Success) study which analyzed the administrative behavior of a national sample of elementary school principals in a simulated school has indicated the importance of sophistication in the use of administrative processes. The eight primary factors identified by the study as being related to success are heavily process-oriented:

Factor A[1]   Exchanging information
Factor B[1]   Discussing with others before acting
Factor C[1]   Complying with suggestions made by others
Factor D[1]   Analyzing the situation
Factor E[1]   Maintaining organizational relationships
Factor F[1]   Organizing work
Factor G[1]   Responding to outsiders
Factor H[1]   Directing the work of others [6]

6. John K. Hemphill, Daniel E. Griffiths, and Norman Frederiksen, *Administrative Performance and Personality* (New York: Teachers College, Bureau of Publications, Columbia University, 1962), pp. 143 ff.

Technical-Managerial Competencies

There are three important aspects of administrative performance related to technical-managerial areas that require continuous improvement. The first involves improved understanding of elementary school operation in relation to technical functions in each administrative task area: instruction and curriculum development, pupil personnel, staff personnel, finance and business management, school plant and auxiliary services, and community relations. Mastery in these areas is essential.

A second aspect of technical competence is concerned with management of the organization. This involves the ability to translate accepted goals and purposes into functions, the assignment of functions to personnel, the fostering of processes to fulfill the functions, the establishment of authority and responsibility patterns, and coordination of the complete educational enterprise.

The third aspect requires penetrating understanding of educational and organizational technologies such as ETV and ITV, autoinstructional hardware and materials, the educational and business uses of computers, team teaching, grouping, large-group instruction, individualization of instruction, and streaming.

Although many of the above competencies are more closely associated with organizational *maintenance* than with *leadership*, they nevertheless comprise a significant dimension of administrative performance in the elementary school principalship.

KNOWLEDGE IN ELEMENTARY SCHOOL ADMINISTRATION

Opportunities for gaining the knowledge desired and needed by elementary school administrators have never been more inviting. In addition to more extensive preservice preparation offerings, these opportunities include conferences, workshops, self-study, visiting in other established institutions, advanced formal study at universities, and work in professional interest groups and associations. All of these sources can make effective contributions to the administrator's knowledge and competence in the purpose, process, and technical-managerial aspects of performance. Each is an important resource for achieving and maintaining a level of operation which will ensure success and satisfaction in administration.

Other useful resources are also available. The social sciences, the humanities, philosophy, and the arts are providing models, concepts, and knowledge which have been found useful in developing competence in administration. Contributions from these sources are being incorporated into many preservice programs. Education departments are appointing professors from these areas to their staffs, and joint appointments with departments of philosophy, social science, and humanities are becoming increasingly common. These changes indicate that the administrator in his own in-service program should range widely in search of new concepts and comprehension.

In turning to other fields for relevant knowledge, the administrator should guard against several dangers. Among these are the dangers of (a) adaptations of alien concepts to the process of education, (b) seeking knowledge solely as an adornment without giving thought to its application, and (c) accepting *processes* from other disciplines as *purposes* in education. If such dangers can be avoided, however, there is much that can be gleaned for administration from these related human studies.

Knowledge and Purpose Definition

Today's elementary school serves a society characterized by interdependence and complexity. Today's rate of change is exponential in character and is touching every stratum of the social order. The demands of society on education are not only increasing in extent but are changing in kind. It is not enough for the schools to prepare students to fill static roles in society. The changes are so rapid that schools must prepare them for unanticipated societal conditions. Moreover, today's educational leaders must develop their capacity to participate in and to influence the activities which direct and shape the accelerating cultural metamorphoses. Knowledge is essential in meeting this new demand effectively.

Albright [7] has listed three categories of concepts needed. The first of these are images, generalized from specifics, of what the major problems are and why these problems have arisen. These concepts are necessary in order that the administrator can deal with real issues rather than with their symptoms. The second category is knowledge of the situation so that the administrator can generate ideas about what can or cannot

7. A. D. Albright, *et al., School Administration and the Human Sciences* (Lexington, Ky.: University of Kentucky, 1961), pp. 115, 116.

be done in any given situation. The third is a system of ideas about what should be. The administrator needs concepts of what characterizes a good society; social goals are what give meaning and purpose to the lives of individuals and organizations. It appears important to stress the administrator's need to achieve a viable synthesis of knowledge, theory, and research if he is to be effective in facilitating development of those policies and purposes that will serve and shape cultural ends. Some sources of relevant knowledge are given below.

From the humanities. A clearly defined framework of values is indispensable to processes of purpose setting and policy definition. A firmly anchored value system will indicate the relevance of educational purposes to the "good" life and the "good" society. For centuries, philosophy and the humanities have been the repositories of civilized thought in relation to value questions. Concepts from these sources may prove indispensable as decisions are made about value-laden issues such as allocation of funds to various facets of education, curriculum emphasis, equal educational opportunity, and excellence in education.

From political science. Agger has observed that the past 25 years have witnessed three major changes in community political processes which pose important implications for educational administrators. First, much decision making that was formerly political is being transformed into administrative decision making. Second, public administrators are acquiring political leadership roles and increasing political influence in both administrative and political decision making. Third, much of what was recently "private" political decision making by relatively consensual political leaderships is being converted into "openly conflictful issues with more competitive leadership situations." [8]

The body of knowledge about political systems is becoming extensive. Since the educational enterprise is both the product of a political system and is in some respects a political system in its own right, effective performance on the part of the administrator will require knowledge of political processes and power systems. Moreover, knowledge of political organization and decision-making processes will contribute a great deal to the administrator's sophistication in educational purpose develop-

8. Robert E. Agger, "Political Science and the Study of Administration," in Lawrence W. Downey and Frederick Enns (eds.), *The Social Sciences and Educational Administration* (Edmonton, Alberta, Canada: Division of Educational Administration, University of Alberta, 1963), p. 57. See also Stephen Bailey *et al., Schoolmen and Politics* (Syracuse, N.Y.: Syracuse University Press, 1962).

ment. Comprehension of power structures, awareness of decision-making processes on public issues, understanding of the interrelationships of political systems at various governmental levels—each of the foregoing appears vital to effective performance.[9]

From sociology. Since the school system is a social system which is in constant interaction with other social systems, the need for sociological concepts in school administration is apparent. Concepts related to organizations, ethnic groups, welfare, specialization and interdependence, urbanization, the influence of bigness in government, industry, and commercial enterprises, developing technologies, race relations, and the family are of significance in education. Merton has listed over 30 areas of sociology in which problems of interest to the school administrator are being studied.[10] More recently Campbell has noted the growing interest of scholars from the social sciences in problems of educational administration: "An increasing amount of attention is being given to problems of educational administration by scholars in the disciplines themselves. While social psychologists have been interested in administration for some time, political scientists and sociologists are increasingly showing a strong interest in school problems." [11] This continuing and emerging interest of social scientists in education as a field of study is continuing to contribute knowledge of considerable relevance to administrative performance.

From economics. For many years, economics has offered concepts that have been utilized both in educational finance and in business management. Contributions from economics which appear highly relevant to purpose definition in education include those dealing with the economic contributions of education,[12] economic changes and their effects on tax systems, allocations of tax resources at various govern-

9. For extensive treatments of these subjects see Ralph Kimbrough, *Political Power and Educational Decision Making* (Chicago: Rand McNally, 1964); Robert S. Cahill and Stephen P. Hencley, *The Politics of Education in the Local Community* (Danville, Ill.: Interstate Printers and Publishers, 1964); Thomas R. Dye, "Politics, Economics, and Educational Outcomes in the States," *Educational Administration Quarterly,* Vol. 3, No. 1, Winter, 1967; Marilyn Gittell and Alan G. Hevesi, *The Politics of Urban Education* (New York: Frederick A. Praeger, 1969).

10. R. K. Merton *et al., Sociology Today* (New York: Basic Books, 1959).

11. Roald F. Campbell, "The Quarterly and the Field," *Educational Administration Quarterly,* Vol. 3, No. 1, Winter, 1967.

12. Theodore W. Schultz, *The Economic Value of Education* (New York: Columbia University Press, 1963). See also American Association of School Administrators, *Education is Good Business* (Washington, D.C.: the Association, 1966).

mental levels,[13] and the economic effects on society of automation, technology, and cybernation.[14]

Knowledge Related to Administrative Processes

Research centering upon administrative processes common to bureaucracies has been conducted in many organizational settings. Such studies have probed the characteristics of bureaucracies, the dynamics of organizational control, individual and group decision making, innovation and change processes, and communication networks and activities. Knowledge of what research offers the elementary school administrator in these and similar areas is fundamental to competent administrative performance in both intraorganizational and extraorganizational settings.

In considering various administrative processes, it is essential that the administrator give attention to both value content and scientific content. The administrator in elementary schools, as elsewhere, is confronted not only with problems of knowing *what is* and *how it may be altered,* but also of *what ought to be* and *how it ought to be altered.* Thus, the administrator must decide not only what it is possible for him to do, but also what is proper for him to do. Successful performance depends on one as much as on the other.

The impact of conceptualization and study relative to the *is* aspect of change processes, for instance, is illustrated in the classification schema presented in Table 14–1. The schema, which was developed by Egon Guba, classifies major concepts and variables which administrators should encompass in relation to innovation and change.

Knowledge in Technical Areas

Although knowledge and skill in defining purpose and in the use of administrative processes are necessary in school administration, they are not sufficient. Of equal importance are knowledge and competence in the technical areas of educational administration. The principal's primary functions in these areas are oriented toward maintaining, facili-

13. National Education Association, Committee on Educational Finance, *Local, State, Federal Partnership in School Finance* (Washington, D.C.: the Association, 1966).

14. See, for example, C. H. Springer, "The Systems Approach," *Saturday Review,* January 14, 1967, pp. 57 ff.; Charles Silberman, "Technology is Knocking at the School House Door," *Fortune Magazine,* August, 1966; Timothy E. Reid, "Automation and Its Impact on Education," *Canadian Education and Research Digest,* Vol. 5, No. 3, September, 1965; Patrick Suppes, "The Computer and Excellence," *Saturday Review,* January 14, 1967, p. 48.

Table 14-1. A Classification Schema of Processes Related

	Development			Dif-
	Research	Invention	Design	Dissemination
Objec-tive	To advance knowledge	To formulate a new solution to an operating problem or to a class of operating problems, i.e., to innovate	To order and to systematize the components of the invented solution; to construct an innovation package for institutional use, i.e., to engineer	To create widespread awareness of the invention among practitioners, i.e., to inform
Criteria	Validity (internal and external)	Face validity (appropriateness — Estimated viability — Impact (relative contribution)	Institutional feasibility — Generalizability — Performance	Intelligibility — Fidelity — Pervasiveness — Impact (extent) to which it affects key targets)
Relation to Change	Provides basis for invention	Produces the invention	Engineers and packages the invention	Informs about the invention

SOURCE: The schema shown was taken from Egon G. Guba, "The Change Continuum and Its Relation to the Illinois Plan for Program Develop-to and Necessary for Change in Education

fusion	Adoption		
Demon-stration	Trial	Installation	Institutionalization
To afford an opportunity to examine and assess operating qualities of the invention, i.e., to build conviction	To build familiarity with the invention and provide a basis for assessing the quality, value, fit, and utility of the invention in a particular institution, i.e., to test	To fit the characteristics of the invention to the characteristics of the adopting institution, i.e., to operationalize	To assimilate the invention as an integral and accepted component of the system, i.e., to establish
Credibility —	Adaptability —	Effectiveness —	Continuity —
Convenience —	Feasibility —	Efficiency —	Valuation —
Evidential Assessment	Action		Support
Builds conviction about the invention	Tries out the invention in the context of a particular situation	Operationalizes the invention for use in a specific institution	Establishes the invention as a part of an ongoing program; converts it to a "noninnovation"

ment for Gifted Children," a paper delivered to a conference on Educational Change, Urbana, Ill., March 1, 1966.

tating, and improving educational opportunity. The elementary school principal's position is made unique by his specialized contributions to instructional improvement, to the development of staff and student potential, and to program development.

Many areas of knowledge are relevant in building competence in the technical tasks of administration. Psychology offers much help in relation to learning theory, instructional methodology, and pupil motivation and guidance. Sociology and political science contribute concepts useful in community decision making and in developing satisfactory community relationships. From economics the administrator can get an understanding of resource development and allocation. Study of social psychology will provide assistance in staff personnel administration. Concepts from each of these fields will contribute strength and sophistication to the professional decisions of the elementary school in the technical areas.

The principal has an unparalleled opportunity to improve instruction and to upgrade teaching-learning situations. He is closest to these situations. Consequently, his competence should include the ability to muster and to deploy existing organizational resources for the improvement and maintenance of teaching-learning opportunities in his school. Keeping current his knowledge of procedures for optimizing the educational output from these resources is an important facet of the principal's performance.

Knowledge concerning the technical areas of elementary school administration would be less than adequate without acquaintance with the changing concepts and technologies underlying elementary education. Changes and innovations affecting this level of education have been discussed in several chapters.

COMMITMENT IN THE PRINCIPALSHIP

The extensive knowledge and competence required in elementary school administration is unlikely to be achieved without long-term perspective, dedication, and commitment. Fortunately, the principalship in American education is being rapidly professionalized; greater and greater numbers of practitioners are indicating their commitment to continuous improvement of professional excellence. The elementary school principalship is becoming a challenge for educators with goals, values, and purpose. It is for those who can tolerate frustration, who are stimulated by challenge, and who are excited by opportunity.

The professional mission of the elementary school principal demands commitments of many kinds; the following, however, appear salient:

1. *Commitment to development of a mature concept of the principal's mission.* Professional commitment along this dimension will require extensive improvement in all the dimensions of administrative performance: policy, process, and technical. Moreover, it will require penetrating analysis of ways in which imperatives such as those suggested by the American Association of School Administrators' Commission can be made operational in elementary schools:

To make urban life rewarding and satisfying
To prepare people for the world of work
To discover and nurture creative talent
To strengthen the moral fabric of society
To deal constructively with psychological tensions
To keep democracy working
To make intelligent use of natural resources
To make the best use of leisure time
To work with other peoples of the world for human betterment.[15]

2. *Commitment to leadership.* Commitment to leadership in elementary school administration will require attention to development and change, as well as to maintenance. There are clear indications of the leadership expectations held for school administrators in the volume of current educational literature devoted to change, in the orientations of current preparation programs, and in the long-range planning activities of school districts.

3. *Commitment to continuous improvement, self-education, and active participation in professional learning activities.* The committed elementary school administrator views learning as a continuous, life-long process. He takes advantage of learning opportunities of all kinds: in his own district, in professionally-sponsored activities, in university programs of study, and in continuous self-study in service.

4. *Commitment to building his profession.* The AASA has listed six criteria which distinguish professions from other vocations, noting that a profession:

a. Differs from other occupations by having a unique body of knowledge that is known and practiced by its members.
b. Is characterized by a strong, voluntary association of its members, active in the regulation of professional entrance requirements.

15. American Association of School Administrators, *Imperatives in Education* (Washington, D.C.: the Association, 1966).

c. Has an enforceable code of ethics.

d. Has a literature of its own, even though it may draw heavily on many academic disciplines for the content.

e. Is ordinarily "in the public service" and is motivated by ideals that transcend purely selfish aims.

f. Is not only professional, but is also perceived by the public as such.[16]

The committed elementary school principal seeks to build his profession in relation to each of the criteria enumerated above. He understands that status is granted to administrators in relation to their preparation, their dedication to administrative excellence, and their consistency in following the ethical standards of their profession.

16. American Association of School Administrators, *Professional Administrators for America's Schools, Thirty-eighth Yearbook* (Washington, D.C.: the Association, 1960), p. 257.

REFERENCES

Albright, A. D., *et al., School Administration and the Human Sciences* (Lexington, Ky.: University of Kentucky, 1961).

American Association of School Administrators, *Professional Administrators for America's Schools, Thirty-eighth Yearbook* (Washington, D.C.: the Association, 1960).

Cahill, Robert S., and Stephen P. Hencley (eds.), *The Politics of Education in the Local Community* (Danville, Ill.: Interstate Printers and Publishers, 1964).

Culbertson, Jack A., and Stephen P. Hencley (eds.), *Preparing Administrators: New Perspectives* (Columbus, Ohio: University Council for Educational Administration, 1962).

Department of Elementary School Principals, National Education Association, *The Elementary School Principalship in 1968* (Washington, D.C.: the Association, 1968).

Department of Elementary School Principals, National Education Association, *Better Principals for Our Schools* (Washington, D.C.: the Association, 1961).

Downey, Lawrence W., and Frederick Enns (eds.), *The Social Sciences and Educational Administration* (Edmonton, Alberta, Canada: Division of Educational Administration, University of Alberta, 1963).

Foskett, John M., *The Normative World of the Elementary School Principal* (Eugene, Ore.: The Center for the Advanced Study of Educational Administration, 1967).

Graff, Orin B., *et al., Philosophic Theory and Practice in Educational Administration* (Belmont, Calif.: Wadsworth Publishing Co., 1966).

Griffiths, Daniel E. (ed.), *Behavioral Science and Educational Administration, Sixth-third Yearbook,* Part II, National Society for the Study of Education (Chicago: University of Chicago Press, 1964).

Hemphill, John K., Daniel E. Griffiths, and Norman Frederiksen, *Administrative Performance and Personality* (New York: Teachers College Bureau of Publications, Columbia University, 1962).

Kimbrough, Ralph B., *Political Power and Educational Decision-making* (Chicago: Rand McNally, 1964).

National Education Association, *The Changing World of the Elementary School Principal,* Parts I and II (Washington, D.C.: the Association, 1968).

University Council for Educational Administration, "Improving Preparatory Programs for Educational Administrators in the United States: Some Action Guides," committee report (Columbus, Ohio: the Council, mimeographed, undated).

Chapter 15

EXCELLENCE IN EDUCATION

V IGOROUS concern for quality in American education is a relatively recent movement. It is only during the last decade that schools have directed critical interest to matters of excellence—and only after social change and vigorous criticism had precipitated controversy concerning the aims, substance, and process of education.

During the 1940's and 1950's, improvements in education were largely quantitative in nature. Maintaining the universality of educational opportunities was a pressing problem which required constant attention to quantitative questions in local school districts. The typical stance toward improvement was to provide greater numbers of teachers, more course offerings, more and larger schools, more books, more equipment, and more buses. Although resources were being allocated to education in ever increasing quantities, serious efforts to structure quality educational programs on the basis of concentrated, programmatic research were rare: less than 0.1 percent of the budgets of local school districts were devoted to research during the 1950's.

More recently, however, both educators and noneducators have evidenced strong interest in educational excellence. The aims, curriculum, process, and outcomes of education have become matters for conscientious and searching appraisal by leaders in education, government, and industry. Social change, national and international tensions, and public criticism and controversy are doubtless responsible for this critical reexamination of education and the restless search for new solutions. Today, governments, industrial corporations, and foundations are all structuring increasing numbers of experimental and developmental projects in education. Educators are being challenged as never before to

332

improve their educational programs at all levels and for all student categories.

CONTINUING QUANTITATIVE EMPHASES

Attention to quantitative concerns has by no means come to an end, however. A number of factors are contributing to a continuing emphasis on quantity during the current decade. Population projections to 1980 predict an annual increase in elementary schools of slightly less than 1 percent, while the high schools and colleges are expected to increase their enrollments by 3 percent and 4 percent, respectively. The concerted movement of people from rural to urban centers continues unabated and estimates are that 95 percent of the total increase in population will be absorbed into the nation's 212 metropolitan areas.[1] This trend will result in continuing problems of numbers for many metropolitan areas and will probably be most acute in suburban school districts.

A second factor that is contributing to an emphasis on quantity is the lack of clarity in societal expectations for schools. The pluralism which characterizes American society has resulted in a number of cross currents of unresolved values and conflicting ideals which have tended to contribute to uncertainty concerning educational goals. Uncertainty about goals for education has been compounded by confusion about where responsibility for goal determination is located. Goodlad has observed that although there exists the tacit assumption that local districts set the goals of education, research indicates that very few of them actually give much attention to the matter.

Many people in most states are saying somewhat resentfully that the federal government is now determining what schools are for. There is some truth in the observation. There is equal truth, however, in the observation that remote curriculum builders in special projects and in publishing houses are determining the actual goals of our schools: goals that come right into the classroom with the materials. We go on espousing the virtues of local control in education while the most important decisions of ends and means are being determined remotely, largely because of local omission.[2]

Since salient goal priorities have tended to remain relatively unclear, the operational goals of schools appear to have the common theme of

1. Edgar L. Morphet and Charles O. Ryan, *Prospective Changes in Society by 1980* (Denver, Colo.: Bradford Robinson, 1966), pp. 52–53.
2. John I. Goodlad, "Innovations in Education," *The Educational Forum*, Vol. 31, No. 3, March, 1967, pp. 282–283.

attempting to be all things to all people. Courses have been added to the curriculum, and more students have been retained for longer periods of time. In short, emphasis on quantity has continued.

A third factor that has contributed to quantitative emphases in the schools is institutionalization. As schools and school systems have grown in size, they have become increasingly bureaucratic in operation. Roles and procedures have assumed forms that were determined initially by the realities of practice but which now possess the force of tradition. The emphasis under such circumstances has been generally upon perfecting old educational models and patterns rather than upon pioneering new models. In most cases, it has been easier to modify what already existed than to seek any radical restructuring of institutionalized patterns.

Still another factor in the emphasis of quantity is the difference in visibility of quantitative and qualitative goals. Society has expected the schools to accommodate the growing student population and to expand the curriculum. Students could not be left out of school. Especially was this true in an era when most categories of employment were closed to those lacking necessary levels of education. The needed increases in budget to accommodate larger numbers of pupils for longer periods of time were relatively obvious, and more or less acknowledged by society. But the added services and budgetary increases needed to provide a better staffed enterprise dedicated to quality were far less obvious and much more difficult to sell to lay school boards and communities.

The effect of these factors has been to inhibit adaptive changes in education other than those associated with increased numbers of students and expanding curricula. Until recently, changes in society associated with knowledge expansions, automation and cybernation, changed vocational patterns, new modes of living, and altered patterns of government went largely unnoticed by those responsible for changing education.

Today's mounting concern for quality in education is finding response from all sections of society. Governmental concern has resulted in increased budgets and numerous new programs at both federal and state levels. School districts are steadily improving programs and adopting innovations at an accelerating rate. Various governmental levels, industry, and educators all appear serious in their concerns for improving the educational output of the nation's public schools.

Lest we become too optimistic about education's future, however, it is well to note that problems that have beset education in the past are likely to continue and may well hamper widespread change. Shortages of quality teachers and outstanding administrators may hamper many attempts to achieve excellence. Adequate financing may be more difficult to obtain, not because we are less affluent, but because the results of money put into quality programs will be neither as obvious nor as immediately discernible as money spent on expansion. The weight of tradition and institutionalization will hinder development. The historical lag between the development of educational ideas and their implementation will also present problems in tailoring new programs. The temper of the times indicates, however, that more and more resources will be allocated to the search for solutions to the many problems standing in the way of quality education in the United States.

EMERGING CHALLENGES

Schoolmen serving in America during the last half of the twentieth century are facing a number of challenges which have little or no precedent in the history of education. One of these is the challenge associated with increasing society's productivity through education. A second is the need to develop new types of educational patterns occasioned by the growth of science and cybernation.

Investment in Human Capital

Although American education has always contained a significant thread of utilitarianism (practical courses have usually been available, land-grant colleges have served the needs of agriculture and the military, and public education has assumed responsibility for educating workers for both business and industry), recognition of education as an investment in the process of production is quite recent and not yet fully developed. The evidence is growing, however, that education is a basic investment in economic growth and productivity.[3] Economists have concluded that education as an investment provides tangible returns at least comparable to investment in other forms of capital, in addition to many secondary benefits. A unique characteristic of investment in human capital is its capacity to yield economic returns in proportion to the amounts invested. In this sense, it is said to be elastic. This elasticity presents a major challenge, both to society and to educators. Since the

3. Harold M. Groves, *Education and Economic Growth* (Washington, D.C.: National Education Association, 1961). See also Don Adams, "Education and the Wealth of Nations," *Phi Delta Kappan*, Vol. 47, No. 4, December, 1965, pp. 169–174.

returns from investment in education are tangible and large, how much of society's resources should be allocated to this important societal function? Recent federal legislation to increase aid to education appears to be a recognition of the importance of investing in human capital through education. The federal viewpoint was expressed by President Johnson in his speech to the Smithsonian Bicentennial Celebration on September 16, 1965:

In our country and in our time, we have recognized, with new passion, that learning is basic to our hopes for America. It is the taproot which gives sustaining life to all our purposes. Whatever we seek to do to wage war on poverty—set new goals for health and happiness—curb crime—and bring beauty to our cities and countryside—all these and more depend on education.

In 1966, and again in 1967, Congress extended the Elementary and Secondary Education Act to provide, among other things, a new formula to aid more of the nation's children from poor families. Money has been allocated for staff, equipment, materials, and construction associated with programs intended to increase the educational opportunities of these children. It is evident that the war on poverty is being coupled with better education for the underprivileged, that both have economic motivations, and that both are receiving their major impetus from the federal government. It is becoming increasingly clear that administrators in the public schools cannot escape responsibility for helping to resolve the twin questions of how much should be invested and which programs should be supported by whom.

Changing Occupational Patterns

Determining the nature, extent, and focus of educational preparation for the mass of young people who will lend stability to the social system in coming decades is a major problem facing educators and society's decision makers. Many unanswered questions exist in relation to (1) the nature of future adult tasks facing today's learners, and (2) the scope of intellectual, social, occupational, and attitudinal preparation for productive living in coming years.

Changing occupational patterns are generating successive impacts throughout the structure of society. The era in which the professional, the highly trained technician, and the skilled craftsman are of unprecedented importance is already with us. Predictions indicate that in large organizations the present work of middle management will be programed; operational researchers and organizational analysts will be highly prized; recentralization will be common; and normal lines of advancement will be drastically curtailed. Other predictions indicate that routine blue-collar and white-collar tasks will be almost depleted by cybernation in two decades; that citizens, though better educated, will lack understanding of a cybernated world; and that the interplay between science and problems of government will be increasingly difficult to grasp.[4] Michael's predictions concerning the magnitude of future changes pose startling challenges to public education:

There will be a small, almost separate, society of people in rapport with the advanced computers. These cyberneticians will have established a relationship with their machines that cannot be shared by the average man any more than the average man today can understand the problems of molecular biology, nuclear physics, or neuropsychiatry. Indeed, many scholars will not have the capacity to share their knowledge or feeling about this new man-machine relationship. . . .

Some of the remaining population will be productively engaged in human-to-human or human-to-machine activities requiring judgment and a high level of intelligence and training. But the rest, whose innate intelligence or training is not of the highest, what will they do? We can foresee a nation with a large portion of its people doing, directly or indirectly, the endless public tasks that the welfare state needs and that the government will not allow to be cybernated because of the serious unemployment that would result. . . .[5]

The improvement of education to meet the future needs of society is a salient problem facing all of the leaders of the educational enterprise. The task will require penetrating insight into the nature of elementary schools as social institutions; deep understanding of the nature and purposes of the evolving society to be served and improved; knowledge of the theoretical bases upon which educational programs may be structured; appreciation of strategies of inquiry that undergird educational programs; familiarity with a broad range of teaching-learning and organizational processes; sophistication in determining the optimum contributions to be made to teaching-learning processes by professionals, organizational arrangements, technologies, and new media; and greatly expanded financial support.

4. Donald M. Michael, *Cybernation: The Silent Conquest* (Santa Barbara, Calif.: Center for the Study of Democratic Institutions, 1962), p. 44.
5. *Ibid.*, pp. 44–45.

TOWARD QUALITY: FINANCIAL SUPPORT

Quality education will not be achieved through tinkering with the status quo; it will require greatly expanded public investments in the educational enterprise. Although the federal government has dramatically increased its support to education, and although more states are using certain nonproperty tax sources of revenue, the main supply of money for education is still from taxes on real property. This latter source of revenue is not only inadequate but unduly restrictive and inelastic for meeting educational projections in a rapidly expanding industrial urban economy. Support derived from property taxes (augmented with limited nonproperty taxes and federal funds) has often been insufficient to deal with major quantitative problems occasioned by rising enrollments, physical plant and site replacements, teacher shortages, and restricted program offerings for the range of abilities represented in school populations.

Although the national average expenditure per pupil in average daily attendance rose from $294 to $533 in the period from 1955–1956 to 1965–1966 (and was expected to rise to $750 by 1975), the gain is more apparent than real. Inflation has tended to offset a large portion of the increase. Moreover, the range in per pupil expenditures from state to state indicates a wide variability in the quality and the kind of education available to children throughout the country. The range is from $318 to $869, as indicated in Table 15–1. Since expenditure per pupil is one of the best indicators of the quality of education offered, it is clear that there are wide disparities in educational opportunity from state to state, and region to region. Some of the implications of inadequate financing in education have been highlighted by Jerry Miner:

The postwar expansion of the educational system has been one of the most striking features of contemporary American society. This expansion is characterized not only by absolute increases in school enrollments and expenditures per pupil, but by rates of increase greater than those of population or of national income. Yet, reports of widespread shortages of teachers and classrooms are only one implication of inadequacies in the present system. *One of the most profound problems of social policy is how to expand and modify the educational system to interact with rapidly changing technology and values.* The financial aspects of this challenge to education are vital because *decisions regarding the magnitude and character of education affect the size, composition, distribution, and rate of growth of income and, there-*

TABLE 15-1. Distribution of Per
Pupil Expenditures in
the States, 1965-1967

Expenditure	No. of States
$300-349	1
$350-399	9
$400-449	4
$450-499	10
$500-549	11
$550-599	7
$600-649	4
$650-699	2
$700-749	1
$750-799	0
$800-849	0
$850-899	1

SOURCE: National Education Association,
Research Division, Research
Bulletin, Vol. 44, No. 1, Febru-
ary, 1966, p. 13.

*fore, have profound influence on the economic welfare of the nation's
citizens.*[6]

The Research Council of the Great Cities Program for School Improvement has noted the general inadequacy of fiscal support for education, and has recommended a number of fiscal policies which would
undoubtedly provide a sound base for movement toward quality education in the United States. Among the fiscal policies recommended by
the Research Council were the following:

1. The fiscal support of public education should be a responsibility shared
   by all citizens in all levels of government.
2. The state program for financial support should recognize the complex
   needs of school systems. But the determination of the need should be
   the responsibility of the local boards of education.
3. The measure of the local school district's ability to contribute to the
   support of education should be in terms of the total burden of local
   government cost borne by the local tax base.
4. Local boards of education should be free from unreasonable restric-

6. Morphet and Ryan, *op. cit.*, p. 298.

tions in the administration of fiscal affairs, from undue controls by other governmental agencies, and from cumbersome legal procedures at state and local levels which thwart effective expression of citizens.

5. The fiscal procedures for adequate school support should provide the school districts with direct access to taxes which can be administered best locally and indirect access to those which can be administered at the state level.

6. The state fiscal plan should include objective procedures to provide adequate funds for operating expenses and capital outlay and debt service payments.

7. The federal government should participate in the support of education when the national interest requires it and when local and state resources are insufficient to provide an acceptable educational program.

8. The level of financial support of public education should be kept responsive to the fluctuations of inflation and deflation in the price structure of the economy.[7]

The Committee on Tax Education and School Finance of the National Education Association has reviewed cost quality relationships and has indicated the relevance of fiscal policies to the attainment of quality education in school districts. Five important conclusions of the Committee were:

1. Pupils on the average make higher scores on tests in the three R's in elementary schools and in the academic subjects in high schools in high schools in high expenditure as compared with low expenditure school systems.

2. Communities spending more per pupil generally get educational programs which take better account of the needs of society and the findings of psychological research on how children learn best. The scope of these school programs includes objectives ranging from excellent teaching of the three R's to such fundamental behavior patterns as good citizenship and the ability to think.

3. The ultimate, or point of diminishing returns, in educational quality has apparently not been reached in even the highest expenditure school districts.

4. The effect of an intelligent, long-range program of adequate financial support in a school system is cumulative and, therefore, especially powerful in its effect on quality. Also, low expenditure, if continued, will greatly reduce quality.

7. Report to the Board of Directors of the Research Council of the Great Cities Program for School Improvement, *Fiscal Policies to Meet the Needs of the Great City School Systems in America* (Chicago: Research Council of the Great Cities Program for School Improvement, 1963).

5. States which make superior provision for the financing of schools rank substantially higher than low expenditure states in educational achievement and in earning power.[8]

Opportunities for educational improvement have escalated in the current decade and can be expected to continue to grow. Realization of education's potential, however, will depend on a core of knowledgeable leaders who are committed to making improvements and who are freed from the stultifying atmosphere of financial scarcity. Until the educational needs of an evolving society are more fully understood; until increased sources of support are available from local, state, and federal governments; until adequate equalized support becomes available for capital outlays, operating costs, and debt service charges; and until education is more universally viewed as an investment rather than a cost, it may be difficult to attain the goal of excellence in elementary education. Without adequate resources, the majority of school districts will be limited to tinkering approaches to quality—with a resultant minimal return.

TOWARD QUALITY: CURRICULUM AND LEARNING THEORY

Important new directions in curriculum reconstruction are emerging to meet the criteria of quality and excellence. The rapid obsolescence of knowledge is already discrediting the notion that the curriculum can consist of a static body of knowledge and ideas which, when mastered, will prepare the individual for effective living. The changing nature of knowledge is bringing realization that today's facts and ideas may be totally inadequate for meeting the challenges of the future. Thus, acquisition of facts is becoming secondary to the development of abilities for using knowledge, analyzing evidence, exercising critical judgment, and reaching sound conclusions. There is an increasing emphasis upon the ability to fit ideas to changing situations and circumstances. Students are learning to apply the important concepts in mathematics and science and the basic themes in the humanities and the social sciences in progressively complex problem situations. The push toward educational excellence is also demanding new criteria for selecting basic ideas and concepts in each subject area, and new patterns for the scope and

8. Committee on Tax Education and School Finance, National Education Association, *Does Better Education Cost More?* (Washington, D.C.: the Association, 1959), pp. 21–37.

sequence of learning experiences. Content in various subject matter fields is being carefully assessed to determine what should be taught and the best way to teach it.

The formulation of new structures of knowledge, the development of "package" courses in various subject fields, and the accelerated trend toward intuitive discovery, reflective thinking, scientific verification, concept formation, and cognitive and symbolic processes all indicate a new interest in the intellectual aims of education.[9] These interests contrast with emphases of the past such as the study and analysis of the aptitudes, the emotional problems, and the educational weaknesses of learners. Moreover, current research is challenging learning principles that have long been in vogue. According to Cronbach, new research evidence is tending to challenge each of the following learning principles.

1. A well-understood verbal generalization is remembered, and aids in adaptation to new conditions.
2. Factual learning or learning that is not clearly understood is quickly forgotten.
3. Learning is shown to be meaningful if the pupil can use his knowledge in new situations, particularly concrete situations.
4. A response that leads to a desired goal will be easier taught than one motivated by external incentives and compulsions.
5. Transfer of learned responses is to be expected only if the later stimulus is much like that on which the person was trained.
6. Pupils should not try tasks where they are unlikely to succeed.
7. Learning occurs through active practice.[10]

Emphasis upon increased understanding of the structure of knowledge systems and strategies of inquiry is also shifting attention away from episodic curricula. The emerging trend is toward more systematic analysis of the important elements of knowledge structures in relation to primitive terms, defined terms, formation rules, transformation rules, postulates, and theorems. Since all organized bodies of knowledge possess unique language systems, or *model* languages, the learner who seeks to

9. See, for example, Stanley Elam (ed.), *Education and the Structure of Knowledge* (Chicago: Rand McNally, 1964); G. W. Ford and Lawrence Pugno, *The Structure of Knowledge and the Curriculum* (Chicago: Rand McNally, 1964): J. Cecil Parker and Louis J. Rubin, *Process as Content* (Chicago: Rand McNally, 1966): J. D. Krumboltz (ed.), *Learning and the Educational Process* (Chicago: Rand McNally, 1965).

10. Lee J. Cronbach, "Issues Current in Educational Psychology," a paper presented at the Social Science Research Council Conference on Mathematical Learning, May 4–6, 1962.

master knowledge systems should progress successfully through each of the following stages of competence and understanding:

1. *Primitive terms*—terms which are undefined in the model language but which are necessary to develop the knowledge system

2. *Defined terms*—terms which are derived from and equivalent to various combinations of primitive terms

3. *Formation and transformation rules*—the language of logic and/or mathematics utilized in working with empirical and conceptual constructs

4. *Postulates*—statements of units and objects, their properties, and their interrelationships; that is, sets of propositions which make it possible to deduce all true statements in the knowledge system

5. *Theorems*—the statements deducible from the postulates

Systematic analyses of knowledge structures will have important implications—not only for teaching-learning processes, but also for programing. Such analyses will ultimately reveal the logical organization or framework of different subject fields and will lead to the development of appropriate teaching-learning strategies for laying a foundation of understanding. The defined terms, the postulates, and the formation and transformation rules will indicate the minimum essential concepts undergirding the knowledge system, and will also provide insights into processes by which conceptual systems are extended and changed.

The new emphases in curriculum and learning theory are being accompanied by basically new approaches to the production of curriculum materials. Traditionally, industry has tended to supply educational materials in terms of textbooks and printed materials, experimental apparatus, and other educational supplies and equipment. These basic materials were then used by teachers to produce their own teaching events. Considerable time and energy were expended at all levels in school districts on program development and synthesis. Although many outstanding programs emerged through these activities, others suffered from lack of specific technical and program building skills and from lack of resources.

Currently, massive resources are being mustered to prepare programs, and program resources of greater sophistication and scope are becoming available. The federal government has become involved in research and development in a number of different program areas. Mergers of a number of large electronic, microfilm, and printing companies have also taken place. These expanded companies are using federal funds and their own resources in the development of educational programs and facilities. Information centers, computer assisted instruction, and simulated school systems are some of the results emerging from this effort. School administrators are aware that the resources available in these government-private enterprise coalitions are far greater than those at the command of any school system.

A fundamental change is also taking place in the way that program content is being altered in elementary education. In the past, program changes in secondary schools have been reflected in more or less degree in elementary schools. Thus, new developments have usually come in science and mathematics; instructional materials "packages" have been emphasized; in-service education of teachers has been stressed; and concepts such as "academic discipline," "structure," "intuitive learning," "discovery," have been widely discussed. However, the twin problems— (1) which primary concepts to include in elementary curriculum as a foundation for the disciplines of secondary curriculum, and (2) which of the many disciplines to include—are forcing a reappraisal of elementary curriculum building processes. Curriculum development is proceeding more slowly than in secondary schools; a more critical attitude is being adopted toward existing curricula, and there is an increasing tendency to plan from the bottom up rather than from the top down with the result that increasing attention is being paid to the developmental characteristics of children.[11]

Program building at the elementary school level requires broad understanding of significant variables affecting human behavior and learning. Attention must be directed to such important considerations as the needs, interests, and developmental levels of pupils; the unique contributions of various program elements to the development of needed knowledge, skills, attitudes, and values; the formulation of clear educational objectives to guide teaching-learning activities; and the evaluation of goal attainment.

The development of understanding and competence in relation to each of the above factors is a formidable task in elementary school administration. Of the factors mentioned, probably none are more critical than those relating to clearly defined objectives, and means for assessing goal achievement. Flanagan has noted some critical interrelationships:

11. John I. Goodlad, "The Curriculum," in *The Changing American School, National Society for the Study of Education Yearbook,* Vol. 65, Part II (Chicago: the Society, 1966).

Unless the status and progress of a student can be evaluated in terms of each specific educational objective, it is extremely difficult to plan a program or determine its effectiveness. Only when instruments which provide meaningful measures of educational objectives are available can an effective instructional program which produces significant student progress be distinguished from a program which represents no improvement but merely innovation and change from former programs.[12]

The important work of reordering knowledge for teaching-learning purposes is underway. As this task proceeds, it promises to usher in new levels of quality in elementary education—in terms of improved curricula and better understandings of learning processes.

TOWARD QUALITY: TECHNOLOGY AND THE REORGANIZATION OF TEACHING AND LEARNING

Far-reaching possibilities for the improvement of elementary education are emerging from growing developments in mass instruction, individual instruction, individualized autoinstruction, and their combinations. In part, the potential stems from the revolution in educational media. Traditional educational media such as books, radios, films and filmstrips, disc recordings, and audio tapes are being rapidly augmented by the addition of television facilities using air-borne and closed-circuit transmission, video tapes, and language laboratories. In the offing are massive developments in programed materials and computer-based instructional materials. Consideration is being given to the problem of how technologies and organizational arrangements in schools might be welded into effective *systems* of instruction. As yet, however, most experimentation with technologies in elementary education has proceeded without the emphasis on instructional systems which the future promises to bring.

As the principles of instructional system design are developed, integrated systems approaches to teaching and learning should emerge with great rapidity. The computerized laboratory for automated school systems (CLASS) at System Development Corporation—with its emphasis on the use of computers, programed instruction, data processing and storage, retrieval and display of information in the teaching-learning

12. John C. Flanagan, "Implications of Research for American Secondary Education," in Stanley Elam (ed.), *New Dimensions for Educational Progress* (Bloomington, Ind.: Phi Delta Kappa, 1962), p. 69.

process—is an example of future trends. As progress is made in identifying the appropriate roles of mass data presentation, individual and small group automated teaching, human interaction, individual study, creative periods, and other elements of importance to teaching-learning processes, the development of integrated instructional systems will be greatly accelerated. From the learner's point of view, future instructional programs will likely be composed of various mixes of mass instruction, individual instruction, automated self-teaching, self-study, and interaction with teachers and other students in a variety of teaching-learning situations. It is also possible that at least some students, even in the primary grades, will consciously help formulate their own educational programs.

Mass Instruction

The impact of new media on education can be gauged in part by the tremendous expansion presently taking place in the audiovisual fields— in accelerated, technological, and media developments; in the growth of local, state, and national AV associations; and in the progress of research in this area.

ETV and ITV. Capability for mass instruction through ETV and ITV is so widely recognized as to require little comment. Airborne television transmission of educational broadcasts has been successfully operated for a number of years. Inherent in space technology is the capacity for worldwide television reception from relay stations on orbiting satellites. Not so spectacular but probably more important for education are local and closed-circuit television facilities.

Proponents of ETV and ITV cite a number of advantages. Students in large numbers can be "exposed to greatness"; masters in the art of teaching can bring their expertise to wide audiences. The medium is highly adaptable for the presentation of details of laboratory work in the physical sciences to large numbers of students at the same time. Moreover, the phenomena and data of the social sciences can be presented in a very impressive and realistic way. Finally, ETV and ITV possess capabilities for introducing flexibility into the teaching-learning process.

Critics of ETV and ITV point to certain limitations. Education is much more than exposure to facts—it involves evaluation, interpretation, and synthesis. Social interaction necessary for social adjustment is all but impossible in mass instructional situations. Thus, such situations may provide little assistance in the acquisition of values, ethics, and moral codes. Mass instructional situations make little provision for active participation by students and the give and take necessary in spirited inquiry. Finally, mass education media have difficulty meeting the need for progressively graded presentations to take care of individual differences among pupils.

ETV and ITV appear to be well suited for certain types of teaching: for demonstrations and presentations of factual material in a wide variety of subject areas. They may hold less promise, however, where interpretations of material are necessary; where fine shades of meaning must be drawn; where analysis, clarification, and judgment are necessary; or where interaction with others is necessary.

Individualized Instruction

Like television, autoinstructional devices are creating unlimited possibilities for new educational patterns in tomorrow's schools. These devices have the capacity to individualize instruction.

Language laboratories and teaching typewriters. These exemplify two of the developments related to individualized instruction. In the former, there is a built-in capability for students to hear sounds, words, and phrases in the language being learned, to reproduce them, and to compare their own pronunciation with a model. Increased sophistication of programs and machines will enable students to carry on conversations and to have their errors in diction and usage corrected. Language laboratories have multiple pupil stations and provide for (1) contact between the control (teacher) station and each pupil station, and (2) facility for controlling a variety of presentations to students individually, or in groups. Each student is provided with a booth, head set, microphone, and recording facilities. These facilities are often augmented by visual aids such as motion picture projectors, overhead projectors, and slide and filmstrip projectors.

Teaching typewriters are devices for teaching typewriting. The material presented and the speed of presentation are gauged by the skill of the learner; errors slow down the rate of presentation, and often result in simpler material being presented. The machine responds to hesitancy and wrong rhythm patterns. In this capacity, it is even more adaptable than a human instructor.

Autoinstructional devices and programed instruction. The idea of teaching machines is not new. Sydney L. Pressey began writing on such devices as early as 1926. B. F. Skinner at Harvard coupled the concept of automated instructional devices with the psychological concept of operant conditioning, thereby stimulating considerable interest and development. In essence, operant conditioning is a selective reinforcement of some of the elements of the learner's operant behavior. Through this process, desirable patterns of behavior (that is, learning) can be established. Operant behavior is that behavior whose form or frequency is affected by consequent conditions. By selecting the most appropriate responses, behavior can be shaped into desirable patterns. This process of shaping, which is called operant condition, formed the basic pattern for the earliest form of programed instruction known as linear programing.

Very small steps in a one-track sequence (with constant reinforcement of correct responses) characterizes linear programing. Reaction to the concept of forcing every learner through the same series of incremental learnings has led to "branching" or "contingency" programs in which alternative instructional routings are possible at various intervals in the program.

Teaching machine programs are alike in that they (1) display learning items, (2) call for student responses, and (3) indicate to students the correctness or incorrectness of responses, thus providing reinforcement of correct behavior. The chief advantage of the better machines is that they can present the displays more efficiently and effectively than is possible with a scrambled book. In a branching program presented in book form, the learner may have to find the next display several pages from the preceding one. Thus, interruptions may be created to his progress through the program. Electronic devices can select and present the next item in micro seconds. More important, however, is the increased capability generated for using displays of other than printed matter. These can include video and audio—tapes, filmstrips, and films. Computers are currently being used on an experimental and trial basis to control the learner's program.

Computer assisted instruction. For a number of years, experimentation and development of computer assisted instruction has been proceeding in several centers. CLASS, at System Development Corporation, has already been mentioned. PLATO and SOCRATES, at the University of Illinois, are further examples. These systems seek to integrate individual autoinstruction with automatic and conventional group instruction. They also encompass data centers to facilitate administration, guidance, and planning.

The primary aim in such systems is flexibility, and thus the central control is a digital computer. Associated with the computer is a switching mechanism called a real time input output transducer. The transducer acts as an intermediary between (1) the computer and the instructional materials being presented, and (2) the recording of student responses by the computer. Other components of the system may include alpha numerical printers, output units, and pupil desks equipped with film viewers and response devices, card punches, flexowriters, and electric typewriters.

The system's output unit can be an individualized filmed item display unit, a random access slide projector and viewing device, closed-circuit television, or the teacher. The closed-circuit television and the random access slide projector can display any type of audiovisual material to the whole class. Control tapes can be loaded on the computer to instruct it as to the way in which student responses should be handled. The tape also controls the order of item presentation and the use of branches built into the program. Moreover, the tape contains instructions about feedback messages for the student. The random access slide projector and the closed-circuit television can be operated by either the computer or the teacher.

The system can provide information to both administration and guidance personnel, in addition to performing instructional tasks. For example, the principal can call upon the computer for information about attendance, registration, classroom scheduling, bus scheduling, teachers' records, financial accounting figures, individual student progress, or any other data amenable to punch-card processing. The information stored on magnetic tape in the computer can also be used by the counselor to give immediate access to grade records, student performance, test scores, biographical data, and student progress at different periods.

The system is planned to provide flexibility in the instruction of whole classrooms of pupils. Since the system provides means for individual presentations to students, it will be possible to teach students either individually or in a group. Moreover, simultaneous, controlled individual instruction will be possible in several subject areas. The computer can be programed in each subject to present each student with material appropriate to his level of proficiency. Thus, a system using a moderately large computer could easily tutor 1,000 or more students simultaneously. If students are receiving the same instructional material concurrently, the number who can be taught depends only on the nature of the student performance analysis required or requested by teachers and administrators.

The complexity of system developments relevant to teaching-learning processes has been illustrated by Stolurow, who posits ten critical requirements for teaching by machine:

1. Display
2. Response
3. Pacing
4. Comparator
5. Feedback

6. Collator-recorder
7. Selector
8. Library or storage
9. Programing
10. Computer [13]

The interrelationships among these requirements are shown in Figure 15–1.

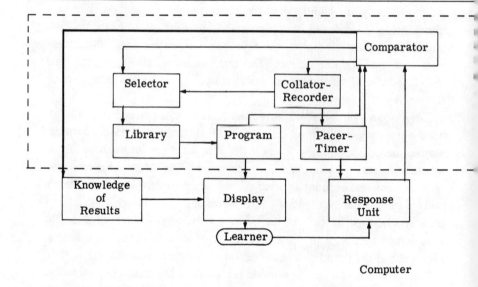

SOURCE: Lawrence M. Stolurow, Teaching by Machine (Washington, D.C.: U.S. Government Printing Office, 1961).

Figure 15-1. Adaptive Teaching Machine System

The goal behind the development of systems is not to replace classroom teachers, but to increase teaching effectiveness with the assistance of advanced technology. Since immediate information about student per-

13. Lawrence M. Stolurow, *Teaching by Machine* (Washington, D.C.: U.S. Government Printing Office, 1961).

formance is available in such systems, teachers can diagnose pupils' difficulties immediately and direct attention and instruction to areas of weakness. Since most clerical tasks, grading, and drill can be handled by the system, teachers can be liberated to perform tasks of a professional nature. The development of systems will undoubtedly lead to tighter organizational arrangements in schools and to greater teacher dependence on district- and state-level instructional planning—especially if stratovision, computer-based machines, and closed-circuit television are incorporated. Thus, the teacher's classroom role may shift extensively from overt teaching toward the management of instructional activities. Opportunities for student independence and creative output may be more difficult to maintain where preprogramed instructional systems are extensively used. Little is known at present about the balance necessary between creative learning and machine-based programed instruction.

The revolution in instruction that will be ushered in by widespread use of systems approaches to learning will present major challenges to administrators of elementary schools. Testing of electronic devices in the instructional process, continuous assessment of the instructional results of system programs, redeployment and regrouping of both teachers and students, maintenance of flexibility in programing and scheduling to fit new instructional patterns, use of self-directed pupil learning in various learning laboratories—these are but a few of the challenges to be met in this area.

TOWARD QUALITY: SCHOOL ORGANIZATION AND FACILITIES

Rich opportunities for the improvement of education lie in those areas of administration which traditionally have been the center of administrative activity, namely organization for instruction and the acquisition and use of educational facilities. A few decades ago the principal was expected to divide the student body into grades, the grades into classes, and to assign the classes to classrooms and teachers. He was also expected to provide teachers with the necessary teaching aids, and with whatever assistance they needed in classroom organization, management, and discipline. More recently, the wisdom of the self-contained classroom type of organization has come under scrutiny. The result has been that several new organization patterns have been developed and tested. These innovations in organization have been adequately supported by new developments in educational technology. In some cases, it is the new technology which makes possible the new pattern of organization.

In addition to the traditional, self-contained classroom type of organization, there are three other organizational patterns which are receiving attention. These organizational patterns are (1) nongraded or continuous progress, (2) dual progress, and (3) team teaching. (See Chapter 6 for an analysis of these patterns). Some of these patterns make almost no additional demands on educational facilities; others require basic and at times expensive modifications in buildings and facilities, especially where technology is incorporated.

The National Education Association's Project on Instruction produced a statement of purpose in the nongraded type of organization:

The vertical organization of the school should provide for the continuous, unbroken, upward progression of all learners, with due recognition of the wide variability among learners in every aspect of their development. The school organization should, therefore, provide for differentiated rates and means of progression toward achievement of education goals.[14]

The continuous progress plan is a system in which an entire school is nongraded, and groups of pupils within a class can progress at their own speed—some completing the programs sooner and others later than the normal rate. Rapid learners may either advance to the junior high school upon completing the elementary program or begin on the junior high school curriculum while in the elementary school.

The continuous progress plan requires more versatility in staff than does the traditional type of organization. However, except for additions to the library and other instructional media suitable for use with slower and faster learners, the requirements for building and facilities are not much different from the more traditional setting. This does not mean that multimedia instructional aids, programed instruction materials, simulation facilities, or even individual instructional materials cannot be used to advantage. It means only that they are not essential in implementing the concept of continuous progress.

The dual progress plan as developed by Stoddard provides two bases for pupil advancement. In language arts and social studies, the process is as in graded schools. In mathematics, sciences, and the fine arts, the plan is one of continuous progress. The plan calls for teacher specializa-

14. National Education Association Project on Instruction, *Schools for the Sixties* (New York: McGraw-Hill, 1963), p. 132.

tion in various curriculum fields and divides the student's time almost equally between the graded and nongraded segments of his program.[15] Thus, the dual progress plan is a modification of the continuous progress plan which includes elements of the traditional. Hence, building and facility requirements for the dual progress plan are similar to those for the continuous progress type of organization.

Team teaching is a phrase of wide currency but variable interpretation. A common but by no means universal definition is that it is a type of organization for instruction in which two or more teachers assume joint responsibility for the education of a group of students. The team is involved in planning, implementing, and evaluating the educational program. It may include senior and junior team members or may be composed of "equals." It may have responsibility for teaching all subject matter areas or may be limited to one or two. The size of the team varies upward from two. Three is common, but some may have 10 members or more.

The most common benefit claimed from team teaching is flexibility. Groups of pupils may be assembled in large auditoria when large-group instruction is effective. On the other hand, teachers may work with individual students when this is necessary and appropriate. Flexibility is also obtained in the amount of time devoted to particular subjects by individual students or by entire classes. Incorporation of individual self-study into the program contributes to flexibility and is also claimed as a secondary benefit.[16]

Because team teaching uses individual, small-group, and large-group configurations for instruction, it makes new and different demands on both building and facilities. Space and materials for individual instruction and autoinstruction are priority requirements. Conference rooms, space for individual viewing of films and filmstrips, soundproof rooms for listening to tapes, laboratories, language laboratories, and studios for individual use are required. Materials for individual study and instruction include films, filmstrips, tapes, models, records, record players, language laboratories, together with the more conventional library materials such as books, charts, and maps. For large-group instruction, large areas equipped with projectors, public address systems, overhead projectors, and oversize models and charts are needed. Space utilization

15. George D. Stoddard, *The Dual Progress Plan* (New York: Harper & Row, 1961).

16. For further information see: David W. Beggs (ed.), *Team Teaching—Bold New Venture* (Indianapolis, Ind.: Unified College Press, 1964).

requires flexibility so that large-group instructional areas can be modified to serve the needs of smaller groups as well.

Administrators who are committed to quality education are aware
of the variety of organizational patterns open to them. They are oriented
to the best in currently available facilities and have an alert perception
of what the future holds when new buildings are planned and new
facilities provided. They are conversant with the efforts of school districts
which have combined the financial resources needed for adequate research and development of buildings and facilities for the schools of
the future.[17]

TOWARD QUALITY: EXCELLENCE IN TEACHING

An important keystone of quality education is excellence in teaching.
Adequate financial support, utilizing of technological advances, development of curriculum and learning theory, and the organization of teaching-learning processes are all necessary ingredients in the search for
quality education. Without quality teaching, however, they are insufficient. Excellence in education is significantly related to the professional
preparation and personal qualities of the teaching force in the educational enterprise.

Improvement of professional standards for teaching will necessitate
critical reappraisal and some reformulation of objectives and practices
in relation to the selection, preparation, employment, and continuing
education of elementary school teachers. Moreover, delineation of clear
standards for the intellectual, scholarly, and personal characteristics required in teaching will also be necessary. No adequate definitions are
available for the level of intellectual ability needed in teaching. Nor has
there been sufficient attention devoted to a delineation of the scholarly,
professional, and personal qualities necessary for optimum performance.
Reformulation of working environments and salary levels to attract and
to retain capable individuals appears necessary. Stress on training programs to incorporate broad liberal education as well as skill development in various teaching-learning strategies appears appropriate.

A number of factors have inhibited the development of general excellence in teaching. Entrance requirements into teacher preparation pro-

17. National Society for the Study of Education; *Sixty-fifth Yearbook,* Part 2;
The Changing American School, 1966: Harold B. Gores, "Schoolhouse in Transition," pp. 146–148.

grams have been characterized by mediocrity. According to Stiles, "the teaching profession has limped along content to admit almost anyone, including rejects from other professional fields." [18] Since teacher preparation programs have often attracted students characterized by poor ability and doubtful potential, large numbers of able young people have tended to reject teaching as a career. Thus, a major factor inhibiting excellence in teaching is related to selection standards in training institutions.

A second factor that has operated to limit excellence is the nature of teacher education programs. Few programs have been intellectually inspiring. The acquisition of substantial bodies of organized knowledge is seldom stressed; demanding levels of intellectual inquiry are infrequently required. Moreover, colleges and universities have seldom involved their ablest scholars in the task of preparing teachers. Chase has noted the results of these shortcomings:

How can we expect to produce stimulating teachers of history unless they are taught by historians of the first rank and inducted by them into the study and criticism of the sources of historical knowledge and the art and science of historical interpretation? Where shall we find teachers who will introduce our children and youth to the great ideas and the noble expressions of ideas in literature, unless scholars who understand the uses and abuses of the art of criticism and retain a fresh and spontaneous enthusiasm for great works participate in the education of teachers? Where will our teachers acquire the ability to develop in their pupils mastery of foreign languages, unless they themselves are taught by those thoroughly at home in the particular languages and cultures of which they are a part? How shall we produce creative teachers of science, unless their education includes contact with genuinely creative scientists and provides the excitement of participating in the discovery of new truths? [19]

A third factor which has inhibited excellence is the low esteem in which teaching is held by the public. One indication of this is the relation of teachers' salaries to those of other professions. The average salaries of teachers clearly indicate that teaching offers substantially smaller economic returns than most other professions. The average salaries of accountants, auditors, attorneys, chemists, engineers, and medical doctors continue to be much above those of teachers.

18. Lindley J. Stiles, "Revolution in Instruction," in B. J. Chandler, Lindley J. Stiles, and John I. Kitsuse (eds.), *Education in Urban Society* (New York: Dodd, Mead & Co., 1962), p. 169.
19. Francis S. Chase, "Universality Versus Excellence," *Education Looks Ahead* (Chicago: Scott, Foresman and Co., 1960), p. 36.

Several studies have shown that standards of selection, preparation, and reward in teaching are directly related to the quality of education available in school districts. Improvements in the quality of teaching personnel result in increased educational achievement among students. For example, Bloom has stated that "a number of different indicators (salary level, professional interests and qualification, etc.) all appear to be related to student achievement and grade standards . . . The quality of the output (student achievement) is highly related to the quality of teachers." [20]

Commitment to Excellence

Movement toward quality through excellence in teaching requires commitments of various kinds:

1. *Commitment to raised standards and rigorous selection procedures for admission to teaching.* Entry standards should match those required for other professions. Not everyone can teach. Candidates should be carefully selected on the basis of academic ability and on the factors of physical, emotional, and mental resiliency. The special qualities of scholarly interest, intellectual ability, and personal characteristics demanded in teaching should be present in good measure. Motivation, ability to work with students and adults, ability and desire to master pertinent fields of knowledge, and the desire to develop pedagogical competence are all required. Careful selection procedures will tend to ensure that candidates have such qualities in acceptable measure.

2. *Commitment to improved preparation programs.* A broad liberal background, intellectually challenging programs of subject matter and pedagogical content—introduced in learning situations which demand acquaintance with strategies of inquiry and pedagogical competence— should become the rule rather than the exception. Improved preparation calls for increased training and more attention to specialization, even for teachers in elementary schools. Reformulation of standards in teacher education will ultimately involve outstanding scholars and educators in teacher preparation programs. The result will tend toward intellectually rigorous curricula where emphasis will be placed upon intellectual inquiry and pedagogical competence as bases for generating and extending knowledge.

20. Benjamin S. Bloom, "Quality Control in Education," *Tomorrow's Teaching* (Oklahoma City, Okla.: Frontiers of Science Foundation of Oklahoma, 1961), p. 45.

3. *Commitment to continuing education of teachers.* Optimum returns from teaching-learning activities demand continuous opportunity for the development of the specialized abilities of teachers. Knowledge obsolescence, coupled with rapid advances and expansions in new knowledge, require that all professionals be actively and continuously engaged in their own professional education. Together with other professionals, teachers must upgrade their professional preparation through in-service preparation programs. Leaders in elementary schools have unique opportunities for extending the in-service development of teaching staff; their roles in promoting instructional excellence are delineated in Chapters 5 and 10.

4. *Commitment to appropriate rewards for teaching excellence.* Both financial and attitudinal rewards are necessary. Salary is important. To rely on nonmonetary rewards to attract and hold teachers has not proven satisfactory. When salaries are adequate, the nonfinancial satisfactions of a teaching career seem convincing; when salaries are low, they appear apologetic. The valuing of teaching excellence should be made evident not only through monetary support but through attitudinal support within the profession and the larger society.

TOWARD QUALITY: INCREASED RESEARCH

Support accorded research in education has not always presented a happy picture. At local levels, 2 to 3 percent of all money spent on education could be allocated to research with great benefits to the educational enterprise. One percent has been suggested as an absolute minimum. Current expenditures at local levels are estimated at less than one fourth of one percent.

Until recently, support from the federal level has also been light. Clark has noted that a decade ago the U.S. Office of Education's research and development expenditures were equivalent to approximately 1 percent of the expenditures for the same purpose in the Public Health Service. The total amount spent for research and development by USOE was less than the amount allocated in agencies such as Commercial Fisheries, the Forest Service, or the Bureau of Sport Fisheries and Wildlife.[21]

21. David L. Clark, "Educational Research: A National Perspective," in Jack A. Culbertson and Stephen P. Hencley (eds.), *Educational Research: New Perspectives* (Danville, Ill.: Interstate Printers and Publishers, 1963), p. 8.

If educational practice is to be solidly based, educational research appears mandatory. The improvement of education will require sustained attention to increased financial support for research; development of facilities for storing and retrieving knowledge; attention to training research workers; and emphasis upon field testing, demonstrating, and disseminating research findings. Fortunately, much is being done to cope with each of these problems. The amounts of money allocated for research through USOE have risen precipitously in recent years. The Educational Research Information Center (ERIC) is being rapidly developed. This automated storage and retrieval system will be used by both researchers and practitioners as a bank of information about research and new developments in education. The Regional Educational Laboratories (REL) and the Research and Development Centers (R & D) are developing rapidly, and good possibilities exist for cooperative patterns of research, development, and field testing involving local, state, and national educational agencies. Although the universities are still oriented for the most part toward the preparation of research generalists, there is some indication that attention will be directed to the preparation of researchers with specialized interests related to (a) producing new knowledge, (b) developing it, (c) diffusing it, and (d) administering it.

As new relationships are developed among the various levels of education, general divisions of labor in relation to the research process should begin to emerge. Basic research and development might fall naturally to the universities, the R & D centers and the REL's. State education agencies, on the other hand, might take responsibility for diffusion, while schools and school districts might concentrate on demonstration and field testing. The lines of functional demarcation will likely provide opportunities for overlap.

A weakness in developing partnerships and compacts is the lack of machinery for structuring coherent policies relating to research processes on the part of various participants and levels of educational government. The pattern of relationships that might exist among federal, state, and local governments to permit these levels to work together in developing policy alternatives concerning research, development, diffusion, and field testing is only now beginning to emerge. There is little tradition or history to go on, but there is a clear need to structure social inventions to handle this problem.

REFERENCES

American Educational Research Association, "Instructional Materials: Educational Media and Technology," *Review of Educational Research,* Vol. 32, No. 2, April, 1962.

Bruner, J. S., *Toward a Theory of Instruction* (Cambridge, Mass.: Harvard University Press, 1966).

Burkhead, Jesse, *Public School Finance* (Syracuse, N.Y.: Syracuse University Press, 1964).

Committee on Tax Education and School Finance, National Education Association, *Does Better Education Cost More?* (Washington, D.C.: the Association, 1959).

Conant, James B., *The Education of American Teachers* (New York: McGraw-Hill, 1963).

Department of Elementary School Principals, National Education Association, *The Elementary School Principalship in 1968* (Washington, D.C.: the Association, 1968).

Educational Facilities Laboratory, *Design for ETV, Planning for Schools with Television* (New York: Dave Chapman, Industrial Design, 1960).

Elam, Stanley (ed.), *Education and the Structure of Knowledge* (Chicago: Rand McNally, 1964).

Finn, James D., and Donald G. Perrin, *Teaching Machines and Programmed Learning, 1962: A Survey of the Industry,* Occasional Paper No. 3, Technological Development Project (Washington, D.C.: National Education Association, 1962).

Ford, G. W., and Lawrence Pugno, *The Structure of Knowledge of the Curriculum* (Chicago: Rand McNally, 1964).

Groves, Harold M., *Education and Economic Growth* (Washington, D.C.: Committee on Educational Finance, National Education Association, 1961).

Krumboltz, J. D. (ed.), *Learning and the Educational Process* (Chicago: Rand McNally, 1965).

National Education Association, *The New Elementary School* (Washington, D.C.: the Association, 1968).

———, *The Nongraded School* (Washington, D.C.: the Association, 1968).

———, *Multi-age Grouping: Enriching the Learning Environment* (Washington, D.C.: the Association, 1967).

Norton, John K., *Changing Demands on Education and Their Fiscal Implications* (Washington, D.C.: National Committee for Support of the Public Schools, 1963).

Parker, J. Cecil, and Louis J. Rubin, *Process as Content* (Chicago: Rand McNally, 1966).

Schramm, Wilbur, *Programed Instruction: Today and Tomorrow* (New York: Fund for the Advancement of Education, 1962).

Schueler, Herbert, *et al., Teacher Education and the New Media* (Washington, D.C.: the American Association of Colleges for Teacher Education, 1967).

Stolurow, Lawrence M., *Teaching by Machine,* Cooperative Research Monograph No. 6 (Washington, D.C.: U.S. Government Printing Office, 1961).

Verduin, John R., Jr., *Conceptual Models in Teacher Education* (Washington, D.C.: the American Association of Colleges for Teacher Education, 1967).

Whitlock, James W., *Automatic Data Processing in Education* (New York: Macmillan, 1964).

INDEX